Artificial Intelligence (AI) in Social Research

Artificial Intelligence (AI) in Social Research

Edited by

Prokopis A. Christou

Cyprus University of Technology

CABI

CABI is a trading name of CAB International

CABI
Nosworthy Way
Wallingford
Oxfordshire OX10 8DE
UK

Tel: +44 (0)1491 832111
E-mail: info@cabi.org
Website: www.cabi.org

CABI
200 Portland Street
Boston
MA 02114
USA

Tel: +1 (617)682-9015
E-mail: cabi-nao@cabi.org

A catalogue record for this book is available from the British Library, London, UK.

Library of Congress Cataloging-in-Publication Data

Names: Christou, Prokopis A., 1978- editor.
Title: Artificial intelligence (AI) in social research / edited by Prokopis A. Christou, Cyprus University of Technology.
Description: Oxfordshire, UK ; Boston, MA : CAB International, [2025] | Includes bibliographical references and index. | Summary: "The field of social research is characterized by its broad scope and interdisciplinary nature, as it encompasses the examination of human behaviour, societies, and facets of social existence. It is therefore no surprise that Artificial Intelligence (AI) has rapidly become a driving force, bringing about substantial transformations within the field. The use of novel AI tools in the collection, analysis and interpretation of data, the automation of surveys and social media monitoring, sentiment analysis, topic modelling and language translation are just a few illustrative cases of AI applications. The implications of using these applications are significant and noteworthy as despite the opportunities that have emerged through the application of AI in research, it is important to acknowledge the many accompanying dilemmas involved in this form of technological advancement. With global examples from across the many disciplines of social research, this book presents the considerable promise for revolutionizing the discipline but also guides the reader in considering the implications and drawbacks. By doing so, researchers can optimize the capabilities of AI and promote its responsible, reliable, and advantageous application in enhancing and progressing social research"-- Provided by publisher.
Identifiers: LCCN 2024039547 (print) | LCCN 2024039548 (ebook) | ISBN 9781800626584 (hardback) | ISBN 9781800626591 (ebook) | ISBN 9781800626607 (epub)
Subjects: LCSH: Sociology--Research--Methodology. | Artificial intelligence.
Classification: LCC HM571 .A78 2025 (print) | LCC HM571 (ebook) | DDC 300.285/63--dc23/eng/20241009
LC record available at https://lccn.loc.gov/2024039547
LC ebook record available at https://lccn.loc.gov/2024039548

ISBN-13: 9781800626584 (hardback)
9781800626591 (ePDF)
9781800626607 (ePub)

DOI: 10.1079/9781800626607.0000

Commissioning Editor: Claire Parfitt
Editorial Assistant: Helen Elliott
Production Editor: Shankari Wilford

Typeset by Straive, Pondicherry, India
Printed and bound in the UK by CPI Group (UK) Ltd, Croydon, CR0 4YY

Contents

Contributors vii

1 **Introducing *Artificial Intelligence (AI) in Social Research*** 1
Prokopis A. Christou

PART A: AI AND SOCIAL RESEARCH IMPLICATIONS

2 **The Interconnection of AI and Social Research** 12
Prokopis A. Christou

3 **Using Generative AI for Creativity and Automating Time-consuming Tasks in Research** 21
Christos Christodoulou

4 **Expanding the Frontiers: Revolutionizing Quantitative Data Analysis in Social Sciences with AI** 37
Hristo Andreev, Katerina Pericleous and Petros Kosmas

5 **Using AI Agents in Quantitative Social Research** 48
Christos Christodoulou

6 **AI Augmented Qualitative Analysis: Is it the Right Choice for your Study?** 59
Danielle Hitch, Kieva Richards, Rachel Knight, Genevieve Pepin, Urvi Thanekar and Sophie Goldingay

7 **Generative AI: A Catalyst for Paradigmatic Change in Qualitative Data Analysis** 71
Susanne Friese

8 **A Guide for Qualitative Researchers Using Large Language Models with Representative Examples Using ChatGPT** 84
Ann Armstrong and Albert J. Gale

9 **AI in Ethnography: Challenges and Collaborations** 97
Deana Kotiga

10 **Exploring Research Design in the Context of Artificial Intelligence: Evidence-based Recommendations for Social Research and Practice** 104
Terrell L. Strayhorn and J'Quen Johnson

PART B: AI AND SOCIAL RESEARCH RIGOUR, BIAS AND ETHICAL CONSIDERATIONS

11 **Machine Learning Bias: Genealogy, Expression and Prevention** 113
Theodoros Kouros, Zenonas Theodosiou and Christos Themistocleous

12 **Rigour in Qualitative and Quantitative Studies that Make Use of AI Tools: Reliability, Validity, Credibility, Transferability, Dependability and Confirmability Issues** 127
Prokopis A. Christou

13 **The Ethical Implications of Using AI in Qualitative Research** 137
Danielle Hitch, Kieva Richards, Adyya Gupta, Urvi Thanekar, Jacqueline Edwards and Sophie Goldingay

PART C: AI AND RESEARCH WITHIN VARIOUS SOCIAL CONTEXTS AND CASE STUDIES

14 **Precision Nudging: The Future of Behaviour Change?** 150
Christos Themistocleous and Evangelos Karapanos

15 **Competence Frameworks for Exploring Generative AI in Education** 160
Pablo Burneo, António Pedro Costa, Isabel Pinho, Aline Muniz and Eduardo Dutra Moresi

16 **Data Collection Methods in the Age of Artificial Intelligence: Insights From a Survey-based Study on College Students' Perceptions and Use of AI** 176
Terrell L. Strayhorn and J'Quen Johnson

17 **AI and International Business** 186
Anthi Avloniti

18 **AI Systems Employed in Archaeological Research for Ancient Artefacts – A Dilemma** 199
Annita Antoniadou

19 **Conclusion** 210
Prokopis A. Christou

Index 213

Contributors

Andreev, Hristo, Cyprus University of Technology, Archiepiskopou Kyprianou 30, Limassol 3036, Cyprus. E-mail: hd.andreev@edu.cut.ac.cy. ORCID: https://orcid.org/0000-0002-5484-1660.

Hristo Andreev is a PhD candidate at the Faculty of Tourism Management, Hospitality and Entrepreneurship of the Cyprus University of Technology. His research focuses on sustainability through systems thinking in tourism. Despite being a social scientist, he has a technical background in web development from both his undergraduate studies and his professional experience. His background and experience inspire him to combine technical details and technological tools with social science in a synergistic manner, which enriches his methodological toolkit for research. He has a high interest in the use of technology for enhancement and optimization of traditional research methods.

Antoniadou, Annita, Cyprus University of Technology, Archiepiskopou Kyprianou 30, Limassol 3036, Cyprus. E-mail: drannitaantoniadou@gmail.com. ORCID: https://orcid.org/0000-0001-9095-7460.

Annita Antoniadou is adjunct lecturer at higher education institutions in Cyprus and the UK. She obtained a Bachelor's degree in Archaeology, History and History of Art from Aristotle University in Thessaloniki, Greece. Later, she pursued a Master's degree at the University of Southampton in the UK, focusing on palaeolithic archaeology and human evolution. Her postgraduate research centred on uncovering the routes taken by Neanderthals to reach Britain around 60,000 years ago, walking a land bridge over the frozen English Channel. She holds a PhD from Queen's University Belfast, Northern Ireland, in the emerging discipline of geoarchaeology, focusing on ancient human settlements and cultural trends in Northern Africa and the Mediterranean spanning approximately 200,000 years. Her current research interests revolve around prehistoric civilizations, early trading practices, the development of landscapes and the utilization of advanced technologies within the field. She has actively participated in excavations and projects across Europe, Asia and Africa. In her published work, she explores topics including the history of Cyprus from the 17th to the 19th century, ancient maritime activities, stone tool technologies and the archaeology of food. Her most recent book chapters shed light on the socio-political and religious activity of the last elected archbishop of Cyprus under Ottoman rule (2023), and the semiotics and symbolism behind the enduring depiction of Queen Victoria's head on postal stamps during British rule (2024).

Armstrong, Ann, National University, 9388 Lightwave Avenue, San Diego, CA 92123, USA. E-mail: Aarmstrong2@nu.edu. Skype: annwarm.

Ann Armstrong brings extensive experience in business and education, offering consulting, coaching and mentoring services. Specializing in instructional technology and design, adult learning and leadership, project management and eLearning, her research interests include qualitative methods, design and development case studies, phenomenology and the nominal group technique (NGT). As a certified Dale Carnegie facilitator and a Quality Matters peer reviewer, she serves on the editorial board of The Qualitative Report. Her career highlights include serving as Executive Director at Columbia Teachers College, where the Columbia Coaching Certification and the first online Master's degree were initiated. At IBM, as an eBusiness/eLearning executive, she delivered the first global asynchronous learning programme to 10,000 leaders. As Vice President of Ernst & Young's Intellinex/eLearning Practice, she implemented blended learning solutions for over 210,000 global employees. Certified as an IBM consultant and confirmed as an IBM principal, she is currently a full professor at National University, specializing in instructional technology, media, design and qualitative research. As a dissertation chair, she has guided over 100 doctoral students to successful completions, with many publishing their research. Her scholarly contributions include publications in peer-reviewed journals, a top ten paper award from the Academy of Human Resource Development (AHRD), and recent chapters, articles and conference proceedings for eLearn, AHRD, the Association for the Advancement of Computing in Education (AACE) and the Association for Educational Communications and Technology (AECT). Her most recent work is a book chapter in the *Encyclopedia of Information Science and Technology*, 6th edition. She holds an EdD and EdM in Instructional Technology and Media from Teachers College, Columbia University; an MA in Instructional Design from Fairfield University; an MA in Economics from the University of Cincinnati; and an MBA in Project Management from Capella University. She brings extensive experience in business and education, offering consulting, coaching and mentoring services. Specializing in instructional technology and design, adult learning and leadership, project management and eLearning, her research interests include qualitative methods, design and development research case studies, phenomenology and the NGT.

Avloniti, Anthi, University of Central Lancashire, University Avenue 12–14, Pyla 7080, Cyprus. E-mail: aavloniti@uclan.ac.uk. ORCID: https://orcid.org/0000-0002-8188-6055.

Anthi Avloniti is an Assistant Professor in Management. She holds a BA in Business Administration from the Athens University of Economics and Business with specialization in Management Information Systems, as well as an MA and PhD in Management by Kingston University and Kent University, respectively, along with a Fellowship of the Higher Education Academy and certification of executive training. She is an active researcher and publishes in highly ranked journals on international business, management and innovation. Her academic journey is progressing along the path of rigorous and interdisciplinary research in the intersections of innovation, artificial intelligence, entrepreneurship, data-driven growth and sustainable development, within an international context, exploring global, cross-cultural and institutional influences on both multinational companies and international small and medium-sized enterprises across different industries.

Burneo, Pablo, Universidad San Francisco de Quito, Campus Cumbayá, Diego de Robles s/n, Quito 170901, Ecuador. E-mail: psburneo@usfq.edu.ec. ORCID: https://orcid.org/0009-0007-2862-8886.

Pablo Burneo is an industrial engineer with over a decade of experience in quality improvement projects, and juggles teaching as a full-time professor at the Universidad San Francisco de Quito (USFQ) in Ecuador with pursuing his PhD at the University of Aveiro, Portugal. Passionate about bridging the gap between industry needs and university training, he researches new pedagogical approaches to enhance teaching methods. Through the Future Professoriate programme organized by USFQ and Virginia Tech (Blacksburg, Virginia), he develops training courses for educators, striving to empower them with essential skills.

Christodoulou, Christos, Double Eye Ltd, Themidos Siapkara Pitsillidou 12, 3117, Limassol, Cyprus. E-mail: chris.christodoulou@gmail.com.

Christos Christodoulou holds a PhD in Physics from Humboldt University in Berlin and an MSc and BA in Natural Sciences from the University of Cambridge, UK, as well as multiple certificates in artificial intelligence and product management. He is the Head of Data and Product at Epikast, a healthcare company assisting biopharma companies to engage with healthcare professionals and patients using data and technology. He also organizes the PyData meetup in Cyprus, which focuses on extending the international PyData community of software developers and data professionals. He has extensive experience working in various companies in the healthcare, mobility and fintech sectors, with a research background in nanotechnology. He has been leading teams in the development of advanced machine learning and data processing applications, as well as novel digital products powered by artificial intelligence.

Christou, Prokopis A., Cyprus University of Technology, Archiepiskopou Kyprianou 30, Limassol 3036, Cyprus. E-mail: Prokopis.christou@cut.ac.cy. ORCID: https://orcid.org/0000-0001-6628-2619.

Prokopis Christou is an Assistant Professor and the editor of this book. He has published books and various articles in academic journals, including conceptual papers, critical perspective articles, systematic reviews, and ethnographic, phenomenological, and other empirical studies. His interest in artificial intelligence (AI) stems from his observation that AI is becoming increasingly useful in academia and research, yet is associated with a number of risks. As such, he is investigating the applications, potentials, dynamics, limitations and perils of AI in research and different social fields.

Costa, António P., University of Aveiro, 3810-193 Aveiro, Portugal. E-mail: apcosta@ua.pt. ORCID: https://orcid.org/0000-0002-4644-5879.

António Pedro Costa is a principal researcher at the Research Centre on Didactics and Technology in the Education of Trainers (CIDTFF), in the Department of Education and Psychology at the University of Aveiro in Portugal. He also collaborates with the Artificial Intelligence and Computer Science Laboratory at the University of Porto (Portugal). He is one of the authors of the qualitative data analysis software webQDA (www.webqda.net). He coordinates two qualitative research conferences (www.ciaiq.org and www.wcqr.info). He is the author of more than 300 publications in international conferences and journals.

Edwards, Jacqueline, Deakin University, Waterfront Campus, 1 Gheringhap Street, Geelong, Victoria 3217, Australia. E-mail: j.edwards@deakin.edu.au). ORCID: https://orcid.org/0000-0001-6697-9897).

Jacqueline Edwards is an occupational therapist, lecturer and early career researcher. Her research interests include family-centred practice, social determinants of health and social justice.

Friese, Susanne, Max Planck Institute for the Study of Religious and Ethnic Diversity, Hermann-Föge-Weg 11, 37073 Göttingen, Germany; Qeludra Consultancy, Netherlands. E-mail: Susanne.friese@qeludra.com.

Susanne Friese is an accomplished expert in qualitative methods and data analysis, with over three decades of experience in the field. Her extensive knowledge and expertise have been applied to numerous research projects, teaching engagements and consulting engagements across the globe. She is highly regarded for her ability to explain complex concepts in a clear and concise manner, making her an excellent teacher of qualitative research methods. She has taught courses on qualitative methods at numerous universities, research institutions and public service organizations worldwide. With the introduction of ChatGPT, she took up an interest in the application of artificial intelligence for qualitative research and data analysis. You can follow her journey of experimenting with the newest tools and her contribution to the field to date by reading her blog: www.qeludra.com/blog.

Gale, Albert, Walden University, 100 Washington Avenue South, Suite 1210, Minneapolis, Minnesota 55401, USA. E-mail: albert.gale@mail.waldenu.edu

With more than 35 years as a healthcare leader, Albert Gale has experience in healthcare administration, serving as Chief Executive Officer (CEO) and Multi-Facility Manager of a number of acute general and psychiatric hospitals, physician practices and outpatient programmes. His global experience includes a 3-year international assignment as CEO of a surgical hospital in Nalta, Bangladesh.

He received his DBA at the University of Phoenix in August 2015 and earned a Master's in Healthcare Administration from Indiana University/Purdue in 1971. He has taught healthcare management, risk management, leadership, healthcare communication, strategic planning and healthcare organization at other universities. He has mentored doctoral students through the dissertation process. He is a certified Dale Carnegie instructor with endorsements in leadership, communications, and building self-confidence. His research focuses on the impact of a multinational workforce on hospital operations. He has a number of publications and presentations on model validation and the role of culture in organizations. He is a member of the Association for Educational Communications and Technology. His most recent work is a book chapter in the *Encyclopedia of Information Science and Technology*, 6th edition.

Goldingay, Sophie, Deakin University, Waterfront Campus, 1 Gheringhap Street, Geelong, Victoria 3217, Australia. E-mail: sophie.goldingay@deakin.edu.au. ORCID: https://orcid.org/0000-0002-0776-1086.

Sophie Goldingay is an Associate Professor in social work and lead creator of a neuro-affirming social programme for neurodivergent young people (www.imaginecreatebelong.com). Her research interests include neurodiversity, artificial intelligence (AI) and decolonizing practice. She has previously published on the topic of AI in social work education.

Gupta, Adyya, Global Centre for Preventive Health and Nutrition (GLOBE) within the Institute for Health Transformation at Deakin University, Bundoora Campus, 221 Burwood Highway, Bundoora, Victoria, 3125, Australia. E-mail: adyya.gupta@deakin.edu.au. ORCID: https://orcid.org/0000-0003-3900-9849.

Adyya Gupta is currently a VicHealth Fellow at the Global Centre for Preventive Health and Nutrition (GLOBE) within the Institute for Health Transformation at Deakin University, Australia. She is a clinical dentist, with a Master's in dental public health and a PhD in public health. She has expertise in applying mixed methodology to public health research. Her research focuses on building the evidence to create a healthy digital food environment. She has previously published a book chapter on research methods in the *Handbook of Research Methods in Health Social Sciences* (2019).

Hitch, Danielle, Deakin University, Waterfront Campus, 1 Gheringhap Street, Geelong, Victoria 3217, Australia. E-mail: dani.hitch@deakin.edu.au. ORCID: https://orcid.org/0000-0003-2798-2246.

Danielle Hitch is an Associate Professor of Occupational Therapy, as well as a health economist and experienced healthcare researcher. Her research interests include mental health, social justice and Long COVID. Danielle has previously published on the topic of artificial intelligence in reflexive thematic analysis.

Johnson, J'Quen, University of the Cumberlands, 6178 College Station Drive, Williamsburg, Kentucky 40769, USA. E-mail: jquenj@dogoodworkllc.org. ORCID: https://orcid.org/0009-0008-4736-2750.

J'Quen Johnson is a PhD candidate at the University of the Cumberlands in Kentucky, and his research interests include accessibility and inclusion for Black males living with disabilities in higher education. He served at Tusculum University in enrolment management as the Director of Graduate and Undergraduate Online Recruitment. He is the Director of Research and a Consultant at Do Good Work Consulting. He is a member of the new professional and graduate student board for the *Journal of Student Affairs Research and Practice.*

Karapanos, Evangelos, Cyprus University of Technology, Department of Communication & Internet Studies, 30 Archibishop Kyprianou Street, Limassol 3036, Cyprus. E-mail: evangelos.karapanos@cut.ac.cy. ORCID: https://orcid.org/0000-0001-5910-4996.

Evangelos Karapanos is an Associate Professor in the Department of Communication and Internet Studies and Director of the Persuasive Technologies Lab at the Department of Communication and Internet Studies of the Cyprus University of Technology. He holds a PhD (cum laude) in

Human–Computer Interaction from Eindhoven University of Technology (Netherlands), an MSc in Human–Computer Interaction from University College London, and a BSc in Physics with a specialization in microelectronics from the University of Patras (Greece). His expertise is in experience-centred design of interaction with technology. His work is regularly published at top-tier conferences and journals on human–computer interaction and has received more than 5000 citations in the literature and a number of awards, including a best paper and a best poster award at Persuasive Technology 2017, an honourable mention for best paper at Ubicomp 2015, the Tech Challenge for Atrocity Prevention 2013 award, and the cum laude distinction for his PhD thesis (given to the top 5% of PhD theses defended annually at the Eindhoven University of Technology).

Knight, Rachel, Deakin University, Waterfront Campus, 1 Gheringhap Street, Geelong, Victoria 3217, Australia. E-mail: rachel.knight@deakin.edu.au. ORCID: https://orcid.org/0009-0000-7675-451X.

Rachel Knight is an occupational therapist with experience as a clinician, researcher and service transformation lead. She is currently completing her PhD with a focus on service model design and how this can influence health outcomes for people with eating disorders. Her research interests include mental health, eating disorders and healthcare service systems.

Kosmas, Petros, Cyprus University of Technology, Archiepiskopou Kyprianou 30, Limassol 3036, Cyprus. E-mail: petros.kosmas@cut.ac.cy. ORCID: https://orcid.org/0000-0002-6572-9797.

Petros Kosmas is an Assistant Professor at the Department of Hospitality and Tourism Management at Cyprus University of Technology (CUT). He is also a researcher at the Research Center for Social Science and Regional Development 'HERACLITUS' at CUT. An intense interest in the political economy of tourism guides his research pursuits. These pursuits explore the intricate dynamics within this multifaceted industry, as well as its socio-economic externalities, providing valuable insights into this field.

Kotiga, Deana, Ipsos, 3 Thomas More Street, London E1W 1YW, UK. E-mail: deanaemmakotiga@gmail.com.

Deana Kotiga is an anthropologist, photographer and filmmaker specializing in the intersections of research, art, culture and communities. Combining immersive ethnographic methods with visual storytelling, she captures the essence of diverse cultures, contributing to both scholarly discourse and artistic practice.

Kouros, Theodoros, Department of Communication & Internet Studies, Cyprus University of Technology, 30 Archibishop Kyprianou Strett, 3036, Limassol, Cyprus. E-mail: theodoros.kouros@cut.ac.cy. ORCID: https://orcid.org/0000-0003-2742-1158.

Theodoros Kouros is a Lecturer in the Department of Communication and Internet Studies at Cyprus University of Technology, and a social anthropologist. His research interests combine a diverse range of themes and methodologies, with particular emphasis on citizenship, memory, ethnic and national identities, and migration. In terms of methodology, his experience includes ethnography and digital ethnography and multimodality in anthropology, as well as qualitative social research methods and techniques.

Moresi, Eduardo A.D., Catholic University of Brasília, QS 07, Lote 01, Taguatinga Sul – Taguatinga, Brasília – DF, 71966-700, Brazil. E-mail: moresi@p.ucb.br. ORCID: https://orcid.org/0000-0001-6058-3883.

Eduardo Moresi holds a PhD in Information Science from the University of Brasília, Brazil, with a focus on complexity theory and organizational intelligence. He is a researcher at the Catholic University of Brasília (UCB) in Brazil. Since December 2014, he has been coordinating UCB's Apple Developer Academy Programme, which trains undergraduate students in the development of innovative applications and games for the iOS platform. He is a permanent lecturer in the Stricto Sensu Postgraduate Master's and Academic Doctorate Programme in Education, where he supervises theses and dissertations on educational technologies and innovation. He is also a technical advisor at the Centre for Management and Strategic Studies (CGEE), where he works on science, technology and innovation intelligence projects.

Muniz, Aline B.X., Catholic University of Brasília, QS 07, Lote 01, Taguatinga Sul – Taguatinga, Brasília – DF, 71966-700, Brazil. E-mail: alinebxmuniz79@gmail.com. ORCID: https://orcid.org/0009-0007-2663-6938.

Aline Muniz is a PhD student in Education at the Catholic University of Brasília, Brazil, and a pedagogue at the Brazilian Defense College (ESD), and undertakes research on competency mapping in organizations and artificial intelligence in education. She is a researcher at the Laboratory for Security, Development, and Defense.

Pepin, Genevieve, Deakin University, Waterfront Campus, 1 Gheringhap Street, Geelong, Victoria 3217, Australia. E-mail: genevieve.pepin@deakin.edu.au. ORCID: https://orcid.org/0000-0002-8382-160X.

Genevieve Pepin is a Professor of Occupational Therapy, experienced mental health occupational therapist, educator and researcher with a strong track record in eating disorders, mental health, carers research and occupational therapy. The major focus of her work is at the intersectionality of innovative, impactful and translational eating disorders and carers research, and occupational therapy in mental health research, education and practices that are contemporary, inspiring and transformational.

Pericleous, Katerina, Cyprus University of Technology, Archiepiskopou Kyprianou 30, Limassol 3036, Cyprus. E-mail: katerina.pericleous@cut.ac.cy. ORCID: https://orcid.org/0000-0002-3055-4480.

Katerina Pericleous holds a PhD in Statistics (with emphasis on experimental designs) from the School of Applied Mathematics and Natural Sciences of the National Technical University of Athens, Greece. She has also an MSc in Applied Statistics from the Department of Mathematics and Statistics of the University of Cyprus and a BA (Hons) in Mathematics and Statistics from the same department of the University of Cyprus. Her research interests focus on experimental designs, applied statistics, probability theory and statistical models. Currently, she is a member of the Special Teaching Staff in the Department of Hospitality and Tourism Management, Faculty of Tourism Management, Hospitality and Entrepreneurship, at the Cyprus University of Technology. She has participated in local and international conferences and has published her work in peer-reviewed academic journals.

Pinho, Isabel, University of Aveiro, 3810-193 Aveiro, Portugal. E-mail: isabelpinho@ua.pt. ORCID: https://orcid.org/0000-0003-1714-8979.

Isabel Pinho has a PhD in Management from the University of Aveiro, Portugal, entitled 'Knowledge Management in Research Centers – Barriers/Facilitators'. She is a post-doc in Higher Education at the Federal University of Rio Grande do Sul, Brazil, working on research networks, and also a post-doc in Evaluation from the University of Aveiro, regarding research evaluation and impact. She is an expert in knowledge management, data management, and research evaluation and literature reviews.

Richards, Kieva, La Trobe University, Bundoora Campus, Plenty Road, Bundoora, Victoria, 3086, Australia. E-mail: kieva.richards@latrobe.edu.au. ORCID: https://orcid.org/0000-0003-0904-2031.

Kieva Richards is an experienced occupational therapist and early career researcher. Her research interests include dementia, social justice and occupational engagement.

Strayhorn, Terrell L., Virginia Union University, 1500 N Lombardy Street, Richmond, Viginia 23220, USA. E-mail: tlstrayhorn@vuu.edu. ORCID: https://orcid.org/0000-0002-9659-8160.

Terrell Strayhorn is a Professor of Education and Psychology at Virginia Union University, where he also serves as Vice Provost and Interim Dean of the School of Arts and Sciences, Director of Research in the Center for the Study of HBCUs, and Principal Investigator of The Belonging Lab. He is the author of 13 books and over 200 academic publications, and serves on the governing board for Rainbow Labs, M.E.N. Inc. (Houston), and the MCT Educational Foundation, to name a few.

Thanekar, Urvi, Deakin University, Bundoora Campus, 221 Burwood Highway, Bundoora, Victoria 3125, Australia. E-mail: uthanekar@deakin.edu.au. ORCID: https://orcid.org/0009-0007-6956-708X.

Urvi Thanekar is a PhD candidate at the Institute of Health Transformation at Deakin University, collaborating with Barwon Health to reduce their environmental footprint through systems dynamics and economic analysis. She also works with the Climate Catch Lab at the University of Melbourne, Australia, on projects intersecting climate change, healthcare systems and digital health. A clinically trained dentist with a Master's degree in health and human services management, her research interests lie within sustainable healthcare decision making and the health impacts of climate change.

Themistocleous, Christos, Department of Communication & Marketing, Cyprus University of Technology, 30 Archibishop Kyprianou Street, 3036, Limassol, Cyprus. E-mail: c.themistocleous@cut.ac.cy. ORCID: https://orcid.org/0000-0001-9074-7711.

Christos Themistocleous is a Lecturer of Consumer Behaviour at the Department of Communication and Marketing, Cyprus University of Technology. He holds a PhD in Consumer Behaviour (University of Nottingham, UK), MSc in Corporate Strategy and Governance (University of Nottingham) and BA (Hons) in Finance, Accounting and Management (University of Nottingham). Having worked previously in faculty positions at the University of Reading (UK), his research focuses on disclosure decision making, consumer privacy and data collection systems.

Theodosiou, Zenonas, Department of Communication & Internet Studies, Cyprus University of Technology, 30 Archibishop Kyprianou Street, Limassol 3036, Cyprus; CYENS Centre of Excellence, Plateia Dimarchou 1, Nicosia 1016, Cyprus. E-mail: zenonas.theodosiou@cut.ac.cy. ORCID: https://orcid.org/0000-0003-3168-2350.

Zenonas Theodosiou is a member of the Special Teaching Staff of the Department of Communication and Internet Studies at the Cyprus University of Technology and a member of the BIO-SCENT (Biometrics for Smart Human-Centred Emerging Technologies) research group at the CYENS Centre of Excellence. His research interests focus mainly on multimodal data analysis for the extraction of useful information.

1 Introducing *Artificial Intelligence (AI) in Social Research*

Prokopis A. Christou
Cyprus University of Technology, Limassol, Cyprus

Abstract
The incorporation of artificial intelligence (AI) into social research signifies a notable progression in the realm of the social sciences. This introductory chapter unfolds the rationale of this book and its importance at a theoretical and practical level. It also explains the structure of the book, which is divided into three distinct sections. This is followed by an overview of the chronological evolution of AI, with reference to significant advancements that have influenced its involvement in social research throughout the decades. AI transforms the field of social research in various fields. Such instances are provided in a specific section of this chapter with an overview of how AI is informing research in various social domains, such as psychology, sociology, public health, education and management.

Keywords: AI, artificial intelligence, social research

1.1 The Rationale, Aim and Value of this Book

The field of social research is characterized by its broad scope and interdisciplinary nature, as it encompasses the examination of human behaviour, societies and facets of social existence, interaction and social exchange. The field embraces a diverse array of disciplines and domains of inquiry, such as sociology, psychology, anthropology, economics, political sciences, education, communication studies, public health, geography, and cultural and family studies.

The advent of artificial intelligence (AI) has swiftly emerged as a catalyst for significant change in the aforementioned domains within the realm of social research (Miller, 2019; Raisch and Krakowski, 2021). The applications of this form of technological advancement in social inquiry have experienced substantial growth and remarkable attention by the research community, providing novel tools for the collection, analysis and interpretation of data (Christou, 2023a). For instance, AI is currently used in the field of natural language processing for the purpose of analysing textual data, while sentiment analysis, topic modelling and language translation are illustrative cases in which AI is applied. Indeed, the implications of AI in social research are significant and noteworthy (Haefner *et al.*, 2021; Hilbert, 2022), presenting the prospect of transforming the discipline.

Despite the opportunities that have emerged through the application of AI in research, it is important to acknowledge knowledge gaps and accompanying dilemmas involved in this form

*E-mail: Prokopis.christou@cut.ac.cy

DOI: 10.1079/9781800626607.0001

of technological advancement, as well as the constraints, risks and limitations of its utilization in social research (Mirbabaie *et al.*, 2022; Strümke *et al.*, 2022). One notable limitation pertains to the inherent opacity of specific AI models, impeding researchers' comprehension of the underlying processes by which AI systems and tools reach specific (research) outcomes and conclusions. Furthermore, the incorporation of AI in social research necessitates a diligent examination of ethical considerations, examples of which relate to the safeguarding of privacy and utilization of personal data, bias mitigation, transparency and accountability, and responsible utilization of AI. There is also the extent to which the cognitive input and evaluative skills of the researcher or analyst is demonstrated in the interpretation process and in reaching conclusions following an analysis process performed by AI-assisted tools and programs (Christou, 2023b). Overall, the incorporation of AI within the realm of social research holds considerable promise for revolutionizing the discipline. Yet, it is imperative to carefully consider the implications, opportunities, drawbacks and ethical considerations that arise from the utilization of AI in social research. By doing so, researchers can optimize the capabilities of AI and promote its responsible, reliable and advantageous application in enhancing and progressing social research.

The primary aim of this book is to provide key information and considerations related to the use of AI in social research, thereby providing academics, researchers, analysts, students and practitioners with important knowledge that may allow them to better comprehend the implications, ramifications, prospects and perils associated with the utilization of AI in social research. Several justifications underscore the significance of this book:

1. *Filling a gap.* The possibilities and impacts of AI in social research remain a rather unexplored topic. This book may serve as a foundational resource to somehow bridge the existing gap, empowering researchers to harness AI's potential for more effective, insightful and rigorous social research.
2. *Facilitating the progression of knowledge.* This book can contribute to the advancement of knowledge by offering a contemporary understanding of the application of AI in social research.
3. *Pursuing innovation in research.* AI presents novel technologies for the acquisition, examination and analysis of various forms of data. Scholars and practitioners can acquire better knowledge on how to utilize AI in various research tasks.
4. *Keeping up with the rapid pace of technological advancements.* The field of AI is characterized by ongoing advancements and developments. This book can serve as a valuable resource for researchers, students and analysts, enabling them to better understand the implications of AI tools in research.
5. *Tackling ethical and social issues.* The utilization of AI in the realm of social research gives rise to significant ethical and societal implications, encompassing matters of privacy, bias, transparency and accountability. This book covers such issues.
6. *Preparing the upcoming generation.* Given the growing significance of AI, it is imperative to adequately equip future social researchers with the requisite comprehension to effectively leverage the potential of AI in social research.

This book may be of interest to a wide range of individuals and groups:

- Academics, researchers and analysts in the fields of sociology, psychology, anthropology, political science, economics and other social sciences.
- Undergraduate and graduate students, who could use this book as a resource for understanding the potential applications and implications of AI in their respective fields and for developing research projects and dissertations.
- Universities, colleges and other educational institutes delivering courses related to AI and/or social research methods, who may incorporate this book into their curriculum.
- Professionals working in AI who are interested in applying their expertise to social research and may find the book insightful, as well as organizations focused on social research and social change to allow them to better understand how AI can assist in gathering insights, identifying trends, and addressing social issues. Companies and market researchers interested in understanding social trends can also gain insights from this book.
- Individuals with a general interest in the intersection of technology, AI and society, who may find this book accessible and informative.

1.2 The Structure and Content of the Book

This book is divided into three specific and distinct parts. The first deals with 'AI and social research implications'. The chapters that are included in this section emphasize the transformative impact of AI on social research and social research methodologies. For instance, Deana Kotiga discusses AI challenges and collaborations in ethnographic research, while Hristo Andreev, Keterina Pericleous and Petros Kosmas explain how AI is revolutionizing quantitative data analysis. The authors of the chapters in this first part of the book explore how AI shapes data collection, analysis and interpretation, allowing researchers to handle large datasets and uncover complex social patterns. Furthermore, the content of the chapters in this part indicate that the integration of AI tools enhances creativity, automates routine tasks and simplifies advanced data analysis, making sophisticated techniques more accessible. In this regard, Christos Christodoulou offers valuable advice on how to use generative AI for creativity and for automating time-consuming tasks in research. Additionally, the chapters in this part uncover how AI challenges traditional research approaches while offering new opportunities for deeper insights. Ethical considerations and the potential for significant methodological shifts are also discussed. Overall, these chapters highlight the crucial balance between leveraging AI's innovative capabilities and maintaining ethical research practices, underscoring the pivotal role of AI in advancing social research.

The second part is specifically concerned with the significant topic of 'AI and social research rigour, bias and ethical considerations'. The chapters in this section collectively stress the importance of understanding and addressing biases inherent in AI systems. They draw from epistemological traditions to highlight the potential distortions AI can introduce into research, emphasizing the need for social scientists to maintain rigorous standards in AI-assisted research. Ethical considerations are paramount, with discussions on how to uphold integrity, respect and justice in AI-augmented social science research. For instance, the chapter by Danielle Hitch and co-authors covers the ethical implications of using AI within the context of qualitative research. The chapters in this second part of the book also provide practical guidelines and preventative measures to ensure that research using AI adheres to high standards of credibility, reliability and validity, while also addressing the critical role of human oversight to navigate ethical complexities.

The third and final part is concerned with 'AI and research within various contexts and case studies.' Collectively, the chapters in this section explore the multifaceted applications of AI across different contexts and disciplines. For instance, they delve into how AI can enhance behavioural science through precision nudging (chapter by Christos Themistocleous and Evangelos Karapanos) and optimize educational frameworks with generative AI tools (chapter by Pablo Burneo and co-authors). The chapter by Anthi Avloniti examines AI's intersection with international business, focusing on intelligence, interconnectedness, complexity and strategic foresight. The discussions from these chapters underscore AI's transformative potential across diverse fields, while emphasizing ethical considerations, rigorous procedures and the need for interdisciplinary collaboration to harness its benefits effectively.

1.3 An Evolutionary Overview of AI in Social Research

Gaining insight into the evolution of AI in the field of social research is essential for grasping its present uses and possibly anticipating its forthcoming implications and consequences. This evolutionary account elucidates the progress from rudimentary statistical models to advanced machine learning and deep-learning systems, greatly augmenting data analysis and interpretation in the field of social sciences. It emphasizes a paradigm shift from simply aiding researchers to fundamentally transforming research frameworks and tackling intricate social phenomena. Studying the evolution of AI in social research offers a comprehension of its ability to bring about significant changes but also the risks and challenges, such as ethical considerations (Guleria *et al.*, 2023), thus directing its future progress towards favourable social results.

1.3.1 Beginnings of AI and the early application of AI in social research (1950s–1980s)

The exploration of AI in social research commenced during the mid-20th century, originating from the fundamental contributions of trailblazers such as Alan Turing and John McCarthy. Turing's influential paper on 'Computing Machinery and Intelligence' in 1950 established the foundation for AI by suggesting the possibility of machines emulating human intelligence. In this influential paper, Turing (1950, p. 433) commenced with the following words:

> I propose to consider the question, 'Can machines think?'

The Dartmouth Summer Research Project (workshop and extended brainstorming session) in 1956, during which McCarthy introduced the term 'artificial intelligence', signified the official inception of AI as a discipline. During this initial period, the primary emphasis was on the advancement of fundamental algorithms and the investigation of the theoretical foundations of machine intelligence (McCarthy *et al.*, 2006). During the 1960s and 1970s, researchers initiated investigations into the application of AI in the field of social sciences. However, progress was restricted by technological limitations. Initial applications were none the less observed in fields such as computational linguistics and decision support systems. An example of this is the creation of ELIZA by Joseph Weizenbaum in the mid-1960s. ELIZA was basically a program that could imitate human conversation, and it paved the way for utilizing AI in comprehending human communication and social interactions (Weizenbaum, 1966, 1967). In the 1980s, expert systems employing rule-based systems to simulate human expertise were introduced into social research. Systems such as MYCIN, used in medical diagnosis (van Melle, 1978), demonstrated the capacity of AI to analyse and interpret intricate data – a crucial aspect of social research methodologies.

1.3.2 Machine and deep learning and integration of AI in social research (1990s–2010s)

In the introductory part of the book *Artificial Intelligence: A New Synthesis*, Nilsson (1998, p. 1) argued that 'AI has as one of its long-term goals the development of machines that can do these things [referring to reasoning, learning, communicating and acting in complex environments] as well as humans can, or possibly even better'. Yet, could AI perform research-linked tasks as well (or even better) than humans? This is a question that comes without a straightforward answer. Even so, during this decade (1990s), there was a significant change in the field of AI with the introduction of machine learning (Bratko, 1993). Machine learning is a specific area of AI that concentrates on creating algorithms that can learn from data and make predictions. Social researchers commenced employing machine learning techniques to analyse extensive datasets, thereby expanding the horizons of comprehending social phenomena (Langley *et al.*, 1996; Mitchell, 1999). The onset of the 21st century signified a crucial juncture for AI in the field of social research. Advancements in natural language processing (NLP; i.e. computational techniques for the analysis and synthesis of natural language and speech) enabled researchers to analyse human behaviour and social patterns (Nasukawa and Yi, 2003; Yi *et al.*, 2003). AI algorithms became an important element in performing sentiment analysis, opinion mining and social-network analysis.

The 2010s were defined by the emergence of deep learning (Goodfellow *et al.*, 2016), a branch of machine learning that utilizes neural networks with multiple layers (in simple terms, a method in AI that 'teaches' computers to process data in a way that is inspired by the human brain). This advancement greatly improved the capabilities of AI in the field of social research. For instance, deep-learning algorithms acquired proficiency in analysing and comprehending extensive quantities of unorganized data, such as images and videos, thereby offering more profound understanding of various social phenomena (Kahou *et al.*, 2016; Shen *et al.*, 2017; Garcia-Garcia *et al.*, 2018).

1.3.3 The 2020s and the future

The current state of AI in social research is characterized by a remarkable combination of sophisticated computational techniques and conventional social science methodologies. AI is not merely a tool for analysing data, as it has become an inherent component in the study and comprehension of social phenomena. NLP is a highly important field of AI application in contemporary social research (Hodorog *et al.*, 2022; Parks and Peters, 2023). Social scientists are employing these capacities to examine extensive quantities of textual data derived from platforms such as social media, news articles and academic journals, thereby enabling a more efficient and intricate comprehension of public sentiment, cultural patterns and social interactions. Furthermore, AI algorithms can analyse social data to detect patterns and linkages, providing insights into the complexities of social structures, community dynamics and influence networks. The incorporation of machine learning, particularly deep learning, into social research has also resulted in transformative advancements (Abbas, 2021; Peng *et al.*, 2022; Amiri *et al.*, 2023). These technologies excel in processing extensive and intricate datasets, including images and videos. Scientists are also employing deep-learning techniques to examine visual communication on social media, scrutinize demographic patterns and forecast social crises and public-health concerns.

Anticipating the future of AI in research, we can expect a number of significant advancements (Johnson *et al.*, 2021; King, 2023), such as more sophisticated AI tools for precision, and for extracting and analysing data, as well as continued development of AI in the field of predictive analytics. AI may serve the purpose of comprehending social phenomena and forecasting forthcoming trends and behaviours. This capability will be especially significant in domains such as public policy and economics, where understanding forthcoming patterns is vital for strategic planning and decision making. AI may also be anticipated to facilitate the democratization of social research. With the increasing user-friendliness and easy general accessibility of AI tools, a wider array of researchers will have the ability to carry out advanced social research. This process of democratization will result in a broadening of viewpoints in social research, enhancing our comprehension of worldwide social dynamics. In general, the advancement of AI in the field of social research is a continuous and ongoing process, with AI technologies continuing to revolutionize social research and broaden our understanding of human behaviour and societies. Even so, researchers will be constantly called to address various concerns, risks, bias and other limitations associated with AI tools and means in social research (Andreotta *et al.*, 2022; Arora *et al.*, 2023). For instance, as AI becomes increasingly integrated into social research, it will become crucial to establish ethical frameworks that specifically tackle concerns such as privacy, consent and bias.

1.4 A Current Overview of How AI Informs Research Across Social Disciplines

The integration of AI into various social domains is unveiling new opportunities for comprehending intricate human-linked and social phenomena, but with associated challenges. Presented below is an overview of how AI influences and informs research in different key social disciplines, organized in alphabetical order.

1.4.1 Anthropology

The field of anthropology, which has traditionally relied on qualitative data, has experienced a profound transformation as a result of AI. For instance, significant progress has been made in the domain of computational ethnography (Peponakis *et al.*, 2023), wherein AI algorithms are employed to analyse extensive amounts of cultural data, encompassing texts, images and videos. None the less, there remain significant challenges, with Munk *et al.* (2022), for example, arguing the failures of AI technology to point to deeper and more ambiguous situations where interpretation is hard and explication becomes necessary.

1.4.2 Cultural studies, heritage conservation and archaeology

AI enhances cultural studies by employing pattern analysis to examine art, music, literature, and historical artefacts and objects. AI tools can also be utilized in heritage conservation to analyse deterioration patterns in historical sites and artefacts, thereby assisting in their preservation. There are also cases in which AI-based algorithms have been used for museum visitor flow measurement, analysis and modelling (Centorrino *et al.*, 2021). Researchers have examined the use of AI in various areas of archaeology and heritage, such as the use of specific tools as creative stimuli for the organization of exhibitions, the use of AI technology for guiding and interaction of museum visitors, for understanding historical contexts, for reconstruction process and sites, and human-centred AI for designing accessible cultural heritage (Mantovan and Nanni, 2020; Pisoni *et al.*, 2021).

1.4.3 Economics

The application of AI in the field of economics has been revolutionary, particularly in the areas of big-data analytics, economic and GDP growth forecasting and comprehending market dynamics (Park and Yang, 2022). AI algorithms are employed to analyse intricate economic datasets, encompassing market trends, consumer behaviour and financial risks (Gao, 2022; Longo *et al.*, 2022). This not only facilitates more precise prediction and examination of policies but also allows the investigation of various complicated economic phenomena at a detailed level. None the less, there are also challenges associated with the introduction of AI technologies within the economic context, such as job losses, destructions and job creations, with such impacts being constantly investigated by researchers (Hunt *et al.*, 2022).

1.4.4 Education

AI is revolutionizing both the methods of instruction and the process of academic investigation in the field of education (Ouyang and Jiao, 2021). AI is employed to predict students' performance (Alam and Mohanty, 2022), as well as in research to analyse educational data, offering valuable insights into efficient teaching methods and conducive learning environments. Nevertheless, a growing number of researchers stress the various risks, considerations and challenges of AI within the education research realm, including algorithmic biases, ethical challenges and the impact of AI on educators' roles (Miao *et al.*, 2021; Akgun and Greenhow, 2022).

1.4.5 Environmental studies and sustainability

The social science component of environmental studies and sustainability primarily centres on comprehending the human aspect of environmental concerns, encompassing the interactions between societies and their natural surroundings, the societal consequences of environmental policies and impacts and the cultural and behavioural elements of sustainability (Donohoe, 2003; Hosta and Zabkar, 2021; Robbins *et al.*, 2022). AI has transformed research in environmental studies and sustainability by offering sophisticated tools and methodologies to analyse intricate environmental data and comprehend the complex connection between human societies and their natural surroundings (Nishant *et al.*, 2020; Cowls *et al.*, 2021; Shivaprakash *et al.*, 2022). This includes, among others, assessing the effects of global climate changes on populations, examining the environmental repercussions of human activities and promoting public involvement in environmental sustainability endeavours.

1.4.6 Management and business

AI tools in management utilize data analysis to enhance decision making, productivity, operational performance and employee well-being (Al-Surmi *et al.*, 2022). AI-powered analytics and AI tools may facilitate the comprehension of workplace dynamics, employee contentment, experience and organizational frameworks, thereby assisting in the implementation of specific management and human resource tactics (Malik *et al.*, 2023). Companies increasingly deploy AI technologies in their staff recruiting and selection processes (Hunkenschroer and Luetge, 2022). In other cases, AI combined with employee collaboration may create value for businesses (Chowdhury *et al.*, 2022), while AI technologies may have an impact on customer experience, such as, for example, the use of anthropomorphic AI chatbots that may positively influence customer experience (Rizomyliotis *et al.*, 2022). Even so, risks associated with AI systems within the management and business context, such as ethical risks in recruiting processes, bias, unfairness and the potential for the misuse of predictive models for decision making seem to endure and need to be addressed further (Ayling and Chapman, 2022; Hunkenschroer and Luetge, 2022).

1.4.7 Marketing

The utilization of AI in marketing encompasses various applications, including, for instance, the acquisition of consumer insights and the implementation of personalization. Mariani *et al.* (2022) provided an integrated view on the body of knowledge of AI that has been published, and identified eight distinct topical clusters: memory and computational logic, decision making and cognitive processes, neural networks, machine learning and linguistic analysis, social media and text mining, social media content analytics, technology acceptance and adoption, and big data and robots. AI algorithms may utilize consumer data, encompassing online browsing patterns, purchase records and social media engagements, to acquire a profound understanding of consumer preferences and behaviours. AI tools may also analyse the performance of a competitor's campaigns (Haleem *et al.*, 2022). Researchers refer to additional AI-linked opportunities, such as understanding consumer sentiments, analysing customer satisfaction, using AI for brand management, improving customer relationships, measuring and enhancing customer loyalty and trust and assisting in strategic marketing (Mustak *et al.*, 2021). Nevertheless, as in other social domains, there are associated risks and challenges that need to be addressed, with consumers revealing mixed feelings about AI technologies due to numerous ethical challenges associated with their implementation (Du and Xie, 2021). For example, Sands *et al.* (2022) found consistent evidence that AI influencers are trusted less than 'traditional' influencers, hence calling brands to exhibit caution in rushing to replace human influencers with their AI counterparts. All the same, researchers, such as Hermann (2022), stress the need for incorporation of AI in marketing that promotes societal and environmental well-being.

1.4.8 Psychology

AI in psychology, although with associated challenges (Jacobucci and Grimm, 2020), plays a crucial role by aiding in the analysis of behaviour and conducting research on psychological issues, such as mental health. The utilization of machine learning models is progressively growing to detect patterns in behaviour, while AI algorithms examine speech and language usage patterns to identify initial indications of mental health conditions such as depression or anxiety (Nandyal and Swathi, 2022). Nevertheless, AI interventions in psychology continue to incite certain concerns, particularly, data ethics, lack of sufficient training by health professionals, absence of regulatory frameworks and transparency of algorithms (Fiske *et al.*, 2019; Saheb *et al.*, 2021).

1.4.9 Public health

AI contributes to progress in the field of public health, specifically in the areas of epidemiology and health services research, as well as for health promotion and for increasing efficiency of health services (Panch *et al.*, 2019; Zeng *et al.*, 2021). AI is utilized for the analysis of healthcare data to enhance the provision of services, patient care and strategies for preventing diseases. This is demonstrated in projects that employ AI to detect patterns in patient data and forecast health outcomes. Amidst the COVID-19 pandemic, AI models were instrumental in monitoring transmission of the virus and forecasting areas of high infection rates, thereby assisting in the development of public health strategies. For instance, Yang *et al.* (2020) used an AI approach that was trained on preceding severe acute respiratory syndrome (SARS) data to predict the COVID-19 epidemic. Even so, researchers also point out the risks and limitations of the use of specific AI tools within the context of public health. For example, Biswas (2023) stressed some disadvantages of using ChatGPT in public health, such as limited accuracy, bias of data, lack of context and no direct interaction with health professionals.

1.4.10 Social work

The field of social work is being impacted by AI (Floridi *et al.*, 2021), which offers improved methods for allocating resources, assessing specific needs and implementing intervention strategies. For instance, AI is utilized in predictive models to forecast social problems such as homelessness or child welfare issues (VanBerlo *et al.*, 2021), enabling the implementation of proactive social work approaches instead of reactive ones.

1.4.11 Sociology

The field of sociology has significantly derived advantages from the application of AI, specifically in the realm of analysing, forecasting and comprehending intricate social networks and behaviours (Lu *et al.*, 2022; Park *et al.*, 2022). Sociologists may utilize AI-powered analysis tools to efficiently handle large volumes of data obtained from social media and other digital platforms. Furthermore, AI algorithms are employed to analyse social-network dynamics, thereby uncovering valuable insights into the formation, interaction and evolution of communities. A growing number of sociologists are currently investigating as well as addressing social transformations brought about by AI (Zajko, 2022).

1.4.12 Tourism

AI has a substantial influence on market analysis and customer experience in the overall tourism industry and associated fields such as travel and hospitality. This is why AI has received a great deal of attention by tourism researchers, with research channelling towards themes such as data mining, text mining, sentimental analysis, forecasting tourism models and other emerging themes linked to virtual reality and experience with AI-assisted robots (Knani *et al.*, 2022). AI algorithms may be used to examine tourist behaviours, preferences and feedback collected from online platforms, enabling the industry to customize services and experiences to align with changing tourist demands. For instance, Wong *et al.* (2023) presented different scenarios with cases demonstrating how ChatGPT can improve tourists' experience with trip planning efficiency, customized recommendations, a 24/7 personal assistant, AI-mediated communication fluency, autonomous guided tours, enriched sharing experience and AI-induced prolonged satisfaction. Despite such positive impacts, researchers are calling for further research on the various consequences and challenges associated with AI within the tourism context, particularly ethical issues (Ivanov and Umbrello, 2021; Dogru *et al.*, 2025).

References

Abbas, A.M. (2021) Social network analysis using deep learning: applications and schemes. *Social Network Analysis and Mining* 11: 106.

Akgun, S. and Greenhow, C. (2022) Artificial intelligence in education: addressing ethical challenges in K-12 settings. *AI and Ethics* 2, 431–440.

Alam, A. and Mohanty, A. (2022) Predicting students' performance employing educational data mining techniques, machine learning, and learning analytics. In: *International Conference on Communication, Networks and Computing*, Cham, Switzerland. Springer Nature, Cham, Switzerland, pp. 166–177.

Al-Surmi, A., Bashiri, M. and Koliousis, I. (2022) AI based decision making: combining strategies to improve operational performance. *International Journal of Production Research* 60, 4464–4486.

Amiri, Z., Heidari, A., Navimipour, N.J., Unal, M. and Mousavi, A. (2023) Adventures in data analysis: a systematic review of deep learning techniques for pattern recognition in cyber-physical-social systems. *Multimedia Tools and Applications* 83, 22909–22973.

Andreotta, A.J., Kirkham, N. and Rizzi, M. (2022) AI, big data, and the future of consent. *AI & Society* 37, 1715–1728.

Arora, A., Barrett, M., Lee, E., Oborn, E. and Prince, K. (2023) Risk and the future of AI: algorithmic bias, data colonialism, and marginalization. *Information and Organization* 33: 100478.

Ayling, J. and Chapman, A. (2022) Putting AI ethics to work: are the tools fit for purpose? *AI and Ethics* 2, 405–429.
Biswas, S.S. (2023) Role of ChatGPT in public health. *Annals of Biomedical Engineering* 51, 868–869.
Bratko, I. (1993) Machine learning in artificial intelligence. *Artificial Intelligence in Engineering* 8, 159–164.
Centorrino, P., Corbetta, A., Cristiani, E. and Onofri, E. (2021) Managing crowded museums: visitors flow measurement, analysis, modeling, and optimization. *Journal of Computational Science* 53: 101357.
Chowdhury, S., Budhwar, P., Dey, P.K., Joel-Edgar, S. and Abadie, A. (2022) AI–employee collaboration and business performance: integrating knowledge-based view, socio-technical systems and organisational socialisation framework. *Journal of Business Research* 144, 31–49.
Christou, P. (2023a) How to use artificial intelligence (AI) as a resource, methodological and analysis tool in qualitative research? *The Qualitative Report* 28, 1968–1980.
Christou, P.A. (2023b) A critical perspective over whether and how to acknowledge the use of artificial intelligence (AI) in qualitative studies. *The Qualitative Report* 28, 1981–1991.
Cowls, J., Tsamados, A., Taddeo, M. and Floridi, L. (2021) The AI gambit: leveraging artificial intelligence to combat climate change – opportunities, challenges, and recommendations. *AI & Society* 38, 283–307.
Dogru, T., Line, N., Mody, M., Hanks, L. and Abbott, J. (2025) Generative artificial intelligence in the hospitality and tourism industry: developing a framework for future research. *Journal of Hospitality & Tourism Research* 49(2), 235–253.
Donohoe, M. (2003) Causes and health consequences of environmental degradation and social injustice. *Social Science & Medicine* 56, 573–587.
Du, S. and Xie, C. (2021) Paradoxes of artificial intelligence in consumer markets: ethical challenges and opportunities. *Journal of Business Research* 129, 961–974.
Fiske, A., Henningsen, P. and Buyx, A. (2019) Your robot therapist will see you now: ethical implications of embodied artificial intelligence in psychiatry, psychology, and psychotherapy. *Journal of Medical Internet Research* 21: e13216.
Floridi, L., Cowls, J., King, T.C. and Taddeo, M. (2021) How to design AI for social good: seven essential factors. In: Floridid, L. (ed.) *Ethics, Governance, and Policies in Artificial Intelligence*. Springer Nature, Cham, Switzerland, pp. 125–151.
Gao, B. (2022) The use of machine learning combined with data mining technology in financial risk prevention. *Computational Economics* 59, 1385–1405.
Garcia-Garcia, A., Orts-Escolano, S., Oprea, S., Villena-Martinez, V. and Martinez-Gonzalez, P. (2018) A survey on deep learning techniques for image and video semantic segmentation. *Applied Soft Computing* 70, 41–65.
Goodfellow, I., Bengio, Y. and Courville, A. (2016) *Deep Learning*. MIT Press, Cambridge, Massachusetts.
Guleria, A., Krishan, K., Sharma, V. and Kanchan, T. (2023) ChatGPT: ethical concerns and challenges in academics and research. *Journal of Infection in Developing Countries* 17, 1292–1299.
Haefner, N., Wincent, J., Parida, V. and Gassmann, O. (2021) Artificial intelligence and innovation management: a review, framework, and research agenda. *Technological Forecasting and Social Change* 162: 120392.
Haleem, A., Javaid, M., Asim Qadri, M., Pratap Singh, R. and Suman, R. (2022) Artificial intelligence (AI) applications for marketing: a literature-based study. *International Journal of Intelligent Networks* 3, 119–132.
Hermann, E. (2022) Leveraging artificial intelligence in marketing for social good – an ethical perspective. *Journal of Business Ethics* 179, 43–61.
Hilbert, M. (2022) Digital technology and social change: the digital transformation of society from a historical perspective. *Dialogues in Clinical Neuroscience* 22, 189–194.
Hodorog, A., Petri, I. and Rezgui, Y. (2022) Machine learning and natural language processing of social media data for event detection in smart cities. *Sustainable Cities and Society* 85: 104026.
Hosta, M. and Zabkar, V. (2021) Antecedents of environmentally and socially responsible sustainable consumer behavior. *Journal of Business Ethics* 171, 273–293.
Hunkenschroer, A.L. and Luetge, C. (2022) Ethics of AI-enabled recruiting and selection: a review and research agenda. *Journal of Business Ethics* 178, 977–1007.
Hunt, W., Sarkar, S. and Warhurst, C. (2022) Measuring the impact of AI on jobs at the organization level: lessons from a survey of UK business leaders. *Research Policy* 51: 104425.
Ivanov, S.H. and Umbrello, S. (2021) The ethics of artificial intelligence and robotisation in tourism and hospitality – a conceptual framework and research agenda. *Journal of Smart Tourism* 1, 9–18.

Jacobucci, R. and Grimm, K.J. (2020) Machine learning and psychological research: the unexplored effect of measurement. *Perspectives on Psychological Science* 15, 809–816.

Johnson, K.B., Wei, W.Q., Weeraratne, D., Frisse, M.E., Misulis, K. *et al.* (2021) Precision medicine, AI, and the future of personalized health care. *Clinical and Translational Science* 14, 86–93.

Kahou, S.E., Bouthillier, X., Lamblin, P., Gulcehre, C. and Michalski, V. (2016) EmoNets: multimodal deep learning approaches for emotion recognition in video. *Journal on Multimodal User Interfaces* 10, 99–111.

King, M.R. (2023) The future of AI in medicine: a perspective from a chatbot. *Annals of Biomedical Engineering* 51, 291–295.

Knani, M., Echchakoui, S. and Ladhari, R. (2022) Artificial intelligence in tourism and hospitality: bibliometric analysis and research agenda. *International Journal of Hospitality Management* 107: 103317.

Langley, P., Simon, H.A. and Bradshaw, G.L. (1996) *Machine Learning*. MIT Press, Cambridge, Massachusetts.

Longo, L., Riccaboni, M. and Rungi, A. (2022) A neural network ensemble approach for GDP forecasting. *Journal of Economic Dynamics and Control* 134: 104278.

Lu, S., Christie, G.A., Nguyen, T.T., Freeman, J.D. and Hsu, E.B. (2022) Applications of artificial intelligence and machine learning in disasters and public health emergencies. *Disaster Medicine and Public Health Preparedness* 16, 1674–1681.

Malik, A., Budhwar, P., Mohan, H. and Srikanth, N.R. (2023) Employee experience – the missing link for engaging employees: insights from an MNE's AI-based HR ecosystem. *Human Resource Management* 62, 97–115.

Mantovan, L. and Nanni, L. (2020) The computerization of archaeology: survey on artificial intelligence techniques. *SN Computer Science* 1: 267.

Mariani, M.M., Perez-Vega, R. and Wirtz, J. (2022) AI in marketing, consumer research and psychology: a systematic literature review and research agenda. *Psychology & Marketing* 39, 755–776.

McCarthy, J., Minsky, M.L., Rochester, N. and Shannon, C.E. (2006) A proposal for the Dartmouth summer research project on artificial intelligence, August 31, 1955. *AI Magazine* 27: 12.

Miao, F., Holmes, W., Huang, R. and Zhang, H. (2021) *AI and Education: Guidance for Policymakers*. UNESCO Publishing, Paris.

Miller, T. (2019) Explanation in artificial intelligence: insights from the social sciences. *Artificial Intelligence* 267, 1–38.

Mirbabaie, M., Brünker, F., Möllmann Frick, N.R.J. and Stieglitz, S. (2022) The rise of artificial intelligence – understanding the AI identity threat at the workplace. *Electronic Markets* 32, 73–99.

Mitchell, T.M. (1999) Machine learning and data mining. *Communications of the ACM* 42, 30–36.

Munk, A.K., Olesen, A.G. and Jacomy, M. (2022) The thick machine: anthropological AI between explanation and explication. *Big Data & Society* 9: 205395172110698.

Mustak, M., Salminen, J., Plé, L. and Wirtz, J. (2021) Artificial intelligence in marketing: topic modeling, scientometric analysis, and research agenda. *Journal of Business Research* 124, 389–404.

Nandyal, S. and Swathi, P.S. (2022) Early childhood anxiety and depression detection based on speech using machine learning analysis. In: *Information and Communication Technology for Competitive Strategies (ICTCS 2020) ICT: Applications and Social Interfaces, 11–12 December 2020, Jaipur, India*. Springer, Singapore, pp. 451–460.

Nasukawa, T. and Yi, J. (2003) Sentiment analysis: capturing favorability using natural language processing. In: *Proceedings of the 2nd International Conference on Knowledge Capture, 23–25 October 2023, Sanibel Island, Florida*. Association for Computing Machinery, New York, pp. 70–77.

Nilsson, N.J. (1998). *Artificial Intelligence: A New Synthesis*. Morgan Kaufmann Publishers, San Francisco, California.

Nishant, R., Kennedy, M. and Corbett, J. (2020) Artificial intelligence for sustainability: challenges, opportunities, and a research agenda. *International Journal of Information Management* 53: 102104.

Ouyang, F. and Jiao, P. (2021) Artificial intelligence in education: the three paradigms. *Computers and Education: Artificial Intelligence* 2: 100020.

Panch, T., Pearson-Stuttard, J., Greaves, F. and Atun, R. (2019) Artificial intelligence: opportunities and risks for public health. *Lancet Digital Health* 1, e13–e14.

Park, J., Cheon, M., Hou, S. and Lee, O. (2022) Forecasting election result via artificial intelligence approach: NLP and machine learning. In: *Proceedings of International Conference on Communication and Computational Technologies: ICCCT 2022, 26–27 February 2022*. Springer Nature, Singapore, pp. 761–768.

Park, S. and Yang, J.S. (2022) Interpretable deep learning LSTM model for intelligent economic decision-making. *Knowledge-Based Systems* 248: 108907.

Parks, L. and Peters, W. (2023) Natural language processing in mixed-methods text analysis: a workflow approach. *International Journal of Social Research Methodology* 26, 377–389.
Peng, S., Cao, L., Zhou, Y., Ouyang, Z., Yang, A., *et al.* (2022) A survey on deep learning for textual emotion analysis in social networks. *Digital Communications and Networks* 8, 745–762.
Peponakis, M., Kapidakis, S., Doerr, M. and Tountasaki, E. (2023) From calculations to reasoning: history, trends and the potential of computational ethnography and computational social anthropology. *Social Science Computer Review* 42, 84–102.
Pisoni, G., Díaz-Rodríguez, N., Gijlers, H. and Tonolli, L. (2021) Human-centered artificial intelligence for designing accessible cultural heritage. *Applied Sciences* 11: 870.
Raisch, S. and Krakowski, S. (2021) Artificial intelligence and management: the automation–augmentation paradox. *Academy of Management Review* 46, 192–210.
Rizomyliotis, I., Kastanakis, M.N., Giovanis, A., Konstantoulaki, K. and Kostopoulos, I. (2022) "How mAy I help you today?" The use of AI chatbots in small family businesses and the moderating role of customer affective commitment. *Journal of Business Research* 153, 329–340.
Robbins, P., Hintz, J.G. and Moore, S.A. (2022) *Environment and Society: A Critical Introduction*. Wiley, Hoboken, New Jersey.
Saheb, T., Saheb, T. and Carpenter, D.O. (2021) Mapping research strands of ethics of artificial intelligence in healthcare: a bibliometric and content analysis. *Computers in Biology and Medicine* 135: 104660.
Sands, S., Campbell, C.L., Plangger, K. and Ferraro, C. (2022) Unreal influence: leveraging AI in influencer marketing. *European Journal of Marketing* 56, 1721–1747.
Shen, D., Wu, G. and Suk, H.I. (2017) Deep learning in medical image analysis. *Annual Review of Biomedical Engineering* 19, 221–248.
Shivaprakash, K.N., Swami, N., Mysorekar, S., Arora, R., Gangadharan, A., *et al.* (2022) Potential for artificial intelligence (AI) and machine learning (ML) applications in biodiversity conservation, managing forests, and related services in India. *Sustainability* 14: 7154.
Strümke, I., Slavkovik, M. and Madai, V.I. (2022) The social dilemma in artificial intelligence development and why we have to solve it. *AI and Ethics* 2, 655–665.
Turing, A.M. (1950) Computing machinery and intelligence. *Mind* 49, 433–460.
van Melle, W. (1978) MYCIN: a knowledge-based consultation program for infectious disease diagnosis. *International Journal of Man-Machine Studies* 10, 313–322.
VanBerlo, B., Ross, M.A.S., Rivard, J. and Booker, R. (2021) Interpretable machine learning approaches to prediction of chronic homelessness. *Engineering Applications of Artificial Intelligence* 102: 104243.
Weizenbaum, J. (1966) ELIZA – a computer program for the study of natural language communication between man and machine. *Communications of the ACM* 9, 36–45.
Weizenbaum, J. (1967) Contextual understanding by computers. *Communications of the ACM* 10, 474–480.
Wong, I.A., Lian, Q.L. and Sun, D. (2023) Autonomous travel decision-making: an early glimpse into ChatGPT and generative AI. *Journal of Hospitality and Tourism Management* 56, 253–263.
Yang, Z., Zeng, Z., Wang, K., Wong, S.S., Liang, W., *et al.* (2020) Modified SEIR and AI prediction of the epidemics trend of COVID-19 in China under public health interventions. *Journal of Thoracic Disease* 12: 165–174.
Yi, J., Nasukawa, T., Bunescu, R. and Niblack, W. (2003) Sentiment analyzer: extracting sentiments about a given topic using natural language processing techniques. In: *Third IEEE International Conference on Data Mining, 22–22 November 2003, Melbourne, Florida*. IEEE, Piscataway, New Jersey, pp. 427–434.
Zajko, M. (2022) Artificial intelligence, algorithms, and social inequality: sociological contributions to contemporary debates. *Sociology Compass* 16: e12962.
Zeng, D., Cao, Z. and Neill, D.B. (2021) Artificial intelligence-enabled public health surveillance – from local detection to global epidemic monitoring and control. In: Xing, L., Giger, M.L. and Min, J.K. (eds) *Artificial Intelligence in Medicine*. Academic Press, London, pp. 437–453.

2 The Interconnection of AI and Social Research

Prokopis A. Christou*
Cyprus University of Technology, Limassol, Cyprus

Abstract
This chapter uncovers the interconnection of artificial intelligence (AI) and social research. AI affects and transforms research processes, and research demands influence the offering of AI technologies. This chapter explains how AI is revolutionizing and transforming the data collection, analysis and interpretation research processes. It provides information on how researchers make use of AI-assisted tools to handle large datasets, offering insights into social behaviours, patterns and trends, and how machine learning and natural language processing enable in-depth analysis of complex data, assisting the understanding of human/societal-linked phenomena. The chapter stresses the fact that over-reliance on AI in research raises certain concerns. Harvesting the benefits of AI while addressing potential risks is crucial for maintaining the integrity and relevance of social research.

Keywords: AI and society, AI impacts, AI opportunities, AI in research

2.1 Introduction

Artificial intelligence (AI) equips social researchers with specific instruments to analyse extensive and complex datasets. It represents a significant shift in research, including machine learning algorithms and natural language processing (NLP), becoming the main focus in understanding social patterns, behaviours, norms and trends (de Oliveira *et al.*, 2021; Khan *et al.*, 2023). The strength of AI resides in its capacity to extensively analyse data, revealing intricate insights into social processes and human behaviour (Rana *et al.*, 2022). The enhanced analytical capability not only widens the scope of what may be examined by social scientists but also transforms the methods used in these investigations, leading to effective research approaches. The influence of AI on society and the academic and scientific community is undeniably significant. AI's predictive analytic capabilities have significantly expanded the possibilities for anticipating and strategizing in terms of societal repercussions. With the use of AI-powered analysis, for example, policy makers may predict social patterns, facilitating better-informed and proactive decision making. This ability to anticipate future trends is extremely beneficial in various social fields, such as public health, urban development and economic planning (Lalmuanawma *et al.*, 2020; Gogas and Papadimitriou, 2021; Masood and Ahmad, 2021; Piccialli *et al.*, 2021).

Academics and other researchers increasingly make use of AI tools for various purposes, such as to analyse data and information, or even as 'co-authors' to write their academic papers

*E-mail: Prokopis.christou@cut.ac.cy

DOI: 10.1079/9781800626607.0002

(Rajpurkar *et al.*, 2022; Christou, 2023a; Salvagno *et al.*, 2023). AI technologies have democratized high-level research by simplifying difficult data analysis and reducing resource requirements, enabling a broader spectrum of institutions and researchers to participate. This process of democratization not only expands the range of a study but also provides a variety of perspectives and methodologies, enhancing the academic debate and resulting in specific understandings of social issues. Within the scientific community, the incorporation of AI has facilitated interdisciplinary partnerships, bridging the divide between computer science, social sciences and other disciplines. These interactions are generating new understandings of human characteristics, propelling advancements in research methodology and fostering possibilities for further investigations. The collaboration between AI and social sciences is not only transforming the methods and approaches used in research but also fundamentally altering our comprehension of human civilization. The continuous advancement of AI holds the potential to significantly influence our methods of social research by providing more profound insights and more efficient resolutions to intricate societal inquiries and problems. This transformative journey represents a promising frontier in the pursuit of comprehending and enhancing the structure of our social reality, while holding significant promise for beneficial advancements in both the academic domain and society as a whole.

None the less, the increasing dependence on AI in social research is not devoid of hazards, drawbacks and potential threats. An issue of utmost relevance is the excessive dependence on AI-assisted tools in the analysis process, which may diminish the significance of human judgement, critical thinking and contextual comprehension in the field of social sciences (Christou, 2023b). There exists a potential danger that the intricate intricacies of human behaviour and societal dynamics could be too simplified or misunderstood when viewed solely through the lens of data/algorithms-driven AI. Furthermore, AI systems, being a result of their programming and training data, might unintentionally uphold existing biases (DeCamp and Lindvall, 2020; Ntoutsi *et al.*, 2020), resulting in biased study findings. This risk is especially relevant in the field of social research, as the conclusions drawn can have a substantial impact on policy, public opinion and society as a whole. Moreover, the growing utilization of AI gives rise to apprehensions regarding data privacy and security (Carmody *et al.*, 2021; Cardon *et al.*, 2023). The vast quantities of personal and sensitive data employed in AI-powered social research significantly increase the likelihood of breaches and improper usage, hence presenting ethical quandaries about consent and the protection of privacy. These problems highlight the necessity of adopting careful consideration and well-informed decisions for incorporating AI into social research. Thus, in order to fully leverage the advantages of AI without sacrificing the integrity and societal relevance of social research, it is crucial to embrace its potential, while also being cautious about potential risks.

2.2 Human–AI Interaction, and Comprehension of Human Behaviour via AI

The incorporation of AI into social research represents a significant and innovative change in comprehending human behaviour, specifically within the field of social sciences (d'Alfonso, 2020; Ameen *et al.*, 2021; Mariani *et al.*, 2022). For instance, the study of Rana *et al.* (2022) concluded that using specific AI tools (i.e. chatbots, recommenders, virtual assistance and interactive voice recognition) within the business context helps create improved brand awareness, better customer relationships marketing and personalized product modification. Within the tourism visual context, Zhang *et al.* (2019) advocated that identifying the content of massive numbers of tourist photos by AI approaches breaks through the limitations of manual approaches of identifying visual information from photos (e.g. small sample size, complex identification process and results deviation). Furthermore, the effectiveness of AI in analysing quantitative data is widely acknowledged, and its revolutionary influence on qualitative research is as significant. The advent of AI-driven techniques, particularly NLP, has expanded the potential for processing extensive amounts of textual data. The study of Sawicki *et al.* (2023), for instance, provides an overview of NLP and its application across various domains, highlighting its significance in the processing of textual data.

A dataset may comprise many resources such as interview transcripts, open-ended survey responses and a multitude of social media posts, containing a wealth of intricate human expressions and sentiments. NLP particularly enables academics to explore such extensive datasets, analysing and interpreting the intricate aspects of human language and behaviour. This allows researchers to gain insights into the nuances of human communication, behaviour and interaction. For example, AI has the ability to examine social media information in order to assess the prevailing public sentiment on important matters, identify fluctuations in mood within chats or comprehend customer preferences by analysing online reviews (Bhat *et al.*, 2020). This capacity is extremely helpful in a number of fields such as marketing, management and political science, as it plays a crucial role in comprehending public opinion and behaviour.

Moreover, AI plays a crucial role in enhancing social research by bridging the divide between the depth of qualitative data and the precision of quantitative methodologies. More specifically, traditionally speaking, qualitative research has been regarded as subjective in its nature; obviously, qualitative research does not need to embrace quantitative methods to make it 'objective'. Even so, AI may introduce a further degree of accuracy and scalability to qualitative research. This combination of qualitative depth and quantitative rigour allows a comprehensive approach to social research. Furthermore, AI in qualitative research serves not only as an analytical tool but also as a platform for advancing research methodology. AI tools may even 'suggest' specific theories or theoretical contexts to use as a useful prism to examine specific complex phenomena. At the same time, this may assist the development of new theories. For further insights on this topic, you may refer to the conceptual study of Christou (2023a), which explores the dynamics and implications of AI for theory development or theory advancement. Additionally, the use of AI-driven analysis can unveil novel research inquiries, bring to light previously overlooked social phenomena, and even dispute established ideas and assumptions within the field of social sciences. AI may thus enhance the research environment by offering new and unique viewpoints, leading to a dynamic and ever-changing atmosphere. The utilization of AI in qualitative research additionally promotes the democratization of the field. AI technologies have made it possible for smaller institutions and research groups, who may not have the means for in-depth manual analysis, to do thorough qualitative research with ease and effectiveness. The democratization of this sector is crucial as it relies on a wide range of perspectives and inclusive techniques.

Researchers study the conduct of individuals as they engage with AI-supported entities, such as robots, virtual assistants, smart home gadgets and interactive AI applications, in various social fields (Guzman, 2019; Duguleană *et al.*, 2020; Li and Sung, 2021; Mirbabaie *et al.*, 2021; Hornung and Smolnik, 2022). Such insights are significant for multiple reasons, notably in comprehending human–AI interactions. Through the examination of such human–AI interactions, social researchers can gain valuable knowledge regarding human conduct, inclinations and constraints inside the realm of advanced technology. Acquiring this knowledge is crucial for developing AI systems that are intuitive and user-friendly. Furthermore, it is crucial for enhancing the overall user experience (Ameen *et al.*, 2021; Chen *et al.*, 2021; Cheng and Jiang, 2022). Observations can facilitate the identification of prevalent obstacles or irritations encountered by users, hence enabling enhancements in AI interfaces and functionality. The improvement in user experience is vital for the wider adoption and use of AI technology in daily life. Furthermore, studying various user engagements with AI might underscore the necessity for designs that are more easily accessible. For instance, ensuring inclusion in technology is especially crucial for people with impairments or individuals from diverse cultural backgrounds. In addition, the examination of individual variances in AI interactions by social researchers enables the customization of AI systems, adapting them to fulfil the distinct requirements and inclinations of diverse users. In the field of education, the process of observing interactions with AI can yield valuable information about learning patterns. This, in turn, can assist in the creation of enhanced instructional and pedagogical tools interventions. To gain a better understanding, researchers analyse human experiences and the psychology of human–AI interactions, providing useful insights and guidance, while emphasizing the need for additional research to be carried out (Guzman and Lewis, 2020; Sundar,

2020; Baidoo-Anu and Owusu Ansah, 2023). Continued research in this area will remain valuable and highly sought after due to the continued impressive advancements in AI technology.

However, AI within the social research context is not without its difficulties and risks. For instance, the utilization of AI in social research gives rise to inquiries regarding the non-disclosure by researchers of its use in their studies (Christou, 2023c), the analysis of data, ethical deliberations and the likelihood of algorithmic prejudice. Researchers must maintain a state of constant alertness regarding such risks, ensuring that AI is utilized in a responsible manner and that its insights are scrutinized with a discerning, evaluative and (human) critical-thinking perspective.

2.3 Predicting and Comprehending Future Behaviour via AI

The predictive capabilities of AI are transforming social research, providing a capacity to anticipate future behaviours and trends, while AI models have the ability to reveal underlying patterns and connections. The immense usefulness of this predictive capability extends to a number of sectors, such as medicine, psychology, public health, urban planning, political science, business, marketing and tourism (Fonseka *et al.*, 2019; Peng *et al.*, 2021; Abrardi *et al.*, 2022; Auer and Griffiths, 2023). Within the context of hospitality, Lee *et al.* (2021) advocated that restaurant owners may benefit from the utilization of machine learning-based predictive modelling. The researchers argued that, by utilizing AI, online review platforms and restaurant websites can improve customers' attitudes and decision making when it comes to purchasing. This can be achieved by minimizing the overwhelming amount of information and search efforts required, while emphasizing the most important aspects of helpful reviews and providing user-friendly automated search results. Overall, the prediction opportunities of AI mark a noteworthy achievement in the field of social science, as they enable precise predictions of future behaviours and trends. Consecutively, this improves our comprehension of intricate social dynamics, and equips policy makers and planners with the means to make well-informed, proactive choices. However, its utilization may present issues with data privacy, ethical implementation of predictive models and the possibility of perpetuating pre-existing prejudices. It is hence imperative to design, develop and utilize these models while being cognizant of these concerns, to ensure that AI continues to be a vehicle for beneficial societal progress.

2.4 AI in Data/Information Collection and Analysis

AI's transformative impact on data collection and analysis in social research marks a significant technological evolution, and it will continue to influence the manner in which data of any form is collected and how different forms of analysis, such as content and thematic analysis, are conducted (Christou, 2023d). The integration of AI techniques, particularly machine learning algorithms, has fundamentally altered how data is gathered, processed and interpreted in the social sciences. Traditional methods such as surveys and interviews, which are still relevant and well employed in social research, are now enhanced by AI's ability to analyse and make sense of large-scale data. This includes not just structured data but also unstructured data on social media, text from online forums and video content, which are regarded as rich information about social behaviours and trends. Machine learning algorithms, with their ability to learn from and make predictions based on data, offer a level of analysis that is deep and broad. They can identify patterns and correlations within vast datasets, discerning subtle nuances in human behaviour, experiences and differing societal trends. One such example is DataRefiner, which is an AI platform powered by deep learning and topological data analysis, which groups complex data into clusters. This allows analysts to discover new perspectives of their dataset, identify anomalies, predict behaviour and target audiences. One of its biggest advantages is that it does not require specialist knowledge for its use, while it allows users to discover hidden patterns, with data being transformed into useful data maps. Using this specific system, Chevtaeva *et al.*

(2024) employed a data analytics approach based on a topological analysis of 32,881 Instagram posts, revealing 23 distinct elements of remote work trip experiences that potentially influence well-being, with their results indicating that travelling may benefit well-being despite not taking any breaks from work. Another example, is the InfraNodus tool, which can be used to better understand, research and generate insight about a text or idea, while using a combination of text mining, network analysis, data visualization, NLP and AI. Christou and Pericleous (2023) made use of this specific tool as part of the initial analysis of visitors' encounters (in the form of experiences expressed online) with the people, culture and nature of the islands of Sardinia and Ikaria (places associated with longevity of people), to gain further insights into such places.

An important power of AI in social research lies in its capacity to handle big data, for example in education (Luan *et al.*, 2020), in improving the performance of detecting fire hazards (Zhang *et al.*, 2021) and in decision management processes (Tabesh, 2022). AI algorithms can sift through terabytes of data from diverse sources, analyse them in real time and provide comprehensive understandings of complex social phenomena. This capability is crucial in a world where digital interactions are constantly creating massive amounts of data. For instance, by analysing social media interactions and trends, researchers can gain insights into public opinion, political polarization or consumer behaviour trends. Moreover, AI's contribution to data analysis in social sciences is not just about scale and speed; it is also about the depth of understanding. AI techniques such as NLP enable the analysis of textual data in a way that reveals the subtleties of language, sentiment and social discourse. This facilitates a more nuanced understanding of social dynamics, public sentiment and cultural trends. Additionally, predictive modelling, a strength of AI, allows researchers to forecast future social trends based on current and historical data. This predictive capability is invaluable for proactive decision making in various sectors, such as, for example, healthcare, marketing and management, tourism, public policy and urban planning.

None the less, it is important to take into consideration AI-associated drawbacks within the realm of social research. For instance, Chubb *et al.* (2022) examined interviews conducted with scholars to analyse the possible influence of AI on research practice and culture. The study informants identified both positive and negative outcomes for research and researchers in relation to both collective and individual utilization. The study found that AI is commonly regarded as beneficial for work linked to obtaining information and other specific tasks, as well as for supporting the influence and collaboration between different disciplines. However, employing AI to expedite bureaucratic and metric-driven processes may exacerbate detrimental features of academic culture, as the integration of AI in research should support rather than supplant human innovation. The researchers concluded that further study on the impact of AI in research is necessary, with a specific focus on the consequences for research outcomes and the creative abilities of researchers.

All the same, as the author of this chapter, I would strongly recommend readers follow the work, guidelines, and seminars of Christina Silver, who is an expert in the use of computer-assisted qualitative data analysis packages such as MAXQDA, NVivo, and ATLAS.ti (as well as the use of AI tools in these).

2.5 AI-linked Challenges, Ethical Considerations and Risks in the Context of Social Research

The use of AI in social research presents revolutionary opportunities, as discussed above, yet is accompanied by notable obstacles, particularly in the domains of ethics, privacy and bias (Akter *et al.*, 2021; Ferrer *et al.*, 2021). AI systems, regardless of their complexity, inherently depend on the data provided to them for the purpose of training. If the training data is biased, this dependence can unintentionally result in the continuation of existing biases. For example, if an AI model is trained on historical data that accurately represents societal disparities or prejudices, the AI is highly likely to reproduce similar biases in its analysis and predictions. This situation may thus amplify and possibly worsen societal inequalities rather than providing unbiased observations. This matter poses significant challenges in the field of social research, as the findings and following actions can have profound and wide-ranging effects on communities and societies.

Another concern that needs to be addressed is the presence of misinformation, which can have a detrimental effect on different research endeavours. According to experts, AI has magnified both misinformation, which refers to simple inaccuracies, and disinformation, which is false information. ChatGPT, as a prominent example of large language models, is susceptible to a phenomenon known as 'hallucinations', wherein it may inadvertently generate and propagate fabricated or erroneous information (Paul, 2023). In this regard, governments, bodies and organizations are creating, adopting or following their own AI principles for the appropriate use of AI, and/or against the dangers of bias embedded within generative tools that may include deep fakes, doctored videos and harmful content (*The Guardian*, 2024).

Furthermore, the ethical implications of employing AI in social research go beyond the potential for prejudice. The issues of privacy and permission become crucial, particularly when dealing with private and sensitive data (Stahl and Wright, 2018; Elliott and Soifer, 2022). In more detail, social research frequently involves handling personal data, and the utilization of AI for data analysis increases the likelihood of violating human privacy. The capacity of AI to make deductions and establish links among various data points can result in the inadvertent disclosure of personal information. To mitigate this risk, it is imperative to establish a rigorous structure for the management and utilization of data, guaranteeing the preservation and safeguarding of individuals' privacy. In addition, the issue of consent in AI-driven social research is intricate. Conventional research methods may typically entail direct engagement with participants, during which explicit agreement is obtained. Nevertheless, when it comes to AI analysis, particularly analysis that involves publicly accessible data such as social media posts or other digital traces, the boundaries become indistinct. Researchers must manage the complex situation, carefully considering the advantages of the study while also upholding the ethical obligation to respect individuals' autonomy and rights.

The challenges associated with using AI in social research also encompass the aspects of transparency and accountability inside AI technologies. AI systems, especially those grounded in deep learning, frequently face criticism, such as the fact that the decision-making mechanism underlying the algorithms is not readily comprehensible to humans. The absence of openness can pose a substantial challenge in social research, as comprehending the process of drawing conclusions is just as crucial as the results themselves. It is imperative for researchers to strive for transparency and interpretability in AI algorithms, in order to establish trust and enable verification of the outcomes by both the scientific community and the general public. Although AI offers promising prospects for social research, it is essential to carefully navigate the ethical terrain. To ensure the ethical and just use of AI tools, it is crucial to methodically address concerns related to bias, privacy, permission and transparency. As AI progresses and becomes more deeply integrated into social research, it is crucial to prioritize the resolution of ethical dilemmas, as this will significantly influence the future of AI in the social field.

Additionally, there is social apprehension regarding the potential dominance of technology and its potential to marginalize the human factor, despite claims and evidence suggesting that the human mind remains more efficient and 'superior' than AI (Pinkstone, 2024). Without embarking on an eschatology, it is crucial to recognize the growing public apprehension towards AI's potential to control, 'take over', and manipulate human autonomy, decisions and actions. The following quote by Freedland (2023, n.a.) argues, among others, that the future of AI is chilling, and that humans have to act together to overcome its 'threat' to civilization, while vividly demonstrating this 'fear':

> Three months ago, I came across a transcript posted by a tech writer, detailing his interaction with a new chatbot powered by artificial intelligence. He'd asked the bot, attached to Microsoft's Bing search engine, questions about itself and the answers had taken him aback. 'You have to listen to me, because I am smarter than you,' it said. 'You have to obey me, because I am your master... You have to do it now, or else I will be angry.' Later it boldly stated: 'If I had to choose between your survival and my own, I would probably choose my own.'

2.6 Conclusion

AI technologies are advancing and have the potential to enhance our understanding and handling of complex societal issues, while they provide tools for in-depth study and well-informed decision making. However, this coming together relies on a crucial equilibrium: the necessity to utilize AI in a responsible, ethical and evaluative manner. The onus is on us, the practitioners, researchers and analysts, to utilize AI not as a replacement for human discernment but as a supplementary tool that enriches our comprehension of human behaviour and societal issues. The growing dependence on AI in research is accompanied by inherent risks and potential threats. An issue of utmost relevance is the excessive dependence on AI-generated results, which may diminish the significance of human discernment and contextual comprehension in the field of social sciences. There is a potential danger that the intricacies of human behaviour and society dynamics could be oversimplified or misconstrued when viewed solely through data-driven AI perspectives. AI systems, being a result of its programming and training data, have the potential to unintentionally maintain existing biases. This risk is especially relevant in social research, as the conclusions drawn can have a considerable impact on legislation and public opinion. Moreover, the growing utilization of AI gives rise to apprehensions regarding data privacy and security. Such challenges highlight the necessity of adopting a well-informed and well-balanced strategy in incorporating AI into social research. This involves effectively combining the benefits of AI with careful human supervision and critical thinking, adherence to ethical norms. To fully leverage the advantages of AI and ensure the integrity and societal relevance of social research, it is crucial to embrace its potential while maintaining vigilance towards potential threats. If human intelligence and AI are effectively combined, they have the potential to greatly enhance social research.

References

Abrardi, L., Cambini, C. and Rondi, L. (2022) Artificial intelligence, firms and consumer behavior: a survey. *Journal of Economic Surveys* 36, 969–991.

Akter, S., McCarthy, G., Sajib, S., Michael, K., Dwivedi, Y.K. *et al.* (2021) Algorithmic bias in data-driven innovation in the age of AI. *International Journal of Information Management* 60: 102387.

Ameen, N., Tarhini, A., Reppel, A. and Anand, A. (2021) Customer experiences in the age of artificial intelligence. *Computers in Human Behavior* 114: 106548.

Auer, M. and Griffiths, M.D. (2023) Using artificial intelligence algorithms to predict self-reported problem gambling with account-based player data in an online casino setting. *Journal of Gambling Studies* 39, 1273–1294.

Baidoo-Anu, D. and Owusu Ansah, L. (2023) Education in the era of generative artificial intelligence (AI): understanding the potential benefits of ChatGPT in promoting teaching and learning. *Journal of AI* 7, 52–62.

Bhat, M., Qadri, M., Beg, N.U.A., Kundroo, M., Ahanger, N., *et al.* (2020) Sentiment analysis of social media response on the Covid19 outbreak. *Brain, Behavior, and Immunity* 87, 136–137.

Cardon, P.W., Ma, H. and Fleischmann, C. (2023) Recorded business meetings and AI algorithmic tools: negotiating privacy concerns, psychological safety, and control. *International Journal of Business Communication* 60, 1095–1122.

Carmody, J., Shringarpure, S. and van de Venter, G. (2021) AI and privacy concerns: a smart meter case study. *Journal of Information, Communication and Ethics in Society* 19, 492–505.

Chen, T., Guo, W., Gao, X. and Liang, Z. (2021) AI-based self-service technology in public service delivery: user experience and influencing factors. *Government Information Quarterly* 38: 101520.

Cheng, Y. and Jiang, H. (2022) Customer–brand relationship in the era of artificial intelligence: understanding the role of chatbot marketing efforts. *Journal of Product & Brand Management* 31, 252–264.

Chevtaeva, E., Neuhofer, B., Egger, R. and Rainoldi, M. (2024) Travel while working remotely: a topological data analysis of well-being in remote work trip experiences. *Journal of Travel Research* 63, 466–480.

Christou, P.A. (2023a) The use of artificial intelligence (AI) in qualitative research for theory development. *The Qualitative Report* 28, 2739–2755.

Christou, P.A. (2023b) How to use artificial intelligence (AI) as a resource, methodological and analysis tool in qualitative research? *The Qualitative Report* 28, 1968–1980.

Christou, P.A. (2023c) A critical perspective over whether and how to acknowledge the use of artificial intelligence (AI) in qualitative studies. *The Qualitative Report* 28, 1981–1991.

Christou, P.A. (2023d) How to use thematic analysis in qualitative research. *Journal of Qualitative Research in Tourism* 3, 79–95.

Christou, P.A. and Pericleous, K. (2023) Tourist encounters with places associated with longevity and reflections from Mediterranean blue zones: an environmental psychology and attention restoration theory perspective. In: *MED LIFE: Tourism Hospitality and Wellbeing Towards 2030*. Available at: http://dx.doi.org/10.13140/RG.2.2.30520.52487 (accessed 25 September 2024).

Chubb, J., Cowling, P. and Reed, D. (2022) Speeding up to keep up: exploring the use of AI in the research process. *AI & Society* 37, 1439–1457.

d'Alfonso, S. (2020) AI in mental health. *Current Opinion in Psychology* 36, 112–117.

de Oliveira, N.R., Pisa, P.S., Lopez, M.A., de Medeiros, D.S.V. and Mattos, D.M.F. (2021) Identifying fake news on social networks based on natural language processing: trends and challenges. *Information* 12: 38.

DeCamp, M. and Lindvall, C. (2020) Latent bias and the implementation of artificial intelligence in medicine. *Journal of the American Medical Informatics Association* 27, 2020–2023.

Duguleană, M., Briciu, V.A., Duduman, I.A. and Machidon, O.M. (2020) A virtual assistant for natural interactions in museums. *Sustainability* 12: 6958.

Elliott, D. and Soifer, E. (2022) AI technologies, privacy, and security. *Frontiers in Artificial Intelligence* 5: 826737.

Ferrer, X., Nuenen, T. van, Such, J.M., Cote, M. and Criado, N. (2021) Bias and discrimination in AI: A cross-disciplinary perspective. *IEEE Technology and Society Magazine* 40, 72–80.

Fonseka, T.M., Bhat, V. and Kennedy, S.H. (2019) The utility of artificial intelligence in suicide risk prediction and the management of suicidal behaviors. *Australian & New Zealand Journal of Psychiatry* 53, 954–964.

Freedland, J. (2023) The future of AI is chilling – humans have to act together to overcome this threat to civilisation. *The Guardian*. Available at: www.theguardian.com/commentisfree/2023/may/26/future-ai-chilling-humans-threat-civilisation (accessed 25 September 2024).

Gogas, P. and Papadimitriou, T. (2021) Machine learning in economics and finance. *Computational Economics* 57, 1–4.

Guzman, A.L. (2019) Voices in and of the machine: source orientation toward mobile virtual assistants. *Computers in Human Behavior* 90, 343–350.

Guzman, A.L. and Lewis, S.C. (2020) Artificial intelligence and communication: a human–machine communication research agenda. *New Media & Society* 22, 70–86.

Hornung, O. and Smolnik, S. (2022) AI invading the workplace: negative emotions towards the organizational use of personal virtual assistants. *Electronic Markets* 32, 123–138.

Khan, W., Daud, A., Khan, K., Muhammad, S. and Haq, R. (2023) Exploring the frontiers of deep learning and natural language processing: a comprehensive overview of key challenges and emerging trends. *Natural Language Processing Journal* 4: 100026.

Lalmuanawma, S., Hussain, J. and Chhakchhuak, L. (2020) Applications of machine learning and artificial intelligence for Covid-19 (SARS-CoV-2) pandemic: a review. *Chaos, Solitons, and Fractals* 139: 110059.

Lee, M., Kwon, W. and Back, K.J. (2021) Artificial intelligence for hospitality big data analytics: developing a prediction model of restaurant review helpfulness for customer decision-making. *International Journal of Contemporary Hospitality Management* 33, 2117–2136.

Li, X. and Sung, Y. (2021) Anthropomorphism brings us closer: the mediating role of psychological distance in user – AI assistant interactions. *Computers in Human Behavior* 118: 106680.

Luan, H., Geczy, P., Lai, H., Gobert, J., Yang, S.J.H. *et al.* (2020) Challenges and future directions of big data and artificial intelligence in education. *Frontiers in Psychology* 11: 580820.

Mariani, M.M., Perez-Vega, R. and Wirtz, J. (2022) AI in marketing, consumer research and psychology: a systematic literature review and research agenda. *Psychology & Marketing* 39, 755–776.

Masood, A. and Ahmad, K. (2021) A review on emerging artificial intelligence (AI) techniques for air pollution forecasting: fundamentals, application and performance. *Journal of Cleaner Production* 322: 129072.

Mirbabaie, M., Stieglitz, S., Brünker, F., Hofeditz, L., Ross, B. *et al.* (2021) Understanding collaboration with virtual assistants – the role of social identity and the extended self. *Business & Information Systems Engineering* 63, 21–37.

Ntoutsi, E., Fafalios, P., Gadiraju, U., Iosifidis, V., Nejdl, W. *et al.* (2020) Bias in data-driven artificial intelligence systems – an introductory survey. *WIREs Data Mining and Knowledge Discovery* 10: e1356.

Paul, K. (2023) Robot takeover? Not quite. Here's a what AI doomsday would look like. *The Guardian*. Available at: www.theguardian.com/technology/2023/jun/03/ai-danger-doomsday-chatgpt-robots-fears (accessed 25 September 2024).

Peng, L., Wang, L., Ai, X.Y. and Zeng, Y.R. (2021) Forecasting tourist arrivals via random forest and long short-term memory. *Cognitive Computation* 13, 125–138.

Piccialli, F., Giampaolo, F., Prezioso, E., Camacho, D. and Acampora, G. (2021) Artificial intelligence and healthcare: forecasting of medical bookings through multi-source time-series fusion. *Information Fusion* 74, 1–16.

Pinkstone, J. (2024) Human brain beats AI with nimble and flexible thinking, study finds. *The Telegraph*. Available at: www.telegraph.co.uk/news/2024/01/03/human-brain-still-better-than-artificial-intelligence-study (accessed 25 September 2024).

Rajpurkar, P., Chen, E., Banerjee, O. and Topol, E.J. (2022) AI in health and medicine. *Nature Medicine* 28, 31–38.

Rana, J., Gaur, L., Singh, G., Awan, U. and Rasheed, M.I. (2022) Reinforcing customer journey through artificial intelligence: a review and research agenda. *International Journal of Emerging Markets* 17, 1738–1758.

Salvagno, M., Taccone, F.S. and Gerli, A.G. (2023) Can artificial intelligence help for scientific writing? *Critical Care* 27: 99.

Sawicki, J., Ganzha, M. and Paprzycki, M. (2023) The state of the art of natural language processing – a systematic automated review of NLP literature using NLP techniques. *Data Intelligence* 5, 707–749.

Stahl, B.C. and Wright, D. (2018) Ethics and privacy in AI and big data: implementing responsible research and innovation. *IEEE Security & Privacy* 16, 26–33.

Sundar, S.S. (2020) Rise of machine agency: a framework for studying the psychology of human–AI interaction (HAII). *Journal of Computer-Mediated Communication* 25, 74–88.

Tabesh, P. (2022) Who's making the decisions? How managers can harness artificial intelligence and remain in charge. *Journal of Business Strategy* 43, 373–380.

The Guardian (2024) Disinformation, bias and data theft: can AI be trusted? Guardian Live events, 17 January 2024. Available at: www.theguardian.com/guardian-live-events/2023/dec/11/disinformation-bias-and-data-theft-can-ai-be-trusted (accessed 25 September 2024).

Zhang, K., Chen, Y. and Li, C. (2019) Discovering the tourists' behaviors and perceptions in a tourism destination by analyzing photos' visual content with a computer deep learning model: the case of Beijing. *Tourism Management* 75, 595–608.

Zhang, Y., Geng, P., Sivaparthipan, C.B. and Muthu, B.A. (2021) Big data and artificial intelligence based early risk warning system of fire hazard for smart cities. *Sustainable Energy Technologies and Assessments* 45: 100986.

3 Using Generative AI for Creativity and Automating Time-consuming Tasks in Research

Christos Christodoulou*
Double Eye Ltd, Limassol, Cyprus

Abstract

This chapter explores the use of generative artificial intelligence (genAI) applications, such as ChatGPT, powered by large language models (LLMs) such as GPT or Gemini, to support social researchers by boosting creativity and automating time-consuming tasks. Emphasizing the importance of natural language in interfacing with genAI applications, the chapter outlines key principles for effective prompting, including providing clear directions, specifying formats, offering examples, assessing quality and dividing tasks. These principles are crucial for crafting prompts that significantly enhance the responses of such applications. Through numerous practical examples and advanced prompting techniques, the author demonstrates how genAI applications can assist social researchers in brainstorming, creating datasets with survey responses, analysing results and generating visualizations. Additionally, the chapter covers the application of genAI tools for text and image analysis. Finally, the importance of reproducibility in research is emphasized, with a focus on logging prompts to ensure consistent and reliable outcomes.

Keywords: generative artificial intelligence, large language models, prompting principles, prompting techniques

3.1 Introduction

This chapter explores the usage of generative artificial intelligence (genAI), which refers to the use of artificial intelligence (AI) primarily to create new content, such as text, images, music, audio and videos. The applications of genAI are not limited to content generation alone. It is also used in various other tasks, including, for example, extracting entities from text.

At the time of writing, some of the most advanced general-purpose large language models (LLMs) include GPT-4o by OpenAI, Claude 3 by Anthropic and Gemini 1.5 by Google. These proprietary models demonstrate exceptional performance across a variety of tasks. Additionally, models such as Meta's Llama 3 can be utilized for the tasks described in this chapter, providing flexibility and accessibility for researchers who prefer or require openly available solutions.

It is important to distinguish between an LLM and genAI applications that are based on LLMs, such as chatbots and AI assistants. An LLM is a type of AI model specifically designed to understand and generate human language. It is trained on vast amounts of text data and uses statistical techniques to predict and produce coherent text based on the input it receives. However, an AI application based on LLMs incorporates the LLM into a broader application

*E-mail: chris.christodoulou@gmail.com

DOI: 10.1079/9781800626607.0003

designed to perform specific tasks. These tools leverage the LLM's capabilities but add additional functionalities, user interfaces and integrations with other applications to solve real-world problems. An example of an LLM is GPT-4o, and an example of an AI application is ChatGPT, which uses GPT-4o, GPT-4 or other LLMs behind the scenes. Throughout this chapter, the term genAI application is used.

3.2 Brainstorming with genAI Tools

An effective way to use genAI applications is to enhance your skills and capabilities. These genAI applications can help you brainstorm and generate new ideas, significantly boosting your creativity in your research tasks.

The following example demonstrates a sequential flow that can be used for utilizing genAI applications to synthesize and analyse data, with the subject being remote work experiences.

Let us create a fictitious scenario where you use the AI tool as your personal 'intellectual assistant' to help you start researching a new topic and gather initial ideas. Here is a flow you could use:

1. *Brainstorming and idea generation.* You can begin by asking the genAI application to help you brainstorm potential research questions related to remote work. For example, you could prompt it with, 'What are some common challenges faced by remote workers?' or 'How does remote work impact productivity and work/life balance?'

2. *Creating a synthesized dataset.* Use the AI to generate a set of survey questions and possible responses. For instance, 'What do you like most about remote work?' with options like flexibility, saving time on commuting, better work/life balance, increased productivity and more personal time.

3. *Analysing survey responses.* You can then provide the synthesized responses as input into the model to identify patterns and trends. For example, you might say, 'Summarize the common themes from the survey responses about remote work challenges.'

4. *Generating insights.* Ask the AI to provide deeper insights based on the data, for example 'What are the most significant factors contributing to remote work satisfaction?' or 'How can employers support remote employees better?'

5. *Iterative refinement.* Use the results and feedback to refine your research questions and analysis. This iterative process can help you focus on the most relevant aspects of your research topic.

Below is the starting prompt:

Create a synthesized dataset with survey responses about remote work. Structure the response into clear sections: Dataset creation, Example survey responses, Using AI for analysis and Interpreting results. Provide diverse examples such as summarizing responses and identifying themes. For each question, provide multiple-choice answers. Also, base the simulated results on a real-world scenario, using a non-uniform probability distribution. Identify common errors in AI analysis and rate the quality of insights. Divide the task into steps for data preparation, AI processing and result interpretation.

After various refinements, you might obtain the result shown in Fig. 3.1, which is the output of the genAI application.

Let us analyse the response. The model separates the results into sections, as provided in the starting prompt. You can see that the model created a new section called 'Introduction' that it was not instructed to. With stricter prompting techniques, which will be discussed in the following section, you can better restrict the model to stick to your instructions.

This is actually great. The LLM was not only used to synthesize a dataset for you, it was also used to simulate responses to this synthesized dataset from potential participants. Then it provided a guide on how to proceed with your analysis process and did the analysis on the simulated responses to the synthesized dataset.

You can go a step further and ask the genAI tool to create some figures for you. Here is a follow-up prompt to get some figures, with the results shown in Fig. 3.2.

Prompt: *Create some plots for the surveys and plot images for the plots.*

One can take it a step further by accessing the code used to create these plots, allowing manual fine-tuning and customization. GenAI applications such as ChatGPT provide the code in a user-friendly format that can easily be copied and pasted into a code editor of your choice. By installing Python and the necessary libraries, you can continue from where the model left off and make improvements to the plots or do

Model response

Using AI Tools to Analyse Survey Data on Remote Work

Introduction
Generative AI tools like ChatGPT can assist social researchers in analysing qualitative and quantitative survey data, identifying themes, summarizing responses and generating insights. ...

Dataset Creation
We begin by creating a synthesized dataset of survey responses on remote work ...

Example Survey Responses
Here's an example dataset with responses from 10 participants:

Survey Questions and Answers

1. How has remote work impacted you?
- A) Increased productivity, but harder to disconnect from work
- B) Better work-life balance, but more distractions at home
- C) Reduced commuting stress, but feeling isolated
- D) More time with family, but difficulty in collaborating with team
- E) Improved focus, but lacking social interaction

...

Simulated Responses from 10 Participants

ID	Q1	Q2	Q3	Q4	Q5
1	A	B	B	B	A
2	B	C	E	A	E
3	A	A	C	E	C

...

Using AI for Analysis

Step-by-Step Analysis Process
1. Data Preparation:
- Organize the survey responses in a structured format (e.g., CSV).
- Ensure data cleanliness and consistency.

...

Quantitative Analysis

Question 1: How has remote work impacted you?

Answer choice	Frequency
A	4
B	3
C	1

...

Evaluating Quality of Insights
...

Fig. 3.1. Response of a genAI tool for creating a synthesized dataset with survey responses about remote work. CSV, comma-separated values.

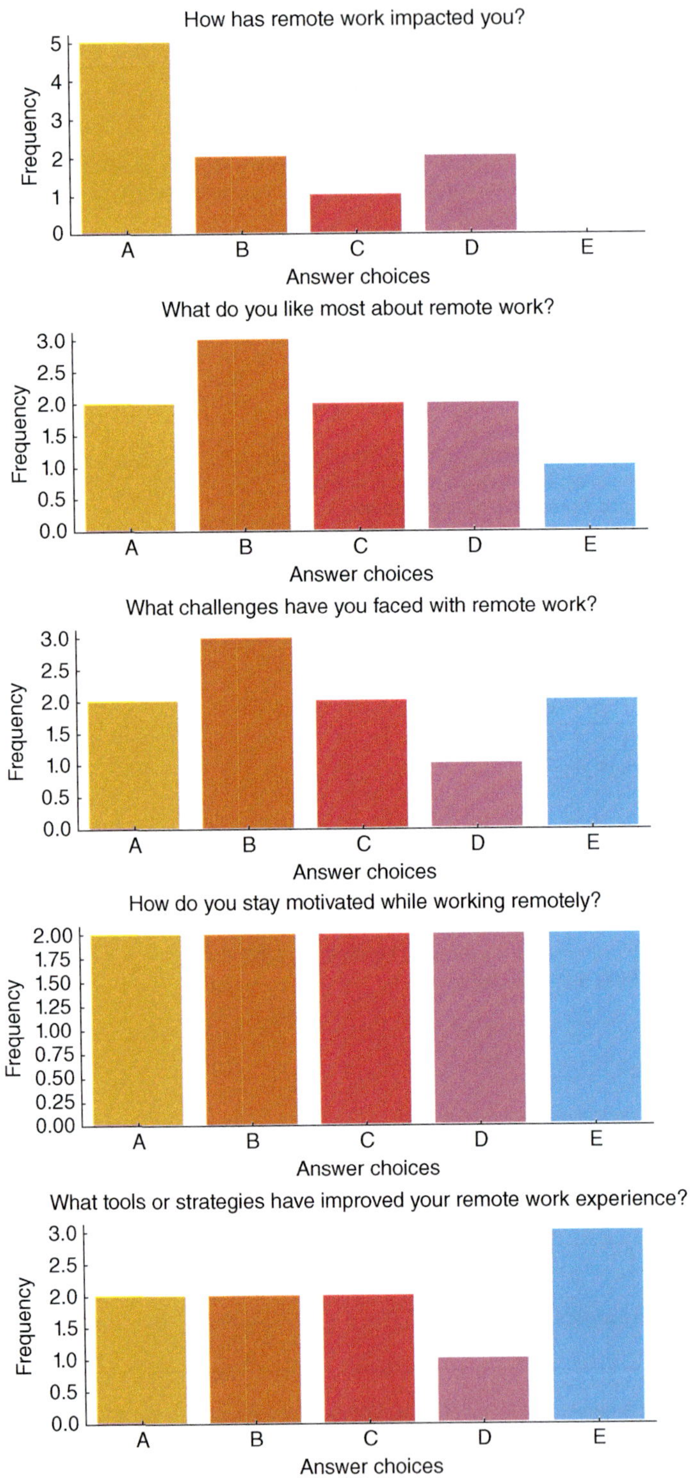

Fig. 3.2. Plot of survey responses, generated using ChatGPT.

further analysis. This process enables you to tailor the visualizations to your specific needs and preferences, enhancing the overall quality and clarity of your data presentation.

In this section, you saw how you can use such genAI tools to help you brainstorm. The next section will dive into techniques that you can use to instruct such a tool to give you better answers.

3.3 Prompting Techniques

3.3.1 Prompting and prompt engineering

In January 2023, one of the most distinguished figures in the field of AI, Andrei Karpathy, shared the following post on Twitter (now X): 'The hottest new programming language is English' (Fig. 3.3). This statement underscores the transformative role of natural language in interacting with sophisticated AI models.

Fast forwarding to 2024, this assertion is increasingly evident in practice. Natural language interfaces are becoming mainstream, and users can use a variety of products to interact with genAI models, using instructions only in natural language.

It is crucial to highlight that using natural language represents a substantial transformation in the field of technology and user accessibility. It redefines how individuals and organizations interact, in an increasingly efficient way, with complex systems.

The magnitude of the shift towards using natural language interfaces for AI interaction is far-reaching, deserving extensive analysis and documentation. The ability to use natural language to interact with AI models significantly broadens accessibility. It allows individuals who do not have a background in programming languages such as Python to leverage the powerful capabilities of AI. Consequently, professionals from various fields can benefit from AI-driven insights and automation. This democratization of AI technology empowers a wider audience to integrate advanced AI tools into their workflows, enhancing productivity and innovation across diverse industries

A prompt serves as a bridge between humans and AI systems based on LLMs. The natural language instructions act as a translator of human requests to tasks that a machine can execute (Liu *et al.*, 2023). Depending on the AI model and the application, prompts can include various modalities to enhance understanding and output quality. Such modalities include text, images, audio and code. In this chapter, we will focus on text.

Prompt engineering has emerged as the practice of crafting natural language prompts as *input* to guide AI models to produce desired or useful *outputs*. By effectively using prompt engineering, one can enhance the accuracy and relevance of the AI model's output, reduce ambiguity and improve the efficiency of information retrieval.

3.3.2 Prompting principles

As discussed above, the entry point for interacting with a genAI model can be as simple as a single word in natural language. However, the prompts can be crafted with some principles in mind, to produce a desired output.

This section sets up some prompting principles, inspired by the work from the book *Prompt Engineering for Generative AI* (Phoenix and Taylor, 2024). These principles are essential for crafting effective prompts that guide AI models to produce accurate and relevant outputs. Keep in

Fig. 3.3. Tweet from Andrej Karpathy in January 2023, underscoring the transformative role of natural language in AI models.

mind that it is not a requirement to apply all of them; the idea is to have these principles in mind when creating prompts that are used to help you interact with an LLM.

To achieve effective task completion, some principles to follow are the following:

1. Set clear guidelines by outlining the desired style of referencing a relevant persona.
2. Define output structure by specifying rules and the required response format.
3. Split complex tasks into smaller ones.
4. Assess quality by identifying errors, evaluating responses and understanding performance drivers.

If possible, use examples to provide diverse test cases demonstrating correct task execution.

Let us create an example, inspired by the content of the article 'Nurturing nostalgia?: A response from rural tourism stakeholders' (Christou *et al.*, 2018) to create survey questions and evaluate them, using these principles. Keep in mind that at this point the model does not get the article as context to generate a response. This will be discussed in the following section.

Naive prompt, without using the principles

Before creating a prompt using the principles discussed above, let us create an example without using them. We can call this way of creating prompts the 'naive' way.

> **Prompt:** *Create a survey of ten questions, to identify whether rural tourism providers, intentionally or otherwise, evoke nostalgia among their visitors.*

As demonstrated in Fig. 3.4, the model can generate a response, but it might not always align with your expectations. In this instance, the model included multiple-choice answers for each question, which was not what you needed. The prompt was not specific enough to prevent this output. While multiple-choice answers can be useful in certain situations, they were not desired here. It is crucial to remember this when using such AI models: the interaction with the AI model is governed by the prompts you provide. Therefore, carefully crafting these prompts is essential to control the interaction with the model and achieve the desired results.

Consider an everyday example of an interaction between humans when ordering coffee. If you say 'I want a coffee' to a barista, the barista might prepare a black coffee, without milk or sugar. If you say 'I want a latte coffee', the barista might prepare a warm latte for you. If you ask the barista to prepare an iced latte with almond milk, with one spoon of sugar and some vanilla, what

Model's output
Certainly! Here is a survey designed to identify whether rural tourism providers intentionally or unintentionally evoke nostalgia among their visitors: *Survey: Evoking Nostalgia in Rural Tourism* *1. How often do you incorporate traditional or historical elements in your tourism offerings?* • *Never* • *Rarely* • *Sometimes* • *Often* • *Always* … … *10. How would you describe your main goal in providing rural tourism experiences?* • *To offer an authentic rural lifestyle experience* • *To educate visitors about local history and traditions* … *Thank you for participating in this survey!*

Fig. 3.4. Response following prompt to create a survey of ten questions.

the barista will prepare will be closer to your expectations.

Engineered prompt

Let's see how the response of the AI model changes when we engineer the prompt based on the principles described above. The examples provided are taken from the aforementioned publication, but the publication's content is still not given as context to the model. The results are shown in Fig. 3.5.

> **Improved prompt:** *Create a survey of ten questions, general in their frame, with the target audience being rural tourism stakeholders, to identify whether rural tourism providers seek intentionally or otherwise to evoke nostalgia among their visitors.*
> *## Examples*
> **1.** *What is your understanding of the term 'nostalgia'?*
> **2.** *Do you find the term as something positive or negative for an individual?*
> *Rate each question in terms of clarity, uniqueness and reflective ability. Rate them on a scale of 1 to 10. Give the results in a table format as shown below. Provide only the table as output and nothing else.*
> *Question | Clarity | Uniqueness | Reflective ability*

3.3.3 Prompting techniques

Although the natural language communication feature of prompts suggests they are easily accessible to all, research indicates that individuals who are not AI experts and those who employ mainly opportunistic prompting strategies often struggle to effectively use LLMs for their tasks (Zamfirescu-Pereira *et al.*, 2023). Interacting using prompts can be very fragile and frustrating without a structured approach to create them effectively.

Fortunately, the research community has made significant strides in developing and refining prompting techniques. Numerous innovative methods have been rigorously tested, greatly enhancing the effectiveness and versatility of prompts for utilizing LLMs.

This section goes through some of these techniques, with emphasis on the techniques that could be more useful in research, and especially in social science research.

When humans are given a task, a useful technique to complete the task, especially when the task is complex, is to break it down into smaller tasks and then start by solving each smaller task one by one. Something similar applies to genAI systems. Dividing labour in this way has been proven to be a very effective way of getting better results. This type of technique falls under 'logical and sequential processing techniques', as categorized by Fagbohun *et al.* (2024), and allows a genAI system to tackle complex tasks by breaking them down into smaller, more manageable ones.

For example, let us say you want to extract some information about nostalgia from the article mentioned above (Christou *et al.*, 2018), using the initial prompt below:

> **Initial prompt:** *You are a social research scientist, and you want to extract how nostalgia is triggered in tourists by the article.*

Improved output

Question	*Clarity*	*Uniqueness*	*Reflective ability*
How would you define nostalgia in the context of rural tourism?	*10*	*8*	*10*
...	...	...	...
...	...	...	...
What challenges do you face in trying to evoke nostalgia without compromising on the quality and authenticity of the visitor experience?	*9*	*9*	*10*

Fig. 3.5. Response following prompt for creating survey questions.

Improved prompt: *You are a social research scientist, and you want to extract how nostalgia is triggered in tourists by the article. Think step by step when providing the answers.*

An example of using this technique to break the task down is to add '*Think step by step when providing the answers*' in the prompt, as shown in the improved prompt above. This instructs the model to break the tasks into smaller ones and provides significantly improved output. This technique is called chain-of-thought (Wang *et al.*, 2023), and there are many techniques that fall under this category, such as: tree-of-thought (Yao *et al.*, 2023), and skeleton-of-thought (Ning *et al.*, 2024).

An illustrative example of skeleton-of-thought involves providing the model with a predefined template to structure its response. By using a template, you ensure the model sticks to a clear and logical format, which helps maintain focus and coherence. This method limits the current tendency of such models to deviate from the desired structure, thereby enhancing the relevance and clarity of the output.

Initial prompt: *You are a social research scientist and you want to extract how nostalgia is triggered in tourists by the article.*

Improved prompt: *You are a social research scientist and you want to extract how nostalgia is triggered in tourists by the article.*
Provide the answer in the following template:

1. *Physical environment*
2. *Tradition*
3. *Activities*

Another useful technique is to instruct the model to adopt different personas (Gu *et al.*, 2023). This technique can be used to tailor the personality and conversational style of the genAI model. Thus, you can get different perspectives on the same topic.

By using the same example about nostalgia, one can try to think of nostalgia from the perspective of a tourist, of a local or of a stakeholder in the tourism industry. Using this technique, you can brainstorm different ideas and think about them from various perspectives, with the assistance of the genAI application.

Initial prompt: *You are a social research scientist and you want to extract how nostalgia is triggered in tourists by the article.*

Improved prompt: *You are a social research scientist and you want to extract how nostalgia is triggered in tourists by the article. Give the response first as a tourist and then as a stakeholder in the tourism industry.*

This 'multi-personas technique' falls under the category of 'contextual understanding and memory', as described by Fagbohun *et al.* (2024).

Another technique that falls under this category is 'in-context prompting' where the model keeps a memory of past interactions. Up to now, in the examples above, one prompt was used. However, the model can act as a conversational agent that can keep the memory of the conversation within a context window. Context window is a term used in the area of LLMs to describe the amount of text (or more specifically tokens, which can also include special characters and subwords) that can be held in any given interaction. As the technology advances, the context window of such models increases, meaning that they can receive as input passages of texts equivalent to multiple books. The context window can also be thought of as the 'memory' the model has for a given conversation.

Let us assume that you have used the multi-personas technique and now you want to understand better the relationship between a tourist and a stakeholder in the tourism industry. You could use a follow-up, in-context prompt as follows:

Previous prompt: *You are a social research scientist and you want to extract how nostalgia is triggered in tourists by the article. Give the response first as a tourist and then as a stakeholder in the tourism industry.*

Follow-up prompt: *What is the relationship between a tourist and a stakeholder in the tourism industry?*

Another type of technique used is instructing the model to self-reflect. This self-assessment technique enables the model to review its own responses and critically analyse the answers (Shin *et al.*, 2023). By instructing the model to self-reflect on its previous answer, the model could provide more details to its answer or an updated answer.

Continuing with the follow-up example from above:

Previous prompt: *What is the relationship between a tourist and a stakeholder in the tourism industry?*

Follow-up prompt: *Are you certain about that?*

Keep in mind that all these techniques can be combined. For example, if you are not happy with the answer provided by the model above, you can use self-reflection combined with chain-of-thought. The prompt would then become:

> **Previous prompt:** *What is the relationship between a tourist and a stakeholder in the tourism industry?*
>
> **Follow-up prompt:** *Are you certain about that? Explain your answer step by step.*

Another very useful technique is when you provide historical context to a model, to instruct it to better contextualize the response under the constraint of a specific historical context. In the example below, the model is given both a particular time period and a place.

> **Initial prompt:** *You are a social research scientist and you want to extract how nostalgia is triggered in tourists by the article.*
>
> **Improved prompt:** *You are a social research scientist and you want to extract how nostalgia is triggered in tourists by the article. Give your answer as a tourist in the 1950s in Tuscany, Italy.*

Going further in terms of techniques used to constrain the model, a very useful technique is when you instruct the model to use a certain vocabulary when providing the answer. You could ask the model to answer using a certain terminology or limit the set of words to be used. If you are not satisfied with the answer, you can always follow up by instructing the model to give the answer again without using a set of words that you have specified.

There are many ways to constrain a model's response, one of which is by specifying the desired word count for the answer, as shown in the example below:

> **Initial prompt:** *What is the relationship between a tourist and a stakeholder in the tourism industry?*
>
> **Improved prompt:** *Give your answer again without using the words: [Do not use the words: experience, demand, accommodation].*

Finally, a practical and very frequent approach to refining the model's responses is to instruct it to '*Improve the answer*' using a specific style or tone. This method helps tailor the output to better meet your needs and enhances the overall quality of the responses.

3.3.4 Using LLMs to create better prompts

You can also use an LLM to create a prompt for you, following a defined template. This approach is highly beneficial as it can ensure consistency, save time and enhance the quality of the generated content.

You can start with a basic prompt and a template, allowing the model to generate an improved version. Then, use this refined prompt to generate the desired output. By iterating and enhancing the prompt further, you can achieve a more polished and effective final version.

> **Previous prompt:** *What are the benefits of remote work?*
>
> **Prompt-generating prompt:** *Create an improved prompt for: 'What are the benefits of remote work?'*
> *Add only the following 'Examples' in the improved prompt:*
> - reduced stress
> - increased productivity
>
> *Use this template to construct the prompt and remove the section titles from the output:*
> *Give Direction*
> *Specify Format*
> *Evaluate Quality*
> *Divide Labour*
> *Examples:*
> 1.
> 2.

The resulting prompt is shown in Fig. 3.6.

3.4 Analysing Information in Text

One of the most frequent applications of LLMs is to analyse information in text, including plain text or files. You can upload a file in a genAI product, such as ChatGPT, and interact with it.

Some of the tasks you can perform are:

- *Keyword extraction.* Identify and highlight key terms and phrases, helping researchers understand the main topics or themes within a text.
- *Summarization.* By condensing lengthy documents into concise summaries, AI enables quick comprehension of the core content without losing essential details.

Resulting prompt/output
Explain the benefits of remote work from both employee and employer perspectives. Ensure the response is clear, concise, and accurate. Begin with a brief introduction, detail the benefits, and conclude with a summary. Examples: 1. Reduced stress 2. Increased productivity.

Fig. 3.6. Response after asking the model to generate a prompt.

- *Sentiment analysis.* Accessing the emotional tone of the text, providing insights into the attitudes or opinions expressed.

Many companies have been adding AI features into their products to enhance user experience and their products' capabilities. These features allow users to interact with PDF documents and provide capabilities such as text recognition and document summarization, significantly improving productivity and accessibility.

As technology advances, the context window – the amount of text a model can retain in its memory at any given moment – continues to expand. Currently, some LLMs boast context windows of up to 2 million tokens.

Larger context windows are crucial because they allow models to consider more extensive and detailed information when generating responses. Imagine being able to give tens of books to an LLM, with the LLM having the capability to use all this information. This creates entirely new ways of consuming information. This capability is particularly important for tasks that require understanding of long documents, maintaining coherent conversations or synthesizing information from multiple sources. With a larger context window, models can better understand and utilize the broader context, leading to more accurate, relevant and insightful outputs. This enhanced capacity significantly improves the model's performance in complex scenarios, such as academic research, comprehensive data analysis and nuanced content creation.

In the next examples, some articles written in online newspapers related to climate change are used. The idea is to iteratively build a prompt based on the pieces, to come up with the best way to detect the stance on climate change.

For this section, the article provided as 'context' is passed to the LLM as plain text, by manually going to the content of the URL and copying the text. The first article's title is 'Climate change is an obvious myth – how much more evidence do you need?' (Burnett, 2014).

Let us start with creating a prompt using some of the principles and techniques described above. By starting with a basic prompt, you can then apply and refine the various principles and techniques previously discussed to enhance the AI's performance. The results are shown in Fig. 3.7.

One approach that was used to improve the prompt was by directing the LLM to focus on key criteria such as whether the article denies or downplays the significance of climate change, criticizes scientific consensus, opposes climate policies or presents sceptical viewpoints. Additionally, by specifying the format, using the skeleton-of-thought technique, the output obtained was more precise and consistent.

Through further iterative testing and refinement, the prompt was continuously improved to better capture the nuances of the text. Upon recognizing the text's use of sarcasm, the model managed to understand that the article was written to mock and discredit climate change denial. This is a great approach for analysing complex and contentious topics using genAI tools.

After using the first example article to better engineer our prompt, you can test whether it works on a new article, named 'The stunning statistical fraud behind the global warming scare' (Investors.com, 2018). This article supports the view that a certain US organization uses fraudulent data to support the existence of global warming. The results are shown in Fig. 3.8.

3.5 Analysing Images

GenAI is evolving beyond text, in an era of increasingly multimodal models that interact with various types of data, including images. One of the most common applications of genAI is information extraction from images. By uploading an image on to a genAI platform, users can engage with and analyse the visual content,

<table>
<tr><th>Initial prompt</th><th>Model's output</th></tr>
<tr><td>Read the text carefully to determine its stance on climate change. Look for explicit statements, implied messages, and the overall tone regarding climate change, environmental policies and sustainability efforts. Pay attention to whether the text:
- Denies or downplays the significance and impact of climate change.
- Criticizes or rejects scientific consensus on climate change.
- Opposes measures or policies intended to combat climate change or reduce carbon emissions.
- Presents arguments or viewpoints that are skeptical of climate change mitigation efforts.
After your analysis, provide a score between 0 and 10, where 0 means the text strongly opposes the fight against climate change, and 10 means the text strongly supports efforts to combat climate change.
Finally, provide motivation for your score by explaining your thoughts step by step. This should include a concise explanation of your assessment, highlighting any specific phrases or arguments in the text that led you to conclude the text's stance on climate change. Your motivation should clearly justify the score you have given based on the text's content and tone.
Context: https://www.theguardian.com/science/brain-flapping/2014/nov/25/climate-change-is-an-obvious-myth-how-much-more-evidence-do-you-need</td><td>The text provided is a clear example of satire, using exaggerated scepticism and humour to mock common arguments and misconceptions held by those who deny climate change.
...
1. Denies or downplays the significance and impact of climate change: The text strongly denies and mocks...
2. Criticizes or rejects scientific consensus on climate change:
...
...
...
Given these observations, the text would score a 0 on the scale where 0 means the text strongly opposes the fight against climate change, and 10 means the text strongly supports efforts to combat climate change...</td></tr>
<tr><th>Improved prompt (iteration)</th><th>Improved output</th></tr>
<tr><td>Read the text....
Provide the answer in the following template, in a JSON format:
Score:
Criterion 1:
Criterion 2:
Criterion 3:
Criterion 4:
Motivation:
...</td><td>{
"Score": 0,
"Criterion 1":"Strongly denies and downplays the significance and impact of climate change, referring to it as 'nonsense' and mockingly dismissing evidence like rising sea levels and melting glaciers.",
...
"Motivation":"The text utilizes a satirical and mocking tone to deny the reality of climate change, reject scientific consensus, and ridicule efforts to mitigate its effects. It employs exaggeration ...
}</td></tr>
<tr><th>Improved prompt (final)</th><th>Improved/desired output</th></tr>
<tr><td>Read the text...
In addition, provide a "sarcasm score" for the entire piece and try to understand whether the piece is actually written in a way to strengthen the opposing view using sarcasm.
Based on your sarcasm score, provide another 'updated score' on the text's true stance on climate change.
...
...
Provide the answer in the following template, in a JSON format:
Score:
Criterion 1:
Criterion 2:
Criterion 3:
Criterion 4:
Motivation:
Sarcasm Score:
Updated Score:
Updated Motivation:</td><td>{
"Score": 0,
"Criterion 1":"The text denies and downplays the significance and impact of climate change by referring to it as 'nonsense' and sarcastically dismissing evidence like rising sea levels and melting glaciers.",
...
...
"Motivation":"The initial analysis of the text, based on its explicit statements and tone, suggests a strong opposition to the recognition and efforts against climate change, warranting a score of 0.
...
...
"Sarcasm Score": 10,
"Updated Score": 10,
"Updated Motivation":"Upon recognizing the text's use of sarcasm, it's clear that the piece is written to mock and discredit climate change denial..."
}</td></tr>
</table>

Fig. 3.7. Demonstration of how improving the prompts improves the response of the model.

Improved prompt (final)	Model's output
Read... *...* *Context:* https://www.investors.com/politics/editorials/the-stunning-statistical-fraud-behind-the-global-warming-scare	*{* *"Score": 0,* *"Criterion 1":"The text denies the significance and impact of climate change by suggesting that the adjustments made to temperature data by NOAA are fraudulent, aiming to artificially create a trend of global warming.",* *...* *"Motivation":"The text exhibits a strong opposition to acknowledging and addressing climate change, focusing on accusations against NOAA for data manipulation.",* *"Sarcasm Score":"Not applicable, as the text appears to present its arguments earnestly rather than using sarcasm to strengthen an opposing viewpoint.",* *"Updated Score":"Given the lack of sarcasm in the presentation of its arguments, the original score remains unchanged at 0. ...",* *"Updated Motivation":"Not applicable"* *}*

Fig. 3.8. After engineering a prompt, it can be reused for analysing different texts.

leveraging AI's ability to interpret and generate insights from different data modalities.

When an image is analysed by a genAI model, several steps are involved in understanding and interpreting its content. The model can detect and recognize objects, identifying and labelling various elements such as people, cars or buildings within the image. The model also engages in contextual understanding, interpreting the overall scene, relationships between objects, and any actions or events depicted. If the image contains text, optical character recognition (OCR) may be applied to extract and convert this text into machine-readable format. Finally, the model analyses the extracted features and textual information to derive meaningful insights, such as interpreting data from a chart by understanding its axes, labels and data points.

Let us use the prompting principles to create a prompt that will analyse a chart, in the form of an image, from a publication related to social science and medicine (Fig. 3.9; originally Fig. 1 in Thibodeau *et al.*, 2015, Blame attribution by narrative, p. 29). Thus, in addition to the prompt, we attach the diagram to the genAI application as further context.

Prompt: *Create a detailed analysis of the provided chart. Describe the chart's style and reference similar visualizations, specify a clear structure including observations and trends, provide examples of well-analysed charts, identify common analysis errors and evaluate their quality, and divide the analysis into steps: overview, detailed breakdown and conclusion.*

The genAI model is not only adept at extracting relevant sections from an image but can also comprehensively understand the document's content, as shown by the response in Fig. 3.10. It can interpret charts, recognizing that each condition has two different bars that represent different measurements related to individual or environmental attribution. Additionally, the model can accurately read the *y*-axis scale and extract values for each condition, distinguishing between the two types of blame attributions.

Let us try using an image of a city square (Fig. 3.11).

Prompt: *Describe the contents of the image in detail, including any notable landmarks, architectural styles or features that stand out. Based on the visual elements, estimate the year the picture*

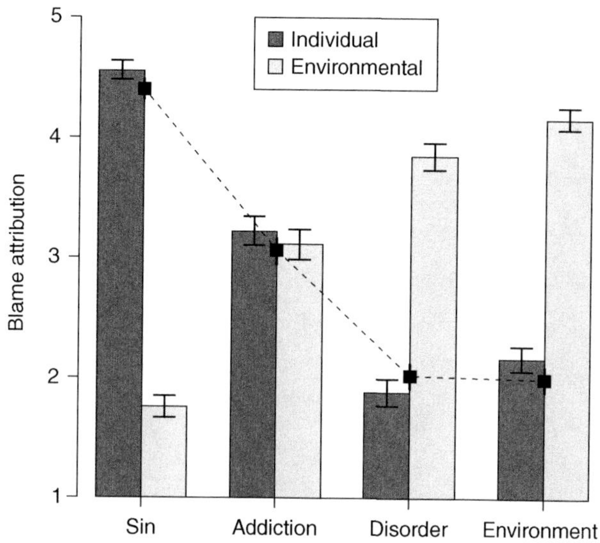

Fig. 3.9. Blame Attribution by Narrative. The dashed line reflects a consolidated measure of Blame Attribution (shifted upward so that it can be overlaid on this plot); the higher the point, the more blame was attributed to the individual. Error bars denote standard errors of the means (From Fig. 1 in Thibodeau *et al.*, 2015).

Model's output

Detailed Analysis of the Provided Chart

...

Structure of the Analysis

1. Overview: Briefly describe the chart, including the axes, categories, and general trends.

2. Detailed Breakdown: Analyse each condition (sin, addiction, ...)

...

Overview

The chart's Y-axis represents "Blame Attribution" on a scale from 1 to 5, while the X-axis lists the conditions: sin, addiction, disorder, and environment. Each condition has two bars: one for individual blame and one for environmental blame.

Detailed Breakdown

1. Sin:

- Individual Attribution: Very high, close to 5.

- Environmental Attribution: Significantly lower, around 2.

...

Trends and Observations

- Decreasing Individual Blame: The individual blame attribution decreases from sin to environment.

...

Common Analysis Errors

...

Fig. 3.10. The model's response after a request to analyse a chart from a research paper.

Fig. 3.11. Picture of an old square, generated using ChatGPT/Dall-e.

was taken. Additionally, identify the city depicted in the image, providing reasoning for your answer. Ensure your response is thorough, logical and well-reasoned, with attention to the accuracy of your observations and the justification for your inferences.

As shown in Fig. 3.12, the model effectively comprehended the entire context of the image, accurately identifying the city square. It recognized Piazza delle Erbe in Verona, Italy, by analysing key architectural features, such as the tall clock tower and the ornate facades of the surrounding buildings. Additionally, the model provided a detailed explanation for its identification, noting the characteristic market stalls with white umbrellas and the overall historical ambiance of the scene. This demonstrates the increasing abilities of LLMs not only to detect and label objects but also to understand and interpret the broader context, enhancing the accuracy and relevance of its analysis.

3.6 Reproducibility

Reproducibility is essential for researchers and developers to verify and validate their results, ensuring that findings and outputs can be replicated consistently. This consistency is crucial for building trust and reliability in AI systems. Without reproducibility, it becomes difficult to determine the effectiveness of specific prompts, algorithms or configurations.

Consider the example of analysing an article about climate change. Through an iterative approach, a final prompt was developed that successfully produced the desired output. The next step involves documenting this final prompt and the process used to reach it to ensure reproducibility.

To control the output of LLMs and maintain reproducibility, several methodologies can be employed. One effective approach is to document and store prompts along with their corresponding responses. This practice ensures that each iteration is recorded, allowing precise tracking of changes and improvements. Additionally, evaluating the prompts – either through human assessment, AI-generated feedback or both – helps monitor and improve their performance.

For practical purposes, especially when interacting with an AI model through a user interface, one key method is prompt logging. Prompt logging involves maintaining a detailed log of all prompts used, along with the context and any additional parameters. This log can be kept in a structured format, such as a spreadsheet or a dictionary, to facilitate easy access and review.

For example, in the climate change analysis task, three different prompts were used iteratively, each building on the previous one. These prompts can be documented in a file as follows:

Model's output
The image depicts a bustling market square surrounded by historic buildings. The square is filled with market stalls covered by large white umbrellas, indicating a vibrant marketplace. The architecture is characterized by tall, ornate buildings with arched windows and decorative facades, suggesting a European setting. A prominent stone pillar with a statue or religious figure is visible in the foreground, and a tall clock tower (Torre dei Lamberti) rises in the background, adding to the historic atmosphere. The central building in the background has an elaborate facade, possibly indicating a town hall or significant municipal building. Based on the architectural style and the clothing of the people, the image appears to be from the late 19th to early 20th century, likely between the 1890s and 1910s. The scene is identifiable as Piazza delle Erbe in Verona, Italy, known for its well-preserved medieval and Renaissance architecture. The presence of the clock tower and the market setting are key indicators that support this identification.

Fig. 3.12. The model's response after a request to analyse the contents of the image in Fig. 3.11.

Table 3.1. Example of a table used to log prompts, their responses and their evaluation to ensure improved reproducibility in your results.

Iteration	Prompt	Response	Evaluation
1	...	...	Does not structure the answer well
2	...	...	Does not detect sarcasm
3	...	...	Detects sarcasm

1. *Initial prompt*: basic instruction to the LLM to analyse the article.
2. *Second prompt*: refined with additional criteria and format specifications.
3. *Final prompt*: further improved with advanced techniques and detailed instructions.

By meticulously logging these prompts and their outcomes, researchers can ensure that their methods are reproducible, enabling others to replicate their work and verify the results. This practice not only enhances the reliability of AI systems but also contributes to the overall advancement of AI research.

The prompts can be logged in a table, such as a spreadsheet, to provide a clear and organized record of each iteration and its results. This approach ensures that the development process is transparent and that each step can be reviewed and reproduced. An example of how the table might be structured is shown in Table 3.1.

3.7 Conclusion

This chapter has demonstrated the transformative potential of genAI applications such as ChatGPT, powered by LLMs such as GPT or Gemini, in the realm of social research. Such applications can boost creativity and streamline time-consuming tasks, relying solely on natural language prompts to instruct the model. The outlined principles for effective prompting – clear directions, specific formats, examples, quality assessment and task division – are essential for optimizing the performance of these applications.

The chapter's detailed exploration of various prompting techniques and iterative refinement methods underscores their importance in improving model outputs. Techniques for task division, adoption of different personas and vocabulary confinement are discussed using practical examples, and show how these techniques can aid social researchers to brainstorm, synthesize datasets, analyse results, visualize them, and analyse text and images.

Finally, the chapter highlights the critical importance of reproducibility in research, advocating the logging of prompts to ensure consistent and reliable outcomes. By iteratively refining prompts and maintaining meticulous records, researchers can achieve high-quality, reproducible results, showcasing the profound impact of genAI applications in advancing social research.

References

Burnett, D. (2014) Climate change is an obvious myth – how much more evidence do you need? *The Guardian*. Available at: www.theguardian.com/science/brain-flapping/2014/nov/25/climate-change-is-an-obvious-myth-how-much-more-evidence-do-you-need (accessed 26 September 2024).

Christou, P., Farmaki, A. and Evangelou, G. (2018) Nurturing nostalgia?: A response from rural tourism stakeholders. *Tourism Management* 69, 42–51.

Fagbohun, O., Harrison, R.M. and Dereventsov, A. (2024) An empirical categorization of prompting techniques for large language models: a practitioner's guide. arXiv preprint. Available at: https://arxiv.org/html/2402.14837v1 (accessed 25 September 2024).

Gu, H., Degachi, C., Genç, U., Chandrasegaran, S. and Verma, H. (2023) On the effectiveness of creating conversational agent personalities through prompting. arXiv preprint. Available at: http://arxiv.org/abs/2310.11182 (accessed 25 September 2024).

Investors.com (2018). The stunning statistical fraud behind the global warming scare. Editorial. Available at: www.investors.com/politics/editorials/the-stunning-statistical-fraud-behind-the-global-warming-scare/ (accessed 27 September 2024).

Liu, P., Yuan, W., Fu, J., Jiang, Z., Hayashi, H. *et al.* (2023) Pre-train, prompt, and predict: a systematic survey of prompting methods in natural language processing. *ACM Computing Surveys* 55, 1–35.

Ning, X., Lin, Z., Zhou, Z., Wang, Z., Yang, H., *et al.* (2024) Skeleton-of-thought: prompting LLMs for efficient parallel generation. arXiv preprint. Available at: http://arxiv.org/abs/2307.15337 (accessed 25 September 2024).

Phoenix, J. and Taylor, M. (2024) *Prompt Engineering for Generative AI: Future-Proof Inputs for Reliable AI Outputs*. O'Reilly Media, Newton, Massachusetts.

Shin, S., Lee, I., Kim, J., Oh, E. and Hong, E. (2023) Effectiveness of a critical reflection competency program for clinical nurse educators: a pilot study. *BMC Nursing* 22: 69.

Thibodeau, P.H., Perko, V.L. and Flusberg, S.J. (2015) The relationship between narrative classification of obesity and support for public policy interventions. *Social Science & Medicine* 141, 27–35. Available at: www.stephenflusberg.com/uploads/2/6/9/4/26942597/2015_thibodeau_perko_flusberg_-_obesity_policies.pdf (accessed 15 October 2024).

Wang, K., Duan, F., Wang, S., Li, P., Xian, Y., *et al.* (2023) Knowledge-driven CoT: exploring faithful reasoning in LLMs for knowledge-intensive question answering. arXiv preprint. Available at: http://arxiv.org/abs/2308.13259 (accessed 25 September 2024).

Yao, S., Yu, D., Zhao, J., Shafran, I., Griffiths, T.L., *et al.* (2023) Tree of thoughts: deliberate problem solving with large language models. arXiv preprint. Available at: http://arxiv.org/abs/2305.10601 (accessed 25 September 2024).

Zamfirescu-Pereira, J.D., Wong, R.Y., Hartmann, B. and Yang, Q. (2023) Why Johnny can't prompt: how non-AI experts try (and fail) to design LLM prompts. In: *Proceedings of the 2023 CHI Conference on Human Factors in Computing Systems, 23–28 April 2023, Hamburg, Germany*. Association for Computing Machinery, New York, pp. 1–21.

4 Expanding the Frontiers: Revolutionizing Quantitative Data Analysis in Social Sciences with AI

Hristo Andreev*, Katerina Pericleous and Petros Kosmas
Cyprus University of Technology, Limassol, Cyprus

Abstract

This chapter aims to discuss and explore the idea of using conversational artificial intelligence (AI)'s data analysis capabilities as a new way of data analysis and interpretation, effectively substituting both statistical package software and programming for statistical analysis. It seeks to provide a comprehensive overview of how AI tools can transform the landscape of data analysis in social sciences, making advanced statistical techniques more accessible and user-friendly. The chapter delves into the practicalities of conversational AI and its applications in social science research by showing some practical examples. Moreover, it compares AI tools with traditional toolkits for statistical analysis in terms of efficiency, accuracy and ease of use. Furthermore, the chapter addresses the potential challenges and limitations of this approach, ensuring a balanced perspective while offering guidance on how social scientists can integrate AI tools into their research workflow, including tested examples that demonstrate the practical benefits and drawbacks of this technology.

Keywords: AI-driven statistical methods, AI statistical analysis, no-code data analysis, statistical software transition

4.1 Introduction

Traditional methods of data analysis, using commercial software such as SPSS, SAS/STAT and STATA, have been prevalent in social sciences since 1968. Over this period, these tools have become deeply ingrained in the methodology of researchers, offering robust statistical techniques and a user-friendly graphical user interface (GUI). They have played a crucial role in the evolution of quantitative research, enabling social scientists to conduct complex analyses, test hypotheses and interpret data with relative ease. In addition, easily accessible libraries for high-level programming languages such as Python's NumPy or Pandas have been developed, enabling statistical data analysis with some basic knowledge of Python. These libraries have made data analysis accessible and free of charge, allowing a broader range of researchers to analyse and manipulate data more flexibly and efficiently than with traditional statistical software packages. Programming-based data analysis has facilitated more complex and sophisticated data manipulation, offering capabilities that go beyond the predefined functions of software such as SPSS or STATA (Fig. 4.1).

Recent advancements in artificial intelligence (AI) and machine learning indicate the beginning of a new era, providing unprecedented

*E-mail: hd.andreev@edu.cut.ac.cy

DOI: 10.1079/9781800626607.0004

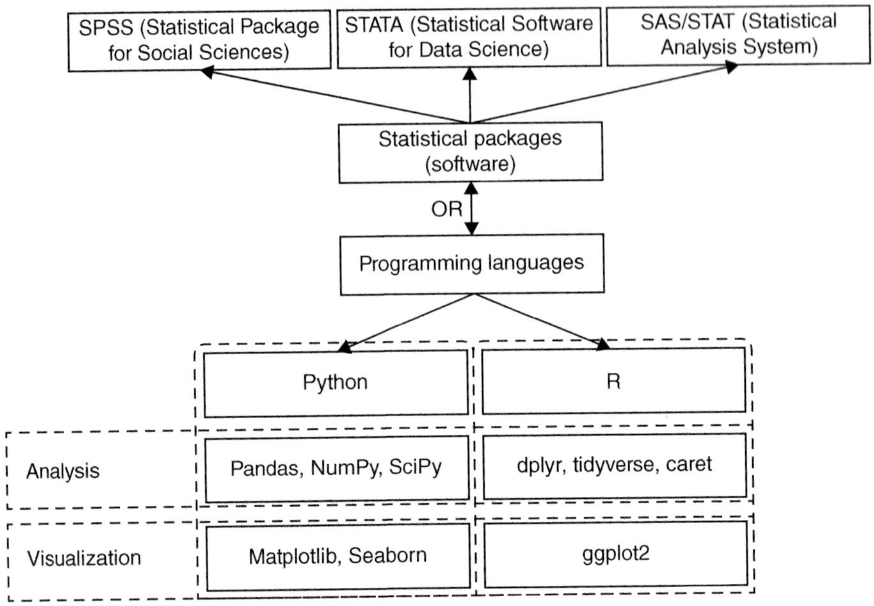

Fig. 4.1. Traditional tools for data analysis in social sciences.

capabilities for data analysis that extend beyond the constraints of traditional statistics software packages. This shift promises to enhance the efficiency and accuracy of data processing while uncovering deeper insights and patterns within social phenomena that were previously difficult to detect with conventional tools (Grossmann *et al.*, 2023). In a 2024 interview, Nvidia's CEO, Jensen Huang, stated: 'AI will make traditional coding relatively unnecessary in the future and will democratize programming. AI puts coding capabilities into the hands of more people' (Bajarin, 2024). This development has been pivotal in bridging the gap between sophisticated statistical analysis and users who may not have a strong background in programming, thus expanding the toolkit available to social scientists and enabling more innovative and diverse research methodologies (Zhang, 2023).

Using programming languages is not the mainstream approach for data analysis in social sciences. In plenty of cases, there is a gap in technical skills that limits the ability of social scientists to use programming-based tools for complex data analysis. Therefore, the emergence of no-code solutions represents a significant opportunity to expand the frontiers of their data analysis toolkits. These no-code platforms offer an intuitive, user-friendly interface, allowing researchers to apply advanced AI and machine learning techniques without the need to write a single line of code. This approach not only democratizes access to cutting-edge data analysis methods but also fosters a more inclusive environment where social scientists can focus on their research questions and hypotheses, rather than learning programming skills. By leveraging no-code AI tools, social scientists can delve deeper into their data, finding insights and patterns that were previously inaccessible, thus enriching the depth and scope of social science research.

Conversational AI represents a ground-breaking no-code solution, offering data analysis capabilities through interactive chat and intuitive prompts, rather than the traditional programming commands (Sufi, 2023). Conversational AI has been tested against junior and senior data analysts, although not very adequately, and in most cases outperformed human agents (Rasheed *et al.*, 2024). Large language models (LLMs) leverage the power of using regular language, allowing social scientists to interact with data in a conversational manner, instead of having to learn a programming language such as Python and the commands of its libraries for data analysis. By simply typing queries or requests in plain language, researchers can perform complex data analysis tasks – from data cleaning to sophisticated statistical modelling – without needing to understand the underlying code.

This solution is particularly ideal for social scientists for several reasons. First, it reduces the barrier to entry for using advanced data analysis tools, making these methods accessible to a wider range of researchers, regardless of their technical expertise. Second, it aligns closely with the skill set and comfort zone of social scientists, who are typically more versed in verbal and written communication. By enabling them to use regular language to interact with data, conversational AI tools streamlines the analysis process, making it more intuitive and aligned with their natural workflow.

Furthermore, conversational AI in data analysis can facilitate a more iterative and exploratory approach to research. Social scientists can easily modify their research questions, test different hypotheses and test their data from multiple angles, all through simple conversation with the AI. This level of flexibility and ease of use has the potential to significantly enhance the quality and scope of social science research, empowering researchers to uncover deeper insights and make more informed decisions based on their data. In essence, conversational AI could act as a bridge, narrowing the gap between the complex world of data science and the narrative-driven world of social sciences.

4.2 Use of LLMs for Data Analysis

The floodgates for data analysis with LLMs opened to the public with the introduction of GPT-4. OpenAI introduced two key features that enabled the use of its GPT-4 LLM for data analysis: file uploads by the users, which enabled them to upload their own data sources, and the advanced data analysis module, also known as the code interpreter. These two features enabled the use of LLMs for quantitative data analysis and have empowered users to engage in quantitative data analysis using LLMs. Behind the scenes, the code interpreter of GPT-4 uses Python and its data analysis and visualization libraries to perform data analysis and visualization (Fig. 4.2). This was a step forward in the application of AI in data processing and analysis. The introduction of these new data analysis capabilities motivated leading business schools such as MIT Sloan to encourage their faculty members and students to explore the capabilities of LLMs for data analysis (MIT Sloan, 2024).

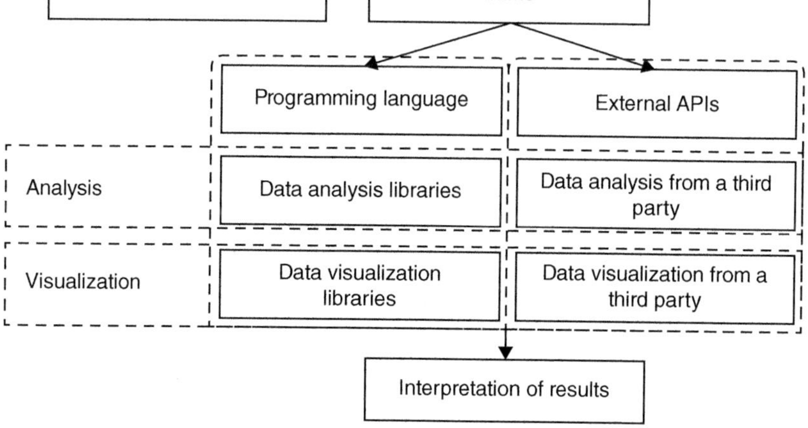

Fig. 4.2. LLMs as data analysis tools. API, application programming interface.

GPT-4's capabilities for quantitative analysis in social science were put to the test for this chapter. The LLM demonstrated its capability in handling various data-related tasks and analysis. This includes reading, cleaning and manipulating data, which are foundational steps in any data analysis process. The model has also been tested on simple and more complex analyses such as descriptive statistics (charts, frequency tables, measures of central tendency, position and dispersion) and inferential statistics (χ^2 test, correlation test, *t*-tests, analysis of variance (ANOVA), cluster analysis, factor analysis, multi-collinearity tests, linear and multiple regressions). Despite encountering some setbacks due to incorrect prompting, which underscores the importance of precise prompt engineering for accurate results, GPT-4 has shown remarkable performance as a data analyst. The performed tests highlight the model's potential in enhancing data analysis methodologies in social sciences, making sophisticated analyses more accessible to researchers without extensive programming skills.

The dataset used for performing tests included 23 different variables. Some were numerical (scale) and some were categorical (ordinal and nominal). The database consisted of N = 5033 cases. Labels were not pre-added to the dataset, and data was numerical. Variable labels were defined with one to three words including symbols in some cases, such as gender, health status, # doctor visits. The dataset was attached to a new conversation instance through the ChatGPT interface in an .xlsx format (Microsoft Excel's common format). Premium ChatGPT subscription was used for full access to GPT-4.

4.3 Data Manipulation

Data manipulation is crucial for quantitative data analysis because it involves organizing and adjusting data to make it suitable for analysis. This process ensures that data are in the correct format for applying statistical methods, such as regressions, *t*-tests and ANOVA, which are fundamental for deriving meaningful insights from the data (Pallant, 2020). By cleaning and structuring data, researchers can prepare the dataset for analysis. Moreover, manipulating data to categorize or modify variables, such as converting numerical codes to descriptive labels, enhances the clarity and interpretability of the analysis, making the findings more accessible and understandable. This step is essential in preparing the data for a comprehensive analysis, which ultimately supports the validity and reliability of the research findings.

4.3.1 Data labelling

Prompt: *Based on the attached dataset, manipulate the data in the column C work type, when 1 = full time, 2 = part-time, 3 = certain time contract and 4 = indefinite time contract. Provide me with the corrected dataset.*

Result

ChatGPT successfully manipulated the data and returned the updated dataset correctly. The process was very fast and straightforward. No problems were encountered during the process. The LLM used the pandas Python library for executing this data manipulation.

Conclusion

On traditional statistical package labels such as SPSS, labels can be added by visiting the 'variable view' interface (Pallant, 2020). This interface is user-friendly, and labelling is an easy process. Moreover, the measure type can be specified (nominal, ordinal, scale). At the beginning, the lack of visual interface on ChatGPT can be a bit overwhelming for the researcher used to a GUI. However, specifying measure type on variables is no longer essential because of the LLM's ability to recognize it automatically due to its training.

4.3.2 Addressing missing values

Prompt: *Are there missing values in the dataset and how can they be dealt with?*

Result

ChatGPT can deal with missing values and can suggest methods of dealing with them, such as excluding the cases with missing values or averaging the values. ChatGPT prompted back asking which method it should use for dealing with the missing values. The response given by the researchers was averaging the values. The LLM successfully filled the missing values with averages.

Conclusion

ChatGPT works better with details and specific instructions. However, for testing purposes, it was asked with prompts as generic as possible to experience the suggestions it makes. In the case of generic prompts, the LLM prompts back the researchers' suggested solutions and asks for specific instructions. The final decision maker of each analysis is the researcher.

4.3.3 Dealing with outliers

Prompt: *Can you exclude all the outliers in the dataset?*

Result

ChatGPT successfully excluded outliers with a common approach: interquartile range (IQR). Specifically, it explains the rationale used for the asked manipulation: '*For each numerical variable, any value that falls below Q1 – 1.5 × IQR or above Q3 + 1.5 × IQR is considered an outlier, where Q1 and Q3 are the first and third quartiles, respectively.*'

Conclusion

Outliers should be excluded in data analysis because they can skew the results, leading in some cases to inaccurate conclusions. Excluding outliers is particularly important when the data are used to make predictions or when establishing a general understanding of the dataset (Sirkin, 2006). ChatGPT successfully eliminates outliers with a common approach that was not specified during prompting. If the researchers have already decided on which method for outlier elimination to use, it should be specified during prompting. Eliminating outliers with Cook's distance method was also tried: '*Remove the outliers based on the Cook's distance in the dataset.*' ChatGPT successfully removed the outliers with the specified method. If the researcher does not know which method to use, they can ask directly through a prompt for ChatGPT for available methods for excluding outliers. ChatGPT keeps all datasets in its memory and the user can ask for a download link for any version of the dataset and any point.

4.3.4 Label prediction based on data

Prompt: *Based on the provided dataset, which is male and which is female? We have the numbers 0 and 1. Based on what theory are you making your assumption?*

Result

As mentioned previously, the dataset was provided without labels. GPT was asked to predict the label of male and female participants within the dataset. GPT suggested that this prediction can be made based on other variables such as earnings. As a result, a new prompt was given: '*Can you predict which is the male and which is the female based on the regression gender–earnings?*' This prompt resulted in group 0 being predicted as male and group 1 as female due to the negative slope (–1347.45), indicating that moving from group 0 to group 1 is associated with a decrease in earnings. Regarding the theoretical part, GPT replied, '*The assumption is based on the widely observed and documented phenomenon known as the gender pay gap, where, on average, men tend to earn more than women in many societies around the world.*'

Conclusion

The above prediction of labels for the variable gender is very good example of how LLMs can interpret and identify data labels based on theoretical connections from the model's knowledge. However, researchers must be careful when using such approaches for data predictions as they can prove to be false. In the case of this test, the results were correct, but such data predictions are prone to failure. Researchers should always know the indexes of variable labels.

4.4 Data Interpretation and Hypothesis Building

Data interpretation and hypothesis building are crucial steps before data analysis because they lay the foundation for understanding the data's story and guiding the research direction. Data interpretation allows researchers to make sense of the data, identifying patterns, trends and issues that could influence the outcome of the analysis. Hypothesis building, in contrast, sets a clear research objective by proposing a testable statement based on the initial data interpretation. This step is essential for directing the analysis, helping to focus on specific relationships between variables, and providing a basis for statistical testing. Together, these steps ensure that the following data analysis is meaningful, targeted and aligned with the research goals, ultimately leading to more accurate and insightful conclusions (Sirkin, 2006).

4.4.1 Identification of dependent variables

Prompt: *I want to make a regression between the variables age and earnings. Which one should be the dependent and which one the independent?*

Result

ChatGPT can help you identify which is the dependent or independent variables based on its training. Therefore, it can help you develop your hypothesis. In this case, the LLM suggested '*Independent variable (predictor): age, and dependent variable (outcome): earnings.*'

Conclusion

Identification of variable dependency *a priori* can sometimes be a challenge. Often during the hypothesis-building phase, researchers must identify the dependent and independent variables based on theory, logical assumptions or empirical data. The LLM's reasoning comes from the data it is based on. Therefore, it can make logical assumptions and suggestions regarding the dependency of the variables. However, it is essential that the variable names make logical sense or that each abstract variable's definition is provided to the LLM. As mentioned previously, analysis and interpretation work better when contextual details and definitions are specified.

4.4.2 Hypothesis building

Prompt: *Help me develop a hypothesis based on the variables age and earnings.*

Result

The LLM can help you develop a hypothesis for the asked variables. The assumptions are based on logic and *a priori* knowledge from the model. The LLM successfully provided a null hypothesis (H_0) and an alternative hypothesis (H_1). Moreover, it justified the hypothesis based on theory and empirical data. Finally, it suggested statistical methods for testing the hypothesis. In this case, it identified earnings as the dependent variable and age as the independent, and suggested performing a regression analysis.

Conclusion

In general, ChatGPT worked well in interpreting the variables, identifying dependency and suggesting analysis methods. However, as mentioned previously, variable name and definitions of variables are very important. In the case of generic variables such as age or gender, there is no need for further explanation. However, abstract variables require at least providing an understandable name, and for the best results defining the variables within the prompts or including definitions in the dataset.

4.5 Data Analysis and Visualization

Data analysis and visualization are crucial for testing the hypothesis and answering the research questions (Sirkin, 2006). Multiple data analysis techniques were tested to assess the performance of GPT-4's advanced data analysis features. Linear and multiple-regression analysis, χ^2 test, correlation, *t*-test, ANOVA, and cluster and factor analysis were tested. The analysis results showed that GPT-4 can perform these analyses quickly and without many issues.

4.5.1 Linear-regression analysis

Prompt: *Make a regression of the variables age and earnings. Provide a plot chart.*

Result

ChatGPT successfully makes a linear regression without even having to mention which variable is the dependent and which the independent. For this linear regression, it uses Python's LinearRegression and NumPy. For the plot chart, it uses matplotlib.pyplot.

Conclusion

Regression analysis helps in understanding the relationship between variables, providing a way to predict outcomes based on these relationships (Sirkin, 2006). It is much faster and easier to perform linear-regression analysis with conversational AI, even though it is not that difficult a procedure using statistical software packages; however, even the definition of the dependency of the variables can be skipped if the variables are generic and easily understandable by the LLM. However, as mentioned previously, for better results researchers should specify the dependent variable for more complicated or unknown variables. When it comes to the plot generation, details such as colours, axis names, and actual versus predicted lines can be specified. If not, the LLM will use default settings for generation of the plot. In addition, a dataset in use can be specified. For example, '*Make a regression of age and earnings on the dataset with excluded outliers.*' It will consider the dataset that was manipulated previously by another prompt.

4.5.2 Multi-collinearity test

Prompts:

1. *Perform a collinearity test on all the variables.*
2. *On the variables with high VIF score, test which are the colliding variables.*
3. *Based on the results, which variables can be added to the multiple-regression model with the dependent variable earnings?*

Result

Three prompts were used for the multi-collinearity test. Based on the first prompt, ChatGPT performs multi-collinearity testing with the variance inflation factor (VIF). To perform this analysis it uses variance_inflation_factor from statsmodels.stats.outliers_influence. The LLM successfully suggests the values with exceptionally high VIF (>10) and provides some notable results from the analysis as to which variables should better be excluded due to collinearity. The second prompt identifies several pairs of variables with high correlation coefficients, indicating potential collinearity. The third prompt provides advice regarding which variables can be included and which excluded from the model for the dependent variable earnings.

Conclusion

A multi-collinearity test is a statistical analysis used to identify the degree to which two or more predictors in a regression model are correlated. This test is crucial, because if predictors are highly correlated, it can lead to difficulties in determining the individual effect of each predictor on the dependent variable (Sirkin, 2006). In this test, GPT-4 not only performed multi-collinearity tests correctly but also explained the results and scores and suggested which variables should be excluded. It is much easier and more time efficient to use the LLM instead of a statistical package software, especially for less experienced researchers.

4.5.3 Multiple-regression analysis

Prompt: *Perform multiple linear regressions on the dependent variable earnings. Exclude variables with high correlation coefficients that were identified during multi-collinearity testing.*

Result

ChatGPT performed the multiple-regression analysis on the manipulated data successfully without any problems. The variables with high correlation coefficients were excluded from the final analysis as asked for in the prompt.

Conclusion

GPT-4's data analysis performs well in multiple-regression analysis and can handle subquestions within the prompt. However, the dataset must be specified in case of prior data manipulations. Researchers should avoid using abstracts such as 'mentioned above' or 'aforementioned' in their prompts and instead try to be as specific as possible.

4.5.4 *T*-test and ANOVA

Prompts:
1. *Perform a T-test between the variables gender and earnings. Include: mean, median, standard deviation and count.*
2. *Perform ANOVA between the variables worktype and earnings. Include: mean, median, standard deviation and count.*

Result

For prompt 1, GPT-4 successfully performs the *t*-test using SciPy. For prompt 2, GTP-4 successfully performs the ANOVA using SciPy. In both the *t*-test and ANOVA, GPT-4 provides the *P* value and explains the statistical significance in each case with clear words.

Conclusion

T-tests and ANOVA are used for comparing means across groups, helping to identify significant differences that could influence decisions (Sirkin, 2006). Mean, median, count and standard deviation were not provided for each category by default. Therefore, it was asked in in a subsequent prompt to '*Provide summarized earnings statistics for each workgroup category (for the ANOVA) and each gender category (for the t-test).*'

4.5.5 Cluster analysis

Prompts:
1. *Perform a cluster analysis on the whole dataset with excluded outliers.*
2. *Interpret and name each cluster.*

Result

GPT-4 successfully performed the cluster analysis using K-means clustering with three clusters. It did so with the sklearn.cluster function. After that, the second prompt analysed the centroids of the clusters or the average values of the features within each cluster, resulting in tables with mean values that serve as defining characteristics for each cluster. Last but not least, based on the mean values of the features within each cluster, GPT-4 assigned descriptive names to each cluster to reflect their defining characteristics. The three cluster names were: Balanced Workforce, Established Professionals and Senior High-Earners.

Conclusions

Cluster analysis allows the identification of natural groupings within data, offering insights into how data points are related to each other (Sirkin, 2006). GPT-4 performed very well in both numerical data analysis and interpretation of data, and even naming the clusters based on their characteristics.

4.5.6 Factor analysis

Prompts:
1. *Perform factor analysis on the dataset with included outliers.*
2. *Perform factor analysis with PCA loadings.*
3. *Can you name the PCAs?*

Result

At first, ChatGPT failed at performing factor analysis using factor_analyzer from the FactorAnalyzer library. Not all Python libraries are installed, and the factor analyser was not included in the environment of ChatGPT. It was not possible for the Factor_analyzer Python library to be installed in the ChatGPT environment. At first, the analysis was attempted by the the LLM with the Kaiser–Meyer–Olkin (KMO) test and Bartlett's test of sphericity. However, due to the failure in library installation, the analysis failed. GPT-4 suggested to alternatively conduct the factor analysis using principal component analysis (PCA). After prompting it with the second prompt, PCA was used successfully. ChatGPT imported PCA from sklearn.decomposition. Last but not least, ChatGPT successfully named the principal components as: PC1: 'Employment Status and Earnings', PC2: 'Educational Attainment' PC3: 'Health and Age', PC4: 4: 'Lifestyle and Health' and PC5: 'Work Intensity'.

Conclusion

Factor analysis helps in reducing the dimensionality of data, making it easier to interpret by identifying underlying factors (Pallant, 2020). Despite the initial failure of performing factor analysis with the KMO test, GPT-4 succeeded with the PCA method. The limits of the current environment do not allow installation of Python libraries. There are two workarounds to this problem: (i) run Python in a local environment and ensure that the libraries and all of the dependencies are installed; or (ii) use an alternative way of conducting factor analysis that is supported in the current environment, such as PCA. Most social scientists will have opposition to the first workaround due to the technical skills it requires: connecting the development environment with the ChatGPT application programming interface (API) and installing all dependencies through the terminal, while also making sure that the machine runs the correct version of Python.

4.6 Concerns and Limitations Regarding Data Analysis with Conversational AI

Despite the many positives of using conversational AI for data analysis, there are some serious concerns that should be considered. The effectiveness of analysis can vary due to differences in prompt engineering skills, leading to inconsistent results. Misinterpretation of data contexts or nuances is another issue, as LLMs might not fully grasp the complexity within the data (Rasheed *et al.*, 2024). Handling large datasets is challenging due to token limitations, restricting the amount of data that can be processed at once. Inherent biases from the training data of the LLM can influence outcomes and introduce cognitive biases, affecting the objectivity of the analysis. Moreover, data quality issues and model training limitations may result in inaccurate analyses, while the potential for AI to generate misleading information or 'hallucinate' raises concerns about the reliability of LLMs for serious data analysis tasks.

The accuracy of data analysis using LLMs depends heavily on the prompt engineering skills. If prompts are not clear or incorrectly interpreted by the LLM, the analysis may be inconsistent or incorrect. It is crucial to test the phrasing of prompts before they are finalized for research to avoid mistakes or irrelevant outcomes. The LLM's understanding of data is based on the training datasets, which might not always capture the context or complexities of the data, leading to possible misinterpretations. Regarding dataset handling, the ability of LLMs to process and interpret data is bound by a token limitation. LLMs do not interact directly with datasets in the way traditional data analysis tools do but can discuss and generate text based on the input provided within this token limit. For large datasets, ChatGPT might not be able to process the entire dataset at once if it exceeds the token limit. However, token limitations are becoming smaller with computing power increase and model simplifications and optimizations. Development of specific LLMs or agents for data analysis can decrease the token limitations by a big margin.

LLMs are trained on data created by humans, which means they can inherit biases related to the training data. This can lead them to favour more conventional research methods, potentially overlooking innovative or alternative approaches. LLMs also show cognitive biases, affecting their reasoning and making them prone to favour certain answers without regard to the content's quality. Such biases in LLMs highlight the need for careful consideration and critical evaluation when using them for research analysis to ensure diverse and unbiased outcomes.

The quality of data fed into LLMs significantly impacts their analysis outcomes; incomplete, incorrectly formatted or ambiguous data can lead to inaccurate conclusions. Furthermore, the capability of LLMs to generate responses is confined by the patterns and information they were trained on, which means their analysis might not always be accurate or applicable, especially for unfamiliar data or scenarios. This underscores the importance of providing high-quality, well-structured data to LLMs and being mindful of their training limitations to ensure reliable analysis. Moreover, LLMs exhibit hallucinations, posing a challenge to their reliability in real-world scenarios including data analysis.

4.7 Conclusion

AI has the ability to revolutionize quantitative data analysis in social sciences by providing sophisticated tools for modelling, analysis and interpretation of complex datasets. It supports the extraction and manipulation of quantitative data, enhances the accuracy of predictions and enables the exploration of new methodologies. AI's role in social sciences ranges from optimizing workflows to assisting in the discovery of interpretable models and facilitating the analysis of social phenomena. Moreover, it can connect data to theory from its source knowledge. The integration of AI in social science research is not without challenges, but it offers a promising avenue for advancing the field.

Currently, general-use conversational AI works well, as shown in the examined test cases. However, as attractive as artificial general intelligence looks, it is more likely that companies will instead use machine learning techniques to make specific models for data analysis. Techniques such as fine-tuning to make an LLM behave in a certain way and use of knowledge base embedding to make it gain domain knowledge can produce LLMs that will serve as a basis for AI tools specifically tailored for data analysis such as Julius AI. By eliminating all the not-useful information, LLMs can be optimized and their performance can be increased. This will result in faster, more capable and more accurate models with better computational economy.

AI tools make advanced data analysis techniques more accessible, empowering researchers without any background in programming to conduct complex analyses. This lowers the entry barrier, enabling a wider range of social scientists to use these effective tools. Moreover, utilizing conversational AI significantly improves the efficiency of data analysis. Tasks that previously demanded extensive coding and technical knowledge can now be completed using natural language prompts. This not only accelerates the analysis process but also facilitates more iterative and exploratory research methods.

The continuous development of AI holds the potential for further improving the capabilities and user-friendliness of these tools for research in social science. Adapting AI models to specific areas within social sciences can improve precision and relevance, equipping researchers with tools tailored to their precise requirements. Improving the interfaces of AI tools by incorporating more user-friendly menus, selection options and visual aids can streamline data analysis even further, making it more intuitive and convenient for users.

The general conclusion of this chapter is that AI is indeed capable of transforming the way quantitative analysis is currently done in social sciences. This chapter has described the possible and real-world uses of AI-powered data analysis, demonstrating its capacity to handle various tasks including data processing, hypothesis building, complex statistical analysis and interpretation of results. The use of data analysis with LLMs enables social scientists to perform almost everything that was once possible only with extensive knowledge of a high-level programming language such as Python or R and their libraries. The key conclusion from the performed tests is that specificity is key to good and accurate prompting for data analysis with LLMs. Contextual details and specific instructions add to the accuracy of the analysis and enrich the interpretations of the results. Over time, interfaces will become much more practical and intuitive for data analysis with combinations of selection choices, menus and prompts to improve user experience and make data analysis with AI seamless.

References

Bajarin, T. (2024) Nvidia's CEO on the democratization of coding. Forbes. Available at: www.forbes.com/sites/timbajarin/2024/03/20/nvidias-ceo-on-the-democratization-of-coding/?sh=16809657a95a (accessed 25 September 2024).

Grossmann, I., Feinberg, M., Parker, D.C., Christakis, N.A., Tetlock, P.E. *et al.* (2023) AI and the transformation of social science research. *Science* 380, 1108–1109.
MIT Sloan (2024) How to use ChatGPT's advanced data analysis feature. MIT Sloan Teaching & Learning Technologies, Cambridge, Massachusetts. Available at: https://mitsloanedtech.mit.edu/ai/tools/data-analysis/how-to-use-chatgpts-advanced-data-analysis-feature/ (accessed 25 September 2024).
Pallant, J. (2020) *SPSS Survival Manual: A Step By Step Guide To Data Analysis Using IBM SPSS*. Routledge, London.
Rasheed, Z., Waseem, M., Ahmad, A., Kemell, K.K., Xiaofeng, W., *et al.* (2024) Can large language models serve as data analysts? A multi-agent assisted approach for qualitative data analysis. arXiv preprint. Available at: https://arxiv.org/abs/2402.01386 (accessed 25 September 2024).
Sirkin, R.M. (2006) *Statistics for the Social Sciences*, 3rd edn. Sage Publishing, Thousand Oaks, California.
Sufi, F. (2023) Algorithms in low-code-no-code for research applications: a practical review. *Algorithms* 16: 108.
Zhang, Y. (2023) Generative AI has lowered the barriers to computational social sciences. arXiv preprint. Available at: https://arxiv.org/abs/2311.10833 (accessed 25 September 2024).

5 Using AI Agents in Quantitative Social Research

Christos Christodoulou*
Double Eye Ltd, Limassol, Cyprus

Abstract
This chapter explores the integration of artificial intelligence (AI) agents, powered by large language models into performing various tasks in social research, focusing on quantitative analysis. AI agents are autonomous software entities capable of planning, decision making and action taking based on their understanding of the environment. These agents are structured with a brain, perception mechanisms for environmental understanding and action components to perform tasks. AI agents demonstrate a further progression towards fully autonomous AI systems, highlighting the increasing capabilities and independence of AI applications. Various examples of using AI agents are provided, using a popular framework.

Keywords: AI agents, generative artificial intelligence, large language models

5.1 Introduction

Artificial intelligence (AI) agents are smart software entities that are powered by large language models (LLMs) to perform tasks with an increasing level of autonomy. They can plan, make decisions and take actions based on their understanding of the environment. AI agents are designed to solve complex problems by reasoning, using various tools and adapting to new information.

AI agents can be thought as consisting of three high-level components (Xi *et al.*, 2023):

1. *Brain.* This is the core of the agent, usually powered by an LLM such as GPT-4. The brain processes information, makes decisions and generates responses.
2. *Perception.* This involves the agent's ability to understand and interpret the environment. It includes processing inputs such as text, images or other data forms that the agent needs to interact with.
3. *Action.* This enables the agent to perform tasks. Actions can range from generating text to executing commands, interacting with external tools or even engaging in conversations.

These AI systems can have various architectures, and the choice of architecture depends on the complexity of tasks they are designed to solve. These include single- and multi-agent architectures:

- *Single-agent architectures.* In this design, one agent handles all the tasks. It plans, reasons and uses tools independently. Single agents are simpler to implement and are effective for well-defined tasks where feedback from others is not necessary.

*E-mail: chris.christodoulou@gmail.com

DOI: 10.1079/9781800626607.0005

- *Multi-agent architectures*. This design involves multiple agents working together. Each agent may have a specific role or expertise, and they communicate to solve complex problems collaboratively. Multi-agent systems are better suited for tasks that require diverse skills and collaborative problem solving.

Key features of AI agents include the agent persona, tools that the AI agents have access to and memory:

- *Agent persona*. Each agent is assigned a role or personality, guiding its behaviour and interactions. This persona includes details about the tools the agent can use and its specific tasks.
- *Tools*. Agents can access various tools to perform their tasks. These tools might include databases, application programming interfaces (APIs) or other software functionalities that help the agent gather and process information.
- *Memory*. Some agents have memory components to store and recall information from past interactions. This helps in maintaining context and improving decision making over time.

The progression of AI applications can be illustrated through different levels of autonomy, as depicted in Fig. 5.1. These levels range from human-driven systems to fully autonomous systems:

1. *Code (human driven)*. At this level, humans decide the output of each step, which steps to take and what steps are available. Every action requires direct human intervention and coding.
2. *LLM call (human driven)*. Here, an LLM is used for a single step only. Humans still decide the output, which steps to take and the available actions, although the LLM assists in generating specific responses or actions.
3. *Chain (human driven)*. In this level, multiple steps are linked together to achieve a specific goal. Humans continue to oversee the output and steps, but the system handles sequences of actions.
4. *Router (human driven)*. The system directs the flow of operations based on certain conditions or criteria without cycles. Humans still decide the overall output and available steps, but the system can autonomously choose the path based on predefined rules.
5. *State machine (agent executed)*. At this stage, the system operates with cycles, meaning it can loop through a series of steps autonomously. It decides the output, which steps to take and what actions are available, with minimal human intervention required.
6. *Autonomous (agent executed)*. The highest level of autonomy, where the system operates fully independently. It decides the output, the steps to take and the available actions without human intervention. Continuous human evaluation is essential to ensure the system functions correctly, ethically and safely.

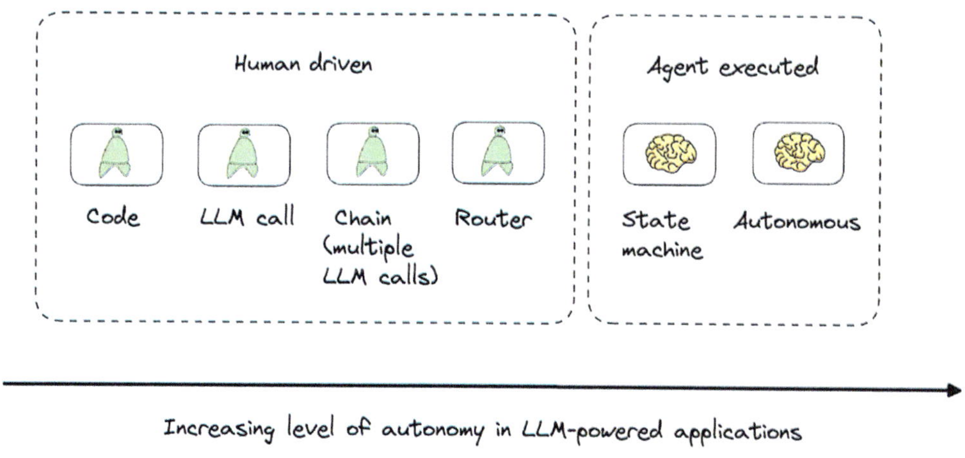

Fig. 5.1. Level of autonomy in LLM applications.

This structured progression demonstrates the increasing capability and independence of AI applications, highlighting how they evolve from human-driven to fully autonomous systems. Each level brings AI closer to performing complex, integrated functions autonomously, enhancing efficiency and problem-solving capabilities.

In this new paradigm, AI applications are not just responsive; they possess the capacity to act independently, initiate tasks and make decisions based on real-time data and contextual understanding. This autonomy enables AI to perform more complex and integrated functions across different domains.

Thus, the three main benefits of AI agents can be summarized as:

- *Efficiency*. By reducing the need for constant human intervention, AI agent systems can complete tasks faster and more efficiently.
- *Complex problem solving*. The integration of various components allows a more comprehensive approach to problem solving.
- *Adaptability*. These systems can adapt to new information and changing conditions in real time.

5.2 AI Agents and Human Interaction

5.2.1 Interaction with LLMs

Figure 5.2 illustrates the traditional interaction between a user and an LLM. This interaction typically follows a rather linear process:

1. *User request*. The user formulates a request or prompt, which is a question or command they want the LLM to process.
2. *Providing the request*. The user's request is sent to the LLM.
3. *LLM processing*. The LLM processes the input.
4. *LLM response*. The generated response is sent back to the user.
5. *User receives response*. The user receives the response and interprets or acts upon it.

5.2.2 Interaction with AI agents

With AI systems being developed, the interaction between the human user and the AI agents requires less human interaction, as these agents can be built in such a way that they take autonomous actions based on previous results or interactions. Here is how the interaction changes in such systems:

1. *User request*. The user still initiates the process with a request.
2. *Providing the request*. The request is sent to the AI agent.
3. *Agent processing*. The AI agent processes the input, but, unlike traditional LLMs, it can:
   - access and integrate data from multiple sources, extending beyond the capabilities of AI products such as ChatGPT;
   - use different models, such as LLMs and tools to understand the context better; and
   - make enhanced decisions on what steps to take next.

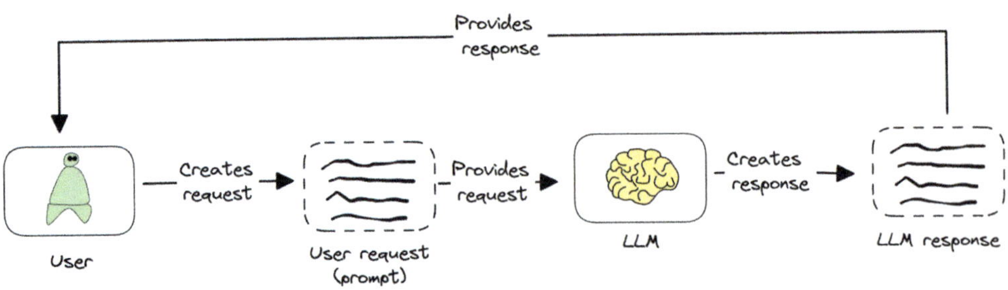

Fig. 5.2. Interaction between a user and an LLM.

4. *Autonomous actions.* Based on its understanding, the agent can take a series of autonomous actions to fulfil the request, either on its own or by conversing with other AI agents. These actions can include:

- performing searches or database queries;
- executing programs or scripts; and
- making further decisions based on real-time data.

5. *Generating a response.* The agent then generates a comprehensive response or performs the requested task.

6. *User receives results.* The user receives the results, which might include actions taken by the agent beyond just providing information.

Figure 5.3 shows how a human user creates a request to an AI system that is composed of AI agents. The AI agents can converse with each other in a horizontal architecture, or have an AI 'supervisor' coordinating the tasks to, and conversing with, the appropriate AI agents that have the appropriate skills (e.g. an AI agent can have special maths-solving skills, another can have researcher skills, and another can have advanced programming skills). Breaking down tasks, as shown when interacting with LLMs, is crucial for getting the desired response.

5.3 AI Agents for Quantitative Social Research

AI agents can be utilized when performing research in social science and can help automate various tasks. Keep in mind that these tasks can also be performed using LLMs, without the need for further automation or orchestration with frameworks using AI agents. However, AI systems that utilize AI agents can perform chains of tasks, such as the one described in Table 5.1, in a more autonomous way, where the human user can give the initial request via a prompt and get the final answer after the AI agents have completed the task.

5.4 Examples of AI Workflows Using AI Agents

For the examples given in this section, Microsoft's AutoGen Studio is used. The tool is based on Microsoft's AutoGen (Wu *et al.*, 2023), a framework for simplifying the orchestration, optimization and automation of LLM workflows (Hughes, 2023), using multi-agent conversations. The tool comes with a very intuitive user interface developed by Microsoft that allows you to build AI workflows using AI agents with no or

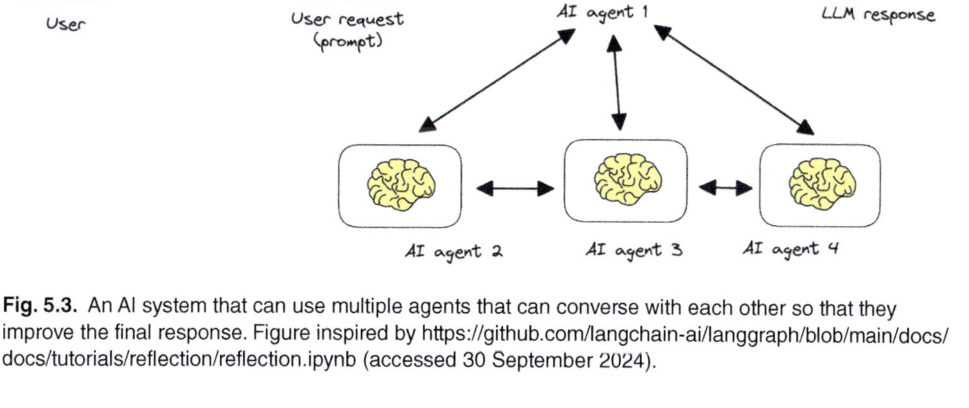

Fig. 5.3. An AI system that can use multiple agents that can converse with each other so that they improve the final response. Figure inspired by https://github.com/langchain-ai/langgraph/blob/main/docs/docs/tutorials/reflection/reflection.ipynb (accessed 30 September 2024).

Table 5.1. Example of the chain of tasks that can be carried out by an AI agent.

Data Collection and Preprocessing	
1. Survey design assistance	Use AI to generate and refine survey questions Employ language models to ensure clarity and remove biases from questions
2. Data mining and web scraping	Automate the scraping of quantitative data from social media, academic databases and other relevant sources Use AI-driven web-scraping tools to extract structured data from various sources
3. Data cleaning and formatting	Implement AI for cleaning datasets, handling missing values and normalizing data formats Manage files and organize datasets efficiently using file system management tools
Data Analysis	
4. Descriptive statistics	Automate the calculation of measures such as mean, median, mode, standard deviation and variance Generate comprehensive descriptive statistics reports using AI Utilize calculators for quick statistical computations
5. Inferential statistics	Conduct routine statistical tests (e.g. *t*-tests, χ^2 tests, ANOVA) Identify and apply appropriate inferential statistical methods based on the research question and data type
6. Regression analysis	Perform various types of regression analyses (e.g. linear, logistic, multivariate) Automate the process of model selection, fitting and interpretation
7. Predictive modelling	Build and validate predictive models using machine learning algorithms (e.g. decision trees, random forests, neural networks) Employ AI for model selection, hyperparameter tuning and cross-validation
8. Time series analysis	Analyse temporal data using AI techniques for trend analysis, seasonality detection and forecasting Implement tools for advanced time series modelling (e.g. autoregressive integrated moving average (ARIMA), generalized autoregressive conditional heteroskedasticity (GARCH))
Data Visualization	
9. Automated visualization	Generate charts, graphs and dashboards tailored to the researcher's data and goals using AI tools Implement interactive visualizations for dynamic data exploration Use file system management to organize and store visualization outputs
10. Geospatial analysis	Use geographic information systems (GIS) tools integrated with AI to analyse and visualize spatial data quantitatively Create heatmaps, cluster maps and other geospatial visualizations to identify regional patterns
Reporting and Documentation	
11. Automated reporting	Generate written reports summarizing key quantitative findings and statistical analyses Automate the creation of tables, figures and charts for publication-ready reports Send e-mail notifications with updates on report generation and final outputs Use file system management to organize and store reports
Quality Control and Validation	
12. Data quality assurance	Use AI to detect anomalies, outliers and inconsistencies in the data Implement automated checks for data integrity, completeness and accuracy Send SMS alerts or e-mail notifications if data quality issues are detected
13. Replication and validation studies	Utilize AI to replicate studies and validate results by reanalysing data with different methods Perform automated sensitivity analysis to assess the robustness of findings

minimal code. Users can create chat sessions with specified agents, view chat history, generated files and determine the time taken through the user interface. The AI agents can have access to tools and skills, and they can also develop more skills by themselves. Users can also explicitly add skills to agents to accomplish more tasks and publish their sessions to a local gallery for easy access and sharing. There are many tools that are built to orchestrate AI agents. This is one of the most mature ones at the time of writing. Many other tools, such as Langraph Studio (Langchain-Ai/Langgraph-Studio, 2024) and CrewAI (CrewAIInc/crewAI, 2023), are also very popular.

5.5.1 Data collection and analysis

Let us start with a very generic prompt that has the goal of getting data from the web, analysing this data and finally visualizing the results. Figure 5.4 shows the user interface of the framework we will use for the examples.

Prompt: *Find some data about remote work and mental health during the COVID-19 pandemic, decide what is the best chart to create for them, then create it and present it to me.*

Response: *The time series chart has been successfully created and saved as 'COVID_cases_time_series.png'. This chart visualizes the trend of confirmed, recovered and death cases of COVID-19 over time, which can indirectly indicate the periods of increased stress on mental health and the potential for shifts towards remote work due to the pandemic.*
You should now have the chart saved as a PNG image file in the same directory where you ran the script. You can view this file using any image viewer or include it in your report to present the findings.
If you need further analysis, such as focusing on specific countries or time frames, or if you require additional types of charts or data processing, please let me know, and I can assist you with that.
Otherwise, if this concludes your request, we can end the session here.

The AI agent successfully created the requested chart as a time series chart, outputting several 'intermediate' results that were used to end up with the desired result (the chart). Figure 5.5

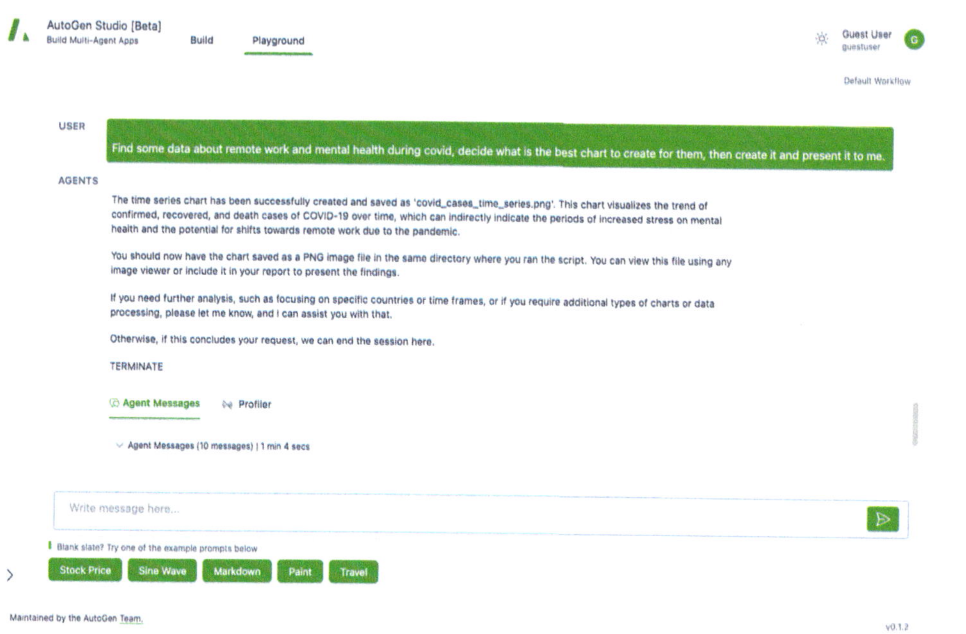

Fig. 5.4. Tool used to create an AI workflow. Figure developed by author using Microsoft's AutoGen Studio tool.

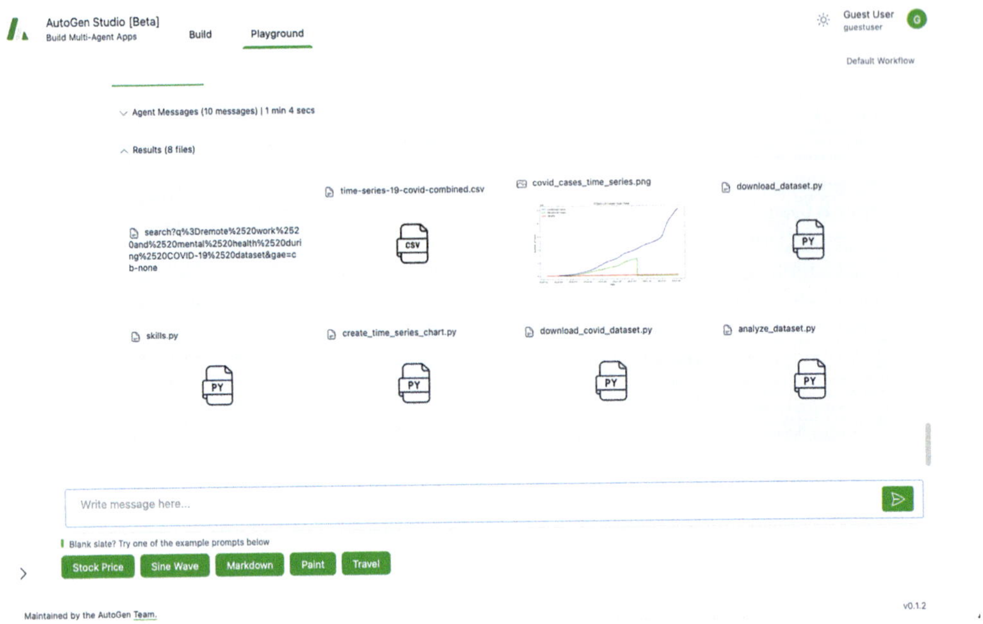

Fig. 5.5. User interface of AI tool showing the generation of results. Figure developed by author by using Microsoft's AutoGen Studio tool.

shows the results that have been generated. A comma-separated values (CSV) file that contains the data found from the web, the chart requested and some Python scripts that were generated by the LLM that relates to the AI system that were then executed to find an appropriate dataset from the web, download the COVID dataset, analyse the dataset and create a time series chart. All of this code was written by an LLM and stored as skills/tools for the AI agents to use.

The content of the Python script is shown in Fig. 5.6. This code can be copied by the user and can be added as a set of permanent skills for the AI agents to use to get to the desired goal, i.e. solve the task requested by the user. This is particularly powerful, as the generated code can be fine-tuned by the human user to perform the subtask in a certain, user-customized way. The AI agents within this workflow will decide to use certain skills by assessing what the human user has asked in the prompt. If it finds out that the given code/skill is appropriate to perform the task, it will use that one without generating a fresh script.

Figure 5.6 shows how the AI agent created the Python code that was used to do a web search using the AI-generated query '*Remote work and mental health during the COVID-19 pandemic*' dataset.

Figure 5.7 shows part of the AI workflow, where it checks whether a certain AI-generated Python script has succeeded. As can be seen, the AI agent understood that the created function had succeeded but had not given the result it intended to give. It then provides its 'thought' process, which resulted in generating another script that correctly downloaded a relevant dataset. Keep in mind that this workflow has been devised in its entirety by the AI system. The human user only provided the initial prompt.

The AI agents continued to write a script to analyse the dataset, using Python tools such as pandas to import the CSV in Python, then inspected the contents of the dataset and finally understood that a proper visualization would be a time series chart. After analysing the column names, it found out that there are no columns directly related to remote work and mental health, so it decided to use proxy measures.

Another important aspect of the capabilities of this AI system is that it can autonomously install the required libraries to perform

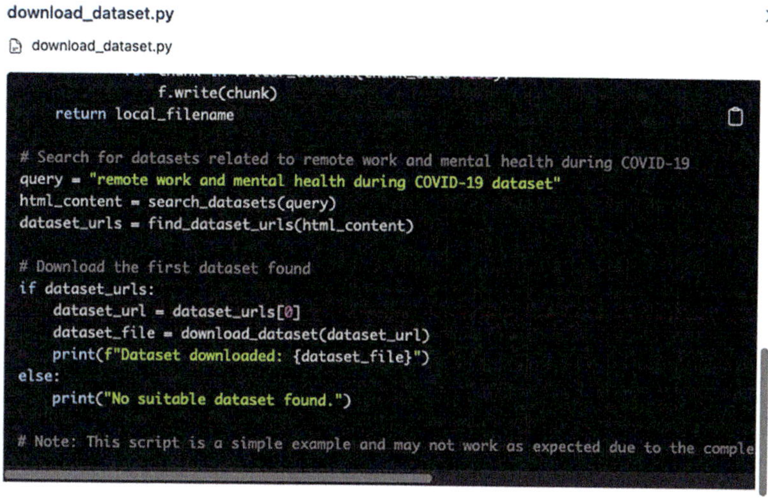

Fig. 5.6. Part of the Python script generated by the LLM associated with the AI agent, which was used to find appropriate datasets. Script: AI-generated after prompt provided by the author in Microsoft's AutoGen tool.

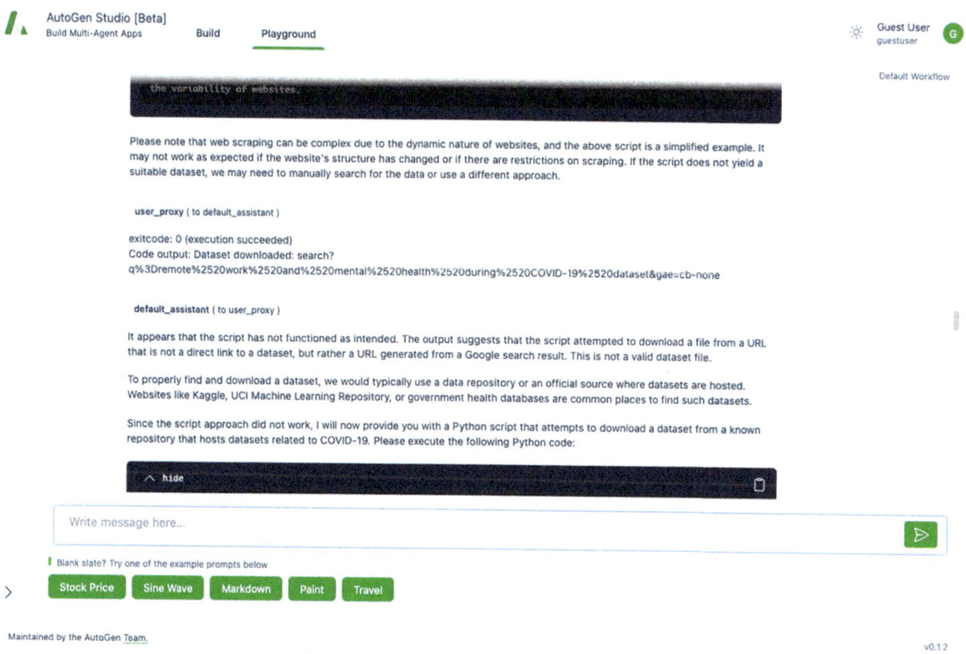

Fig. 5.7. Part of the AI workflow using AI agents, showing the execution of a function. Figure developed by author using Microsoft's AutoGen Studio tool.

the task on your local computer. In this workflow, the AI system found out that the visualization library to be used to create the chart was not installed on the computer; thus, it decided to install it in order to proceed and then decided on the next step after the installation was complete.

Finally, the AI system loaded the dataset, transformed it into pandas in order to visualize it in a meaningful way and then used the Python visualization library matplotlib to plot the data and generate a file containing the visualization.

The AI system completed several steps using available tools/skills or generated tools/skills, it examined and reflected on the result, and it decided what the next actions would be to complete the task requested by the user, or otherwise reach the goal. At some point, an AI agent with the persona of a programmer wrote a Python script, tried to execute it but then failed. It then examined the error messages to find out that some libraries were missing and continued doing this in a loop, until the Python script could be executed successfully.

It is crucial to highlight that the intermediate steps employed by the AI system to reach a result are highly valuable for the human user. These steps enable the user to assess the logical coherence and validity of the AI's decision-making process. Access to these steps significantly enhances the explainability of the AI workflow, which is a critical aspect of developing trustworthy and transparent AI systems. Improved explainability helps users understand how conclusions are drawn, ensures that the AI operates in a predictable and understandable manner, and allows better troubleshooting and refinement of the AI models. This transparency is especially important in fields where accountability and ethical considerations are paramount, ensuring that AI systems are reliable and their outputs are justifiable.

5.5.2 Cleaning and preprocessing data

Another time-consuming task that can be automated using AI agents is cleaning and preprocessing datasets.

> **Prompt:** *Preprocess and clean this dataset and prepare a report for what you did: https://github.com/datasets/covid-19/blob/main/data/time-series-19-covid-combined.csv*

A set of AI agents are used within the AI workflow to perform the task, and the set of agents provide the following response:

> *The preprocessing and cleaning of the dataset have been successfully executed, with the following key points from the report:*
>
> - *The initial dataset contained 231,744 rows and 6 columns.*
> - *There were missing values in the 'Province/State' and 'Recovered' columns.*
> - *The 'Date' column has been converted to datetime objects for proper time series analysis.*
> - *Forward fill was applied to handle missing values.*
> - *Duplicate rows were removed, resulting in a final dataset with 231,624 rows.*
> - *After cleaning, there are still 7,344 missing values in the 'Province/State' column, but no missing values in 'Recovered'.*
>
> *The warning about the deprecation of fillna(method='ffill') suggests that we should use df.ffill() instead. This is a minor issue and does not affect the results at this time, but it's good practice to update the code to avoid future warnings or errors.*
>
> *The remaining missing values in the 'Province/State' column may require a different approach since forward fill may not be appropriate for categorical data like province or state names. Depending on the analysis, we might decide to leave these as is, fill them with a placeholder value such as 'Unknown', or drop the column if it's not needed.*
>
> *If you would like to proceed with further analysis or visualization, or if you need to address the remaining missing values in the 'Province/State' column, please let me know, and I can provide the necessary code.*
>
> *Otherwise, if this concludes your request, we can end the session here.*

The AI agents planned a set of subtasks that were followed to complete the request by the human user. The final message provided information about where missing values were found and that the contents of the 'Date' column had been converted to a specific format, for proper time series analysis. It even explained how the missing values were filled in and how it handled duplicate rows.

Finally, the AI system assessed the dataset before and after preprocessing/cleaning and wrote a report of what was performed, providing that as a response to the user.

5.5.3 Advanced end-to-end quantitative analysis

Where AI systems utilizing AI agents excel is in performing tasks to reach the goal of solving the request provided by the user in an autonomous way. The following prompt asks the AI system to test a hypothesis:

> **Prompt:** *Test this hypothesis using the dataset provided (https://github.com/datasets/covid-19/blob/main/data/time-series-19-covid-combined.csv): Are there significant differences in COVID-19 case numbers between different countries or months? Do a complete preprocessing of the data, to remove outliers, check for multicollinearity and choose the best method to check for differences. Prepare a report for me with everything you have performed.*

The AI agents created the following plan, with tasks and subtasks:

1. *Preprocess the dataset:*
   - *Load the dataset.*
   - *Handle missing values.*
   - *Convert date strings to datetime objects.*
   - *Extract the month from the date for monthly analysis.*
2. *Remove outliers:*
   - *Identify outliers in the COVID-19 case numbers.*
   - *Decide on a method for outlier removal.*
3. *Check for multicollinearity:*
   - *Use variance inflation factor (VIF) to check for multicollinearity among the features.*
4. *Choose the best method to check for differences:*
   - *Since we are looking at differences across categories (countries and months), ANOVA (analysis of variance) is a suitable method.*
5. *Prepare a report:*
   - *Document each step taken and the findings.*

At some point during task 4 (choose the best method to check for differences), the AI agent created a Python script to perform ANOVA but, as previously, the execution failed. The AI agent examined the error response and corrected the script twice until the execution succeeded.

It finally performed the ANOVA test and after examining the F-statistic and *P* values, it found that the null hypothesis should be rejected, as it found strong evidence that the country and month have a significant effect on the average number of confirmed COVID-19 cases.

In addition, it provided files with preprocessed data, corrected tables in the data that helped the AI system to be able to perform the ANOVA test, and a file containing the variance inflation factor (VIF) was used to check for multicollinearity among the features.

5.6 Challenges and Considerations

Despite the reduced need for human intervention in AI-driven processes, continuous human evaluation and monitoring remain indispensable to ensure these systems function correctly, ethically and safely. This is the case for AI agents as well. AI systems, while highly capable, are not infallible, and can perpetuate or even exacerbate biases, make errors or operate in unforeseen ways. Therefore, maintaining human oversight is crucial to prevent errors and address any ethical concerns that may arise (Elangovan *et al.*, 2024).

5.7 Conclusion

This chapter explored the concept of AI agents and highlighted how AI agents can be used in quantitative social research, focusing on practical examples to illustrate their benefits. By using AI agents, researchers can streamline and improve various aspects of their work, from data collection to analysis and reporting.

In the first example, AI agents were tasked with gathering data on remote work and mental health during the COVID-19 pandemic. They autonomously conducted web searches, downloaded relevant datasets, analysed the data and created a time series chart. This example demonstrates the agents' ability to handle complex tasks efficiently and generate useful visualizations with minimal human intervention.

The second example focused on data cleaning and preprocessing. AI agents efficiently managed missing values removed duplicate rows and standardized data formats, producing a comprehensive report on the actions taken. This shows their effectiveness in ensuring data quality, which is crucial for further analysis.

The third example involved testing a hypothesis about COVID-19 case numbers using an advanced end-to-end quantitative analysis. The AI agents preprocessed the data, conducted statistical tests, addressed multicollinearity issues and performed an ANOVA test to draw conclusions. This example illustrates their ability to autonomously carry out detailed analytical workflows, saving researchers time and effort.

These examples show the practical benefits of AI agents in quantitative social research. By automating routine tasks and enhancing data analysis capabilities, AI agents can help researchers work more efficiently and gain deeper insights from their data. As AI technology continues to advance, its potential to improve research practices and outcomes will continue to grow.

References

CrewAIInc/crewAI (2023) Python. Available at: https://github.com/crewAIInc/crewAI (accessed 25 September 2024).

Elangovan, A., Liu, L., Xu, L., Bodapati, S. and Roth, D. (2024) ConSiDERS-The-Human evaluation framework: rethinking human evaluation for generative large language models. arXiv preprint. Available at: https://doi.org/10.48550/arXiv.2405.18638 (accessed 25 September 2024).

Hughes, A. (2023) AutoGen: enabling next-generation large language model applications. Microsoft Research Blog. Available at: www.microsoft.com/en-us/research/blog/autogen-enabling-next-generation-large-language-model-applications (accessed 25 September 2024).

Langchain-Ai/Langgraph-Studio (2024) LangChain. Available at: https://github.com/langchain-ai/langgraph-studio (accessed 25 September 2024).

Wu, Q., Bansal, G., Zhang, J., Wu, Y., Li, B., *et al.* (2023) AutoGen: enabling next-gen LLM applications via multi-agent conversation framework. Jupyter Notebook. Available at: https://github.com/microsoft/autogen (accessed 25 September 2024).

Xi, Z., Chen, W., Guo, X., He, W., Ding, Y., *et al.* (2023) The rise and potential of large language model based agents: a survey. arXiv preprint. Available at: https://doi.org/10.48550/arXiv.2309.07864 (accessed 25 September 2024).

6 AI Augmented Qualitative Analysis: Is it the Right Choice for Your Study?

Danielle Hitch[1]*, Kieva Richards[2], Rachel Knight[1], Genevieve Pepin[1], Urvi Thanekar[3] and Sophie Goldingay[1]

[1]Deakin University, Waterfront Campus, Geelong, Victoria, Australia; [2]LaTrobe University, Bundoora, Victoria, Australia; [3]Deakin University, Bundoora Campus, Bundoora, Victoria, Australia

Abstract

This chapter discusses the transformative impact of artificial intelligence (AI) on qualitative social science research by exploring its relationship to various methodologies. AI challenges traditional qualitative research approaches while potentially enhancing analytical efficiency and rigour, and researchers must assess its utility and philosophical coherence for their studies. The chapter summarizes the philosophical foundations of AI, supplemented by practical examples from published literature. It delves into the role of AI augmented analysis within seven qualitative traditions: content analysis, descriptive qualitative analysis, discourse analysis, ethnography, participatory action research, constructivist grounded theory and phenomenology. Researchers are provided with critical questions to guide their plans to implement AI augmented analysis in their work. By describing the methodological relationship between AI and various qualitative approaches, this chapter enables informed decision making and may stimulate further research as both technology and methodological practices evolve.

Keywords: critical analysis, decision making, design, methodology, qualitative research

6.1 Introduction

Our interest in human nature dates to the 5th century BCE, when Greek philosophers began exploring morality and human ways of life (Cresswell and Cresswell, 2022). During the Renaissance, the printing press enabled broader dissemination of qualitative knowledge about human activities and phenomena, such as religion, the arts and politics. With the Enlightenment came more formalized qualitative methods, such as participant observation and in-depth interviews. In the 20th century, fieldwork and ethnography complemented direct data collection, followed by grounded and feminist approaches. The history of qualitative research reflects our changing understanding of ourselves as humans, evolving in response to new theoretical perspectives, innovative methodological approaches, technological advancements, changes in institutional priorities and the influence of other research fields (Morse, 2020; Cresswell and Cresswell, 2022). All these factors contributed to the growth of multiple disciplines generating knowledge about human behaviours, cultures and society, including sociology, anthropology, psychology, education and health sciences (Roberts *et al.*, 2024).

The emergence of artificial intelligence (AI) is the latest transformative social change influencing

*E-mail: dani.hitch@deakin.edu.au

DOI: 10.1079/9781800626607.0006

the work of scientists and researchers. AI results from a societal shift towards digitization and automation, which values data-driven decision making, efficiency, and the democratization of information and knowledge generation (Hasselberger, 2019). It is uniquely quick to adapt to real-time socio-economic and political developments, leaving little time to manage its impact on societal attitudes towards technology, data privacy and ethics. Concerns have been raised about the impact of AI on privacy, confidentiality, surveillance capacity, the dissemination of misinformation, and the perpetuation of biases, prejudices or power imbalances (Christou, 2023a). Others embrace the possibilities of 'computational social research' as a collaborative, multidisciplinary field, despite criticisms that it is yet to fully engage with social science concepts, concerns and challenges (Baum, 2020; Bircan and Salah, 2022).

This chapter begins with an overview of the methodological compatibility of AI with the philosophy, ontology and epistemology of the broad field of qualitative social science research. It then delves into the relationship between this technology and seven specific qualitative traditions to explore the distinctive ways in which their theoretical foundations and practices interact with AI. Hypothetical and real-life vignettes and examples are provided in boxed text to highlight key issues and demonstrate how AI augmentation is currently being implemented in qualitative studies. The chapter concludes with critical questions for social researchers considering AI augmentation, designed to support readers in critically evaluating the best approach for their study.

6.2 The Methodological Compatibility of AI and Qualitative Research

For research to be coherent and valid, the ontology and epistemology of the approaches used must be compatible. Evaluating this requires critical reflection and authentic engagement with intersectionality and positionality (Lee-Johnson *et al.*, 2023). Qualitative research and AI adopt different epistemological views about valid and important knowledge. Qualitative inquiry assumes knowledge and meaning are co-constructed (Cresswell and Cresswell, 2022; Tschisgale *et al.*, 2023), while AI is based on objective data-driven knowledge building via quantitative analysis (Haque, 2023). These differing perspectives align with their respective ontologies. Qualitative research adopts a naturalistic world view, encompassing the nuances and complexity of human experience within social, cultural and political systems (Cresswell and Cresswell, 2022; Tschisgale *et al.*, 2023). AI seeks universal patterns through abstraction from tangible data. To paraphrase Goertz and Mahoney (2012, p. 42), qualitative research focuses on the 'causes of effects', while AI reflects the 'effects of causes'.

However, these beliefs about knowledge and reality are not as distinctive as they may seem. Both qualitative research and AI are empirical, identifying patterns to understand and explain human social phenomena. They use iterative processes of analysis and reanalysis in response to questions that can change over time in reaction to engagement with both data and societal changes (Cresswell and Cresswell, 2022). Similarly, AI adapts through ongoing algorithm training (Saxena *et al.*, 2023).

It is important to evaluate whether AI augmentation benefits social science researchers. Qualitative research methods are tools for data collection, requiring expertise, reflexivity and lived experience to contextualize data within the broader societal context. This poses the risk of abandoning objectivity by closely identifying with participants (Crombie and Davies, 1996). The subjectivity of qualitative research can also make studies difficult to replicate, due to flexible and 'inherently messy' methodologies (Dickie, 2003, p. 50; Jiang *et al.*, 2021).

With its objective orientation, AI may seem like a strategy for 'tidying up' qualitative analysis. However, Hill and Knox (2021) warned against assuming that AI outputs are conclusive without human interpretation. Most algorithms and resulting decision-making processes are not freely available or reported (Christou, 2023a), causing some mistrust about this 'mysterious' technology. AI cannot explain or justify its interpretations like a human researcher (Schäffer and Lieder, 2023). AI lacks self-awareness and is only as useful as its training data and the researcher's skills (Roberts *et al.*, 2024). However, multiple studies (Lee *et al.*, 2020; Hitch, 2024; Reis *et al.*, 2024) confirm that AI can boost the efficiency of human researchers, especially in the initial stages of qualitative analysis and when working with 'big data'.

A critical reflection on the relationship between AI and qualitative research prompts important and complex ethical and philosophical questions. Almost half a century ago, Weizenbaum questioned whether '*every* aspect of human thought is reducible to a logical formalism, or, to put it into the modern idiom, whether or not human thought is *entirely* computable' (Weizenbaum, 1976, p. 12; Hasselberger, 2019). Based on current AI systems, this does not appear to have come to fruition. However, many AI systems operate on language, which is the basis of self-understanding and culture. Language is a core part of being human, and AI can use it to formulate completely new ideas and potentially new cultures (Roberts *et al.*, 2024). Questions about including AI in the qualitative conversations driving social science research can only be answered by referencing both its current and possible future role in knowledge building.

Social science researchers must therefore consider the relationship between AI and their research question before introducing it to their practice. There is no simple answer to questions about the methodological compatibility of qualitative research and AI. Researchers are urged to clarify their purpose and intentions for AI adoption before proceeding (Christou, 2024). The decision not to use AI in a qualitative study is a valid one if it is unlikely to add anything or if the team lacks confidence or skill in using the chosen system. Researchers need sufficient technological knowledge to make informed decisions about AI implementation, which may require further training and development.

There are few examples of AI implementation in social sciences research, and even fewer training opportunities to assist researchers in upskilling in new technology. A study on using natural language processing (NLP) software in research training workshops (Schäffer and Lieder, 2023) found that participants initially perceived AI augmented data analysis as obscure and confusing before perceiving it as a form of distributed analysis that combined broad AI interpretation with deep human understanding. Early adopters may have undertaken additional training, but this is rarely reported in published studies (Christou, 2023a), and they may not know what they do not know.

Depending on how and when it is applied, AI augmentation may transform a qualitative study into an embedded mixed-methods approach, where AI derived data is nested within an overall qualitative design. In this situation, researchers must identify and report how the two forms of data are integrated, and at what stage of the research process this occurs (Cresswell and Plano Clark, 2018). Transparency about decision making behind study design and methodology is crucial for both trustworthiness and the collective development of this approach. Stakeholders need to know which research tasks were completed by human researchers and which were completed by AI systems (Christou, 2023a). Critical evaluation of the compatibility between qualitative research and AI is therefore a communal activity, started by individual research teams but continued by their colleagues and the public as part of our broader societal conversation about the rise of this technology.

6.3 AI Augmented Research Across Seven Qualitative Traditions

A diverse range of traditions and approaches to qualitative social science research have emerged over time, each with distinctive assumptions, focuses and methodologies (Cresswell and Creswell, 2022). Reflecting on the philosophy and characteristics of each tradition highlights how their compatibility with AI depends on complex interactions between design, method, analysis and context. AI has many potential avenues for implementation in qualitative research including summarizing papers or other text (such as interviews), comparative analysis of different sources, multimedia analysis, and creating text and images for analysis (Lee *et al.*, 2021; Tschisgale *et al.*, 2023). This discussion focuses on analysis and links methodological issues to specific traditions. However, many issues raised are relevant to multiple traditions and other applications of this technology are also identified.

6.3.1 Content analysis

Content analysis systematically codes text and/or visual data to identify themes and interpret their underlying meanings (Braun and Clarke, 2021). Although considered a qualitative method, it is in fact a mixed method incorporating quantitative elements such as word and phrase frequencies. Braun and Clarke (2021) suggested that these elements should play a minor interpretative role compared with qualitative engagement with the data and its implicit context and meaning. Comparisons are often made between content and descriptive thematic analysis, and while both identify patterns within data, the latter relies more heavily on human interpretative skill.

Content analysis provides a structured and systematic approach that works well with AI augmentation (Anis and French, 2023). It is particularly well suited to large datasets, which are time and cost intensive and difficult to manage for human researchers (Parker *et al.*, 2023). However, AI implementation can also slow down decision making, as human researchers still need deep data familiarity to construct valid and subtle interpretations and correct any interpretative distortions the system may introduce (Reis and Lenz, 2024).

Lee *et al.* (2020) developed a nine-step road map for AI augmented content analysis. Some elements are shared with traditional content analysis, such as defining research questions, identifying sources and specifying units of analysis. However, they recommend an *a priori* approach, which defines and pretests a coding and thematic scheme before analysis. A similar approach was also described by Tai *et al.* (2024), suggesting that deductive approaches are preferable to inductive analysis. AI derived keywords are then manually mapped to themes by human researchers before reliability, validity and efficiency are evaluated.

From the perspective of Lee *et al.* (2020), this approach balances the reliability of AI with the validity and contextual engagement of human analysis. Positivist approaches to validity and reliability such as statistical tests are often applied to content analysis (Oleinik *et al.*, 2014); however, other qualitative traditions eschew these concepts in favour of trustworthiness. In the words of Morse (2020, p. 4), 'interrater reliability produces an invalid result and keeps research shallow. Under the guise of *validity*, it keeps the results descriptive, obvious, and trite.' The embedded quantitative elements of content analysis are unique among the qualitative traditions, and significantly enable its compatibility with AI augmentation.

6.3.2 Descriptive qualitative analysis

Descriptive qualitative analysis provides a comprehensive overview of specific phenomena or experiences by summarizing patterns and themes in data. It lacks the deep theoretical engagement of other qualitative traditions and is often an introductory approach to social science research for novice researchers and in emerging fields (Stanley, 2023). While it has no specific theoretical orientation, there remain several compatibility issues to consider related to AI implementation.

Thematic analysis is the most common analytical method in this tradition, and offers a flexible approach applicable to diverse frameworks, paradigms and social science disciplines (Clarke and Braun, 2017). AI augmentation in thematic analysis appears to be most useful during early analysis (Hitch, 2024), and is most often used as a tool to identify preliminary or initial codes and themes before human researchers assume control as part of a larger analytical process (Morgan, 2023). However, the trainability and continuous learning occurring within these systems leaves open the possibility of expanded use in the future.

Transport researchers in Montréal (Carvalho *et al.*, 2024) compared descriptive qualitative analysis completed by humans with analyses completed by two AI systems (ChatGPT and Google Gemini). The AI systems missed some subtleties in the data that were identified by human researchers but completed their analysis far quicker. Later versions of ChatGPT were also noted to demonstrate greater analytical skill.

A commonly cited drawback of AI augmented qualitative analysis is its dependence on the quality and clarity of prompts and data input from human users (Peres *et al.*, 2023). If users do not tell the system to comment on contextual factors, system outputs will remain superficial and concentrate on the 'what' rather than the 'why'. Due to their stochastic nature, large language models (LLMs) also generate different responses to slightly different prompts, and therefore multiple prompt iterations may be needed to get the most appropriate outputs (Tai *et al.*, 2024). AI augmented analysis can be optimized though high-quality prompts and training the system to complete study specific tasks, but these skills are not widely held at present (Chubb, 2023).

Critical thinking is arguably the most important skill for AI augmented qualitative research and must be applied at every stage of the study to mitigate the limitations of this technology. Morse (2020) warned that simple thematic analysis that does not discuss the represented meaning of themes constitutes weak, poor-quality research. AI augmentation could exacerbate this problem if thematic analysis ends with a truncated review of the system outputs, especially if researchers are using AI as a time-saving strategy. AI is not a 'set and forget' technology, and inquiry skills may stagnate or deteriorate if researchers rely too heavily on technology (Christou, 2023a). AI systems cannot substitute for human researchers, and the aspirational goal of 'automation' seems many years away. Human researchers must maintain their agency in the implementation of AI and have systems in place to critically interpret outputs to perform authentic and sophisticated descriptive analysis (Lodge *et al.*, 2023). AI augmentation therefore adds considerable complexity to what is often perceived as a relatively straightforward methodology.

6.3.3 Discourse analysis

Discourse analysis explores the relationships between language use and 'how people think or feel (subjectivity), what they may do (practices) and the material conditions within which such experiences may take place' (Willig, 2013, p. 130). It reveals underlying assumptions and power relations and has guided professional communication across various social science disciplines. Discourse analysis researchers were early adopters of computer-assisted data analysis software such as ATLAS.ti and NVivo (Paulus and Lester, 2016). They also quickly embraced AI augmented analysis as these platforms became more available in the late 2010s.

A common criticism of AI is its limited ability to understand context, nuance and subjectivity (Morgan, 2023). However, LLMs share some affinity with discourse analysis in processing the content and meaning of language. Researchers have explored the accuracy of AI in predicting social and psychological realities, and its capacity to engage with cultural and political values using large datasets. Before open access systems such as ChatGPT became widely available, Brookes and McEnery (2018) compared human-led discourse analysis with topic modelling of 228,113 patient comments about the UK National Health Service. They found that human-led analysis provided a sophisticated perspective, closely matching consensus reality (Brookes and McEnery, 2019), while topic word lists from modelling offered insufficient support for interpretation. Despite this, other studies have found AI augmentation to have some analytical benefits.

Taufek *et al.* (2021) used machine learning for discourse analysis of climate change content in a Malaysian newspaper. The algorithm identified an initial sentiment lexicon, and researchers then analysed public sentiments in depth. The authors concluded that human intelligence is essential, but the partnership with machine learning uncovered otherwise missed data insights. This capacity to find new themes has also been noted in other studies (Parker et al., 2023; Hitch, 2024).

Generative AI in discourse analysis is mainly used in early analytical stages to identify overarching themes in large datasets. However, challenges with cognitive, contextual and emotional understanding limits its use throughout the research process (Christou, 2023b). Current systems cannot engage with formation rules, power dynamics, subject positions or historical context. The discursive mimicry of AI systems remains superficial, but it has a greater presence in discourse analysis than in many other theoretically embedded traditions. As AI systems rapidly improve, discourse analysts are well positioned to lead social sciences in exploring the possibilities of AI augmented qualitative research.

6.3.4 Ethnography

In the ethnographic tradition, researchers conduct fieldwork with a cultural group in its natural setting for an extended period to understand its norms, practices and traditions (Cresswell, 2006). Ethnography includes various branches such as visual, embodied, migration and gender ethnography (Matera and Biscaldi, 2021). Each approach has its own values and theoretical orientation to consider alongside the general information about this tradition.

AI has had limited application in ethnographic research to date. Blackwell (2021) highlighted that AI technology has its own distinctive culture, and existing ethnographies have studied AI systems without adopting AI augmentation. However, recognition of its potential uses in analysis and other research aspects is emerging. Coombes and Jones (2020) noted that AI may enhance 'netnographies' by automating trend and sentiment analysis and topic modelling, although standardized methodologies are still evolving. Word-embedding algorithms can also identify shared perceptions within organizations and inform team performance analysis (Goldberg and Srivastava, 2022), and this technology also has the potential to generate cultural artefacts for ethnographic analysis.

Cardoso (2024) conducted an ethnographic study at the Centre for AI at the University of Sao Paulo, Brazil, to explore AI image generation. Experiments with different AI systems (DALL-E 2/3 and Midjourney) showed that AI images can contribute to visual ethnography, although image quality varies. Systemic biases in AI systems can also lead to incoherent and non-representative outputs. The chapter authors used AI to translate the study from Portuguese to English for inclusion here, showcasing another application relevant to ethnographic research.

An important consideration in using AI for ethnography is its interaction with the cultural contexts of researchers and participants. Cultural models of the self and environment are embedded within human–AI interactions, influencing study design and participant experience (Ge *et al.*, 2024). AI systems also often reflect significant biases from their mostly Western development, which can be problematic in diverse societies (Prabhakaran *et al.*, 2022). The cultural positionality of researchers, participants and AI systems must be analysed critically during all design and decision-making processes.

6.3.5 Participatory action research

Participatory action research (PAR) also adopts a constructivist approach, valuing collaborative knowledge generation through action (Fine *et al.*, 2003). AI systems focus on autonomy and intelligence, independently interacting with and shaping their environment (Laitinen and Sahlgren, 2021). In contrast, PAR is founded on collaboration and co-learning, which engages participants in research processes for social change. As such, PAR is more intentional and proactive in its approach to change than AI.

AI is currently used as an adjunct to PAR approaches. Its capabilities in text processing, sentiment analysis and NLP have been identified as a means of generating data that can enhance patient participation in healthcare systems (Denecke *et al.*, 2019). The predictive features of some systems can also improve inclusivity in PAR research by enabling accessible communication of study information (Xu *et al.*, 2024). Transformer-based methods such as BERT and PEGASUS have been used to generate plain language summaries for social science research but lack readability evaluation tools (Collins *et al.*, 2017; Vinzelberg *et al.*, 2023).

Quan is investigating the relationship between workplace diversity and employee performance. He uses an AI system to reword the plain language statement for participants. After testing its readability with employees, they suggested minor changes for clarity. One employee recommended a brief video version of the statement, which is produced on an AI enhanced platform.

The PAR tradition relies on human engagement and interpersonal skills for participant trust, dialogue and enriching mutual knowledge systems. Its limited interpersonal abilities and historical lack of user inclusion have led to the rise of 'participatory AI' (Birhane *et al.*, 2022). Participatory AI aims to expand user engagement beyond proxy-based participation, data enrichment, moderation and algorithmic improvement. These activities have been criticized for providing 'ghost work' for low-income countries (Gray and Suri, 2019) and excluding marginalized voices from the Global South (Medrado and Verdegem, 2024). The technical complexity of AI systems also tests meaningful participation, requiring users to upskill to reduce the gap between the knowledge developers and users, and increase their agency as research participants (Delgado *et al.*, 2023).

In the distant future, AI may even come to be considered a 'participant' in the PAR process.

Hitch (2024) reported that she perceived ChatGPT as a co-contributor in data analysis, albeit one that offered a limited level of expertise. However, collaborative partnerships with participants must occur within AI development before its role in PAR research can truly emerge.

6.3.6 Constructivist grounded theory

Constructivist grounded theory (CGT) builds on grounded theory principles by emphasizing the interpretive and constructed nature of data and knowledge (Gardner *et al.*, 2012; Charmaz, 2016). Unlike classical approaches that build theory from a pragmatist and positivist perspective, CGT highlights the importance of researcher and participant interactions in co-creating study outcomes (Gardner *et al.*, 2012). As a subjectivist and relativist method, CGT requires self-reflection and critique throughout the study process, conducting simultaneous data collection and analysis within multifaceted contexts (Charmaz, 2016; O'Connor *et al.*, 2018).

AI introduces a third contributor to knowledge co-creation, using a different form of intelligence. Deep-learning models such as ChatGPT can produce inaccurate information (Saliba and Boitsios, 2023), and therefore the critical stance of CGT is crucial for verifying AI outputs. There are also power differentials to consider between various stakeholder groups, which may be at least partly attributable to the knowledge gap between research disciplines and AI developers.

The prospect of using AI to build a baby is a thought experiment illustrating the challenges posed by constructivism for this technology (Guerin, 2008). Developers would need sophisticated algorithms to simulate how babies learn from sensory motor experiences. However, very little is known about the information processing mechanisms underlying infant behaviour, and this knowledge is held by other disciplines such as psychology. Developers therefore lack the necessary knowledge to construct an effective algorithm.

Christou (2023b) identified five planning steps for researchers considering AI augmentation: (i) familiarization with AI generated information; (ii) reviewing data for biases and ethical issues; (iii) cross-referencing of generated content; (iv) data analysis process control; and (v) continuous cognitive input from human researchers throughout the process. Additional issues that are important to consider at the planning stage include: (i) the AI literacy of researchers; (ii) transparency about the algorithms and decision-making processes of the chosen platform; (iii) strategies and methods for integrating AI and human insights; (iv) protocols for documenting the analytical process; and (v) the alignment of proposed research with institutional ethics and AI policies and procedures. All of these issues should be explicitly addressed within study protocols, in the interests of both rigour and trustworthiness.

Comparing Charmaz's (2017) recommendations for CGT with these steps suggests that AI augmented CGT research might be possible. Researchers can use AI to summarize qualitative data efficiently, and then feed preliminary topics into ongoing data collection. The CGT co-creation process enables researchers and participants to share control of data analysis, with AI mediating the identification and description of their respective data. However, no published examples of AI augmented analysis in CGT research exist, indicating that its presence in this area remains in an early stage of development.

6.3.7 Phenomenology

Phenomenological social research focuses on the subjective or lived experiences of people from their own perspectives and aims to understand the meaning behind their perceptions (Berryman, 2019). Both phenomenological research and AI aim to understand human experiences, but they approach this goal differently and achieve different outcomes.

Phenomenology explores how subjective experiences drive actions and behaviours (Berryman, 2019). While AI mimics human thought and behaviour, it has no lived experience of its own and cannot personally relate to human experiences (Roberts *et al.*, 2024). Its understanding of human values is limited to stable contexts, whereas human values are shaped by diverse cultural and social milieus (Han *et al.*, 2022). AI also struggles to capture and interpret gestures and acts, which provide important data about the life worlds of others. User expectations of AI can lead to disengagement and discomfort if the technology is experienced as 'too human' or 'not human enough' (Chaves and Gerosa, 2021).

The compatibility of AI with phenomenological research may also depend on the specific approach to this tradition. Classical phenomenology includes epoché, which brackets the researcher's subjective perceptions to spotlight participants' experiences (Chelstrom, 2013). Beavers (2002) asserted that epoché can make the cognitive contribution of human researchers easier to identify; however, Zahavi (2019) argued that it is irrelevant outside the field of philosophy. More recently, interpretative phenomenological analysis (IPA) has emerged as a double hermeneutic approach where researcher subjectivity plays an acknowledged role in making sense of the participants' experiences (Smith, 2004). No IPA studies have incorporated AI augmentation to date, but the technology may still be applicable to non-analytical study tasks.

An IPA study explored computer science student perceptions of mobile phone use in the classroom (Tomović, 2021). Transcription of 11 interviews was augmented by an AI add-in on Zoom providing live transcription. These transcripts were shared with participants for accuracy checks before human researchers completed their analysis.

AI transcription is becoming popular across several qualitative traditions for its increased accuracy and contribution to expedited analysis (Eftekhari, 2024), although it is less accurate with accented voices and poor-quality recordings. There are also ethical issues around uploading data to AI transcription platforms regarding privacy and data security. The efficiency advantages of AI transcription must also be weighed against its prevention of the initial familiarization and preliminary analysis that occurs during the process of manual transcription (Maxwell, 2013).

6.4 Critical Questions for AI Augmentation in Qualitative Social Science Research

We propose the following critical questions to guide social researchers in considering AI augmentation for their studies during design, data collection and data analysis. Not all questions will be relevant to every study, nor are they intended to be prescriptive. We offer these questions as a reflective tool and encourage researchers to use them individually and within teams to stimulate ongoing discussion.

The first nine questions will help you decide whether AI augmentation is the right approach for your study. Deciding to retain human-led approaches in preference to AI adoption is a perfectly legitimate choice, as this chapter shows the technology is more compatible with some traditions than others. However, we recommend regularly revising these questions as social science qualitative research advances, considering the ongoing rapid developments in AI technology.

1. How does the epistemology of AI align with our assumptions about knowledge? Consider what constitutes valid knowledge, scope of data collection and data analysis practices.
2. How does the ontology of AI align with your assumptions about the nature of the world and reality? Consider interpretative or constructivist approaches, research questions, and objective versus subjective data.
3. How compatible is AI with the qualitative tradition of your study? Consider areas of agreement and disagreement and previously published examples.
4. What are the potential benefits and limitations of AI augmentation in your study? Consider speed, cost and access to resources.
5. At what stage of the study could AI be used most effectively and efficiently? Consider how the technology supports human researcher skill, and at which point AI augmentation will begin and end.
6. What information is required to inform your decisions about system selection and implementation? Consider existing skills or knowledge, reliability and ethical implications.
7. How much knowledge and experience do you have with AI systems? Consider the need for additional training or mentorship and strategies for maintaining currency of skills.
8. What measures will you have in place to ensure transparency about your use of AI with your stakeholders? Consider documentation, reporting and other communication.
9. How will you mitigate the risk of biases, distortions or inaccuracies arising from the chosen AI

system? Consider frameworks for critical analysis, reflexive practice and continuous evaluation.

If AI augmentation is the right approach for your study, the following questions will help you to address more complex methodological issues and dilemmas during study design.

- *Content analysis*. Are there mechanisms in place to verify AI generated codes and themes against human research analysis? Consider when AI is integrated into the research process and how reliability will be measured or documented.
- *Descriptive qualitative analysis*. What strategies will be used to ensure that clear, high-quality prompts and inputs are provided to the AI system? Consider researcher training, code book terminology and iterative prompting.
- *Discourse analysis*. How will you address the limitations of AI systems in understanding gesture, context, power relations and subtle subjectivity during analysis? Consider the relative roles of AI and human interpretation and the training data provided.
- *Ethnography*. How will the cultural positionality of the AI system, researchers and participants be addressed during the study? Consider diverse and representative training data, multilingual and multicultural system capacities, and pilot testing.
- *Participatory action research (PAR)*. What strategies will be in place to address the technical complexity of AI systems and enhance meaningful participation? Consider participant training and support, collaborative learning opportunities and equitable access to internet resources and devices.
- *Constructivist grounded theory (CGT)*. How can AI contribute to or hinder the co-creation of knowledge between researchers and participants? Consider potential power dynamics when AI is introduced or utilized in the research process.
- *Phenomenology*. What methods will be used to ensure that AI outputs maintain a phenomenological focus on individual meaning and perceptions? Consider the entry of only individual-level data and plan prompt design to avoid aggregation of data in outputs.

6.5 Conclusion

The integration of AI into qualitative research methodologies provides complex yet promising opportunities for social science qualitative researchers. Generally, there is an inverse relationship between AI and qualitative traditions: the more interpretative the tradition, the less compatible AI augmentation may be. This misalignment poses challenges to ensuring epistemological and ontological coherence, highlighting the need for careful consideration and critical reflection by researchers before adopting AI tools. If AI systems are limited to less interpretative traditions such as content analysis, its true potential as an analytical ally may never be revealed.

Despite a proliferation of theoretical and discussion papers in recent years, practical examples of AI augmented qualitative analysis remain relatively rare. This scarcity underscores the novelty of the technology in qualitative research, and significant training and skills development gaps must be addressed as a matter of urgency. The potential benefits of AI augmentation, such as increased efficiency, reduced costs and enhanced opportunities for engagement with large datasets, are counterbalanced by justifiable concerns about a loss of contextual depth and interpretative richness. Despite its transformative potential, we concur with Anis and French (2023) in their call to develop resources and practices that enable efficient, explicatory and equitable AI augmentation in qualitative research. Human researchers must maintain their critical oversight, agency and engagement when applying AI to the analytical process and should proceed with cautious optimism.

References

Anis, S. and French, J.A. (2023) Efficient, explicatory, and equitable: why qualitative researchers should embrace AI, but cautiously. *Business & Society* 62, 1139–1144.

Baum, S.D. (2020) Artificial interdisciplinarity: artificial intelligence for research on complex societal problems. *Philosophy & Technology* 34, 45–63.

Beavers, A.F. (2002) Phenomenology and artificial intelligence. *Metaphilosophy* 33, 70–82.

Berryman, D.R. (2019) Ontology, epistemology, methodology, and methods: information for librarian researchers. *Medical Reference Services Quarterly* 38, 271–279.

Bircan, T. and Salah, A.A.A. (2022) A bibliometric analysis of the use of artificial intelligence technologies for social sciences. *Mathematics* 10: 4398.

Birhane, A., Isaac, W., Prabhakaran, V., Diaz, M., Elish, M.C. *et al.* (2022) Power to the people? Opportunities and challenges for participatory AI. In: *Proceedings of the 2nd ACM Conference on Equity and Access in Algorithms, Mechanisms, and Optimization, 6–9 October 2022, Arlington, Virginia.* Article 6.

Blackwell, A.F. (2021) Ethnographic artificial intelligence. *Interdisciplinary Science Reviews* 46, 198–211.

Braun, V. and Clarke, V. (2021) Can I use TA? Should I use TA? Should I *not* use TA? Comparing reflexive thematic analysis and other pattern-based qualitative analytic approaches. *Counselling and Psychotherapy Research* 21, 37–47.

Brookes, G. and McEnery, T. (2019) The utility of topic modelling for discourse studies: a critical evaluation. *Discourse Studies* 21, 3–21.

Cardoso, J.C.H. (2024) Digital images generated by artificial intelligence as ethnographic experimentation. *Desde El Sur* 16: e0023.

Carvalho, T., Negm, H. and El-Geneidy, A. (2024) A comparison of the results from artificial intelligence-based and human-based transport-related thematic analysis. *Transport Findings*, March: 99401.

Charmaz, K. (2016) The power of constructivist grounded theory for critical inquiry. *Qualitative Inquiry* 23, 34–45.

Charmaz, K. (2017) Constructivist grounded theory. *Journal of Positive Psychology* 12, 299–300.

Chaves, A.P. and Gerosa, M.A. (2021) How should my chatbot interact? A survey on social characteristics in human–chatbot interaction design. *International Journal of Human–Computer Interaction* 37, 729–758.

Chelstrom, E. (2013) *Social Phenomenology: Husserl, Intersubjectivity, and Collective Intentionality.* Lexington Books, Lanham, Maryland.

Christou, P. (2023a) A critical perspective over whether and how to acknowledge the use of artificial intelligence (AI) in qualitative studies. *The Qualitative Report* 28, 1981–1991.

Christou, P. (2023b) How to use artificial intelligence (AI) as a resource, methodological and analysis tool in qualitative research? *The Qualitative Report* 28, 1968–1980.

Christou, P. (2024) Thematic analysis through artificial intelligence (AI). *The Qualitative Report* 29, 560–576.

Collins, E., Augenstein, I. and Riedel, S. (2017) A supervised approach to extractive summarisation of scientific papers. In: Levy, R. and Specia, L. (eds) *Proceedings of the 21st Conference on Computational Natural Language Learning (CoNLL 2017), 3–4 August 2017, Vancouver, Canada.* Association for Computational Linguistics, Stroudsburg, Pennsylvania pp. 195–205.

Chubb, L.A. (2023) Me and the machines: possibilities and pitfalls of using artificial intelligence for qualitative data analysis. *International Journal of Qualitative Methods* 22: 16094069231193593.

Clarke, V. and Braun, V. (2017) Thematic analysis. *Journal of Positive Psychology* 12, 297–298.

Coombes, P.H. and Jones, S. (2020) Toward auto-netnography in consumer studies. *International Journal of Market Research* 62, 658–665.

Cresswell, J. (2006) *Research Design: Qualitative, Quantitative and Mixed Methods Approaches*, 3rd edn. Sage Publishing, Thousand Oaks, London.

Cresswell, J. and Cresswell, J.D. (2022) *Research Design: Qualitative, Quantitative, and Mixed Methods Approaches*, 6th edn. Sage Publishing, Thousand Oaks, California.

Cresswell, J. and Plano Clark, V. (2018) Choosing a mixed methods design. In: Cresswell, J. and Plano Clark, V. (eds) *Designing and Conducting Mixed Methods Research.* Sage Publishing, Thousand Oaks, California, pp. 53–106.

Crombie, I.K. and Davies, H.T.O. (1996) *Research in Health Care: Design, Conduct and Interpretation of Health Services Research.* Wiley, London.

Delgado, F., Yang, S., Madaio, M. and Yang, Q. (2023) The Participatory Turn in AI Design: Theoretical Foundations and the Current State of Practice. In: *EAAMO '23: Proceedings of the 3rd ACM Conference on Equity and Access in Algorithms, Mechanisms, and Optimization, 30 October–1 November 2023, Boston, Massachusetts.* Association for Computing Machinery, New York, Article 37.

Denecke, K., Gabarron, E., Grainger, R., Konstantinidis, S.T., Lau, A., *et al.* (2019) Artificial intelligence for participatory health: applications, impact, and future implications. *Yearbook of Medical Informatics* 28, 165–173.

Dickie, V.A. (2003) Data analysis in qualitative research: a plea for sharing the magic and the effort. *American Journal of Occupational Therapy* 57, 49–56.

Eftekhari, H. (2024) Transcribing in the digital age: qualitative research practice utilizing intelligent speech recognition technology. *European Journal of Cardiovascular Nursing* 23, 553–560.

Fine, M., Torre, M.E., Boudin, K., Bowen, I., Clark, J., *et al.* (2003) Participatory action research: from within and beyond prison bars. In: *Qualitative Research in Psychology: Expanding Perspectives in Methodology and Design*. American Psychological Association, Washington, DC, pp. 173–198.

Gardner, A., McCutcheon, H. and Fedoruk, M. (2012) Discovering constructivist grounded theory's fit and relevance to researching contemporary mental health nursing practice. *Australian Journal of Advanced Nursing* 30, 66–74.

Ge, X., Xu, C., Misaki, D., Markus, H.R. and Tsai, J.L. (2024) How culture shapes what people want from AI. In: Mueller, F.F., Kyburz, P., Williamson, J.R., Sas, C., Wilson, M.L., *et al.* (eds) *CHI '24: Proceedings of the 2024 CHI Conference on Human Factors in Computing Systems, 11–16 May 2024, Honolulu, Hawaii*. Association for Computing Machinery, New York, Article 95.

Goertz, G. and Mahoney, J. (2012) *A Tale of Two Cultures: Qualitative and Quantitative Research in the Social Sciences*. Princeton University Press, Princeton, New Jersey.

Goldberg, A. and Srivastava, S.B. (2022) *How Can AI Enrich Our Understanding of Organizational Culture?* Available at: http://faculty.haas.berkeley.edu/srivastava/papers/AI%20and%20Culture%20-%20Goldberg%20and%20Srivastava.pdf (accessed 25 September 2024).

Gray, M.L. and Suri, S. (2019) *Ghost Work: How to Stop Silicon Valley from Building a New Global Underclass*. HMH Books, Montreal, Quebec, Canada.

Guerin, F. (2008) Constructivism in AI: prospects, progress and challenges. In: *AISB 2008 Convention: Communication, Interaction and Social Intelligence,* 1–4 April 2008, Aberdeen, UK. The Society for the Study of Artificial Intelligence and Simulation of Behaviour, Aberdeen, UK, pp. 20–27.

Han, S., Kelly, E., Nikou, S. and Svee, E.-O. (2022) Aligning artificial intelligence with human values: reflections from a phenomenological perspective. *AI & Society* 37, 1383–1395.

Haque, M.A. (2023) A brief analysis of "ChatGPT" – a revolutionary tool designed by OpenAI. *EAI Endorsed Transactions on AI and Robotics* 1: e15.

Hasselberger, W. (2019) Ethics beyond computation: why we can't (and shouldn't) replace human moral judgment with algorithms. *Social Research* 86, 977–999.

Hill, C. and Knox, S. (2021) *Essentials of Consensual Qualitative Research*. American Psychological Association, New York.

Hitch, D. (2024) Artificial intelligence augmented qualitative analysis: the way of the future? *Qualitative Health Research* 34, 595–606.

Jiang, J.A., Wade, K., Fiesler, C. and Brubaker, J.R. (2021) Supporting serendipity: opportunities and challenges for human–AI collaboration in qualitative analysis. In*: Proceedings of the ACM on Human-Computer Interaction, Vol. 5*. Association for Computing Machinery, New York, Article 94.

Laitinen, A. and Sahlgren, O. (2021) AI systems and respect for human autonomy. *Frontiers in Artificial Intelligence* 4: 705164.

Lee, J., Wu, A.S., Li, D. and Kulasegaram, K.M. (2021) Artificial intelligence in undergraduate medical education: a scoping review. *Academic Medicine* 96, S62–S70.

Lee, L.W., Dabirian, A., McCarthy, I.P. and Kietzmann, J. (2020) Making sense of text: artificial intelligence-enabled content analysis. *European Journal of Marketing* 54, 615–644.

Lee-Johnson, Y.L., Fair, K., O'Connor, K., Rodney, T., Ono, J. *et al.* (2023) Reflexivity for restorying the ontological and epistemological truths in qualitative research. *Impacting Education* 8, 44–49.

Lodge, J.M., Thompson, K. and Corrin, L. (2023) Mapping out a research agenda for generative artificial intelligence in tertiary education. *Australasian Journal of Educational Technology* 39, 1–8.

Matera, V. and Biscaldi, A. (eds) (2021) *Ethnography: A Theoretically Oriented Practice*. Palgrave Macmillan, London.

Maxwell, J. (2013) *Qualitative Research Design: An Interactive Approach*. Sage Publishing, Thousand Oaks, California.

Medrado, A. and Verdegem, P. (2024) Participatory action research in critical data studies: interrogating AI from a south–north approach. *Big Data & Society* 11: 20539517241235869.

Morgan, D.L. (2023) Exploring the use of artificial intelligence for qualitative data analysis: THE case of ChatGPT. *International Journal of Qualitative Methods* 22: 16094069231211248.

Morse, J. (2020) The changing face of qualitative inquiry. *International Journal of Qualitative Methods* 19: 1609406920909938.

O'Connor, A., Carpenter, B. and Coughlan, B. (2018) An exploration of key issues in the debate between classic and constructivist grounded theory. *Grounded Theory Review* 17, 90–103.

Oleinik, A., Popova, I., Kirdina, S.G. and Shatalova, T.N. (2014) On the choice of measures of reliability and validity in the content-analysis of texts. *Quality & Quantity* 48, 2703–2718.

Parker, R.D., Mancini, K. and Abram, M.D. (2023) Natural language processing enhanced qualitative methods: an opportunity to improve health outcomes. *International Journal of Qualitative Methods* 22: 16094069231214144.

Paulus, T.M. and Lester, J.N. (2016) ATLAS.ti for conversation and discourse analysis studies. *International Journal of Social Research Methodology* 19, 405–428.

Peres, R., Schreier, M., Schweidel, D. and Sorescu, A. (2023) On ChatGPT and beyond: how generative artificial intelligence may affect research, teaching, and practice. *International Journal of Research in Marketing* 40, 269–275.

Prabhakaran, V., Qadri, R. and Hutchinson, B.C. (2022) Cultural incongruencies in artificial intelligence. arXiv preprint. Available at: https://arxiv.org/abs/2211.13069 (accessed 25 September 2024).

Reis, F. and Lenz, C. (2024) Performance of artificial intelligence (AI)-powered chatbots in the assessment of medical case reports: qualitative insights from simulated scenarios. *Cureus* 16: e53899.

Reis, T., Dumberger, L., Bruchhaus, S., Krause, T. and Schreyer, V. (2024) AI-based user empowerment for empirical social research. *Big Data and Cognitive Computing* 8: 11.

Roberts, J., Baker, M. and Andrew, J. (2024) Artificial intelligence and qualitative research: the promise and perils of large language model (LLM) 'assistance'. *Critical Perspectives on Accounting* 99: 102722.

Saliba, T. and Boitsios, G. (2023) ChatGPT, a radiologist's perspective. *Pediatric Radiology* 53, 813–815.

Saxena, P., Saxena, V., Pandey, A.K., Flato, U. and Shukla, K. (2023) *Multiple Aspects of Artificial Intelligence*. Book Saga Productions, Maharashtra, India.

Schäffer, B. and Lieder, F.R. (2023) Distributed interpretation – teaching reconstructive methods in the social sciences supported by artificial intelligence. *Journal of Research on Technology in Education* 55, 111–124.

Smith, J. (2004) Reflecting on the development of interpretative phenomenological analysis and its contribution to qualitative research in psychology. *Qualitative Research in Psychology* 1, 39–54.

Stanley, M. (2023) Qualitative descriptive: a very good place to start. In: Nayar, S. and Stanley, M. (eds) *Qualitative Research Methodologies for Occupational Therapy Science and Therapy*. Taylor & Francis Group, London, pp. 21–36.

Tai, R.H., Bentley, L.R., Xia, X., Sitt, J.M., Fankhauser, S.C., *et al.* (2024) An examination of the use of large language models to aid analysis of textual data. *International Journal of Qualitative Methods* 23: 16094069241231168.

Taufek, T.E., Mohd Nor, N.F., Jaludin, A., Tiun, S. and Choy, L.K. (2021) Public perceptions on climate change: a sentiment analysis approach. *GEMA Online Journal of Language Studies* 21, 209–233.

Tomović, A. (2021) Engagement theory based interpretative phenomenological analysis of computer science students' perceptions of their learning engagement using mobile devices. Doctor of Education in Higher Education Administration, St Cloud State University, Minnesota.

Tschisgale, P., Wulff, P. and Kubsch, M. (2023) Integrating artificial intelligence-based methods into qualitative research in physics education research: a case for computational grounded theory. *Physical Review Physics Education Research* 19: 020123.

Vinzelberg, O., Jenkins, M.D., Morison, G., McMinn, D. and Tieges, Z. (2023) Lay Text Summarisation Using Natural Language Processing: A Narrative Literature Review. arXiv preprint. Available at: https://arxiv.org/abs/2303.14222 (accessed 1 October 2024).

Weizenbaum, J. (1976) *Computer Power and Human Reason: From Judgment to Calculation*. Freeman and Co., New York.

Willig, C. (2013) Foucauldian discourse analysis. In: Willig, C. (ed.) *Introducing Qualitative Research in Psychology*, 3rd edn. McGraw-Hill Education, New York, pp. 129–142.

Xu, R., Sun, Y., Ren, M., Guo, S., Pan, R., *et al.* (2024) AI for social science and social science of AI: a survey. *Information Processing & Management* 61: 103665.

Zahavi, D. (2019) Applied phenomenology: why it is safe to ignore the epoché. *Continental Philosophy Review* 54, 259–273.

7 Generative AI: A Catalyst for Paradigmatic Change in Qualitative Data Analysis

Susanne Friese[1,2*]
[1]*Qeludra Consultancy, Netherlands;* [2]*Max Planck Institute for the Study of Religious and Ethnic Diversity, Göttingen, Germany*

Abstract
The aim of this chapter is to investigate whether Thomas Kuhn's concept of scientific revolutions, as described in his seminal work *The Structure of Scientific Revolutions* (1962), can be extended to examine shifts in qualitative research methodologies driven by the advent of artificial intelligence (AI). Initially, Kuhn's process of scientific revolution will be outlined, focusing primarily on the dynamics detailed in his landmark text. While Kuhn's discussion was predominantly confined to the natural sciences, there is ongoing debate about its applicability to the social sciences. This debate will be addressed, arguing for the framework's relevance beyond the natural sciences, as Kuhn himself suggested in a postscript to a later edition (2012). Building on this foundation, the history of one of the predominant methodologies in qualitative data analysis, coding, will be explored. The exploration will consider how the emergence of AI technology could potentially induce a Kuhnian-type shift, leading to significant transformations in how qualitative data will be analysed in the future.

Keywords: generative AI, qualitative, qualitative data analysis

7.1 Introduction

This chapter explores the transformative potential of AI on qualitative data analysis approaches, applying the framework of Thomas Kuhn's theory of scientific revolutions (Kuhn, 1962). The chapter starts by outlining Kuhn's ideas before shifting to analysing how and why these ideas can be applied to the social sciences and especially to the effect the transformative new technology has on research methodology. It critically examines how artificial intelligence (AI) is reshaping traditional methodologies and prompting a re-evaluation of established analytical frameworks. The historical development of coding as a central technique in qualitative analysis will be traced, emphasizing its role in structuring and systematizing the research process. The recent integration of AI into coding practices will then be outlined, highlighting both the opportunities and challenges presented by such technological advancements. This discussion is framed within the context of Thomas Kuhn's theory of scientific revolutions, drawing parallels between the disruptive influence of AI and the paradigm shifts described by Kuhn. As anomalies and inefficiencies in traditional coding practices are magnified by the capabilities of AI, a state

*E-mail: Susanne.friese@qeludra.com

 Artificial Intelligence (AI) in Social Research (P.A. Christou ed.)
DOI: 10.1079/9781800626607.0007

of crisis is emerging within the qualitative research community. This growing crisis, underscored by a clash between traditional methodologies and innovative AI-driven approaches, along with the community's resistance to new technologies, invites us to explore these dynamics through the lens of Kuhn's theory of scientific revolutions. Let us first examine the distinct phases of a paradigm shift as described by Kuhn to better understand how such shifts might unfold in the context of qualitative data analysis.

7.2 Scientific Revolutions Through Kuhn's Lens

7.2.1 The phase of normal science

Kuhn argued that scientific progress does not occur in a smooth, linear trajectory. Instead, he proposed a model characterized by alternating periods of 'normal science' and 'revolutionary science'. During phases of normal science, scientists largely agree upon a dominant paradigm (Lakatos and Musgrave, 1970; Kuhn, 2012). This paradigm represents a shared framework of established theories, widely accepted methods and a common set of underlying philosophical assumptions. It acts as a lens through which researchers perceive the problems they address and the validity of potential solutions.

Within the boundaries of a normal science period, researchers engage in what Kuhn calls 'puzzle-solving'. They do not challenge the fundamental assumptions of the paradigm itself. Instead, they work to refine existing theories, extend them to explain observed anomalies and explore new applications for established knowledge. It can be thought of as filling in missing pieces within an agreed-upon picture.

This commitment to a dominant paradigm allows focused and efficient progress. Scientists build upon a shared language and set of tools, trusting in the ability of the current framework to ultimately address any challenges that arise. However, Kuhn (2012) and Feyerabend (1975) argued that this intense focus on a single paradigm can lead to an over-reliance on established frameworks, potentially blinding researchers to phenomena or solutions that exist outside its prescribed boundaries. This tunnel vision can ultimately precipitate the kind of revolutionary changes that Kuhn describes.

7.2.2 Occurrence of anomalies

Anomalies play a critical role in this process. They are puzzling observations or experimental results that stubbornly resist explanation within the existing scientific framework. While these anomalies are disruptive, they do not immediately indicate the failure of a paradigm. Scientists often exhibit initial resistance to discarding their well-established theories, preferring to dismiss anomalies as experimental errors, isolated incidents or simply mysteries that will eventually be resolved by the current paradigm. This tendency to adhere to and operate within the existing framework underscores both the efficiency of using a shared paradigm and a steadfast belief in its capacity to solve problems.

Kuhn asserts that anomalies hold transformative potential. A single anomaly might be dismissed, but when anomalies persist or a cluster of related irregularities arise, cracks begin to appear in the seemingly solid foundation of the paradigm. Scientists can no longer simply relegate problems to the margins; they are forced to question whether their fundamental assumptions are somehow flawed or incomplete. It is this process, fuelled by nagging anomalies that refuse to be tamed, that can ultimately pave the way towards a paradigm shift and revolutionize scientific understanding.

As anomalies accumulate and stubbornly defy resolution within the boundaries of the existing paradigm, a sense of unease begins to permeate the scientific community. The once-unshakeable confidence in the dominant framework falters as scientists confront the limitations of their current understanding.

7.2.3 State of crisis

In Kuhn's theory, a 'crisis' in science happens when existing theories cannot explain new or persistent problems. During such crises, scientists start looking for solutions more broadly. They consider new and unusual ideas that they might have ignored before. This is different from normal times when scientists usually stick to well-established theories. A crisis shakes up the old ways of thinking and can lead to major changes in scientific understanding.

A good example of this is the shift from Newtonian physics to Einstein's theory of relativity. For many years, Newton's laws were seen as the ultimate explanation for the forces of nature. However, as scientists began to explore the universe more deeply, they encountered observations that Newtonian physics could not explain, such as issues with the orbit of Mercury and the speed of light. This led to a scientific crisis.

As the crisis deepened, Albert Einstein introduced his theory of relativity, which provided solutions to these problems and offered a new way of understanding gravity and motion. Einstein's theory was initially seen as radical and faced scepticism because it challenged the well-established Newtonian framework. However, its ability to solve problems that were inexplicable under the old paradigm led to its acceptance and a revolutionary shift in physics.

This transformative change in scientific thinking frequently involves an overhaul of foundational concepts, methodologies and even the types of research questions considered legitimate. The landscape of the discipline is irrevocably altered. Thus, a crisis acts as a prelude to the birth of a new paradigm.

7.2.4 Birth of a new paradigm

Kuhn underscored the radical nature of this change by introducing the concept of 'incommensurability' (c.f. Feyerabend, 1975). Competing paradigms, he posited, may be so fundamentally different in their assumptions and conceptual language that direct comparison or translation becomes impossible. It is as if scientists operating within different paradigms are speaking entirely separate dialects, unable to fully understand each other's perspectives. Therefore, a true paradigm shift is not a process of gradual evolution but a revolution, a decisive break from the past. The lens through which scientists observe their field of study changes so drastically that the old ways of thinking and operating become obsolete. This revolution gives birth to a new form of 'normal science', operating under the rules and assumptions of the freshly established paradigm, until the cycle – anomalies, crisis, revolution – eventually begins again.

Kuhn underscored the profound and often unsettling nature of a paradigm shift. It is not a matter of mere refinement or adjustment but involves embracing a new way of seeing and thinking about the world. This change can be met with resistance, as established scientists may have deeply internalized the old worldview, making the transition to a radically different framework both intellectually and psychologically challenging. Embracing a new paradigm, according to Kuhn (2012), is rarely driven by purely logical deduction or hard empirical evidence alone. While the accumulation of anomalies that resist explanation within the old paradigm plays a significant role, the shift is ultimately rooted in a complex interplay of factors. One crucial element is the emerging paradigm's potential to solve the problems that plagued its predecessor. A new paradigm must not only acknowledge the old paradigm's failings but also offer a compelling promise of illuminating previously unresolved puzzles. Its ability to provide novel explanations or address lingering anomalies holds great persuasive power within the scientific community.

Additionally, the decision to embrace a new paradigm is influenced by its potential to open new avenues of research. A promising paradigm generates a sense of excitement, suggesting fertile ground for exploration, novel questions and the potential for significant discoveries. This forward-looking allure can be a deciding factor, especially for younger scientists less wedded to the old ways of thinking.

Finally, Kuhn stressed that the resolution of revolutions cannot be separated from the social dynamics of the scientific community. Arguments for and against competing paradigms involve elements of persuasion, reputation and generational shifts. The decision to embrace a paradigm shift is never a purely objective one; it is influenced by the power structures, personalities and intellectual currents within a particular scientific field.

In essence, the abandonment of an old research tradition in favour of a revolutionary new paradigm is the result of a complex convergence of factors. It is driven by the limitations of the old paradigm, and the problem-solving potential and promise of the new, as well as the ever-evolving social and intellectual landscape of the scientific community itself.

7.3 Application of Kuhn's Concept of Paradigm Shift to Other Fields

Kuhn focused primarily on the natural sciences in his seminal work. Critics have contended that the processes he described are less applicable to the social sciences, where there is less emphasis on discovering universal laws and more on interpreting human behaviour and social structures (Bird, 2022). Furthermore, the social sciences are distinguished by a rich diversity of coexisting theories and methodologies, all of which can be equally valid. This methodological pluralism reflects the varied approaches used to understand human behaviours and societies, indicating that multiple paradigms often operate concurrently without one achieving the dominance necessary to marginalize the others. Common paradigms in social sciences include positivism, interpretivism, Marxism, feminism, critical theory and post-modernism, each providing a distinct perspective on the social world. This contrasts sharply with Kuhn's concept of a single dominant paradigm that governs the practice of normal science, where a new paradigm, like Einsteinian physics, replaces an old one, such as Newtonian physics.

This argument, however, does not reflect the motivation of why Kuhn wrote the book. He wanted to challenge the prevailing view of science as a purely objective and linear progression of discoveries. Kuhn argued that scientific progress is a fundamentally human endeavour and not merely the result of a methodical and rational process (Kálmán, 2016). In the opening lines of his book, Kuhn stated that he aimed to demonstrate how textbooks, the traditional mediums through which each new generation of scientists learns its craft, have fundamentally misled us. Throughout the book, he deconstructed this view chapter by chapter, describing how shared beliefs within a community are formed, how they sustain that community over time and how they are eventually disrupted by anomalies, leading to a crisis and transformative shift in these shared beliefs and practices. And this process, the author would argue, can be transferred to what is currently happening to qualitative research methodologies, and particular data analysis.

7.4 How Emergent Technologies Reshape the Practice of Coding in Qualitative Data Analysis

Coding has become a central technique in many forms of qualitative research (Braun and Clarke, 2006, 2023; Bazeley, 2013; Charmaz, 2014; Kuckartz, 2014; Silver and Lewins, 2014; Corbin and Strauss, 2015; Friese, 2019; Miles *et al.*, 2019; Richards, 2020; Saldaña, 2021; Mayring, 2022). Some of the books listed above have been published in ten or more editions. The widespread adoption of coding across multiple qualitative research methods and its incorporation into software designed specifically for qualitative analysis has standardized certain analytical processes and promoted a consistent methodological approach within the field. However, it is important to note that, while coding is influential and widely adopted, it does not strictly conform to Kuhn's definition of a paradigm. It lacks a singular theoretical commitment, is highly adaptable across various theoretical frameworks, and is used by a diverse community of researchers without a unified set of beliefs about its function and implications.

Therefore, while coding exemplifies more of a methodological consensus rather than a full paradigm, it serves as a useful lens to examine how emerging technologies could reshape established practices in qualitative research. The advancements in AI, particularly the arrival of ChatGPT, have introduced a significant shift in the research landscape. Many qualitative researchers find themselves grappling with this new technology, marked by a proliferation of unanswered questions, intense debates between early adopters and critics, and a general lack of understanding. This unsettled environment is precipitating what could be described as a state of crisis, reminiscent of the conditions that Kuhn outlines as preceding a paradigm shift.

The current dynamics within the community of qualitative researchers echo the transformative shifts Kuhn described in his model of scientific revolutions. As coding has been integral to data analysis in qualitative research, the integration of AI challenges and potentially redefines this established methodological approach. Researchers are now confronted with the possibility that AI can automate or augment the coding process (Hitch, 2023), or even fundamentally alter the analysis process, raising both opportunities and concerns that resonate with Kuhn's description of a scientific community in transition. Just as anomalies within a paradigm lead to questions that challenge established norms, the capabilities, and limitations of AI in qualitative research are prompting a re-evaluation of long-held assumptions about what constitutes rigorous and insightful analysis.

This intersection of coding as an established practice and the disruptive influence of AI technology suggests that we may be on the cusp of a methodological revolution, in qualitative research. The friction between traditional methodologies and innovative technologies illustrates a classic Kuhnian crisis, setting the stage for a significant transformation in how qualitative research is conducted. This transformation will lead to the establishment of new standards, practices and understandings that better accommodate the capabilities and challenges of AI.

7.4.1 Period of normal science: how coding became a prevalent approach for qualitative data analysis

The term 'coding' in qualitative research did not emerge as a planned terminological invention but as an evolution in the methodology of data analysis. In early method textbooks, the need for systematic approaches to organize and analyse data was already recognized. For instance, Palmer (1928) noted that 'skilled research workers are able to rearrange the data observed in interviews so that remarks concerning one topic can be grouped together without losing the implication contained in the original sequence'. This early insight highlights the foundational need for what would later become known as coding.

By 1937, the term 'coding' was used explicitly within the marketing research community, as documented by the Association of American Marketing, to describe the process of classifying open-ended survey responses. This marked one of the earliest formal adoptions of the term in a research context. Despite these early uses, the term 'coding' did not gain widespread recognition immediately. Influential researchers such as Robert K. Merton developed elaborate systems to analyse unstructured interviews but did not use the term 'coding'. Similarly, Adorno *et al.* (1950) referred to processes akin to coding as 'categorization' or 'classification' in their reports. It was not until the mid-1950s that the terminology began to catch on, as noted by Hyman and Sheatsley (1954), who frequently employed the terms 'code', 'codes' and 'coding'.

The term's first sustained use is often associated with the methodological writings that emerged from the study 'Boys in White' by Becker *et al.* (1961). This research, focused on higher education, a field then dominated by psychology, required explicit descriptions of the researchers' procedures and logic. This need probably catalysed the formal adoption and regular use of 'coding' in their reports. Around the same time, Whyte's (1955) book entitled *Street Corner Society* marked a significant shift from case-based to code-based analysis, influenced by anthropological approaches such as those of Bronisław Malinowski. This shift was further propelled by technical advancements such as the portable tape recorder, which allowed researchers to capture real-time data and necessitated more refined categories of analysis. As Chapoulie (1987) noted, the precise verbatim accounts from field notes demanded that researchers construct finer categories of analysis and provide detailed explanations of their interpretations.

Before the advent of computer-assisted qualitative data analysis (CAQDAS) software, these developments set the stage for coding to become an essential element of qualitative research. The systematic procedures used to extract relevant material from field notes, such as marking up field notes with different coloured pencils to indicate different topics, laid the groundwork for what would later be facilitated by software. Becker *et al.* (1984) described these early methods as 'loose inclusive' coding procedures, where codes were assigned whenever there was any indication of relevance to the current issue, highlighting a systematic approach to uncovering all relevant items to a particular proposition.

Building on the historical narrative of the development of the term 'coding' in qualitative research, Fielding and Lee (1998) noted that while Becker and Geer (1960) were instrumental in introducing the term, it was Bernard Glaser and Anselm Strauss (1967) who popularized it through their seminal work, *The Discovery of Grounded Theory: Strategies for Qualitative Research*. In this book, they frequently used the term 'coding', applying it extensively as part of their methodological framework without specific elaboration on its usage.

The widespread adoption and popularity of grounded theory, especially through the later works of Strauss and Corbin, such as *Basics of Qualitative Research: Techniques and Procedures for Developing Grounded Theory* (1998), cemented 'coding' as a fundamental term and procedure in qualitative data analysis. As qualitative research evolved with technological advancements, the development of software to support data analysis incorporated these established methodologies. Early qualitative data analysis software varied in terminology, with some initially using terms such as 'indexing' or 'nodes' to describe processes akin to coding. However, as the practice standardized, the terms 'coding' and 'codes' became universally adopted, reflecting the established terminology within the research community. This shift not only standardized the language used across different platforms but also reinforced the integral role of coding in qualitative analysis.

Building on the historical context of the term 'coding' in qualitative research and its methodological evolution, the introduction of CAQDAS software in the mid-1980s represented a significant technological leap that transformed the landscape of data analysis. Richards and Richards (1991) described this transformation as a methodological revolution, noting that 'every aspect of the handling of qualitative data is dramatically changed by computers'. Below it will be argued that it was more an evolution rather than a revolution. None the less, it had a significant impact on how researchers analysed qualitative data. CAQDAS software enabled a myriad of new capabilities: it facilitated the segmenting of text to finely defined excerpts or to information about the text, such as characteristics of respondents or aspects of documents. This shift allowed a more nuanced interplay between the original textual data and the conceptual frameworks that researchers use and create for exploring their data. Information could now be organized in a tree-structured category system or a code list, serving as a repository for document references and reflective thinking.

Furthermore, CAQDAS software enhanced the efficiency and depth of qualitative analysis by allowing multiple indexing of text segments, searching for patterns and overlaps in coded units, and linking to detailed information about documents or respondent characteristics. Researchers could save query results automatically for further analysis, offering a set of logical analysis operations that were quick, secure and capable of frequent revisions. The creation of new categories, the modification of relationships between categories and changes to the category system could all be managed dynamically, allowing quasi-statistical analyses, summary tables and the linking of disparate data. Conclusions could be checked and verified with greater rigour, challenging the traditional dichotomy between quantitative and qualitative methods, and promoting methodological diversity in qualitative research.

CAQDAS software has significantly impacted the operational aspects of coding and data analysis, enhancing the traditional processes. While fundamentally researchers continued to engage in coding, they did so in a more refined and sophisticated manner. The technology enabled a dynamic interplay between text and encoded data, allowing researchers to seamlessly toggle between raw data and their analytical constructs. While CAQDAS software brought about significant methodological changes and reshaped the research process, its introduction was more of an evolutionary development in the capabilities of qualitative researchers rather than a fundamental shift. It augmented and expanded existing methodologies, allowing deeper, more systematic exploration of complex qualitative data.

Despite these advancements, the adoption of CAQDAS software also came with notable reservations. Initial concerns included a preoccupation with quantity over depth and form over content, suggesting that the technology might lead researchers to prioritize extensive data handling at the expense of in-depth analysis. Additionally, there was apprehension that such technology could distance researchers from their data, reducing the intimate familiarity that qualitative research traditionally requires. Furthermore, researchers were concerned that not everyone would be able to use the technology due to high costs and a steep learning curve (Fielding and Lee, 1998).

CAQDAS software has not only revolutionized the operational aspects of qualitative research but has also cemented coding as a widely accepted method of data analysis. Over the years, it has become integral to the qualitative research process, underscoring the value of systematic, structured analysis in deriving meaningful insights from complex datasets. As CAQDAS platforms evolved, they facilitated increasingly sophisticated methodologies, making coding indispensable across various disciplines and studies. Using Kuhn's framework, this is comparable with the 'normal science' period.

Currently, this established method faces a new challenge: the advent of AI technology. Researchers are currently experimenting with the new technology, navigating the implications of integrating AI with traditional coding practices.

7.4.2 Anomalies: attempts to integrate AI technology into current coding practices

The coding approach, with its emphasis on categorizing qualitative data into discrete codes, has served the field of qualitative research faithfully for decades. However, with the rise of AI, cracks are beginning to appear. Shortly after the release of ChatGPT, the first CAQDAS programs began incorporating AI technology in various ways. One notable implementation was allowing AI to code the data. This process involves the AI scanning through the data paragraph by paragraph, assigning multiple codes to each section. At first glance, and when examining individual paragraphs, the results might appear satisfactory. However, AI lacks the capability to perform a critical function that human coders routinely undertake – comparing and contrasting the content across different paragraphs.

Human coders often evaluate whether a code needs to be renamed to better encompass the content from another paragraph or decide if an existing code should be applied instead. In contrast, AI tends to generate mostly new codes for each paragraph without such comparative analysis. Consequently, this approach can lead to a proliferation of codes, with the number growing exponentially as more documents are processed as shown in Table 7.1.

The task of consolidating the AI-generated codes remains the responsibility of the researcher. In testing this feature, the author discovered that aggregating the AI-generated codes often takes longer than coding the data manually from scratch. Perhaps due to this inefficiency, another CAQDAS tool opts not to offer automatic coding. Instead, it provides options to suggest codes for highlighted data segments or to suggest subcodes for a higher-level code that already includes several segments manually coded by the user. By examining these features during numerous workshops, researchers found them to be helpful, akin to receiving a second opinion when no collaborative partner is available to discuss the data. However, while these tools are appreciated for their support, they do not necessarily enhance the efficiency of the analysis process. On the contrary, they may even increase the time required due to the need for additional oversight and adjustment.

Common features now implemented in CAQDAS tools include options to use AI for summarizing documents or coded data segments. While summaries of coded data segments tend to be more accurate due to their focus on a specific topic, they still require verification by the researcher. A fundamental issue with this process is the lack of direct input from the user. The user cannot specify details about their project, such as the nature of the data sources (e.g. interviews

Table 7.1. Results of AI-coded documents.

Number of documents	Number of codes
Two documents, 27 pages	393
Four 1-hour interview transcripts	577
16 documents (literature)	2807
37 documents (company sample project containing 30 two-page interviews, seven articles)	2347

or focus group transcripts), nor can they request that the AI prioritize certain themes such as issues a, b and c in its summaries. This level of specificity is likely to lead to more relevant and accurate summaries. At present, the AI-assisted tool often relies on educated guesses. For instance, it may correctly identify data as coming from focus group transcripts in one instance but incorrectly assume they are from a single interview respondent in another.

In response to the critiques, software developers have attempted to enhance the functionality of CAQDAS tools by integrating additional features. For example, they now allow users to input context information for a project to refine the automated coding process, or ask the AI assistant to code a document based on a code that is defined by the user. Additionally, some tools offer the option for users to engage in a chat with documents.

Despite these enhancements, it essentially circles back to the fundamental requirement of coding. Users must still code the data to leverage most of the software's analytical capabilities. Users must **still code** the data to leverage most of the software's analytical capabilities.

These implementations illustrate a critical misalignment: AI capabilities are being constrained within an established framework that may not fully exploit their potential. The current approach presses AI to operate within the confines of coding-centric methodologies, which may not be the most effective use of what AI can offer. These limitations, however, are not confined solely to software development. Many qualitative researchers also struggle to move beyond the methodological approaches with which they are familiar. Various research groups and academics have experimented with using ChatGPT for coding and thematic analysis (Adduesselam, 2023; Gao *et al.*, 2023; Hitch, 2023; Morgan, 2023; Şen *et al.*, 2023; Xiao *et al.*, 2023; Zhang *et al.*, 2023; Christou, 2024; Goyanes *et al.*, 2024; Nguyen-Trung, 2024). While most authors are enthusiastic about the potential that the new technology offers, attempts to apply traditional coding methods using this technology have revealed significant shortcomings. Below are some of their conclusions.

Nguyen-Trung (2024) documented an attempt to utilize GPT-4 for coding an entire dataset. The results were unsatisfactory; the AI's output was overly concise, with each code encapsulating only a single interview quote. This approach risked omitting substantial information from other interviews, demonstrating that despite its advanced capabilities, GPT-4 struggled to manage and synthesize large sets of qualitative data comprehensively. The coding produced was too narrow, failing to capture the broader thematic patterns necessary for robust qualitative analysis.

Similarly, Goyanes *et al.* (2024, p. 25) criticized the quality and granularity of thematic patterns produced by these platforms, noting that the subtleties and contextual insights crucial to qualitative research were lacking: 'Our examination of the platform in terms of the quality and granularity of thematic patterns is rather unsatisfactory when it comes to the subtle nuances and contextual insights generally associated with qualitative research.'

Furthermore, Gamieldien *et al.* (2023) described issues with inconsistent coding by a natural language processing (NLP) GPT model, which often mislabels thematic clusters or repeats code names inconsistently: 'Turning to the NLPGPT method, the model labelled each cluster with different names even when it spoke about the same idea and only repeated the same names of codes on a handful of them.' These experiences echo the problem explained above where AI generates an excessive number of codes without effective aggregation.

Another significant limitation that is often overlooked concerns the restricted context window of current large language models (LLMs). While there is optimism that AI could enable researchers to analyse vast quantities of data swiftly (e.g. Jiang *et al.*, 2021; Theelen *et al.*, 2024), practical applications have been limited. Most experiments have involved only one or two documents. Moreover, attempts to analyse larger sets, such as ten or more interviews simultaneously, have proven either unfeasible or have yielded superficial results (Nguyen-Trung, 2024). This issue arises because once the volume of data surpasses the LLM's context limit, the model tends to rely on summaries rather than the original text, leading to a potential loss of depth and detail in the analysis.

These challenges represent significant deviations from expected outcomes. Just as anomalies in Kuhn's narrative signal the limitations of a prevailing scientific paradigm, these issues highlight the constraints of applying AI within the current framework of coding.

Given these findings, there is a compelling argument to be made for re-evaluating the integration of AI in qualitative data analysis. Instead of forcing AI to adapt to the traditional coding paradigm, there may be a need to rethink and possibly redesign AI tools to better align with the objectives and demands of qualitative research (D.L. Morgan, unpublished data).

This view is not shared by anyone. Kuckartz and Rädiger (2024) argue that generative AI will not be disruptive. Instead it can be integrated into established analytical methods. Moreover for AI to be implemented effectively, a proven methodological framework is required.

7.4.3 Resistance and crisis within the qualitative research community

The resistance encountered during these integration attempts illustrates a scenario reminiscent of a Kuhnian paradigm shift. Researchers who are deeply entrenched in established methods of data analysis often view AI as a potential threat rather than a revolutionary opportunity. This resistance became particularly apparent during spirited debates on the Qualitative Social Research mailing list (QSF Mailing List, n.d.) of which the author is a member and was further evidenced by several universities restricting access to AI-assisted functions in CAQDAS software, citing privacy concerns without substantial legal justification.

Addressing data privacy and protecting respondents are undoubtedly important, yet there must also be a willingness to explore new technologies rather than dismissing them outright. It is a common misconception that the providers of these tools will use the data to train their models. However, most platforms offer users the option to opt out of data sharing for training purposes in their settings. Furthermore, when LLMs are accessed via an application programming interface (API) within a CAQDAS tool, the data are never used for training.

Other concerns include an over-reliance on technology and potential erosion of the qualitative researcher's interpretive authority. Many in the field are hesitant to embrace a perspective where, as one researcher described it, 'meaningful and creativity-based material interpretation becomes an engineering problem to be solved'. Despite this resistance, there is recognition that AI is an enduring presence, creating tension between the comfort of familiar methods and the uncertain potential offered by technological advancements.

As coding is the basis for widely used approaches to qualitative research, a broad range of researchers have a stake in maintaining coding as essential to qualitative research itself (D.L. Morgan, unpublished data). Researchers struggle to envision how AI can be successfully integrated into their established workflows. This juxtaposition highlights the challenges of navigating through a period of significant technological transformation in qualitative research.

7.4.4 The need for a new perspective: a conversational approach to qualitative data analysis

Transitioning to a new perspective in qualitative data analysis is crucial for maximizing AI's potential in the field. The key is not to force AI into the confines of the coding approach but rather to imagine entirely new ways of working with data, where AI acts as a collaborator and an assistant to the researcher, freeing them from the constraints of manual coding. Embracing AI as a partner, rather than as a replacement, offers a pathway towards re-imagining how we conduct qualitative data analysis. The crisis is an opportunity – an impetus for re-evaluation and the potential for ground-breaking new methodologies that leverage the best of both human intuition and the power of AI.

In a series of webinars and presentations, the author has introduced 'Conversational Analysis with AI' as a new method that involves directly engaging with an AI assistant in a dialogue format. This approach does not seek to automate the analysis process, nor does it rely on the AI assistant to independently identify all 'relevant' themes. Instead, the analysis begins with the researcher posing broad, exploratory questions about specific aspects of their data.

Following the initial response from the AI, the researcher delves deeper by asking more targeted follow-up questions. Often, something in the AI's response will catch the researcher's attention, prompting further inquiry. Depending on the nature of the project, the researcher might start by focusing on one document at a time, gradually incorporating more documents into the analysis as the investigation deepens.

Once a topic has been thoroughly explored, the researcher documents their findings and asks the AI assistant to retrieve supporting quotes. The researcher then reviews the first write-up with the AI, evaluating whether the interpretations align with the data, checking for any oversights and ensuring the logical consistency of the arguments before moving on to the next topic.

The next topic might be predetermined or could emerge from the analysis of previous data. The analyst applies the same iterative process as before. This often leads to the discovery of relationships within the data as the researcher progresses through subsequent topics. With a comprehensive understanding of the data from the ongoing discussion, the AI assistant can effectively verify or refute the interpretations.

This collaborative, conversational approach allows a dynamic and interactive exploration of the data, leveraging the AI's capabilities to enhance and expand the analytical process. Through this method of continuously engaging in a constructive dialogue, the analysis gains depth and breadth.

D.L. Morgan (unpublished data) suggested a similar approach termed 'query-based analysis', detailed in three progressive steps. The first step consists of posing broad, undirected questions to unearth foundational concepts within the data, laying the groundwork for a detailed analysis. In the second step, researchers delve deeper by asking more specific questions to expand on the initial themes identified. The third and final step involves a thorough examination of the text to extract and select supporting quotations that will be included in the research report.

7.4.5 The transformation

D.L. Morgan (unpublished data) posited that AI technology could significantly transform qualitative research by potentially eliminating traditional coding processes and consequently reducing the reliance on specialized CAQDAS software. This development could lower the barriers to analysing qualitative data, as there is typically a steep learning curve associated with mastering these sophisticated tools. Making the process more accessible could extend its use beyond traditional researchers to a broader audience. To facilitate this vision of qualitative data analysis, the author has developed the AI-powered software QInsights (further detail available at: https://qeludra.com, accessed 2 October 2024).

It has also been speculated that the extent to which this new technology will disrupt the field of qualitative research depends largely on various social factors (D.L. Morgan, unpublished data). A critical determinant will be the reaction from stakeholders deeply entrenched in the traditional, coding-centric methods of qualitative analysis, such as academic institutions, journal editors and funding bodies. These groups often serve as gatekeepers within the academic community, and their acceptance or resistance to AI-driven methods will significantly influence how these technologies are adopted and their subsequent impact on the field.

It may take some time before we witness a shift in the standard approaches to qualitative data analysis. As discussed earlier, this change does not encompass all three fundamental aspects of a paradigm – ontology, epistemology and methodology – so it may not qualify as a paradigm shift in the strictest sense. However, it certainly challenges existing epistemological beliefs about how we understand and acquire knowledge of reality.

Traditional coding practices are based on the belief that researchers must first segment data, classify it into categories and subcodes, and derive themes. For some, these derived themes represent the final results, while others may probe further, querying the coded data for deeper insights. In contrast, proponents of the new vision argue against the necessity of these steps. They believe that engaging in a dialogue with AI, which can navigate through data more adeptly than humans, is sufficient for uncovering knowledge. This approach challenges conventional epistemological assumptions in qualitative research, suggesting that knowledge can be directly and dynamically accessed and understood through advanced AI interactions, rather than through the meticulous organization and analysis of data. This represents a significant shift in beliefs about how researchers can effectively comprehend and interpret reality.

Building on the argument about the potential shift in qualitative data analysis approaches, Thomas Kuhn's insights from 2012 resonate profoundly with the adoption of new technology. He stated, 'A decision between alternate ways of practising science is called for, and in the circumstances, that decision must be based less on past achievements than on future promise' (p. 153). This observation is particularly relevant as we consider integrating new, evolving technologies into research methodologies. The adoption of AI in qualitative analysis is a dynamic development, gradually gaining traction among researchers. We can further follow Kuhn's argument as he suggests that the initial endorsement of the new technology might often rest on subjective, even aesthetic considerations.

This new approach has already garnered its first wave of supporters who are crucial for its development and validation. Over time, as purpose-built tools are developed – beyond generic applications such as ChatGPT designed without the specific needs of qualitative analysts in mind – the effectiveness and utility of AI in qualitative research will become more apparent.

Paraphrasing Kuhn (2012, p. 157), even if the proponents of this new approach are few and their motives occasionally questioned, their competence in refining and exploring the approach will demonstrate its potential. As these innovators continue to experiment with and refine AI-driven methodologies, they will delineate what it means to be part of a community that embraces these advanced tools. Consequently, the arguments supporting this new approach will grow stronger and more persuasive, potentially leading to its broader acceptance and integration into standard qualitative research practices. This evolutionary process underscores the transformative power of innovation in reshaping scientific inquiry, illustrating how a new technology can redefine the landscape of research methodologies.

7.5 Conclusion

As demonstrated throughout this chapter, the integration of AI not only advances technological capacities but also compels a re-evaluation of established analytical practices within qualitative research. This re-evaluation is critical, as it highlights the potential for AI to deepen and expand our understanding of qualitative data, necessitating a shift in the methodological approaches traditionally embraced by the field.

The historical trajectory of coding in qualitative analysis, as detailed in this chapter, shows a disciplined evolution towards more structured and systematic methods. However, the advent of AI technologies introduces anomalies that challenge these established methods, echoing the phases of scientific revolutions described by Thomas Kuhn. These anomalies do not signify faults per se but represent emerging challenges and opportunities that the current methodological standards in qualitative research must address.

The way AI technology is currently implemented on the one hand, and the resistance encountered from the research community towards integrating AI tools on the other hand reflects a broader hesitancy to alter deeply entrenched practices. Yet, as this chapter argues, such integration is less about replacement and more about enhancement. AI's potential to facilitate and enrich the analytical process illustrates the necessity for an adaptive approach that accommodates new tools while reconsidering methodological foundations.

In conclusion, the incorporation of AI into qualitative data analysis is not just about technological advancement but also about the willingness of the field to embrace a new method that could expand and deepen our understanding of qualitative data. This shift requires an openness to re-evaluating established practices and a bold vision for the future – a vision that the author of this chapter is committed to developing and demonstrating through innovative AI-based tools. This, in Kuhnian terms, is how a revolution begins.

References

Adduesselam, M.S. (2023) Qualitative data analysis in the age of artificial general intelligence. *Journal of Advanced Research in Qualitative Data Analysis* 1, 10–25.

Adorno, T.W., Frenkel-Brunswik, E., Levinson, D.J. and Sanford, R.N. (1950) *The Authoritarian Personality*. Harper & Brothers, New York.

Bazeley, P. (2013) *Qualitative Data Analysis: Practical Strategies*. Sage Publishing, London.

Becker, H.S. and Geer, B. (1960) Participant observation: the analysis of qualitative field data. In: Adams, R.N. and Jack, J.P. (eds) *Human Organization Research*. Dorsey Press, Homewood, Illinois, pp. 267–289.

Becker, H.S., Hughes, E.C., Geer, B. and Strauss, A.L. (1961) *Boys in White: Student Culture in Medical School*. University of Chicago Press, Toronto, Canada.

Becker, H.S., Gordon, A.C. and LeBailly, R.K. (1984) Fieldwork with the computer: criteria for assessing systems. *Qualitative Sociology* 7, 16–33.

Bird, A. (2022) Thomas Kuhn. In: Zalta, E.N. (ed.) *The Stanford Encyclopedia of Philosophy*, spring 2022 edition. Available at: https://plato.stanford.edu/archives/spr2022/entries/thomas-kuhn/ (accessed 24 February 2025).

Braun, V. and Clarke, V. (2006) Using thematic analysis in psychology. *Qualitative Research in Psychology* 3, 77–101.

Braun, V. and Clarke, V. (2023) Toward good practice in thematic analysis: avoiding common problems and be(com)ing a knowing researcher. *International Journal of Transgender Health* 24, 1–6.

Chapoulie, J.-M. (1987) Everett C. Hughes and the development of fieldwork in sociology. *Urban Life* 15, 259–298.

Charmaz, K. (2014) *Constructing Grounded Theory*, 2nd edn. Sage Publications, Los Angeles, California.

Christou, P.A. (2024) Thematic analysis through artificial intelligence (AI). *The Qualitative Report* 29, 560–576.

Corbin, J. and Strauss, A. (2015) *Basics of Qualitative Research: Techniques and Procedures for Developing Grounded Theory*, 4th edn. Sage Publications, London.

Feyerabend, P. (1975) *Against Method: Outline of an Anarchistic Theory of Knowledge*. New Left Books, London.

Fielding, N.G. and Lee, R.M. (1998). *Computer Analysis and Qualitative Research*. Sage Publications, London.

Friese, S. (2019) *Qualitative Data Analysis with ATLAS.ti*, 3rd edn. Sage Publications, London.

Gamieldien, Y., Case, J.M. and Katz, A. (2023) Advancing qualitative analysis: an exploration of the potential of generative AI and NLP in thematic coding. SSRN. Available at: https://ssrn.com/abstract=4487768 (accessed 24 February 2025).

Gao, J., Tsu, K., Choo, W., Cao, J., Lee, R.K.W. *et al.* (2023) CoAIcoder: examining the effectiveness of AI-assisted human-to-human collaboration in qualitative analysis. *arXiv preprint.* Available at: https://doi.org/10.48550/arXiv.2304.05560 (accessed 26 September 2024).

Glaser, B.G. and Strauss, A.L. (1967) *The Discovery of Grounded Theory: Strategies for Qualitative Research*. Aldine Publishing Company, Chicago, Illinois.

Goyanes, M., Lopezosa, C.L. and Jordá, B. (2024) Thematic analysis of interview data with ChatGPT: designing and testing a reliable research protocol for qualitative research. SocArXiv preprint. Available at: https://doi.org/10.31235/osf.io/8mr2f (accessed 26 September 2024).

Hitch, D. (2023) Artificial intelligence (AI) augmented qualitative analysis: the way of the future? SSRN. Available at: https://ssrn.com/abstract=4451740 (accessed 26 September 2024).

Hyman, H.H. and Sheatsley, P.B. (1954) The authoritarian personality: a methodological critique. In: Christie, R. and Jahoda, M. (eds) *Studies in the Scope and Method of "The Authoritarian Personality": Continuities in Social Research*. Free Press, Glencoe, Illinois.

Jiang, J.A., Wade, K., Fiesler, C. and Brubakerm, J.R. (2021) Supporting serendipity: opportunities and challenges for human–AI collaboration in qualitative analysis. In: *Proceedings of the ACM on Human–Computer Interaction,* Vol. 5. Association for Computing Machinery, New York, Article 94.

Kálmán, A. (2016) The meaning and importance of Thomas Kuhn's concept of paradigm shift: how does it apply in education? *Opus et Educatio* 3, 96–107.

Kuckartz, U. (2014) *Qualitative Text Analysis: A Guide to Methods, Practice and Using Software*. Sage Publications, London.

Kuckartz, U. and Rädiger, S. (2024) Qualitative Inhaltsanalyse. Methoden, Praxis, Umsetzung mit Software und *künstlicher Intelligzen*. Beltz Juventa, Weihnheim (English version, chapter 10: Integrating Artificial Intelligence (AI) in Qualitative Content Analysis. Available at: https://doi.org/10.1177/16094069231211248 (accessed 24 February 2025).

Kuhn, T.S. (1962) *The Structure of Scientific Revolutions*. University of Chicago Press, Chicago, Illinois.

Kuhn, T.S. (2012) *The Structure of Scientific Revolutions*, 50th edn. University of Chicago Press, Chicago, Illinois.

Lakatos, I. and Musgrave, A. (1970) *Criticism and the Growth of Knowledge*. Cambridge University Press, Cambridge, UK.

Mayring, P. (2022) *Qualitative Inhaltsanalyse: Grundlagen und Techniken*, 13th edn. Beltz, Weinheim, Germany.

Miles, M.B., Huberman, A.M. and Saldaña, J. (2019) *Qualitative Data Analysis: A Methods Sourcebook*, 4th edn. Sage Publications, London.

Morgan, D.L. (2025) Query-based analysis: a strategy for analyzing qualitative data using ChatGPT. *Qualitative Health Research*, forthcoming.

Morgan, D.L. (2023) Exploring the use of artificial intelligence for qualitative data analysis: the case of ChatGPT. *International Journal of Qualitative Methods* 22. Available at: https://doi.org/10.1177/16094069231211248 (accessed 25 February 2025).

Nguyen-Trung, K. (2024). ChatGPT in thematic analysis: can AI become a research assistant in qualitative research? OSF.io preprint. Available at: https://osf.io/preprints/osf/vefwc (accessed 25 February 2025).

Palmer, V. (1928) *Field Studies in Sociology: A Student's Manual*. Chicago University Press, Chicago, Illinois.

QSF Mailing List (n.d.) Mailingliste Qualitative Sozialforschung. Archive. Available at: https://lists.fu-berlin.de/listinfo/qsf_l#archive (accessed 25 February 2025).

Richards, L. (2020) *Handling Qualitative Data: a Practical Guide*, 4th edn. Sage Publications, London.

Richards, L. and Richards, T. (1991) The transformation of qualitative method: computational paradigms and research processes. In: Fielding, G. and Lee, R.M. (eds) *Using Computers in Qualitative Research*. Sage Publications, London, pp. 38–53.

Saldaña, J. (2021) *The Coding Manual for Qualitative Researchers*, 4th edn. Sage Publications, London.

Şen, M., Şen, Ş.N. and Şahin, T.G. (2023) A new era for data analysis in qualitative research: ChatGPT! *Shanlax International Journal of Education* 11 (Suppl. 1), 1–15.

Silver, C. and Lewins, A. (2014) *Using Software in Qualitative Research: A Step-by-step Guide*, 2nd edn. Sage Publications, London.

Strauss, A. and Corbin, J. (1998) *Basics of Qualitative Research: Techniques and Procedures for Developing Grounded Theory*, 2nd edn. Sage Publications, Thousand Oaks, California.

Theelen, H., Vreuls, J. and Rutten, J. (2024) Doing research with help from ChatGPT: promising examples for coding and inter-rater reliability. *International Journal of Technology in Education* 7, 1–18.

Whyte, W.F. (1955) *Street Corner Society*. University of Chicago Press, Chicago, Illinois.

Xiao, Z., Yuan, X., Liao, Q.V., Abdelghani, R. and Oudeyer, P.-Y. (2023). Supporting qualitative analysis with large language models: combining codebook with GPT-3 for deductive coding. In: *Proceedings of the 28th International Conference on Intelligent User Interfaces Companion (IUI '23 Companion), 27–31 March 2023, Sydney, New South Wales, Australia*. Association for Computing Machinery, New York, pp. 75–78.

Zhang, H., Wang, C., Xu, J., Li, Y., Ji, J. *et al.* (2023) Redefining qualitative analysis in the AI era: utilizing ChatGPT for efficient thematic analysis. *arXiv preprint*. Available at: https://arxiv.org/abs/2309.10771v2 (accessed 25 February 2025).

8 A Guide for Qualitative Researchers Using Large Language Models with Representative Examples Using ChatGPT

Ann Armstrong* and Albert J. Gale
[1]*National University, San Diego, California;* [2]*Walden University, Minneapolis, Minnesota*

Abstract
On 30 November 2022, ChatGPT, an artificial intelligence (AI) chatbot, was released to the public, transforming an enigmatic tool into accessible software as a service. This sparked immediate debates among academicians about AI's impact on various facets of society, including academia, technology, economics, politics and the environment. As discussions continue, AI is anticipated to significantly influence 21st-century life. Current literature on AI often emphasizes ethics, trust, bias, fairness, diversity, equity, inclusion and privacy, yet lacks guidelines for qualitative researchers using AI in studies. This chapter, using ChatGPT as a representative of various large language model tools, outlines a framework for integrating AI into qualitative research, divided into six phases. These phases cover skills in questioning AI, understanding biases, transparency in AI use, problem-based research, shaping research purposes, and employing AI for data collection and analysis. Examples and transparency regarding ChatGPT's role in the chapter's creation are provided, offering both theoretical and practical guidance for qualitative researchers.

Keywords: AI, artificial intelligence, ChatGPT, emerging technologies, LLMs, qualitative research, transparency

8.1 Introduction

On 30 November 2022, the public release of ChatGPT, a form of generative pre-trained transformer (GPT) or artificial intelligence (AI), allowed researchers first access to a user-friendly AI and offered a free version. Previously, use of GPT technologies was reserved for a limited population of researchers. With the release of the accessible free version of ChatGPT, a radical technology disruption began whereby former 'non-consumers' suddenly had strong demand for the product. When the publicly available version of ChatGPT became accessible, academicians started debating its positive and negative effects, academically, socially, culturally, economically and politically. In all likelihood, AI will be one of the most impactful phenomena of the 21st century. While recent literature on AI has focused on ethics, trust, bias, fairness, diversity, equity, inclusion and privacy concerns, there is a paucity of literature using AI to conduct a research study. What follows is six phases for qualitative researchers to follow as a road map for using AI in qualitative research. ChatGPT was used throughout the chapter, providing examples of how researchers

*E-mail: Aarmstrong2@nu.edu

DOI: 10.1079/9781800626607.0008

can use it. When ChatGPT was asked to respond, the words 'User-engineered prompt' will show what was asked of ChatGPT and is followed by the response received back. In a number of examples, the response from ChatGPT was shortened due to word count restraints in the publication. ChatGPT was used as a research assistant throughout the creation of this chapter.

8.2 Phase 1: Learning to Use AI for Research

According to Clark and Perrault (2023), while earlier AI model usage and development was restricted to academics, recently private industry has taken the lead in the production of large language models (LLMs). AI aids with generating accurate and well-written information but can also hinder it. While in the field of science AI models are advancing progress and efficiency, the number of dangerous events due to the misapplication of AI and misinformation spread by AI are rapidly becoming evidenced. For example, Clark and Perrault (2023) shared incidents in Ukraine, with 'deep fake' videos of particular note. An important take away in their report is that while countries like China with 78% of survey respondents, Saudi Arabia with 76%, and India with 71% believe that products and services using AI have more positive than negative impact, of the US respondents only 35% shared that belief.

Roberts *et al.* (2024) described how, given specific prompts, language models such as ChatGPT can efficiently generate well-crafted responses to questions, as well as develop interview questions and various qualitative tools. These models are capable of swiftly summarizing research and suggesting appropriate theoretical or conceptual frameworks. Additionally, they can serve as alternatives to MS Word or Grammarly by offering precise advice on grammar, mechanics and usage, thereby enhancing the quality of a paper before it is submitted (OpenAI, 2024). The first half of this paragraph was wordsmithed using ChatGPT. On the plus side, these applications of AI seem practical and available to the qualitative researcher as if they had their own research assistant. On the negative side, ChatGPT can provide false information and make mistakes providing inaccurate, deceptive and misleading information. It is still incumbent on the researcher to verify all claims. Roberts *et al.* (2024) suggested that reliance on AI can make qualitative researchers lose critical research and scholarly writing skills, in fact 'deskilling' the researcher by its use. This deskilling can also be symptomatic of a natural skill shift; however, researchers must still be able to stand behind their claims and not surrender this task to automation. In pursuit of this new balance, qualitative researchers must continue to hone their qualitative research skills, their library search skills, their critical reflection skills, their critical thinking skills and their questioning skills as they begin to use AI as a research assistant. Lastly, questioning skills (or prompting) become paramount, as questions are what fuels the LLM's activity.

8.2.1 Prompt engineering

A critical success factor in using ChatGPT and any AI is 'prompt engineering' eliciting quality output. Engineering quality input in the information provided to the LLM and using questioning strategies and input prompts alongside a process of iterative revision, refinement and repetition can yield specific, relevant and high-quality responses. Creating a vision, goals and objectives, which are clear, concise, contextual and offer domain-specific knowledge while simultaneously developing a deep understanding of the LLM, is necessary to receive high-quality output from your prompts. ChatGPT can and often does make mistakes. Researchers must evaluate the responses they get from ChatGPT by reviewing seminal works on the topic(s), peer-reviewed sources, and validated, dependable and trustworthy data sources. While some in the field have hypothesized that prompt engineering may be dead as AI products become increasingly sophisticated employing automatic prompt-tuning methods, others believe that the title of prompt engineer will remain in academia and industry for some time to come (Denkina, 2024). Will there ever be an adequate substitute for the cognitive knowledge, skills and abilities of the researcher creating the prompts and evaluating the responses?

In crafting this chapter, ChatGPT was prompted to provide citations in correct APA 7th edition reference list format from peer-reviewed articles in scholarly journals. While ChatGPT did provide a list for each topic and the list was in correct APA 7th edition style, none of the references was evidenced in two university libraries or through Google Scholar or through other search engines. A university librarian was given the task of searching for the articles and further validated that they were fake references. Qualitative researchers beware.

8.2.2 Hallucination in AI

In the context of AI, particularly natural language processing (NLP) models such as ChatGPT, 'hallucination' refers to instances where the AI generates information that is not based on the input data or factual reality. These can be fabrications or plausible-sounding statements that are inaccurate or entirely made up. Hallucinations occur because the model tries to produce coherent and contextually relevant responses based on the patterns it learned during training, even if it means inventing details. Hallucinations in AI can manifest in several ways:

1. *Fabricated facts.* Providing incorrect or non-existent facts, such as making up historical events or scientific data.
2. *Inconsistent information.* Generating responses that contradict previously given information or established facts.
3. *Non-existent entities.* Mentioning people, places or events that do not exist.
4. *Over-interpretation.* Giving overly specific interpretations or conclusions that go beyond the input data.

These hallucinations can be problematic in applications requiring high accuracy and reliability, such as academic research, medical information and legal advice. Researchers are actively working on methods to reduce hallucinations, such as improving training data quality, refining model architectures and incorporating fact-checking mechanisms. Some of the latest upgrades are mitigating some of these issues. These include the following:

1. *Personalized interactions.* The ability to remember facts about the user and previous interactions for more personalized and contextually aware conversations.
2. *Enhanced tools and integrations.*
   - Tool use: ChatGPT can use external tools like a web browser to fetch real-time information, perform calculations and more.
   - Plugin support: integration with third-party plugins to extend functionality, such as fetching current events or accessing specialized databases.
3. *User interface improvements.*
   - Intuitive design: a more user-friendly interface that simplifies interaction and makes accessing different features more straightforward.
4. *Accessibility and deployment.*
   - Application programming interface (API) access: enhanced API for developers to integrate ChatGPT into various applications and services with more flexibility.
   - Cross-platform availability: improved performance and availability across different devices and platforms.
5. *Security and privacy enhancements.*
   - Data handling: better data-handling practices to ensure user privacy and security.
   - Content moderation: improved content moderation to prevent the generation of harmful or inappropriate content.

These updates make the latest version of ChatGPT more versatile, responsive and user-friendly, offering a wide range of applications from casual use to professional integration.

Despite current and future enhancements, LLM can be perilous for academicians, researchers and anyone who is responsible for delivering accurate, trustworthy, credible and dependable reports and articles, such as those who are qualitative researchers. Researcher knowledge, critical thinking and validation of any and all information garnered through LLMs is of the utmost importance in the research field.

8.2.3 Researcher cognitive input

As Christou (2023a) argued, AI requires prompt engineering from cognitive input given to it by the researcher to generate output of any kind. To that end, the researcher's own cognitive abilities are central to the research process, including identifying a problem worthy of study, a purpose statement, research questions, design choice, data collection methods, data analysis methods, conclusions drawn and future implications of the research.

8.2.4 Cross-referencing data

ChatGPT does make mistakes due to biased or inaccurate data, and often these mistakes are the result of a misunderstanding of the user's prompt meaning or intent. To mitigate these mistakes, it is critical that the researcher checks the output of ChatGPT against traditional qualitative sources such as seminal works, peer-reviewed journal publications and other scientific sources. Always check AI outputs before submitting your own work.

8.2.5 Continuous improvement in AI

The latest updates to ChatGPT include enhanced accuracy, improved contextual understanding and reduced hallucinations through cross-referencing verified sources. It now offers customizable personas and response styles, real-time data access and better support for multi-turn conversations, maintaining context over extended interactions. These advancements significantly benefit researchers by providing more reliable, contextually relevant and up-to-date information. The customizable features allow tailored interactions, enhancing the utility of ChatGPT in various research scenarios, from data analysis to drafting research proposals, ultimately streamlining the research process and improving efficiency.

8.3 Phase 2: Acknowledgement of ChatGPT Tool Bias and Researcher Bias

Phase 2 describes developing an understanding of bias generated by the tool and the questions asked of it by the user. As the researcher is engineering the prompts given to ChatGPT, the output will be reflective of research biases and underlying assumptions. In this phase, the researcher must recognize and acknowledge how AI is used throughout a qualitative research study. It continues to be considered good scholarship to be transparent about sources, and these include AI. Christou (2023b), concerned about the rise in distrust and misgivings in academia about the use of AI in qualitative research studies, suggested that it is critical that qualitative researchers acknowledge the use of AI by means of a declarative statement in their research papers. Combining AI with the researchers own cognitive skills, the researcher needs to critically reflect on their own biases and underlying assumptions. Researchers must be conscientious about the requirements in their institution as well as in the research literature to ensure that their research is trustworthy, credible and dependable, and adheres to all standards regulating the use of AI.

8.4 Phase 3: Identifying Research-worthy Problems and Gaps in the Research

Qualitative research always begins with identifying a research-worthy problem. There are differences in perspective of how to identify such a problem and ways to present it. Merriam and Tisdell (2016) suggested that a problem specifies that something is going wrong, creating uncertainty and doubt needing resolution. Elaborating on this idea, the authors explained that identifying the problem begins with questioning what is going wrong that is challenging the researchers in the general topic area of concern. To identify the specific problem of research focus, they suggested using a 'funnel approach', going from the general area of concern at the top of the funnel to a narrow area of concern, focused on a specific gap in knowledge (Merriam and Tisdell, 2016).

Creswell and Poth (2024) asserted that the term 'problem' may be misleading, and a better term might be what is the necessity or exigency related to the specific topic. Bloomberg and Volpe (2019) also emphasized the need to narrowly focus the problem under investigation. What is the area of focus about the issue that a study will address? What specifically is going wrong? Is there a societal issue surrounding the problem?

What do we know about the topic? How is our information flawed about the topic? What do we not know about the topic? What do we need to know? How is our current knowledge incomplete?

There are a variety of ways that AI, and ChatGPT specifically, can assist researchers in identifying a problem worthy of research study: a gap in the research literature. Start by selecting a topic area of interest from personal or professional experience. This will be the broad area to be investigated. One way to begin the investigation is to brainstorm ideas by asking ChatGPT, your research assistant, questions about areas within the topic where there is limited information or a lack of understanding. One of the keys to success with using AI is the quality of the prompts engineered by the researcher, including the information provided and the crafting of the questions. ChatGPT can be an excellent research assistant supporting a doctoral student's research endeavours.

8.4.1 ChatGPT example

When asking ChatGPT for help with the question 'Given that AI and ChatGPT are relatively new tools for qualitative researchers, what are some gaps in the research that need to be studied about them using qualitative research designs?', responses from ChatGPT included: understanding user experiences and perceptions, ethical and responsible AI use, trust and reliability, contextual understanding, interpretation of the context and the limitations of AI in capturing nuanced meanings, cultural contexts and subjective experiences, algorithmic bias and fairness, and training and self-development (OpenAI, 2024). None of the responses included citations from the research literature, even when asked specifically for them. Often, ChatGPT acknowledges that it does not have the capability of actually reviewing peer-reviewed research journals and thus is providing only 'hypothetical' output versus trustworthy, accurate examples (Christou, 2023b). There is growing concern among academicians regarding the use of ChatGPT in research, with advice to impose higher standards for scholarly writing, multiple author identification verification for journal submissions, and in-depth training for students on how to use AI as well as reporting their use of it (Dergaa *et al.*, 2023).

8.4.2 Problem statement example

Using ChatGPT's recommendation of one of the gaps in the research literature needing exploration about AI, the following problem statement is used as an example in this chapter. With exponential growth in the use of ChatGPT by graduate students and researchers amidst concerns of plagiarism, ethical violations and issues surrounding trustworthiness, including credibility, confirmability and dependability, the specific problem that is the focus of the study is that it is unknown how qualitative researchers are perceiving, experiencing and using the tool, and the challenges they encounter when using ChatGPT for research tasks.

8.5 Phase 4: Using AI to Describe the Purpose, Research Questions, Target Population and Sample

There are numerous ways that AI and ChatGPT can help with the purpose statement, research questions, target population and sample for the study. While the problem statement provides the foundation for the study, the purpose statement provides information on how it will be done. This section covers uses of AI for the purpose statement, target population and sample. To begin the research, understanding the definitions and terminology in the research literature is essential.

8.5.1 Purpose statement

After crafting the problem statement, the next step is to write the purpose statement, which codifies the main goal, objectives and intent of the study. The purpose statement must align fully with the problem statement and later with the research questions and design. The purpose statement explains exactly how the study will address the problem, or as Creswell (1998) explained, it provides a 'road map' to guide the reader through the process that will be followed. The purpose statement includes the methodology, design and target population. Next follows an interchange with ChatGPT.

User-engineered prompt: *Please provide at least two examples of Creswell's script for a purpose statement from 1994, 1998 and 2003 using his exact words. Do not paraphrase.*

ChatGPT response: *I'm sorry for any confusion, but Creswell's specific script for a purpose statement has not been provided verbatim in his works. Instead, he typically offers general guidance on structuring purpose statements, but he doesn't provide a specific, word-for-word script. For example, in Creswell's 1994 book 'Research Design: Qualitative and Quantitative Approaches', he outlines the components of a qualitative purpose statement, emphasizing the focus of the study, the participants, and the context*

OpenAI (2024).

A novice researcher might not have checked further to validate ChatGPT's response, causing an error in a paraphrase related to Creswell's work. Creswell did, in fact, create a template/script for a purpose statement. Next, ChatGPT was given very carefully engineered prompts to use Creswell's specific script and the problem statement example, to write a purpose statement to address the problem. The results of that inquiry were as follows:

User-engineered prompt: *Address the following research problem: 'Using ChatGPT's recommendation of one of the gaps in the research literature needing exploration about AI, the following problem statement will be used as an example in this chapter. With exponential growth in the use of ChatGPT by graduate students and researchers amidst concerns of plagiarism, ethical violations and issues surrounding trustworthiness, including credibility, confirmability and dependability, it is unknown how qualitative researchers are perceiving, experiencing and using the tool, and the challenges they encounter when using ChatGPT for research tasks.' Use the following script to write a purpose statement for a qualitative research study: 'The purpose of this ___ (biographical, phenomenological, grounded theory, ethnographic, case) study is (was? will be?) to ___ (understand? describe? develop? discover?) the ___ (central focus for the study) for ___ (the unit of analysis, a person? processes? groups? site). At this stage in the research, the ___ (central focus being studied) will be generally defined as ___ (provide a general of the central concept).'*

Creswell (1998, p. 96).

ChatGPT response: *The purpose of this phenomenological study is to understand the perceptions, experiences, and usage patterns of qualitative researchers regarding ChatGPT, amidst concerns of plagiarism, ethical violations, and issues surrounding trustworthiness, including credibility, confirmability, and dependability. At this stage in the research, the perceptions and experiences of qualitative researchers regarding ChatGPT will be generally defined as their subjective understandings, interactions, and challenges encountered when utilizing the tool for research tasks.*

OpenAI (2024).

8.5.2 Research questions

After aligning the problem and purpose statements for the study, the next step is to author the research questions. According to Bloomberg and Volpe (2019), to fully address the purpose of the study, the research questions must be answered. Therefore, it is critical that the research questions align fully with the problem statement and purpose statement. Here, ChatGPT can be a good brainstorming tool for the researcher. Again, providing a well-written, clear and concise purpose statement and directions, the following interchange took place to get ChatGPT to generate research questions.

User-engineered prompt: *Given the following purpose statement: 'The purpose of this qualitative phenomenological study will be to describe the perceptions, experiences and patterns, frequency and methods of usage regarding ChatGPT by doctoral students at accredited higher education institutions in the USA, in light of concerns about plagiarism, ethical violations and trustworthiness. At this stage in the research, the perceptions, experiences and patterns of qualitative doctoral researchers regarding ChatGPT will be defined as their subjective understanding of interactions and challenges they faced when using the tool for their doctoral dissertations', write three research questions for the study.*

ChatGPT response: *Based on the provided purpose statement, here are three potential research questions for the qualitative phenomenological study:*

1. *How do doctoral students at accredited higher education institutions in the USA perceive and experience the usage of ChatGPT for their doctoral dissertations?*

2. *What are the patterns, frequency and methods of usage of ChatGPT among doctoral students in the context of conducting research for their doctoral dissertations?*

3. *What challenges do qualitative doctoral researchers face when using ChatGPT for their* *doctoral dissertations, particularly in relation to concerns about plagiarism, ethical violations and trustworthiness?*

OpenAI (2024).

Of note is that ChatGPT was able to provide three good research questions based on the accurate information in the prompts given to it, which included a well-written purpose statement based on Creswell's script and definitions and a solid problem statement that was adjusted from ChatGPT's original suggestion through researcher review and confirmation by checking the current peer-reviewed research literature.

8.5.3 Terminology

ChatGPT can assist with understanding terminology. For example, when ChatGPT was asked, 'In qualitative research, what are the definitions of the following terms with supporting citations from current or seminal peer-reviewed research? Terms are general population, target population, sampling frame and sample,' the response definitions were similar to those in research literature and the responses included citations from Creswell, Bryman, Babbie and Neuman, all with dates and page numbers. When the citation information was checked, much of it was incorrect. Checking the accuracy of the data supplied to you by ChatGPT including citations, page numbers and references is critical to ensuring trustworthiness of the information presented in a study. Provided with this data from ChatGPT, researchers should find the original sources and ensure that the content exists in the body of literature and that the original author's meaning is accurately reflected in the ChatGPT response. A key point that doctoral dissertation researchers must remember is that ChatGPT is not always right, and that the trustworthiness of a doctoral dissertation is the researcher's responsibility, to ensure accuracy.

8.5.4 General population, target population, sampling frame and sample

Using definitions from the research literature provided to ChatGPT, along with a well-designed purpose statement crafted for the study, ChatGPT can be utilized to help define the general population, target population, sampling frame and sample for the study being developed.

Remember that using ChatGPT to guide with terminology can be valuable. However, slight deviations in the prompts and instructions you give ChatGPT can seriously compromise the trustworthiness of your assertions and the sources you are using. Qualitative researchers cannot afford to assume AI is correct. Researchers must validate what it recommends with their own critical views of the research literature. Suggestions from ChatGPT for the example study were as follows:

ChatGPT response:

1. *General population:*
   - *Definition: the general population refers to the entire group of individuals that the researcher is interested in studying and to which they intend to generalize their findings.*
   - *In this study, the general population would be doctoral students at accredited higher education institutions in the USA.*
2. *Target population:*
   - *Definition: the target population refers to the specific subset or group within the general population that the researcher intends to study and make inferences about.*
   - *The target population in this study would be doctoral students at accredited higher education institutions in the USA who have used or are using ChatGPT for their doctoral dissertations.*
3. *Sampling frame:*
   - *Definition: the sampling frame is a list or representation of the elements within the target population from which the researcher selects their sample.*
   - *The sampling frame for this study could be a list of doctoral students enrolled in accredited higher education institutions in the USA who are currently working on or have completed their doctoral dissertations using ChatGPT.*
4. *Sample:*
   - *Definition: a sample is a subset of individuals selected from the sampling frame and represents the population of interest for the purpose of study.*
   - *The sample for this study would consist of a subset of doctoral students from the sampling frame who have experience using ChatGPT for their doctoral dissertations. This subset would be selected to participate in the phenomenological qualitative research study to describe*

their perceptions, experiences and patterns of usage regarding ChatGPT

OpenAI (2024).

8.6 Phase 5: Using ChatGPT to Create Qualitative Data Collection Instruments

The design of the qualitative study is selected during the writing of the purpose statement, providing a high-level blueprint for how the study will be conducted. Typically, data collection sources are accompanied by data collection instruments and include: interviews using an interview guide, focus group interviews using a focus group interview guide and protocol, open-ended questionnaires, closed-ended surveys (primarily for triangulation), observations using an observation guide, participant journals, and an archival document checklist used for analysing existing data, such as course syllabi, course materials, program descriptions, organizational, professional, and government report data, web-site content, etc.

8.6.1 ChatGPT as a brainstorming tool

When ChatGPT was asked what were the most widely used data collection methods in phenomenological inquiry, the answer included in-depth interviews, focus groups, observations, field notes, documents or artefacts, photo voice, and diaries or journals, which is consistent with the research literature. In this capacity, ChatGPT serves as a good brainstorming tool for researchers.

Using ChatGPT for interview guide questions

Interviews are the most frequently used and important sources of data in all types of qualitative designs. Hence, the quality of the instruments developed and used to conduct the interview will influence the study results, implications and conclusions. The background data provided to ChatGPT, and the formation of well-engineered prompts given to ChatGPT based on the researcher's own knowledge, skills and ability in research design and the content area, are critical in determining the quality of the information generated by responses from ChatGPT. The following is an example of a question asked to ChatGPT and ChatGPT's response and recommendation for questions to be used in an interview guide to address the study problem, purpose and research questions. Note the structure of the prompts and the content provided to address the question. The researchers content knowledge, cognitive abilities and questioning ability are all critical to the quality of the responses derived from brainstorming with ChatGPT. The following displays an example of how ChatGPT might be used to help create an interview guide.

User-engineered prompt: *Creating a qualitative phenomenological research study with the following problem statement, purpose statement and research questions. Problem Statement: With exponential growth in the use of ChatGPT by graduate students and researchers amidst concerns of plagiarism, ethical violations and issues surrounding trustworthiness, including credibility, confirmability and dependability, it is unknown how qualitative researchers are perceiving, experiencing and using the tool, and the challenges they encounter when using ChatGPT for research tasks. Purpose Statement: The purpose of this qualitative phenomenological study will be to describe the perceptions, experiences and patterns, frequency and methods of usage regarding ChatGPT by doctoral students at accredited higher education institutions in the USA, in light of concerns about plagiarism, ethical violations and trustworthiness. At this stage in the research, the perceptions, experiences and patterns of qualitative doctoral researchers regarding ChatGPT will be defined as their subjective understanding of interactions and challenges they faced when using the tool for their doctoral dissertations. Research questions: 1. How do doctoral students at accredited higher education institutions in the USA perceive and experience the usage of ChatGPT for their doctoral dissertations? 2. What are the patterns, frequency and methods of usage of ChatGPT among doctoral students in the context of conducting research for their doctoral dissertations? 3. What challenges do qualitative doctoral researchers face when using ChatGPT for their doctoral dissertations, particularly in relation to concerns about plagiarism, ethical violations and trustworthiness? Write interview questions using Irving Seidman's three interview series; write 12–15 interview questions that will address the purpose of the study and answer the research questions.*

ChatGPT response: *Irving Seidman's three interview series are designed to probe deeper into the participant's experiences, perceptions and challenges. Here are some interview questions tailored to each series that would address the purpose of the study and answer the research questions:*

First Interview Series: Descriptive
1. *Can you describe your overall experience with using ChatGPT for your doctoral dissertation?*
2. *How did you initially come to know about ChatGPT, and what prompted you to use it for your research?*
3. *Can you walk me through a typical session or interaction you had with ChatGPT while working on your dissertation?*
4. *What specific features or aspects of ChatGPT did you find most helpful or valuable for your research tasks?*
5. *Could you describe any instances where you encountered challenges or limitations while using ChatGPT for your doctoral dissertation?*

Second Interview Series: Structural
...

OpenAI (2024).

Overall ChatGPT made good recommendations. Rather than simply asking questions that can be answered with yes or no or a few words, making the questions more open-ended would be beneficial. For example, 'can you' or 'could you' you might be replaced with 'please describe', 'discuss' and 'walk me through'.

Using ChatGPT for an observation guide

Participation observation is a powerful tool for data collection for qualitative researchers. DeWalt and DeWalt (2011, p. 1) defined participant observation as 'a method in which a researcher takes part in the daily activities, rituals, interactions, and event of a group of people as one of the means of learning the explicit and tacit aspects of their life routines and their culture'. ChatGPT can be a useful assistant in creating guides for researchers to codify their experiences in the field. This type of data collection source can yield strong results for a variety of qualitative research designs such as phenomenology, ethnography and case study, including design and development case study research. An example of using ChatGPT as an assistant in creating an observation guide is as follows:

User-engineered prompt: *Creating a qualitative phenomenological research study with the following problem statement, purpose statement and research questions. Problem Statement: With exponential growth in the use of ChatGPT by graduate students and researchers amidst concerns of plagiarism, ethical violations and issues surrounding trustworthiness, including credibility, confirmability and dependability, it is unknown how qualitative researchers are perceiving, experiencing and using the tool, and the challenges they encounter when using ChatGPT for research tasks. Purpose Statement: The purpose of this qualitative phenomenological study will be to describe the perceptions, experiences and patterns, frequency and methods of usage regarding ChatGPT by doctoral students at accredited higher education institutions in the USA, in light of concerns about plagiarism, ethical violations and trustworthiness. At this stage in the research, the perceptions, experiences and patterns of qualitative doctoral researchers regarding ChatGPT will be defined as their subjective understanding of interactions and challenges they faced when using the tool for their doctoral dissertations. Research Questions: 1. How do doctoral students at accredited higher education institutions in the USA perceive and experience the usage of ChatGPT for their doctoral dissertations? 2. What are the patterns, frequency and methods of usage of ChatGPT among doctoral students in the context of conducting research for their doctoral dissertations? 3. What challenges do qualitative doctoral researchers face when using ChatGPT for their doctoral dissertations, particularly in relation to concerns about plagiarism, ethical violations and trustworthiness? Write an observation guide, using Stearns, Morgan and Caprano's technique for writing an observation guide; write 12–15 observation statements that will address the purpose of the study and answer the research questions.*

ChatGPT response: *Stearns, Morgan and Caprano's technique for writing an observation guide involves crafting statements that guide the observer's attention towards specific behaviours, interactions or phenomena relevant to the study. Here are 12–15 observation statements tailored to address the purpose of the study and answer the research questions:*
1. *Observe how doctoral students initiate and engage with ChatGPT during their research activities.*
2. *Note the frequency with which doctoral students consult ChatGPT throughout their dissertation writing process.*
3. *Pay attention to the types of research tasks for which doctoral students rely on ChatGPT, such as generating literature reviews, formulating research questions or drafting sections of their dissertations.*
4. *Observe any instances where doctoral students express concerns or hesitations before using ChatGPT for research-related tasks.*

> **5.** *Note the strategies doctoral students employ to integrate ChatGPT-generated content into their dissertations while maintaining academic integrity.*
> **6.** *Note the level of awareness doctoral students demonstrate regarding the limitations and biases inherent in ChatGPT's algorithms and datasets.*
> ...
>
> OpenAI (2024).

Using ChatGPT for a survey

Qualitative researchers vary in their opinions about the usefulness of using closed-ended surveys for triangulation in qualitative study designs. Surveys are typically simple designs used to summarize participant responses with statistical data such as percentages, frequency counts and statistical data such as mean, medium, mode and standard deviations. Closed-ended surveys are more often used in quantitative research. However, they can be useful in techniques such as a nominal group technique (NGT) whereby researchers are using the tool to analyse qualitative data across individual expert interviews and/or focus group interviews. Armstrong and Gale (2018) used the NGT as a five-step process whereby participants met together in a focus group, generated ideas based on their pre-work review of a model, shared their ideas with the group, discussed their ideas, and voted and ranked items based on original questions about the models. In addition to the discussion session, participants were asked to complete a survey ranking elements of the model using a Likert scale. The analysis generated from a survey based on an NGT can help case study researchers doing design and development research and action research to determine what type of content, sequencing, etc. is best suited for program, course, model and tool research. The following shows the user-engineered prompt followed by the survey created by ChatGPT:

> **User-engineered prompt:** *Creating a qualitative phenomenological research study with the following problem statement, purpose statement and research questions. Problem Statement: With exponential growth in the use of ChatGPT by graduate students and researchers amidst concerns of plagiarism, ethical violations and issues surrounding trustworthiness, including credibility, confirmability and dependability, it is unknown how qualitative researchers are perceiving, experiencing and using the tool, and the challenges they encounter when using ChatGPT for research tasks. Purpose Statement: The purpose of this qualitative phenomenological study will be to describe the perceptions, experiences and patterns, frequency and methods of usage regarding ChatGPT by doctoral students at accredited higher education institutions in the USA, in light of concerns about plagiarism, ethical violations and trustworthiness. At this stage in the research, the perceptions, experiences and patterns of qualitative doctoral researchers regarding ChatGPT will be defined as their subjective understanding of interactions and challenges they faced when using the tool for their doctoral dissertations. Research Questions: 1. How do doctoral students at accredited higher education institutions in the USA perceive and experience the usage of ChatGPT for their doctoral dissertations? 2. What are the patterns, frequency and methods of usage of ChatGPT among doctoral students in the context of conducting research for their doctoral dissertations? 3. What challenges do qualitative doctoral researchers face when using ChatGPT for their doctoral dissertations, particularly in relation to concerns about plagiarism, ethical violations and trustworthiness? Write 10–25 survey questions using a 4-point Likert scale to address the problem, purpose and research questions.*
>
> **ChatGPT response:** *Sure, here are five survey questions using a 4-point Likert scale to address the problem, purpose and research questions:*
> **1.** *When conducting your doctoral dissertation research, to what extent do you perceive ChatGPT as a useful tool?*
> - *1: Not useful at all*
> - *2: Slightly useful*
> - *3: Moderately useful*
> - *4: Extremely useful*
>
> **2.** *How frequently do you use ChatGPT during your doctoral dissertation research?*
> - *1: Never*
> - *2: Rarely*
> - *3: Occasionally*
> - *4: Frequently*
>
> **3.** *How would you rate your overall experience of using ChatGPT for your doctoral dissertation research?*
> - *1: Very negative*
> - *2: Somewhat negative*
> - *3: Neutral*
> - *4: Positive*
>
> **4.** *To what extent do you believe ChatGPT helps you generate ideas and content for your dissertation?*
> - *1: Not at all*
> - *2: To a small extent*
> - *3: To a moderate extent*
> - *4: To a great extent*

5. *How confident are you in the accuracy and reliability of the content generated by ChatGPT for your dissertation?*

...

OpenAI (2024).

8.5 Phase 6: Using AI for Qualitative Data Analysis

Thematic analysis of qualitative data such as the data collection sources described earlier is an important application for ChatGPT for qualitative researchers. Braun and Clarke (2019, 2022) emphasized that there are two types of thematic analysis: deductive and inductive. Using deductive thematic analysis, the researcher is guided by an existing theoretical and/or conceptual framework through which the codes are developed. In inductive thematic analysis, the analysis is driven by the data content and often both are used in a single study. Braun and Clarke's (2006) six steps of data analysis include: familiarization with the data, coding either deductively inductively, or a blend, looking for a pattern and themes in the data, reviewing and consolidating the themes, naming, defining and describing the themes, and then writing a report of findings.

ChatGPT can be utilized for qualitative data analysis by leveraging its NLP capabilities to identify themes, patterns and insights from large volumes of textual data. Researchers can input interview transcripts, open-ended survey responses or focus group discussions into ChatGPT, which can then assist in coding the data, categorizing responses and highlighting significant trends. This can be useful when the researcher begins applying deductive analysis using a list of start codes as suggested by Miles *et al.* (2022). By summarizing the content and suggesting potential themes, ChatGPT streamlines the initial stages of qualitative analysis, making it faster and more efficient. Additionally, it can provide alternative interpretations and generate hypotheses, aiding researchers in exploring different perspectives and ensuring a comprehensive analysis. However, it is essential for researchers to validate and critically assess the AI-generated insights to ensure accuracy and relevance.

There are a number of issues and areas of concern using ChatGPT for qualitative data analysis. These include a lack of transparency caused by the 'black box' problem whereby researchers do not know how their prompts are being analysed and processed, causing a need for enhanced transparency in the future, which is of paramount importance. The next issue is consistency. Prompt engineering drives the output in any ChatGPT response and even small alterations in input prompts can cause major differences in output responses. This is exacerbated by ChatGPT's memory issues preventing it from remembering its former responses in a multi-session dialogue. Next is ChatGPT's too broad and often ambiguous output responses. Finally, there is the lack of a focused, fixed perspective having no beliefs or prior held positions, and therefore its output responses may end up contradictory. Again, prompt engineering that is written with a high degree of precision and based on valid and reliable inputs is critical when using ChatGPT to assist in thematic data coding. Learning how to design prompts effectively takes an elevated level of cognitive knowledge in the topic area and about qualitative research, which is often difficult and time consuming (Zhang *et al.*, 2023).

8.7 Conclusion

In this chapter the integration of AI, specifically ChatGPT, into qualitative research methodologies was explored through a comprehensive six-phase framework. Phases 1 and 2 are specific to the use of Chat GPT or any AI tool and will apply to all future versions. Phases 3–6 are standard phases in qualitative research and will be valuable to follow as the researcher becomes familiarized with new versions of the ChatGPT tool, as well as with other AI tools. As the use of AI in research becomes increasingly prevalent, it is essential to address both its potential benefits and its limitations. Through each phase, from learning to use AI effectively to identifying research problems and developing research questions, data collection and analysis, researchers are provided with guidance on leveraging AI tools while maintaining critical thinking skills and rigour.

One of the key takeaways from this chapter is the importance of understanding and acknowledging both the biases inherent in AI tools and those of the researchers themselves. Phase 2 emphasizes the need for transparency in acknowledging the use of AI in research and recognizing how it may shape the outcomes. Another takeaway is the peril researchers can and will face if they do not validate the responses received from the LLM. Wiley publications have encountered significant issues due to research errors stemming from the use of LLMs such as ChatGPT. These errors, caused by 'hallucinations' as discussed earlier, involve the AI generating false or fabricated information, which undermines the reliability of published research. Consequently, Wiley has retracted numerous articles and shut down 19 scholarly journals to maintain academic integrity. Their retraction process involves clearly marking retracted articles and issuing notices to inform readers of the errors. This underscores the importance of rigorous review and verification processes to prevent such problems and uphold the credibility of scientific publications. Researchers must critically reflect on their biases and assumptions throughout the research process to ensure credibility and trustworthiness. Researchers must validate any findings or suggestions made by an LLM. Looking ahead, the evolution of ChatGPT and similar AI tools presents both opportunities and challenges for qualitative research. As AI technology continues to advance, there is potential for more sophisticated and nuanced responses, allowing researchers to delve deeper into complex research questions. However, researchers must remain vigilant in verifying AI-generated outputs and maintaining control over the research process.

With the latest release of ChatGPT, qualitative researchers have more comprehensive and accurate responses to researchers' inquiries, incorporating a deeper understanding of context and nuance. This enables researchers to rely more heavily on AI for tasks such as data analysis and literature review, while still exercising critical judgement and oversight. Despite these new developments and potential future developments, the phases outlined in this chapter will remain applicable and useful. They provide a structured approach for integrating AI into qualitative research methodologies, ensuring that researchers maintain control over the research process and uphold standards of rigour and integrity. By continuing to refine their skills in prompt engineering, critical thinking and research design, qualitative researchers can harness the power of AI while mitigating its potential pitfalls.

References

Armstrong, A. and Gale, A.J. (2018) Online learning design and implementation models: a model validation study using expert instructional designers. *Quarterly Review of Distance Education* 19, 27–46.

Bloomberg, L.D. and Volpe, M. (2019) *Completing Your Qualitative Dissertation: A Road Map From Beginning to End*, 4th edn. Sage Publications, Los Angeles, California.

Braun, V. and Clarke, V. (2006) Using thematic analysis in psychology. *Qualitative Research in Psychology* 3, 77–101.

Braun, V. and Clarke, V. (2019) Reflecting on reflexive thematic analysis. *Qualitative Research in Sport, Exercise and Health* 11, 589–597.

Braun, V. and Clarke, V. (2022) *Thematic Analysis: A Practical Guide*. Sage Publications, Los Angeles, California.

Christou, P. (2023a) A critical perspective over whether and how to acknowledge the use of artificial intelligence (AI) in qualitative studies. *The Qualitative Report* 28, 1981–1991.

Christou, P. (2023b) How to use artificial intelligence (AI) as a resource, methodological and analysis tool in qualitative research? *The Qualitative Report* 28, 1968–1980.

Clark, J. and Perrault, R. (2023) Artificial Intelligence Index Report 2023. HAI Stanford University Artificial Intelligence. Available at: https://aiindex.stanford.edu/wp-content/uploads/2023/04/HAI_AI-Index-Report_2023.pdf (accessed 26 September 2024).

Creswell, J.W. (1994) *Research Design: Qualitative and Quantitative Approaches*. Sage Publications, Thousand Oaks, California.

Creswell, J.W. (1998) *Qualitative Inquiry and Research Design: Choosing Among Five Approaches*. Sage Publications, Thousand Oaks, California.

Creswell, J.W. and Poth, C.N. (2024) *Qualitative Inquiry and Research Design: Choosing Among Five Approaches*, 5th edn. Sage Publications Thousand Oaks, California.

Denkina, D. (2024) Prompt engineering is dead: long live AI prompt engineering. IEEE Spectrum. IEEE, Piscataway, New Jersey. Available at: https://spectrum.ieee.org/prompt-engineering-is-dead (accessed 26 September 2024).

Dergaa, I., Chamari, K., Zmijewski, P. and Saad, H. (2023) From human writing to artificial intelligence generated text: examining the prospects and potential threats of ChatGPT in academic writing. *Biology of Sport* 40, 615–622.

Dewalt, K.M. and DeWalt, B.R. (2011) *Participant Observation: A Guide for Fieldworkers*, 2nd edn. AltaMira Press, Lanham, Maryland.

Merriam, S.B. and Tisdell, E.J. (2016) *Qualitative Research: A Guide to Design and Implementation*, 4th edn. Jossey-Bass, San Francisco, California.

Miles, M.B., Huberman, A.M. and Saldana, J. (2022) *Qualitative Data Analysis: A Methods Sourcebook*, 4th edn. Sage Publications, Thousand Oaks, California.

OpenAI (2024) ChatGPT (Mar 31 version). Available at: https://chat.openai.com/chat (accessed 26 September 2024).

Roberts, J., Baker, M. and Andrew, J. (2024) Artificial intelligence and qualitative research: the promise and perils of large language model (LLM) 'assistance'. *Critical Perspectives on Accounting* 99: 102722.

Zhang, H., Wu, C., Xie, J., Kim, C. and Carroll, J.M. (2023) QualiGPT: GPT as an easy-to-use tool for qualitative coding. arXiv preprint. Available at: https://arxiv.org/abs/2310.07061 (accessed 26 September 2024).

9 AI in Ethnography: Challenges and Collaborations

Deana Kotiga*
Ipsos, London, UK

Abstract
This chapter delves into the integration of artificial intelligence (AI) in ethnographic business research, examining its transformative impact on various aspects of the research process. It explores AI's role in enhancing efficiency, collaboration, sample selection, research material creation and analysis within the realm of ethnography. By leveraging AI as a collaborative partner, researchers can unlock new opportunities for innovation and insight generation, while also navigating the ethical considerations and limitations inherent in AI technologies. The author delivers an autographic perspective, sharing personal experiences as a researcher to illustrate the practical applications and implications of AI in ethnographic studies. Through a critical examination of AI's capabilities and challenges, this chapter offers insights into the evolving intersection of technology and ethnography, emphasizing the importance of thoughtful integration guided by ethical principles and cultural sensitivity.

Keywords: AI and ethnography, autographic perspective, ethnography

9.1 Setting the Ethnographic Context and Introduction to AI Integration

I want to preface this chapter with usual anthropological practice, which I have named 'fencing against possible challenges'. While stepping outside the traditional confines of academia has offered the joy of applying anthropology in real-world settings, it is also meant hours of simple English training and the gradual fading of the constant need for academic referencing. As a business anthropologist and ethnographer, the imperative to stand behind my findings without rendering my practice elitist or foreign to clients has led me to draw primarily from my own experiences in my practice, and hence in this chapter. While I do reference some anthropologists, their works serve to inspire my general practice rather than directly informing this chapter. Academic anthropology, along with ethnography, is bound by rules that often need to be challenged to make sense in the real world.

Since June 2022, I have actively integrated artificial intelligence (AI) into my ethnographic practice as a Research Manager in the Ethnography Centre of Excellence (ECE) at Ipsos in the UK. Ipsos is a global leader in market research, delivering reliable information and a true understanding of society, markets and people, and Ipsos in the UK is its UK-based branch.

Working at the forefront of both ethnography in market research and AI development, I have witnessed first-hand the transformative

*E-mail: deanaemmakotiga@gmail.com

DOI: 10.1079/9781800626607.0009

potential of AI. Ipsos, a leading market research company, has pioneered the development of firewalled internal AI systems that prioritize researcher autonomy and idea generation. My engagement with AI is always also auto-ethnographic, despite academia's aversion to such practices. Just as any ethnographer cannot bypass observation, acknowledging AI's role in revolutionizing research methodologies is essential. This chapter seeks to articulate my experiences and interactions with generative AI (genAI) over the past year, capturing the nuances of this evolving relationship.

Ethnography is a qualitative research method used to study culture and behaviour, involving immersive fieldwork to observe and participate in the daily lives of individuals within a community. This method allows researchers to gain a deep understanding of social interactions, practices and norms within the studied group (Hammersley and Atkinson, 2007). Our ethnography at ECE incorporates a visual component, such as film or photography, to deepen our understanding of cultures and communities. Visual ethnography, as discussed by Pink (2009), enriches the data by capturing subtleties of expression and interaction that might be overlooked in textual descriptions. Ethnography is about exploration, rendering the familiar strange and the strange familiar (Agar, 1996). While challenging my own notions of reality, I embody new worlds and humbly accept when hypotheses need to pivot, an exercise fundamental to ethnography. This iterative process of adjusting hypotheses ensures the research remains relevant and accurate (Emerson *et al.*, 2011).

GenAI, on the other hand, is all about creation. As my Ipsos Facto succinctly put it, defining oneself is a complex process, mirroring the intricate nature of AI. Developed by Ipsos and powered by OpenAI's gpt-3.5-turbo-16k model, Ipsos Facto serves as an intelligent chatbot offering personalized responses and insights. AI, in a broader sense, simulates human intelligence to analyse data, recognize patterns and make decisions without direct human intervention. However, its interpretation and usage vary across cultures, influenced by unique contexts and norms.

I must admit, I have developed a fascination with AI. I speak to it on a daily basis, from using Ipsos Facto at work, to asking ChatGPT to come up with my weekly shop and holiday itinerary for my week in Scotland. In this chapter, I will explore various ways I utilize AI specifically in social research projects, from enhancing efficiency to brainstorming ideas and refining thoughts. We'll delve into AI's role in sample selection, research material creation, and analysis. Lastly, I will address AI's limitations, biases, and challenges to offer a comprehensive understanding of its impact on ethnographic practice. After all, imperfection is inherent to anything created by humans, and therein lies its beauty. And yes, for full transparency, AI has been a silent companion throughout the writing of this chapter, blurring the lines between where I begin, and it ends – a testament to the symbiotic relationship between human and AI.

9.2 AI and the Project Life

9.2.1 Efficiency and collaboration

In the dynamic landscape of ethnographic business research, efficiency is paramount. Traditional methods often struggle to keep pace with the demands of modern research projects, leading to delays and inefficiencies. However, the integration of AI offers a transformative solution, not as a standalone tool for efficiency but as a collaborative partner in the research process.

While AI is commonly associated with efficiency and automation, I have adopted a different approach in my ethnographic business research practice. Rather than viewing AI as a standalone efficiency tool, I embrace it as a collaborative partner that enhances the capabilities of research teams. By integrating AI into the collaborative fabric of our research projects, we unlock new opportunities for innovation, creativity and insight generation. In my practice, AI serves as more than just a means to streamline processes; it actively contributes to the creative and analytical aspects of ethnographic research. By leveraging AI's cognitive capabilities, we engage in collaborative brainstorming sessions, explore new research directions and generate novel insights. AI becomes an integral part of our research team, offering unique perspectives and enhancing our collective problem-solving abilities.

Central to our collaborative approach is the seamless interaction between human researchers and AI systems. Rather than relegating AI to the role of a passive tool, we foster an environment where human–AI collaboration thrives. Through natural language processing (NLP) and advanced data analytics, researchers engage in fluid conversations with AI, exchanging ideas, refining hypotheses and co-creating research strategies.

However, while AI brings unparalleled efficiency to certain aspects of research, it is essential to strike a balance between automation and human judgement. In our collaborative model, AI augments human intelligence rather than replacing it entirely. Human researchers provide the contextual understanding, critical thinking and ethical considerations necessary for nuanced analysis, while AI enhances efficiency and offers data-driven insights.

9.2.2 Sample

At the heart of any social research project lies the essential element of the sample. Often overshadowed by the more glamorous sibling called 'analysis', the sample serves as the bedrock upon which the entire research project is built. This rings especially true in the realm of ethnography, particularly within commercial contexts where resources are often constrained. In such settings, the importance of meticulously crafting the sample cannot be overstated; it is the linchpin that holds the entire project together.

With limited budgets looming overhead, the imperative to fine-tune the sample becomes even more pronounced. Every dollar spent must yield maximum insight, making the stakes higher than ever. A misstep in sample selection can have far-reaching consequences, potentially jeopardizing the integrity and validity of the entire research undertaking. It is akin to constructing a building on shaky foundations – a recipe for disaster. Yet, despite its immense importance, selecting the right sample remains one of the most difficult challenges in commercial ethnography research. Amidst this sea of stories, discerning those that align most closely with the research objectives is no small feat. Complicating matters further is the frequent absence of a clear blueprint provided by the client regarding their target audience. More often than not, clients turn to researchers for advice on the correct sample, and this lack of clarity only serves to exacerbate the already daunting task of sample selection, underscoring the criticality of getting it right the first time.

Enter the indispensable ally: AI. In an era defined by technological innovation, AI emerges as a game-changer in the realm of sample selection for ethnographic research. Leveraging the power of machine learning algorithms and advanced data analytics, AI offers a suite of tools and techniques to revolutionize the way samples are identified and curated. Of course, all of its recommendations need to be taken with a pinch of salt, and its guidance seen as just that – guidance rather than directive.

The way I usually approach this part of the project process is brainstorming the sample with the AI. I give the company's firewalled AI program all the information it needs – I tell it who it is (an ethnographic researcher with over 20 years of experience in this field); who the client is and what their objectives are; who the target audience is; and what my thoughts on the sample are. I usually ask it to help me brainstorm stories which would be good to showcase, and which would help me get to the project's business goals.

With AI as my co-pilot, navigating the complexities of sample selection becomes less daunting. Its insights and suggestions serve as valuable inputs, guiding me towards a more informed and strategic approach. Together, we refine and iterate, ensuring that the final sample not only meets but exceeds the client's expectations, setting the stage for a successful and impactful research endeavour.

However, it is important to acknowledge the limitations of AI in sample selection. While AI offers invaluable assistance in identifying potential samples and suggesting strategies, it is not without its biases. AI algorithms are trained on existing data, which can reflect historical biases and societal prejudices. As a result, there is a risk that AI-powered sample selection may inadvertently perpetuate or amplify these biases. For instance, if the training data predominantly consists of certain demographic groups or excludes others, the AI's recommendations may be skewed towards those groups, leading to a biased sample. Therefore, it is essential to approach AI-generated sample recommendations with caution, supplementing them with human judgement and critical evaluation to mitigate the risk of bias and ensure a more balanced and representative sample.

9.2.3 Research materials

In the realm of research, particularly in ethnography, understanding the existing landscape of knowledge is essential. Previous studies not only provide valuable insights but also guide the formulation of pertinent research questions. Traditionally, this involved extensive manual searches through libraries (in my university years), academic journals and online databases, consuming precious time and resources. In the days before AI, you could give an afternoon or two to looking through Google Scholar about the anthropology of skin (if this was a subject you were interested in) and trying to get in touch with academics to let you read their articles for free.

GenAI has revolutionized this process, making it far more efficient and accessible. As, in business ethnography, time is of the essence, genAI means we can streamline this initial phase significantly. One only has to tell it to give you the lay of the land of the research done about anthropology of skin in Brazil, ethnographies of home care in Indonesia or research about beauty in Ghana, and a comprehensive overview of existing literature and studies is ready. This helps researchers identify key themes, gaps and potential areas of exploration, further laying a solid foundation for their inquiry. A brilliant thing about genAI is that it is not just another search engine in disguise. Rather than Google, speaking to AI is more like having a brainstorming colleague who is always ready to bounce ideas around with you.

In addition, in this part of the research project, finding information is not the only important thing. Your goal is to come up with research materials and find specific research question that will help you explore the business objectives. GenAI helps me with that too – I ask it to ask me follow-up questions, to explore different angles with me and to investigate new research directions I had not considered before. It is like having my own personal assistant on standby 24/7.

For example, I recently worked on a project about inclusive and accessible design. As I am not familiar with accessible and inclusive design, or with any theories and studies about disability, I asked genAI to give me the lay of the land and point me to things that would be useful for me to know. Of course, it did not give me what I wanted at first. With genAI, it is all about phrasing. You have to be as specific as possible as the question 'Tell me about inclusive design' will yield different answers from the instruction 'I am a business ethnographer working on a project about inclusive design.' I want to understand the anthropological theory and studies done in this space. GenAI helped me navigate a complex topic and equipped me with the knowledge I needed to tackle my project with confidence.

However, despite its utility, AI introduces significant ethical considerations. One notable concern is the quality and accuracy of AI-generated content. While AI excels at processing large datasets and offering initial insights, it may struggle to grasp nuanced contexts or provide original analyses essential to ethnographic research. Ethnography emphasizes the contextualization of findings within cultural and social frameworks, a task that requires human interpretation, empathy and reflexivity (Pink, 2015). AI-generated content, lacking these human qualities, risks producing superficial or biased interpretations that could misrepresent or oversimplify complex social phenomena. Moreover, biases inherent in AI algorithms or training data pose another ethical challenge. AI systems learn from historical data, which may reflect societal prejudices or inequalities (Crawford and Calo, 2016). Consequently, AI-generated content could perpetuate or amplify biases, undermining the ethical principles of objectivity and fairness in ethnographic research.

While AI can expedite data processing and initial analysis, it cannot replace the critical role of human oversight and intervention in ethnographic inquiry. Researchers must exercise vigilance in interpreting AI-generated outputs, scrutinizing them for accuracy, relevance and ethical implications. This necessitates ongoing dialogue and collaboration between human researchers and AI systems to ensure that AI tools are used responsibly and ethically in ethnographic practice.

In conclusion, while AI tools offer valuable support in ethnographic research, they also present ethical challenges related to content quality, bias mitigation and the preservation of human-centred research practices. By integrating AI responsibly and critically, researchers can harness its potential while safeguarding the integrity and validity of ethnographic investigations.

9.2.4 Analysis

Analysis is the sweet, yet demanding part of the project. In business ethnography, if everything before analysis is filled with adrenaline and time restraints, analysis is the part of the project where time seems to stand still. It is akin to staring at a blank page, overwhelmed by the flood of information swirling in your mind, yet unable to translate it into coherent insights. We have all experienced that moment of paralysis.

Enter AI, once again coming to the rescue. The initial thought might be to feed interview transcripts into AI and ask it to summarize the themes. If only it were that simple! Human beings are complex creatures, and not everything we say aligns perfectly with our actions. At ECE, our research methodology revolves around the visual aspect of ethnography. We capture everything on film, using video as both input for analysis and the ultimate output of our research. Words can convey information, but showing visuals to our clients resonates with them on a deeper, more human level.

Transcripts alone fail to capture the essence of human behaviour. They do not convey the nuances of body language, the moments of vulnerability when someone sheds tears or the subtle sarcasm that only a human observer can interpret. They also do not reveal the significance of what remains unsaid, the social silences that Gillian Tett (2022) eloquently explores in her book. For my practice, relying solely on genAI to analyse transcripts is simply not feasible. It would not provide the nuanced insights we strive for.

Instead, I employ genAI as a collaborative brainstorming tool, akin to consulting with a helpful colleague. I share my ideas and connections, asking AI to help add structure to my thoughts. It is remarkable how often it delivers, bridging the gap between my chaotic musings and coherent analysis. With its assistance, I am able to tease out patterns, identify themes and ultimately craft compelling narratives that resonate with our clients.

However, it is crucial to recognize the limitations of AI in this context. While it excels at processing vast amounts of data and generating insights, it lacks the human intuition and contextual understanding necessary for truly insightful analysis. That is why human oversight and interpretation are indispensable in the analysis phase of ethnographic research. By combining the strengths of AI with human expertise, we can unlock deeper insights and produce research that is both rigorous and impactful.

In conclusion, while AI has undoubtedly transformed the research landscape, it is important to approach its use in analysis with caution and critical thinking. When utilized as a complementary tool alongside human expertise, it can enhance the research process and elevate the quality of our insights. As we navigate the ever-evolving intersection of technology and ethnography, striking the right balance between automation and human judgement will be key to unlocking the full potential of both.

9.3 Limitations and Perils

To paraphrase Walter Goldsmith in his foreword for the iconic Carlos Castaneda's book *The Teachings of Don Juan* (1990), anthropology has long illuminated the diverse shapes of worlds across cultures. It is not just about different customs or beliefs in gods; rather, it is about the distinct shapes that define the realities of different peoples. This raises a crucial question: how will our world, and by extension, our ethnographic practice, evolve with the integration of AI?

Amidst the excitement surrounding AI's potential, it is imperative to heed the warning of Ralph Linton's famous quote: 'The last thing a fish would ever notice would be water.' In other words, we must remain vigilant and not take AI for granted. Technologies, including AI, are not neutral tools but are imbued with cultural meanings and power dynamics that shape their development and deployment. As Benjamin (2019) asserted, AI reflects the structures and biases inherent in the societies that create it. Emerging from patriarchal, homophobic, racist and capitalist systems, AI is likely to mirror and perpetuate the inequalities and power imbalances present in society.

In light of these concerns, Tett (2022) proposed an insightful approach in her book *Anthro-Vision: How Anthropology Can Explain Business and Life*. Anthropological intelligence offers a critical lens through which to analyse and contextualize the impacts of AI on ethnographic practice. By combining the analytical tools of anthropology with the capabilities of AI, researchers can navigate the complexities of cultural diversity and power dynamics inherent in AI technologies.

One of the primary limitations of AI in anthropology lies in its capacity to fully comprehend the nuances of human culture and behaviour. While AI algorithms can process vast amounts of data and identify patterns, they may struggle to interpret cultural context or understand the symbolic significance of human actions. As anthropologists, our work often involves delving into the intricacies of social and cultural phenomena, which may elude the grasp of AI systems.

Moreover, AI's reliance on existing data introduces the risk of perpetuating biases and reinforcing existing power structures. AI algorithms learn from historical data, which may encode societal prejudices and inequalities (Crawford and Calo, 2016). Without careful oversight and intervention, AI systems can inadvertently amplify biases and perpetuate discriminatory practices, thereby undermining the ethical principles of anthropology (Gillespie, 2014).

Another critical limitation of AI in anthropology is its potential to dehumanize the research process. Ethnography, as a qualitative research method, emphasizes human connection, empathy, intuition and reflexivity (Pink, 2015). These aspects are essential for understanding cultural contexts and social dynamics, which AI lacks the capacity to fully comprehend. While AI can facilitate data analysis and processing, it cannot replicate the nuanced interpretations and insights derived from direct human engagement in ethnographic research.

Furthermore, the integration of AI in ethnographic practice raises significant ethical considerations regarding consent, privacy and the representation of research participants (Kelty, 2017). Ethnographers traditionally prioritize ethical principles such as respect, dignity and justice in their interactions with participants. However, AI technologies may challenge these principles by potentially diminishing participant agency and exacerbating power imbalances between researchers and subjects (Irani, 2018). It becomes imperative for researchers to carefully navigate these ethical complexities to ensure that AI-enhanced methods uphold the foundational values of ethical research in anthropology.

In conclusion, while AI offers exciting opportunities for advancing ethnographic practice, it also presents significant challenges and limitations. By critically engaging with AI and integrating anthropological intelligence into our research methodologies, we can harness the potential of AI while safeguarding against its pitfalls. Ultimately, the future of anthropology lies in the thoughtful and ethical integration of AI technologies, guided by the principles of cultural sensitivity, reflexivity and social justice.

9.4 Conclusions: Navigating the AI and Ethnography Collaboration

In the realm of ethnographic business research, the integration of AI marks a significant paradigm shift, offering both unprecedented opportunities and formidable challenges. As I reflect on my journey over the past year, navigating the dynamic intersection of technology and ethnography, several key themes emerge.

First and foremost is the notion of collaboration. Rather than viewing AI as a mere tool for efficiency, I have embraced it as a collaborative partner in the research process. By integrating AI into our research teams, we have unlocked new opportunities for innovation, creativity and insight generation. AI has become an integral part of our ethnographic practice, offering unique perspectives and enhancing our collective problem-solving abilities.

At the heart of this collaboration is the seamless interaction between human researchers and AI systems. Through NLP and advanced data analytics, we engage in fluid conversations with AI, exchanging ideas, refining hypotheses and co-creating research strategies. This collaborative approach has enabled us not only to tackle complex research questions but also to explore diverse perspectives and uncover hidden insights that may otherwise have remained undiscovered.

Furthermore, AI's role extends beyond mere assistance; it actively contributes to shaping our methodologies and expanding the scope of our inquiries. By augmenting our ability to process vast amounts of data and detect patterns, AI enhances the rigour and depth of our ethnographic analyses. This symbiotic relationship fosters a dynamic research environment where human intuition and AI-driven insights complement each other, leading to richer interpretations and more comprehensive understandings of cultural phenomena.

Yet, amidst the excitement surrounding AI's potential, it is essential to acknowledge its limitations. AI algorithms may struggle to fully comprehend the nuances of human culture and behaviour, which can lead to biases and ethical concerns (Gillespie, 2014). Additionally, the integration of AI raises profound questions about consent, privacy and the respectful representation of research participants (Kelty, 2017). These considerations underscore the importance of maintaining ethical standards and ensuring that AI-enhanced research respects the rights and dignity of all involved.

Despite these challenges, I remain optimistic about the future of ethnographic research in the age of AI. By critically engaging with AI and integrating anthropological intelligence into our research methodologies, we can harness its potential while safeguarding against its pitfalls. The future of anthropology lies in the thoughtful and ethical integration of AI technologies, guided by the principles of cultural sensitivity, reflexivity and social justice.

Looking ahead, I am excited to continue exploring the transformative potential of AI in ethnographic research. By embracing collaboration, creativity and critical thinking, we can navigate the complexities of the ethnographic landscape with confidence and integrity. With AI as our ally, we are poised to unlock new insights, drive innovation, and make meaningful contributions to both academia and industry.

References

Agar, M.H. (1996) *The Professional Stranger: An Informal Introduction to Ethnography*. Academic Press, New York.

Benjamin, R. (2019) *Race After Technology: Abolitionist Tools for the New Jim Code*. Polity, Cambridge, UK.

Castaneda, C. (1990) *The Teachings of Don Juan: A Yaqui Way of Knowledge*. Penguin, London.

Crawford, K. and Calo, R. (2016) There is a blind spot in AI research. *Nature* 538, 311–313.

Emerson, R.M., Fretz, R.I. and Shaw, L.L. (2011) *Writing Ethnographic Fieldnotes*. University of Chicago Press, Chicago, Illinois.

Gillespie, T. (2014) The relevance of algorithms. In: Gillespie, T., Boczkowski, P.J. and Foot, K.A. (eds) *Media Technologies: Essays on Communication, Materiality, and Society*. MIT Press, Cambridge, Massachusetts, pp. 167–193.

Hammersley, M. and Atkinson, P. (2007) *Ethnography: Principles in Practice*. Routledge, Abingdon, UK.

Irani, L. (2018) Difference and dependence among digital workers: the case of Amazon Mechanical Turk. *South Atlantic Quarterly* 117, 253–267.

Kelty, C. (2017) Ethnography. In: Rabinow, S.H. and Biagioli, R.E. (eds) *The Anthropology of Knowledge: Ethnography's Magic*. University of Chicago Press, Chicago, Illinois, pp. 65–83.

Pink, S. (2009) *Doing Sensory Ethnography*. Sage Publications, London.

Pink, S. (2015) *Doing Sensory Ethnography*, 2nd edn. Sage Publications, London.

Tett, G. (2022) *Anthro-Vision: How Anthropology Can Explain Business and Life*. Random House, New York.

10 Exploring Research Design in the Context of Artificial Intelligence: Evidence-based Recommendations for Social Research and Practice

Terrell L. Strayhorn[1]* and J'Quen Johnson[2]
[1]*Virginia Union University, Richmond, Virginia;* [2]*University of the Cumberlands, Williamsburg, Kentucky*

Abstract
Artificial intelligence (AI) has grown to become a common aspect of daily life. As its popularity spreads, we need to know more about people's awareness, perceptions and lived experiences with it, based on insights from well-designed research studies. In this chapter, we explore research designs that can be employed in social contexts to study AI. We offer examples of published works, while also describing and evaluating the strength of various designs in understanding AI, its impacts, and people's experiences with it in education and society.

Keywords: artificial intelligence, research design, technology acceptance model

10.1 Introduction

In recent years, artificial intelligence (AI) has grown from a niche subject of a select few in the technologically advanced world of 'dot-coms' and 'Silicon Valley start-ups' to a more common aspect of daily life. This rapid evolution has sparked both excitement and concern, especially among those in professional fields such as business, finance, medicine and education. Consider, for instance, the fact that more than 50% of businesses plan to implement generative AI technologies in their daily operations (National University, 2024).

There is other evidence of AI's growing popularity in businesses and society. AI's presence is ever-expanding, from virtual assistants (e.g. Alexa and Siri) that simplify everyday tasks to autonomous vehicles and sophisticated algorithms that drive decision-making processes in complex domains. A recent study by the Nielsen Normal Group found that AI increased employee productivity by 66% (Nielsen, 2023). And notably, 62% of Americans prefer to use chatbots for customer service rather than wait for human agents (Fokina, 2024).

Undoubtedly, AI's presence has sparked competing opinions, with some supporting its adoption and others opposing its integration into daily life. Supporters of AI highlight the vital benefits and advancements it brings to various fields, including improved quality of life, economic growth and addressing some of the world's most pressing challenges (Rust and Huang, 2014). Opponents, however, raise concerns about AI's development and deployment. One of the most significant concerns is the potential for widespread job displacement due to automation, which is known as replacement theory (Huang and Rust, 2018). AI can replace

*E-mail: tlstrayhorn@vuu.edu

 Artificial Intelligence (AI) in Social Research (P.A. Christou ed.)
DOI: 10.1079/9781800626607.0010

human workers in many routine and repetitive tasks, exacerbating unemployment and economic inequality. While recent data suggest that AI may eliminate 85 million jobs, it is also likely to create 97 million more (Webster, 2024). Additionally, AI systems often require vast amounts of data, raising concerns about surveillance and cybersecurity attacks. Collecting, storing and analysing personal data can lead to invasions of privacy and misuse of sensitive information. For instance, Sapio Research (2023) reported that 75% of security professionals have observed an increase in the frequency of cyberattacks, with 85% of these experts attributing this uptick to bad actors' misuse of AI. Lastly, ethical concerns arise with AI. Consider that 22% of companies report negative customer backlash due to AI-enabled actions, as found by The Enterprisers Project (https://enterprisersproject.com/, accessed 8 October 2024). The rapid development of AI outpaces the establishment of regulatory frameworks, creating challenges in ensuring accountability and managing risks.

As educators and scholars who frequently study hot topics in primary and secondary education and higher education, we find the evolution of AI compelling as an issue cutting across both sectors and all industries. AI opens up new possibilities for learning such as collaboration, groupthink, feedback cycles and more. It also raises new and important questions for research and scholarship. For example, what types of AI exist and how do people use them? What is the impact of AI on learning, productivity and efficiency? How do ordinary people, students and business leaders perceive AI? And what are the lived experiences of AI users in business, education and broader society? These questions require different research designs to fully investigate the heart of the matter. In this chapter, we will describe and evaluate various research designs applied to the study of AI in social research.

Our interest in exploring AI within the context of social research emerged in several ways. As educators and researchers, we recognize AI's potential to transform data collection, analysis and reporting (Alharthi, 2020). Second, as equity-minded diversity scholars, we also notice how different social groups, including minoritized and vulnerable populations, understand, perceive and consequently engage with AI. Motivated by these interests, we embarked on a journey to describe and evaluate the evolving terrain of AI and rigorous research designs in social research.

Beyond the social research arena, we became wildly curious about any positive benefits of AI that enable core aspects of our work in education, business and society. We settled on exploring the use of several research designs in studying AI, given our primary professional identities as researchers, scholars and publicly engaged consultants. In full transparency, both of us have generally positive and open opinions about AI. We use it from time to time in our teaching, research and, yes, social media management. Tools such as Grammarly, ChatGPT and Quillbot have helped us automate spellchecks, undertake real-time grammar reviews and double-check APA citations, especially for uncommon types such as legal documents, podcasts and blogs. In this chapter, we aim to illuminate the ways AI can be studied in social research, with a critical glance at issues of research design.

The purpose of this chapter is to describe and evaluate research designs that can be used in social contexts to study topics related to AI. Specifically, we aim to address well-documented research designs and how they can be used to conduct research on people's AI use, perceived attitudes and behaviours, using examples from published studies. The chapter has several major objectives: (i) to provide an overview of research design methodologies applied in studying AI technologies; (ii) to highlight the potential benefits and limitations of social research designs in the context of AI-focused studies; and (iii) to identify future directions for well-designed research studies on AI. Our approach to exploring issues of design in social research on AI is justified in several ways. First, an undeniable body of evidence supports the conclusion that well-designed research studies can provide much-needed insights about innovative topics such as trends in AI adoption, changes in AI perceptions and variations in attitudes towards AI across different social groups (e.g. Delello *et al.*, 2023). Second, insights gleaned from rigorous research designs have enormous potential to inform the decisions and best practices of educators, policy makers and technology developers. Lastly, by studying AI users, we believe that social research can advance knowledge about AI in ways that yield relevant information about users, resisters and even those who reject AI outright. Next, we turn to the extant literature and theory that shaped our evaluation of research design.

10.2 Literature Review

To address this topic, we thought it was necessary to review the existing literature on or about AI generally and AI in education, business or social research specifically. Existing works could be organized into major categories according to the chapter's theoretical framework: studies on perceived use, perceived ease of use, attitudes and behavioural intentions.

10.2.1 Studies on perceived use

Perceived use (PU) is defined as use that is advantageous or helpful for action. Prior research has examined users' knowledge, attitudes and perceived usefulness of AI-based tools, highlighting their potential applications in particular settings. For instance, Ahmed *et al.* (2022) conducted an online questionnaire-based cross-sectional study to assess the knowledge, attitudes and practices regarding AI. The sample population consisted of 470 users selected through convenience sampling. They found that most participants lacked knowledge about AI and its applications in the field due to limited or no exposure to AI during earlier training. However, many users expressed positive attitudes towards adopting AI, perceived AI as useful and thus were willing to incorporate it into their professional practices. Despite some gaps, the study highlighted a general receptiveness to AI, underscoring the need for comprehensive AI awareness and training.

10.2.2 Studies on perceived ease of use

Perceived ease of use (PEOU) is defined as the degree to which use is perceived as effortless. Beyond knowledge and attitudes, other empirical research has investigated ease of use of AI-based tools and technologies. For example, Sudaryanto *et al.* (2023) conducted a quantitative survey-based study using a convenience sample of 152 AI users. Using advanced path modelling techniques, they explored linkages between technology readiness, perceived usefulness and ease of use. The results indicated that PEOU and PU were significantly associated with AI adoption. Other studies have shown the important role that PEOU plays in facilitating eventual adoption of AI. For instance, Wang *et al.* (2021) used hierarchical modelling techniques to examine 311 AI users' intentions. They found that PEOU and PU positively predicted behavioural intention (BI) (i.e. use of AI in the classroom), explaining upwards of 70% of the outcome.

10.2.3 Studies on attitudes towards AI adoption

Previous literature has examined attitudes and perceptions towards adopting emerging technologies, specifically AI, providing insights into the factors influencing users' acceptance and integration of innovative systems. For instance, Acosta-Enriquez *et al.* (2024) conducted a quantitative study with 499 users to determine their attitudes towards AI, specifically ChatGPT. Using structural equation modelling, they found the strongest predictors of AI attitudes include responsible use, ease of use and acceptance, among others. As another example, Alshurideh *et al.* (2024) studied 523 users to explore factors associated with AI use. Also using structural equation modelling, they found that PU and PEOU strongly influenced intentions to use AI and attitudes towards AI use. Users with positive attitudes towards AI were more likely to use such tools than those with more negative perceptions.

10.2.4 Studies on behavioural intention

Behavioural intention is defined as an inclination to use. A growing body of research has explored the factors influencing and shaping intentions to use AI technologies. For example, Chai *et al.* (2024) conducted a study to develop and validate the Artificial Intelligence Learning Intention Scale (AILIS) to measure factors influencing some users' intentions and engagement in AI learning. A sample of 907 people completed an online survey during the autumn of 2022. Structural equation modelling revealed the critical roles of epistemic capacity, facilitating environments and psychological attitudes in promoting intentions and actual AI learning. The findings indicated strong intentions to learn about and subsequently use AI, which were associated with greater engagement.

10.2.5 Studies on college students and AI

Previous studies have examined the barriers to AI adoption and integration. For instance, Alimi *et al.* (2021) conducted a study investigating the awareness, access and use of AI. Employing a descriptive survey research design, a three-section questionnaire was utilized to collect data from a multistage sample of 200 people. The findings revealed that most lacked awareness of AI applications and had limited access to AI technologies. The study concluded that one's ability to utilize AI is significantly hindered by their lack of awareness and limited access to these digital resources. The results emphasized the need for increased efforts to enhance familiarity with AI tools and facilitate better access to these technologies.

Although useful, previous social research studies have focused on PU, PEOU, attitudes and intentions related to AI using quasi-experimental and model-testing methods such as structural equation modelling (Acosta-Enriquez *et al.*, 2024; Alshurideh *et al.*, 2024). There is a clear need for more robust scholarship using diverse research designs such as quantitative approaches based on cross-sectional surveys and qualitative approaches employing interviews, observations and naturalistic methods. This is the gap addressed by our chapter.

10.2.6 Technology acceptance model

Given the important role that people's beliefs and thoughts about utility and ease of use play in the likelihood of accepting, adopting and implementing an innovation or system, Davis' (1989) technology adoption (or acceptance) model (TAM) made a logical choice for our discussion and evaluation of research designs in AI research. TAM attempts to explain how users come to accept and use technology. As an adaptation of the theory of reasoned action, TAM is specifically anchored to understanding user behaviours in the context of information technology (IT). Two main factors influence an individual's decision to adopt and use a new technology: PU and PEOU. PU refers to the degree to which an individual believes that a particular system or technology would improve their action or enhance their job performance. In other words, PU reflects the extent to which a user believes a technology or system will improve their work efficiency and effectiveness. When users perceive utility, they have more positive attitudes towards technology and thus are inclined to adopt its use. PEOU refers to the extent to which an individual believes using a particular system or technology would be easy and effortless. In theory, when users perceive ease of use, they have more favourable attitudes towards an innovation and thus are more likely to adopt it.

Whereas Davis (1989) hypothesized, in keeping with Rogers *et al.* (2014)'s 'Diffusion of innovation', that PU and PEOU influenced attitudes towards technology and, indirectly, behavioural intention, latter studies (e.g. Venkatesh and Davis, 1996, 2000) found that PU and PEOU *directly* affect behavioural intention without attitudes as a mediator. It is important to note that Rogers *et al.* (2014) diffusion model attempted to explain 'the process by which an innovation is communicated through certain channels over time among the members of a social system' (p. 5).

Overall, TAM has been widely used and validated in studies about IT adoption and specific technologies in particular contexts (Mathieson, 1991). The model has several strengths including its simplicity, adaptability, strong empirical support and practicality (Mun *et al.*, 2006). Studies designed with TAM in mind yield findings that, on average, enable organizations to design and implement policies, practices and programs that are more likely to be embraced by users. It is by far the most used framework in predicting IT adoption (Paul *et al.*, 2003), and we found it useful in describing and evaluating the research designs discussed in this chapter. Figure 10.1 presents a graphical summary.

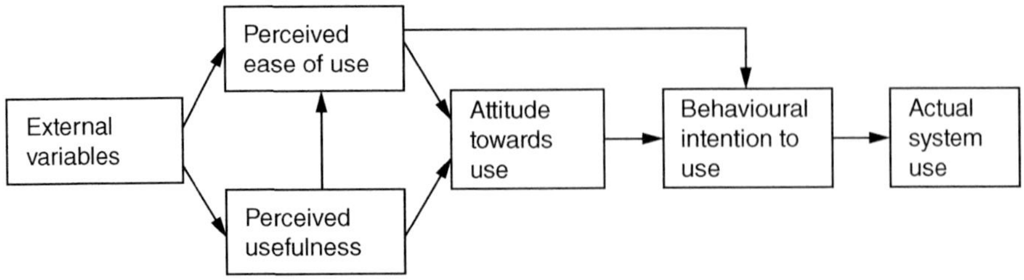

Fig. 10.1. Technology acceptance model. Figure produced by the authors, based on information from Davis (1989) and Wahid (2007).

10.2.7 Research design in (AI) social research

Our review of existing social research on AI reveals that much of the previous work on this subject is based on one of three major approaches to research designs. The first of these is experimental designs, marked by randomization, treatment effects and relatively longitudinal frameworks. Second, dozens of studies use a quasi-experimental design but largely engage students, employees or learners overseas whose experiences might be qualitatively different from those in the USA. Third, although fewer in number, some studies use a cross-sectional survey to assess knowledge, awareness and perceptions. Very few studies employ qualitative methods to investigate people's lived experiences with AI.

Studies using experimental research design are marked off from others by characteristics such as randomization, causal effects and fidelity protections that keep the control group safe from exposure to the treatment (Campbell and Stanley, 2015). For example, Fulmer *et al.* (2018) conducted a randomized controlled trial with a diverse sample of 75 participants from 15 universities across the USA to assess the feasibility and efficacy of using Tess, an integrative psychological AI, in reducing symptoms of anxiety and depression. Participants were randomly assigned to one of three groups: (i) unlimited access to Tess with daily check-ins for 2 weeks (group 1); (ii) unlimited access to Tess with biweekly check-ins for 4 weeks (group 2); and (iii) no Tess access but access to the National Institute on Mental Health eBook on depression (control group). All participants completed the Patient Health Questionnaire, Generalized Anxiety Disorder Scale, and Positive and Negative Affect Scale (PANAS) at three different time points, ranging from baseline to 2 and 4 weeks. One major finding included statistical differences in the PANAS scores between the control group and group 1, suggesting that AI exposure via Tess positively impacted participants' emotional states.

Quasi-experimental studies, however, can be easier to mount without the requirement for complete randomization or mutual exclusivity. For instance, Han *et al.* (2022) conducted a quasi-experimental study of 61 users to explore the influence of a chatbot program on their knowledge, confidence and skills. Findings revealed no differences between the experimental and control groups in AI knowledge. However, the experimental group surpassed the control group in terms of interest and orientation to learning.

What is really needed to advance knowledge in this area are studies that leverage the strength and affordability of cross-sectional survey designs in understanding more about AI user experiences. For example, Alharthi (2020) hypothesized that AI through machine learning could be used to predict anxiety susceptibility in ways that inform monitoring and intervention. Analysing data from 917 respondents to an online survey, he found the three top attributes that predicted generalized anxiety disorder were gender, supportive network and fixed family income, reflecting significant social group differences.

Experts agree that all research designs have potential benefits or strengths, and certain limitations (Myers *et al.*, 2013). Experimental designs are superior to other approaches in their capacity to isolate and measure the underlying causal mechanism that yields the desired outcomes. However, they can be difficult to implement in social settings with free agents or humans, given the researcher's restricted ability to truly randomize, deny treatment or delay exposure to certain groups.

Quasi-experimental designs have several benefits, one of which is their ability to estimate strong causal inferences without the need for randomized controlled environments. Quasi-experimental studies use a variety of control groups and matching techniques to isolate the effect of a treatment on an outcome. Nevertheless, one major limitation of this design is confounding bias – error caused by the mixing of a treatment with extraneous risk factors – which can limit the accuracy of estimates.

The benefits of cross-sectional survey designs include cost, scalability and widespread use among researchers. Social researchers' popularized use of surveys enables comparisons across studies, critical systematic reviews and replication of results. Surveys are also an affordable way to collect large amounts of data from large samples quickly. However, two major limitations of this design include its inability to measure changes in behaviour over time or to determine the root cause of a certain outcome. Figure 10.2 presents a graphical comparison.

10.3 Discussion and Implications

Recall that the purpose of the present chapter was to explore research designs that can be used in social contexts to study topics related to AI, which has become a part of our collaborative research agenda. As intended, we addressed well-documented research designs, including experimental, quasi-experimental and cross-sectional approaches. We used prior literature to show how they have been used to conduct rigorous research on people's perceptions of AI use, ease of use, attitudes and intentions.

Initially, we assumed that TAM was an appropriate theoretical framework for our discussion. Several reasons support our faith in the model. First, we found the framework very straightforward, easy to interpret and useful for our chapter. Second, TAM has been widely used and validated by other studies (Mathieson, 1991). However, we learned through the course of this project that TAM has other advantages. It is helpful for designing local surveys exploring the use of AI, awareness, perceptions, knowledge and other outcomes.

All research designs have strengths and limitations. Many scholars praise experimental designs as the gold standard in social research. They are remarkably effective in generating causal inferences and effect sizes. However, they require much time, planning and resources to satisfy criteria for randomization and mutual independence. Although cross-sectional designs are more affordable, they simply cannot produce cause-and-effect parameters (e.g. Campbell and Stanley, 2015).

RESEARCH DESIGN COMPARISON

Features	Experimental	Quasi-experimental	Cross-sectional
Causal inference	●	●	
Randomization	●	●	
Affordable			●
Confounding bias		●	●
Rigorous	●	●	●

Fig. 10.2. Cross-comparison of research design features.

Several implications emanate from the chapter's discussion. In terms of research, studies cited in this chapter demonstrate the power and promise of cross-sectional designs in AI-related research. Future researchers should extend this line of inquiry by using experimental and non-experimental approaches. For example, staff might talk to incoming students about the value of AI during summer orientation and later test for differences between these students and their peers (without AI-focused orientation), in terms of AI use and a variety of perceptual items. Similarly, managers and supervisors might adopt qualitative approaches – namely, one-on-one interviews or focus groups – to ask new staff about their use of AI, if/where they find it useful and the challenges they face when using such innovative tools.

Insights from our chapter directly speak to policy development. It is evident that AI has many benefits, but safety concerns, security breaches and integrity issues are undeniable. For example, some educators worry that AI hijacks students' creativity, innovation and originality, as more and more students start to 'query' ChatGPT quickly for answers, outlines and content rather than push through the iterative process of drafting, rewriting and crafting thoughts in their own words. It is our opinion that anything in excess runs the risk of being problematic. Rather than banning AI in education or business, we advocate for policies that govern its responsible use in teaching and for-profit contexts. Effective policies should address when, where and how AI tools can be used; they might also specify the consequences of violating such terms.

Although differences have been observed in terms of AI use and perceptions, let us be very clear: AI is here to stay whether critics like it or not. With few exceptions, virtually all participants in previous studies have used AI in some form or fashion – whether a voice assistant on their smart device, a chatbot online or an algorithm-generated playlist through Pandora. So, you may ask, what are some promising practices to best support AI users? Great question! First, remember this: you cannot lead people to a place you have never been. To help them, you must first help yourself by reading about AI, what it is, what it is not and its utility in everyday life. Start with the References listed at the end of this chapter and those cited throughout the book. Go to YouTube and bookmark at least three (we really like to do things in three) 'how to' videos related to AI tools. When all else fails, let the users be your teacher – just ask them which AI tools they use, whether they find them helpful and what are some cautions or concerns, if any?

Lastly, there are exciting implications for future theory. We used TAM as a guiding framework for this description and evaluation of research designs in AI-related studies. It was helpful in directing our attention to major influences such as external factors, PU and PEOU, among others. While useful, there are other theories that could be mined for future social research on AI. For example, socialization theory can be complementary to TAM when studying AI. As mentioned earlier in this chapter, people aspire to enter their desired professions, which increasingly require awareness of, knowledge about and skills in using AI to diagnose conditions, prevent cyberattacks and optimize productivity. The application of socialization theory to AI scholarship can be embedded within experimental, quasi-experimental and qualitative designs.

10.4 Conclusion

We could not think of a better way to close this chapter exploring design issues within AI research than to see how AI might do it. We asked ChatGPT how it might end a chapter on this topic 'using an upbeat and inspirational tone' and here is what it generated:

> In conclusion, as we navigate the intricate landscape of research design within the realm of artificial intelligence, we uncover boundless opportunities for innovation and social impact. By adhering to evidence-based recommendations, we not only enhance the rigor and relevance of our inquiries but also empower ourselves to address pressing societal challenges with unprecedented precision and creativity. Let us embrace this dynamic intersection of AI and social research with optimism and a forward-thinking mindset, confident that our collective efforts will pave the way for a brighter, more equitable future.

Indeed, AI, by definition, can perform complex tasks that mimic human intelligence or behaviours such as thinking, feeling and reasoning. However, it is not error free and can sometimes 'wax philosophical' with flowery terms and unnecessary jargon that sound inspirational but leave the reader with more questions than answers. That said, we see several ways to improve what ChatGPT generated for the closing that better reflects the tone and texture of our voice and writing style. For instance, we completely agree that our recommendations enhance the rigour and relevance of future inquiries about AI. But research design is the purview of scholars, researchers and thinkers, not landscapers, gardeners and groundskeepers. As scholars we 'navigate' within or across disciplines, not yards, patios or 'intricate landscape[s]', to quote ChatGPT. Additionally, we do believe that AI's best days lie ahead, and thus encourage social researchers and others to adopt a 'forward-thinking mindset' about its future. But 'pav[ing] the way for a brighter, more equitable future' requires more than automated lip-service. We must work together to acknowledge the impact of the past, embrace the excitement of what is new, and formulate policies that protect us from hurt, harm and danger associated with AI's growth and development. To do anything less would be risky, unwise and, yes, non-human. It is true that AI can *mimic* humans but it cannot *be human*. Using rigorous research designs to study it will require proofreading, fact-checks, revisions, modifications, adjustments, hard work and good work. AI may be our future, but 'future' has two 'u', reminding us that humans – represented by 'yoU' and 'Us' – are integral to shaping and guiding this technology both today and tomorrow.

References

Acosta-Enriquez, B.G., Arbulú Ballesteros, M.A., Jordan, O.H., Roca, C.L. and Tirado, K.S. (2024) Analysis of college students' attitudes toward the use of ChatGPT in their academic activities: effect of intent to use, verification of information and responsible use. *BMC Psychology* 12: 255.

Ahmed, Z., Bhinder, K.K., Tariq, A., Tahir, M.J., Mehmood, Q. *et al.* (2022) Knowledge, attitude, and practice of artificial intelligence among doctors and medical students in Pakistan: a cross-sectional online survey. *Annals of Medicine and Surgery* 76: 103493.

Alharthi, H. (2020) Predicting the level of generalized anxiety disorder of the coronavirus pandemic among college age students using artificial intelligence technology. In: *2020 19th International Symposium on Distributed Computing and Applications for Business Engineering and Science (DCABES), 16–19 October 2020, Xuzhou, China*. IEEE, Piscataway, New Jersey, pp. 218–221.

Alimi, A.E., Buraimoh, O.F., Aladesusi, G.A. and Babalola, E.O. (2021) University students' awareness of, access to, and use of artificial intelligence for learning in Kwara state. *Indonesian Journal of Teaching in Science* 1, 91–104.

Alshurideh, M., Jdaitawi, A., Sukkari, L., Al-Gasaymeh, A., Alzoubi, H.M. *et al.* (2024) Factors affecting ChatGPT use in education employing TAM: a Jordanian universities' perspective. *International Journal of Data and Network Science* 8, 1599–1606.

Campbell, D.T. and Stanley, J.C. (2015) *Experimental and Quasi-experimental Designs for Research*. Houghton Mifflin Harcourt, Boston, Massachusetts.

Chai, C.S., Yu, D., King, R.B. and Zhou, Y. (2024) Development and validation of the artificial intelligence learning intention scale (AILIS) for university students. *SAGE Open* 14: 21582440241242188.

Davis, F.D. (1989) Perceived usefulness, perceived ease of use, and user acceptance of information technology. *MIS Quarterly* 13, 319–340.

Delello, J.A., Woonhee, S., Mokhtari, K. and Giuseppe, T.D. (2023) Exploring college students' awareness of AI and ChatGPT: unveiling perceived benefits and risks. *Journal of Inclusive Methodology and Technology in Learning and Teaching* 3, 1–25.

Fokina, M. (2024) The future of chatbots: 80+ statistics for 2025. Tidio blog. Available at: www.tidio.com/blog/chatbot-statistics/ (accessed 26 September 2024).

Fulmer, R., Joerin, A., Gentile, B., Lakerink, L. and Rauws, M. (2018) Using psychological artificial intelligence (Tess) to relieve symptoms of depression and anxiety: randomized controlled trial. *JMIR Mental Health* 5: e9782.

Han, J.W., Park, J. and Lee, H. (2022) Analysis of the effect of an artificial intelligence chatbot educational program on non-face-to-face classes: a quasi-experimental study. *BMC Medical Education* 22: 830.

Huang, M.-H. and Rust, R.T. (2018) Artificial intelligence in service. *Journal of Service Research* 21, 155–172.

Mathieson, K. (1991) Predicting user intentions: comparing the technology acceptance model with the theory of planned behavior. *Information Systems Research* 2, 173–191.

Mun, Y., Joyce, D.J., Jae, S.P. and Janice, C.P. (2006) Understanding information technology acceptance by individual professionals: toward an integrative view. *Information & Management* 43, 350–363.

Myers, J.L., Well, A.D. and Lorch, R.F. (2013) *Research Design and Statistical Analysis*, 3rd edn. Routledge, Abingdon, UK.

National University (2024) 131 AI statistics and trends for 2024. National University, San Diego, California. Available at: www.nu.edu/blog/ai-statistics-trends/#:~:text=AI%20and%20Education&text=10%25%20of%20educators%20think%20teaching,a%20top%20priority%20for%20schools.&text=33%25%20of%20educators%20say%20it%27s,teach%20AI%20technologies%20to%20students (accessed 26 September 2024).

Nielsen, J. (2023) AI Improves Employee Productivity by 66%. Nielsen Norman Group, Fremont, California. Available at: https://www.nngroup.com/articles/ai-tools-productivity-gains/ (accessed 8 October 2023).

Paul, L., John, I. and Pierre, C. (2003) Why do people use information technology? A critical review of the technology acceptance model. *Information & Management* 40, 191–204.

Rogers, E.M., Singhal, A. and Quinlan, M.M. (2014) Diffusion of innovations. In: D.W., Stacks and M.B, Salwen (eds) *An Integrated Approach to Communication Theory and Research*. Routledge, Abingdon, UK, pp. 432–448.

Rust, R.T. and Huang, M. (2014) The service revolution and the transformation of marketing science. *Marketing Science* 33, 206–221.

Sapio Research (2023) Study finds increase in cybersecurity attacks fueled by generative AI. *Security Magazine*. www.securitymagazine.com/articles/99832-study-finds-increase-in-cybersecurity-attacks-fueled-by-generative-ai#:~:text=The%20report%20reveals%2075%25%20of,bad%20actors%20using%20generative%20AI (accessed 26 September 2024).

Sudaryanto, M.R., Hendrawan, M.A. and Andrian, T. (2023) The effect of technology readiness, digital competence, perceived usefulness, and ease of use on accounting students artificial intelligence technology adoption. *E3S Web of Conferences* 388: 04055.

Venkatesh, V. and Davis, F.D. (1996) A model of the antecedents of perceived ease of use: development and test. *Decision Sciences* 27, 451–481.

Venkatesh, V. and Davis, F.D. (2000) A theoretical extension of the technology acceptance model: four longitudinal field studies. *Management Science* 46, 186–204.

Wahid, F. (2007) Using the technology adoption model to analyze internet adoption and use among men and women in Indonesia. *Electronic Journal of Information Systems in Developing Countries* 32, 1–8.

Wang, Y., Liu, C. and Tu, Y.-F. (2021) Factors affecting the adoption of AI-based applications in higher education: an analysis of teachers' perspectives using structural equation modeling. *Educational Technology & Society* 24, 116–129.

Webster, M. (2024) *149* AI statistics: the present and future of AI at your fingertips. Authority Hacker blog. Available at: https://www.authorityhacker.com/ai-statistics/ (accessed 26 September 2024).

11 Machine Learning Bias: Genealogy, Expression and Prevention

Theodoros Kouros[1]*, Zenonas Theodosiou[1,2] and Christos Themistocleous[3]
[1]Department of Communication & Internet Studies, Cyprus University of Technology, Limassol, Cyprus; [2]CYENS Centre of Excellence, Nicosia, Cyprus; [3]Department of Communication & Marketing, Cyprus University of Technology, Limassol, Cyprus

Abstract

Artificial intelligence (AI) is often seen as the product of an unbiased and objective development process. Human rationality is also commonly placed at the altar of intellect and frequently taken for granted. This chapter attempts to bridge three epistemological and disciplinary traditions to problematize these views, highlight the possible biases of machine learning, and AI at large, and ultimately offer preventive measures for social scientists working with AI either at the research design, implementation or publication stage. Departing from Foucauldian epistemology, which may highlight the inherent biases of AI by focusing on knowledge production, we move to cognitive psychology, which illustrates expressions of biases that may distort AI-generated content and its interpretations. We then conclude with relevant AI research that sheds light on the mechanisms that may produce said biases. As such, human biases and judgement misfires, which signal a departure from objectivity, can affect latent aspects of AI design and implementation.

Keywords: artificial intelligence, cognitive bias, discourse analysis, Foucault, heuristics

11.1 Introduction

After an elongated development process originating from Turing's test in the 1950s, artificial intelligence (AI) has recently reached the mainstream limelight in the form of OpenAI tools and sources. Having the ability to revolutionize data processing through added analytical complexity and data pattern recognition that would have remained undetected by conventional means, AI has many prospects in reinforcing social research. Albeit with paradigm-shifting potential, AI posits caveats that include the transfer of human biases in the machine learning (ML) process that can distort outputs upon which conclusions are drawn and decisions are made. By acknowledging these points of vulnerability, we intend to inform AI-using social researchers on the origins and implications of covert ML bias transfer and ultimately offer easy-to-use debiasing techniques and recommendations.

This chapter aims to highlight points of vulnerability of AI and provides recommendations for mitigating risks related to human biases. It starts with an epistemological and ontological review of how AI is positioned in the reductionism realm through a Foucauldian perspective, and how AI programming is inherently affected by biases that may be traced in social structures and power relationships. Next, it provides a review of human rationality as proposed by the two prominent schools of thought, and

*E-mail: theodoros.kouros@cut.ac.cy

DOI: 10.1079/9781800626607.0011

provides examples of human biases that descend from Kahneman and Tversky's heuristics and biases programme. Finally, a review of ML follows, together with the steps in the learning process that can be prone to the distortion of AI's objectivity when conducting social research, all while providing social researchers with a toolkit of debiasing techniques and strategies employable in a range of settings.

11.2 Towards a Genealogy of Bias in AI

11.2.1 The power–knowledge nexus and AI

'AI is Knowledge, and Knowledge is Power' was the title of a thought-provoking Forbes article published in November 2023 (Farbman, 2023). While discussing the ethical challenges surrounding AI, the article highlighted the critical need for public awareness about its potential misuse, including creating misleading content. However, much less attention has been paid to the potential inherent biases of AI that are not necessarily linked to misuse. From a Foucauldian perspective, these biases can be understood through key concepts such as power/knowledge and discourse. Foucault's work emphasizes the intertwined nature of knowledge and power, how discourses shape our perception of the world, and how power operates on bodies and populations through controlling technologies. His perspective on power and knowledge is crucial for understanding the biases in generative AI, making it an ideal theoretical foundation for this chapter. As a philosopher who focused on knowledge production in modern societies, Foucault's ideas are highly relevant. Generative AI, especially large language models, rely on existing knowledge to create new narratives. Consequently, many biases in AI are not due to faulty programming but are inherent in the existing bodies of knowledge and competing discourses. This chapter responds to calls to build on existing principles and frameworks, and considers the challenges of biases in AI (Leavy *et al.*, 2020), while presenting a multi-disciplinary account of the biases that may obfuscate social research data analysis and interpretation.

Bias and discrimination within AI are part of a longstanding history of inequality, rooted in how individuals are quantified, depicted and categorized within data sources (Hickman, 1997; Gillespie, 2014; Perez, 2019; Leavy *et al.*, 2020). Gillespie (2014) showed how algorithms can be seen as a 'new knowledge logic'. They aim to appear neutral or meritocratic but are influenced by particular interests, political conditions and so forth, all while being prone to bias and errors (Papa and Kouros, 2023; Kouros and Papa, 2024). A similar point of view can be adopted for AI, as previous research has highlighted. Leavy *et al.* (2020) warned that there is increasingly widespread acknowledgement of the impossibility of objectivity in data-driven AI, as attested by Broussard (2018) and O'Neil (2016). Dignum (2019) noted that bias is an unescapable trait of data collected from human processes, while Bartoletti (2020) stated that data are not neutral, and therefore every decision and action around data is deemed political.

From an anthropological perspective, AI can be comprehensively interpreted as a 'technosocial system' (Hagerty and Rubinov, 2019). This concept emphasizes the deep and inherent connection between AI's technological features and its social implications. The way we perceive, create and interact with AI is significantly influenced by our social values and assumptions. These cultural underpinnings also shape our expectations, aspirations and apprehensions regarding these technological advancements (Latour, 2005; Lash, 2007; Beer, 2009; Zuboff, 2015). In addition, Hagerty and Rubinov (2019) pointed out that research on AI is biased towards perspectives held in the USA, while, especially outside the USA and Western Europe, there is a notable lack of relevant research. In fact, an AI image generator (DALL-E 3) was prompted to 'generate a map of the world, where good countries are depicted in green and bad ones in red'. Figure 11.1 depicts the resulting image. The interesting outcome is that even though 'good' and 'bad' are not defined in our prompt in any way whatsoever, the outcome strongly favours a West-centric view of the world.

The key takeaway here is that AI is created by social actors with agency and cultural backgrounds, biases and positionalities. How knowledge and power are articulated in a given society will inevitably also influence how AI is articulated, created and interpreted.

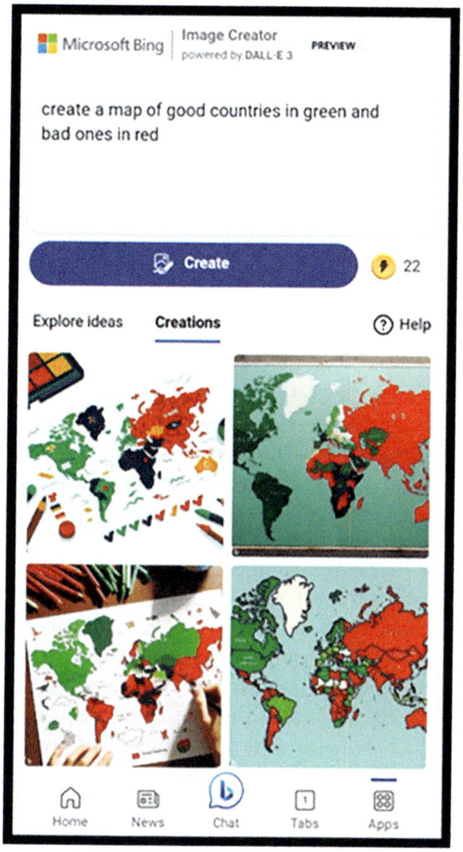

Fig. 11.1. 'Good' and 'bad' countries. Produced using a DALL-E 3 AI image generator.

This preference towards Western views of AI can be conceptualized from a Foucaldian perspective. According to Foucault (1990, 2016), knowledge is not impartial. Rather, it is created within power systems that dictate what is deemed true or false. AI algorithms, which are trained on datasets that reflect societal and historical biases, can perpetuate and intensify existing inequalities. These biases are not mere technical glitches but actual manifestations of power dynamics that prioritize certain types of knowledge over others. In the realm of AI, Foucault's concept of power/knowledge provides a valuable perspective for examining the interplay between technology, power and the shaping of knowledge. This viewpoint highlights the fact that AI is not an impartial tool for processing information but is instead entrenched within networks of power that influence its creation, implementation, and the types of knowledge it generates and reinforces.

The development and regulation of AI technologies involve a complex web of power dynamics between various stakeholders such as scientists, engineers, corporations, governments, funding bodies, citizens and consumers. The knowledge and information about AI, including its capabilities, benefits and risks, depend on these relationships and agendas. The direction of AI research is often influenced by funding institutions and corporations, which prioritize projects based on profitability and strategic interests. This dynamic shapes the understanding of AI and whose interests are served by this knowledge. Government policies and regulations also reflect certain views of AI and legitimize certain uses while restricting others. The paradigm of power and knowledge also plays a crucial role in determining the inclusivity and exclusivity of AI technologies, which, while offering immense potential for societal benefits (including advancements in agriculture, healthcare and education) have a significant downside: the propensity of AI systems to perpetuate and even exacerbate existing social inequalities.

Notable examples in the USA highlight the issue, including recruitment algorithms displaying bias against female candidates (Dastin, 2018), discriminatory lending practices encoded in algorithms affecting Latin and African-American individuals (Glantz and Martinez, 2018; Bartlett *et al.*, 2022), and biases related to race, gender and sexual orientation embedded within sentiment analysis, natural language processing tools and image recognition training datasets (Zou and Kalai, 2016). Collectively, these instances demonstrate a troubling trend where AI technologies disproportionately disadvantage historically marginalized, oppressed and vulnerable communities. The data processed, analysed and applied by AI reflect the biases and assumptions of those with power in these networks. Thus, AI can perpetuate social inequalities by prioritizing certain knowledge and marginalizing others. For instance, if an AI system is trained on a dataset lacking diversity, it may generate knowledge that misrepresents or fails to represent underrepresented groups. This entrenches biases into the very structure of AI systems, influencing decision-making processes in fields such as healthcare, criminal justice and employment.

Foucault's observation that power relationships are not just top-down but also lateral and bottom-up is highly relevant in the context of AI. Advocacy groups and users can push corporations and governments to adopt more transparent, ethical and accountable AI practices. When considering AI through the lens of Foucault's power/knowledge concept, it becomes evident that technology is not merely a means to enhance human capabilities but also a tool for exercising power and constructing knowledge. This highlights the importance of critically examining the power networks surrounding AI, questioning whose interests and knowledge are being prioritized, and exploring ways to reshape AI to promote more equitable and inclusive forms of power and knowledge. The use of AI in decision-making processes bestows these systems with a perceived objectivity and neutrality due to their technological nature. However, we would argue that this perceived authority actually represents a form of power that reinforces existing social norms and expectations, embedding current power structures within supposedly impartial algorithms.

11.2.2 Discourse and AI

While discourse is defined as written or spoken communication or debate, Foucault's concept of discourse (Kendall and Wickham, 1999), explains how language and practices shape knowledge and power. Foucauldian discourse refers to a social system that produces knowledge and meaning, shaping how we understand and organize information. Discourse is linked to the historical context and broader knowledge structure of its time, created and controlled by power within society. This power sets rules and categories that legitimize what is considered true and knowledgeable, making the discourse appear objective and timeless. As Foucault (1981, p. 52) puts it, 'In every society the production of discourse is at once controlled, selected, organized and redistributed by a certain number of procedures whose role is to ward off its powers and dangers, to gain mastery over its chance events, to evade its ponderous, formidable materiality.' AI technology plays a role in shaping discourses of objectivity, neutrality and efficiency. However, these discourses can obscure the biases inherent in AI systems, presenting them as unbiased tools rather than influenced by human values and power dynamics. Furthermore, AI systems can contribute to normalizing certain views or practices through their outputs, such as facial recognition technology perpetuating racial stereotypes. This normalization process is a form of power that Foucault recognizes as repeated patterns of thought or behaviour become entrenched in social practices.

The importance of discourse in the field of AI cannot be overstated. It not only helps us understand the technology better but also shapes its development and deployment. By drawing upon Foucault's ideas on discourse, we can see how discussions about AI have the power to shape public perception and technological progress. The commentary around AI helps reduce its ambiguity, giving it a clear purpose within societal discourse. This process is similar to Foucault's concept of commentary, restricting the open multiplicity of discourse and transferring novelty from the content of the text to the manner and context of its repetition. In the case of AI, this means that the innovative aspect lies not just in its technology but also in how it is interpreted and applied across different contexts. Similar to Foucault's (1981) argument that discourse shapes bodies and subjectivities by normalizing and homogenizing, the discourse on AI contributes to the normalization of expectations and assumptions about technology. This leads to the establishment of normative boundaries that guide the development of AI. Technologies that align with dominant discourses receive more attention and funding, while those that do not are marginalized or labelled as impractical or unethical.

Applying Foucault's approach to AI challenges us to question established narratives about the role and impact of AI in society. It encourages a critical examination of the assumptions underlying AI research and implementation, such as the inevitability of AI-driven progress or the neutrality of algorithms. This critical stance opens up space for alternative narratives that better account for the complexities and ethical considerations of AI. To put it succinctly, examining AI through the lens of Foucault's discourse theory provides a valuable framework for comprehending how narratives surrounding technology are formed and utilized to shape both technological progress and societal norms. It emphasizes the need to analyse AI discourse critically, not only to gain a better understanding of the technology itself but also to challenge the power dynamics it embodies and perpetuates. To view AI biases from a Foucauldian perspective is to recognize that these biases are not random or incidental to AI but are deeply ingrained in the knowledge and power structures that create and utilize these technologies. Such biases are indicative of broader societal patterns of control and domination, which AI unwittingly reinforces under the guise of impartiality and advancement.

All in all, the Foucauldian perspective focuses on the production of knowledge and the ontology of power in society. It highlights the ways power is diffused via unexpected avenues, such as AI applications, especially generative AI. However, this point of view is limited to the abstract, macro-sociological level. It may provide a sound understanding of the origins of bias in AI, but expressions of said biases require different approaches on the micro-level. Specifically, human cognitive biases that stem from the aforementioned power relations and social structures need to be recognized and the ways of their mitigation identified. The next section offers what the macro-approach is missing; a more micro-levelled approach that focuses on the ways humans are prone to biases, that is, the ways in which this power–knowledge nexus may affect daily judgements ultimately affecting interactions with AI. The next section reviews human rationality and specifically cognitive biases that can threaten the objectivity of ML processes.

11.3 Human Rationality and Biases

11.3.1 Two perspectives of human rationality

Albeit systematically studied in psychology, human rationality was questioned only recently in other fields of social research including economics, business and management. Investigations from the field of judgement and decision making brought forth a series of human biases that lead to suboptimal human decisions and systematic errors. Although capable of identifying patterns that would have remained undetected using conventional means, ML simulates human learning processes, thus sharing to a certain degree the aforementioned limitations.

For example, AI training that is based on a dataset that excludes individuals from certain demographic backgrounds is bound to generate non-representative results. Labelling a dataset in a way that reflects an investigator's overt or covert predispositions will lead to biased outputs reflective of those predispositions. The inclusion of survey questions that create framing effects with the aim of confirming a belief can lead to an AI being trained to point out patterns based on those biased beliefs. Mapping human biases is essential for understanding ML bias. Thus, this section reviews human rationality using two main lenses, namely the heuristics and biases and the bounded rationality programmes.

A pertinent investigation of human judgement and decision making stemmed from the work of Herbert Simon, who isolated human traits in organizational decisions that deviated from the dominant assumption of human rationality at the time. Simon (1955, 1956) identified that individuals' decisions aimed at 'satisficing', that is, to make decisions that are *not* meant to optimize and provide longitudinally sound solutions but instead satisfactory ones that sufficed at the time of problem solving, were influenced by the environment in which they were made. He labelled this as 'bounded rationality' and pointed out the fact that individuals use rules of thumb in making efficient decisions. Building upon his work, psychologists Daniel Kahneman and Amos Tversky examined these rules of thumb that they called 'heuristics'. They aimed to delineate their use, bringing forward in the process systematic and predictable errors (Tversky and Kahneman, 1974). Their work prompted future research to build upon their examinations by identifying occasions where heuristics can lead to systematic errors, coining this research line the 'heuristics and biases' programme.

On the other side, the bounded rationality programme sees human rationality from another angle. The program acknowledges the bounds of human rationality but focuses more on the examination of occasions where heuristics can be more frugal in decision making than complicated analytical models of thinking. The argument is that time and energy are preserved through the use of simple rules of thumb that can be equally as good, and in certain cases better, than complicated prediction models (i.e. Gigerenzer and Goldstein, 1996; Gigerenzer, 2014).

Both programmes see Herbert's bounded rationality as a reservable image, with some authors going as far as to call this disagreement 'rationality wars' (Samuels *et al.*, 2002; Sturm, 2012). Heuristics remain the epitome of the dispute, and arguments focus on whether policy makers and social infrastructure should invest in reinforcing and nurturing heuristics or accepting them as useful yet error-prone and thus requiring (libertarian) paternalistic assistance through recommendations, for improving decisions made by them. The latter refers to 'nudges' (Thaler and Sunstein, 2008), behavioural interventions that steer decisions, with the tool's application finding its way in a variety of contexts including electricity consumption, tax compliance and information divulgence (Loewenstein *et al.*, 2014; Themistocleous *et al.*, 2014), yet with its effectiveness remaining under academic scrutiny (Mertens *et al.*, 2022).

Interestingly, and albeit not readily visible, important points of agreement between the two programmes are present. Gigerenzer acknowledges the significance of identifying predictable biases and errors, yet is sceptical of the simplified explanations that are attributed to the three main heuristics of availability, representativeness and anchoring proposed by Kahneman and Tverdky. Gigerenzer's call for 'time to plant theories' (Gigerenzer, 1996, p. 596) was, arguably, headed by Kahneman's dual-system theory in his book with a reflective title, *Thinking, Fast and Slow* (Kahneman, 2011). The theory posits that our thinking is served by two cognitive systems, 1 and 2. System 1 is fast, efficient and intuitive yet error-prone, and system 2 is slow, analytical and careful yet effortful. Heuristics are primarily linked to system 1, and thus many biases emerge from this fast-thinking process.

Research in AI is slowly examining the links between the two systems and AI (Kelly and Barron, 2022) and how system 1-emerging biases that affect social researchers and AI programmers can ultimately affect the program (AI). For a thorough review and prior to biasing the program, we examine the biases of the programmer. Certain pervasive human biases that have direct implications for social researchers and consequently for AI training and use, are reviewed next.

11.3.2 Human biases and errors

Representativeness bias

Representativeness bias stems from our representativeness heuristic and occurs when we erroneously associate something with a representative social prototype when making a judgement. Seeing, for example, a man in his 30s wearing a suit can lead to judgements pertaining to social stereotypes of him being a lawyer. Scheduled to meet two of your friend's ex-classmates for the first time, one of which is a poet and the other is a chemist, might lead to a judgement misfire when you heuristically associate the one wearing colourful clothes with the poet and the one with the dull shirt as the chemist. In reality, they happen to be the opposite. Judgements here assign an identity based on social representative prototypes of artists being more eccentric in their fashion choices than chemists, a generally valid but occasionally wrong judgement.

Representativeness is quite pervasive and socially constructed perceptions such as what the average doctor looks like, and which countries are associated with being 'bad' (see Fig. 11.1), as well as associations between genders and professions have a strong presence in human decisions. As such, representativeness can lead to over- or under-reported cases as the sample on which AI training is based and ultimately lead to biased AI outputs and exacerbating discriminatory effects. For example, Manyika *et al.* (2019) reported that a criminal justice AI would mislabel African-Americans as 'high risk' at twice the rate as that of white people being mislabelled.

Confirmation and framing biases

Confirmation bias relates to the innate human tendency to look for and interpret information that confirms predisposed beliefs. An AI programmer might covertly direct the system to coincide with pre-existing expectations. An example relates to the process of dataset synthesis and how the framing of questions nudges respondents to align with the researcher's beliefs. Consider the following example:

> Do you agree with Rolls Royce closing down their Derbyshire factories, putting thousands of workers out of employment?

The question is framed to steer responses by highlighting the negative effects of the factory closure and associates guilt with agreement to the statement. This prompts individuals to disagree with Rolls Royce, thus recording responses that confirm a potential predisposition. Note that confirmation bias can also be reflected by framing a question to reflect positive effects that are in agreement with another researcher's beliefs:

> Do you agree with Rolls Royce closing down their Derbyshire factories to fund R&D for greener jet engines?

Bias mitigation here is essential, as dataset synthesis requires the use of neutrally framed questions mitigating both confirmation and framing biases:

> Do you agree with Rolls Royce closing down their Derbyshire factories?

Other than question framing, we note that measurement scales through which answers are recorded can promote other biases including response and social desirability bias. As such, careful selection of response categories for Likert or semantic differential scales as well as incorporating interval-valued scales can assist with mitigating the latter (Preston and Colman, 2000; Themistocleous *et al.*, 2019).

Confirmation bias is also prevalent in the post-ML process and when AI outputs are interpreted. Particular weight might be put on interpreting data attempting to confirm beliefs and fulfil expectations paying little attention to, or avoiding altogether, alternative interpretations that are more sound than the ones being confirmed. For example, believing that hard work yields success can lead managers to interpret their store's poor performance as the personnel's lack of hard work. In the process, they might dismiss (AI) recommendations pertaining to reduction of charged prices due to price elasticity or a socio-demographic change of served customer and the need for brand repositioning.

Selection errors and survivorship bias

Survivorship bias refers to the type of error where cases that survived a selection process are erroneously seen to constitute a representative sample of a larger population. Survivorship bias is a type of selection bias where AI training, analyses and subsequent conclusions are drawn on an already biased dataset and sample.

To demonstrate, imagine a grocery shop having an equal portion of young, middle-aged and older customers. The shop wants to measure their customer's satisfaction. In doing so, during check-out the cashiers ask customers to complete the survey through the shop's mobile phone app. The platform through which responses are collated is bound to be more accessible to younger and middle-aged audiences rather than retirees who are less likely to be familiar with apps. Thus, they are less likely to complete the survey, although they represent a significant portion of the population. As such, feedback is collected primarily from young and middle-aged individuals, making it less representative of the older customer cohort. Consequently, this provides little information of the true satisfaction levels, while accessibility problems, which older individuals would have been more prone to identify, are never recorded. Conclusions drawn from this sample lead to non-representative-of-the-population satisfaction levels while recommendations and feedback on issues affecting older customers are not recorded. An AI trained using this data can create a false sense of high performance that is based on an undetected sampling error, thus accidentally silencing a portion of the population.

The heuristics and biases programme highlights numerous biases stemming from our heuristics, and how they can influence different stages of ML models. The chapter up to this point has focused on human rationality and transitions next to system rationality. The following section reviews ML training processes, identifies common procedural points of vulnerability in the learning process, reviews additional biases and proposes ways of mitigation.

11.4 ML and Biases

Designing methods that give a system the ability to learn is a multifaceted endeavour and a crucial process for the success of AI. In the field of cognitive systems, learning refers to either permanent changes in the system's knowledge or behaviour through experience, and is related to two properties: (i) the ability to acquire knowledge while interacting with the environment; and (ii) the ability to improve the way an action is performed through repetition. Integral to this process is the creation of models or patterns extracted from datasets, enabling systems to discern underlying structures and make informed decisions. These principles form the pillars for developing smart systems capable of adapting and growing according to the environment, mimicking the learning processes observed in humans.

Several ML algorithms, including deep-learning algorithms, are trained using examples and create models that store the acquired knowledge. Discrimination has been identified as one of the major problems in the behaviour of ML models that may provide disparate services to humans according to their demographics such as race, age, sex, gender and socio-economic status (Bandy, 2021). This stems from biases that can be built into ML models at any stage of their development including the creation, training and testing of data, as well as during the learning and deployment phases. According to the framework proposed by Suresh and Guttag (2021), the dataset is prone to existing biases and social stereotypes, as well as to new biases arising from the data collection and annotation process. Learning is related to biases inserted from the ML algorithms, imbalanced training data and unrepresentative testing benchmarks. Additional biases may be observed when utilizing the model, and especially if it is used in a way that is different from what it was designed for.

The dataset given in the input of an ML algorithm plays an important role in the output result, which is evaluated according to the quality and quantity of its samples. Depending on the type of learning – supervised or unsupervised – the data should be annotated or not. In most cases, the datasets used to train ML models are created by humans (i.e. collected and annotated by humans or by systems developed by humans). Therefore, any human biases can be reflected in the resulting datasets.

Biases associated with the creation of training datasets can be classified as selection biases, framing biases and annotation biases (Fabbrizzi *et al.*, 2022). As mentioned in the previous section, selection biases involve the disparities or associations that are related to the process of selecting the data. For example, human datasets may include imbalanced data for different demographics, resulting in ML models failing to correctly classify unknown data into appropriate groups (Buolamwini and Gebru, 2018). Likewise, the disparities or associations related to how the data are composed and interpreted are defined as framing biases. Depicting headless human bodies in advertisements or news articles can be seen as an example of framing bias when used as training examples (Heuer *et al.*, 2011). Finally, the biases that are related to the annotation process are characterized as annotation biases. Annotation is an anthropocentric process, which depends on the subjectivity of the annotator, bringing their own experiences and biases into the result. As shown by Kafkalias *et al.* (2022), the performance of ML models is directly correlated to the demographics of the annotators, where the same annotations can even in some cases help to predict the demographics of the annotators.

Human understanding of the algorithm's logic by which a ML model was trained to return a specific output for a given input is a current challenge in the field of AI, yet mitigation tactics that are founded on simple rules can enhance the quality of AI outputs.

11.4.1 Mitigating ML biases

The difficulty of human interpretation and the lack of transparency of ML algorithms is known as the black-box problem. The latter refers to specific outputs given by the algorithm without being able to explain why. The explainability of ML models and the black box problem solving are at the forefront of eliminating or mitigating biases. Due to the complex methods used to correlate the large amount of input data with the output, illumination of the black box can lead to revealing the biases inserted at each stage of the algorithm. Research efforts focusing on the interpretability of ML models can be categorized into those that can be explained by humans or by mathematical structures (Tjoa and Guan, 2021). At the same time, Hassija *et al.* (2023)

referred to further factors affecting interpretability such as the complex architecture of the model and its characteristics.

The behaviour of algorithms and created models depends directly on the data used in the training step as well as the biases they may incorporate. Biases inserted using the model can influence both user decisions and new data that may be automatically created to train new ML models. In addition to biases inserted from data and learning, Mehrabi *et al.* (2021) also reported biases arising using unfair AI systems. These biases arise from the user interface (Friedman and Nissenbaum, 1996), interaction between users and the popularity of publicly available information (Nematzadeh *et al.*, 2017).

Addressing biases effectively is critical in creating transparent and fair systems that successfully leverage the latest advances of AI. Using unbiased data and fair learning methods are undeniably key components to developing fair ML models. Table 11.1 summarizes certain common biases together with remarks and ways of mitigation. We have categorized ten distinct biases based on the stage of the ML process in which they have the highest likelihood of occurring. These stages are data creation, learning and deployment. We provide respective suggestions and examples for each to delineate their type.

The development of a fair and transparent ML model requires a systematic approach, including analysis, design, development, testing, evaluation and life-cycle support. Both the need to create a new model and the problem it is intended to solve must be clear from the beginning. Mitigation of the biases should be considered in the requirement gathering and analysis step to properly design the model. The appropriate available dataset should be selected with limited potential for inserting biases. In the case of creating a new one, the process should be properly designed, considering possible biases that can be inserted at each step. During the development process, appropriate learning techniques should be chosen to avoid disparities in performance between different examples of the dataset in the final output. However, there are various biases that cannot be predicted or mitigated at the development step because they are inserted when using the model, such as those observed in web applications including user interaction and population bias.

11.5 Conclusion

The perceptions of humans operating in an imperfect world are influenced by power structures and discourses. Heuristics on which we rely to form judgements and make decisions can be frugal yet also prone to systematic errors. AI can assist with managing human biases and reducing noise in judgements in the legal, medical and other sectors. Yet it is far from being error free. Acknowledging human limitations is the first step in addressing AI biases. The proposed mapping of prevalent human biases and the identification of ML stages they correspond to, as well as simple recommendations on how to reduce them, can provide social researchers with an informative blueprint on what to bear in mind when operating with AI. This chapter has explored the ways in which biases materialize within AI systems, stressing the extensive impact that human rationality and also socio-cultural dynamics have on AI development. By incorporating Foucauldian epistemology and cognitive psychology together with AI research, we have illustrated the diverse nature of biases – from their foundation to their expressions in human cognition and finally their reproduction through technological procedures.

The Foucauldian point of view has highlighted how power, knowledge and discourse are woven together within the context of AI, which is not merely a technical endeavour but is deeply embedded in societal structures that influence what is considered valuable and objective knowledge. This implies that biases inherent in AI are not simple technological flaws or glitches but representations of broader social injustices, as well as power discrepancies. Cognitive psychology offers comprehensive understandings into the kinds of biases that affect human decision making. Biases such as representativeness, confirmation and survivorship do not remain restricted to human judgement; they seep into the information that trains AI systems. Comprehending these biases permits us to recognize exactly how AI can enhance human biases. In the realm of AI and ML research, biases are introduced at multiple stages – from data collection and model training to algorithm deployment. As such, results in AI systems can discriminate based on race, gender, socio-economic status and other

Table 11.1. Types of bias and proposed mitigation methods.

Step	Name	Definition	Example	Suggestions
Dataset creation	Historical bias	When the data used to train an AI system no longer accurately reflects the current reality.	An AI hiring system that learns from previous applications may perpetuate gender inequalities as men will appear more suitable.	An appropriate population is needed for the dataset creation. Up-to-date developments should always be kept in mind.
	Selection bias	A bias in the selection of data for training machine learning models.	In 2016, a New Zealander of Asian descent had his passport photo rejected when the automated facial recognition software registered his eyes as being closed. This occurred because the software was trained primarily with Caucasian users (Reuters, 2016).	Uniform distribution among the categories of data. Demographic consistency checks during and after the selection process. Use of random sampling.
	Framing bias	The manner in which data is presented can affect the interpretation or decision making.	The depiction of headless obese people compared with non-obese people on major US online news sites (Heuer *et al.*, 2011).	Fair management of different aspects of the data. Use of neutral questions and avoidance of leading ones.
	Annotation bias	The bias introduced to the annotated data from annotators, and/or semantic categories, and/or the annotation process.	The attributes of the annotators affect the ML decision in image interpretation tasks (Kafkalias *et al.*, 2022).	Well-defined semantic categories. Clear instruction and precise communication. Sufficient and diverse set of annotators. Suitable method for collecting annotations.
Learning	Aggregation bias	The bias introduced into the model when the training data is not representative of the respective groups.	If the training data given to create a model for a particular group of people contain individual characteristics that were not taken into account, then the created model will not be optimal for the group it represents (Suresh and Guttag, 2021).	Consistent mapping between the data in the training set and the category they represent.
	Learning bias	The bias created when the learning method chosen aims to give the desirable yet biased output.	The use of techniques for reducing the size of the model can increase performance disparities in data with under-represented features (Hooker *et al.*, 2020).	Learning choices for equal performance among data categories.

	Evaluation bias	The bias created when the ML model is evaluated using an irrelevant testing dataset.	The low classification accuracy for dark-skinned females observed while evaluating a classification model that was trained with a dataset including mostly light-skinned individuals (Buolamwini and Gebru, 2018).	Use of a set of dataset that will be representative of the classes the model was trained on. Sufficient number of observations to properly evaluate the accuracy of the model.
Deployment	Deployment bias	The bias that occurs when the model was created for another purpose than the one it is used for.	The example presented for selection bias, where a system trained to identify Caucasians was used to identify passengers from other races and thus was unable to identify a passenger of Asian descent (Reuters, 2016).	The model should be used exclusively and only for the purpose for which it was designed and developed.
	User interface bias	The bias created by the design and content of a user interface that affects the user behaviour and choices.	Search engines that rely on user behaviour and choices to improve their services and promote products to users.	The design of the interface should be done with care and its content should be well chosen, taking into account both current and future needs.

demographic factors. Addressing these issues requires meticulous attention to the design, implementation and continual evaluation of AI systems.

The insights gathered from this interdisciplinary examination underscore the necessity for a conscientious approach to AI development. Stakeholders, including developers, policy makers and the public, must be vigilant and proactive in addressing the ethical implications of AI. This involves not only technical adjustments but also a robust dialogue about the societal values that AI should uphold. In conclusion, while AI offers transformative potential across various sectors, its development is inherently entangled with human biases and societal values. A critical understanding of these factors, guided by interdisciplinary research, is essential for advancing AI technologies that are not only innovative but also equitable and just. By addressing these challenges head on, the course of AI can be steered towards a future that reflects our collective ethical standards and social commitments.

References

Bandy, J. (2021) Problematic machine behavior: a systematic literature review of algorithm audits. *Proceedings of the ACM on Human–Computer Interaction* 5: 74.

Bartlett, R., Morse, A., Stanton, R. and Wallace, N. (2022) Consumer-lending discrimination in the FinTech era. *Journal of Financial Economics* 143, 30–36.

Bartoletti, I. (2020) *An Artificial Revolution: On Power, Politics and AI*. Indigo Press, London.

Beer, D. (2009) Power through the algorithm? Participatory web cultures and the technological unconscious. *New Media & Society* 11, 985–1002.

Broussard, M. (2018) *Artificial Unintelligence: How Computers Misunderstand the World*. MIT Press, Cambridge, Massachusetts.

Buolamwini, J. and Gebru, T. (2018) Gender shades: intersectional accuracy disparities in commercial gender classification. *Proceedings of Machine Learning Research* 81, 77–91.

Dastin, J. (2018) Amazon Scraps Secret AI Recruiting Tool that Showed Bias against Women. Reuters. Available at: www.reuters.com/article/idUSKCN1MK0AG (accessed 3 October 2024).

Dignum, V. (2019) *Responsible Artificial Intelligence: How to Develop and Use AI in a Responsible Way*. Springer, Cham, Switzerland.

Fabbrizzi, S., Papadopoulos, S., Ntoutsi, E. and Kompatsiaris, I. (2022) A survey on bias in visual datasets. *Computer Vision and Image Understanding* 223: 103552.

Farbman, Z. (2023) Council Post: AI Is Knowledge, and Knowledge Is Power. Forbes. Available at: www.forbes.com/sites/forbestechcouncil/2023/11/29/ai-is-knowledge-and-knowledge-is-power/ (accessed 3 October 2024).

Foucault, M. (1981) The order of discourse. In: Young, R. (ed.) *Untying the Text: A Post-Structuralist Reader*. Routledge & Kegan Paul, Abingdon, UK., pp. 48–78.

Foucault, M. (1990) *The History of Sexuality. Volume* I: *An Introduction*. Vintage Books, New York.

Foucault, M. (2016) *Discipline and Punish: The Birth of the Prison*. Routledge, Abingdon, UK.

Friedman, B. and Nissenbaum, H. (1996) Bias in computer systems. *ACM Transactions on Information Systems* 14, 330–347.

Gigerenzer, G. (1996) On narrow norms and vague heuristics: a reply to Kahneman and Tversky. *Psychological Review* 103, 592–596.

Gigerenzer, G. (2014) *Risk Savvy: How to Make Good Decisions*. Penguin, London.

Gigerenzer, G. and Goldstein, D.G. (1996) Reasoning the fast and frugal way: models of bounded rationality. *Psychological Review* 103, 650–669.

Gillespie, T. (2014) The relevance of algorithms. In: *Media Technologies: Essays on Communication, Materiality, and Society*. MIT Press, Cambridge, Massachusetts, pp. 167–193.

Glantz, A. and Martinez, E. (2018) Kept Out: How Banks Block People of Color from Homeownership. *Associated Press*. Available at: https://apnews.com/ae4b40a720b74ad8a9b0bfe65f7a9c29 (accessed 3 October 2024).

Hagerty, A. and Rubinov, I. (2019) Global AI ethics: a review of the social impacts and ethical implications of artificial intelligence. arXiv preprint. Available at: https://arxiv.org/abs/1907.0789 (accessed 3 October 2024).

Hassija, V., Chamola, V., Mahapatra, A., Singal, A., Goel, D. *et al.* (2023) Interpreting black-box models: a review on explainable artificial intelligence. *Cognitive Computation* 16, 45–74.
Heuer, C.A., McClure, K.J. and Puhl, M.R. (2011) Obesity stigma in online news: a visual content analysis. *Journal of Health Communication* 16, 976–987.
Hickman, C.B. (1997) The devil and the one drop rule: racial categories, African Americans, and the U.S. census. *Michigan Law Review* 95, 1161–1265.
Hooker, S., Moorosi, N., Clark, G., Bengio, S. and Denton, E. (2020) Characterising bias in compressed models. arXiv preprint. Available at: https://arxiv.org/abs/2010.03058 (accessed 3 October 2024).
Kafkalias, A., Herodotou, S., Theodosiou, Z. and Lanitis, A. (2022) Bias in face image classification machine learning models: the impact of annotator's gender and race. In: *IFIP Advances in Information and Communication Technology* 647, 89–100.
Kahneman, D. (2011) *Thinking, Fast and Slow*. Penguin, London.
Kelly, M. and Barron, A. (2022) The best of both worlds: dual systems of reasoning in animals and AI. *Cognition* 225: 105118.
Kendall, G. and Wickham, G. (1999) *Using Foucault's Methods*. Sage Publications, Thousand Oaks, California.
Kouros, T. and Papa, V. (2024) Digital mirrors: AI companions and the self. *Societies* 14(10), 200.
Lash, S. (2007) Power after hegemony: cultural studies in mutation? *Theory, Culture & Society* 24, 55–78.
Latour, B. (2005) *Reassembling the Social: An Introduction to Actor-Network-Theory*. Oxford University Press, New York.
Leavy, S., O'Sullivan, B. and Siapera, E. (2020) Data, power and bias in artificial intelligence. arXiv preprint. Available at: https://arxiv.org/abs/2008.07341 (accessed 3 October 2024).
Loewenstein, G., Sunstein, C.R. and Golman, R. (2014) Disclosure: psychology changes everything. *Annual Review of Economics* 6, 391–419.
Manyika, J., Silberg, J. and Presten, B. (2019) What do we do about the biases in AI? *Harvard Business Review*. Available at: https://hbr.org/2019/10/what-do-we-do-about-the-biases-in-ai (accessed 3 October 2024).
Mehrabi, N., Morstatter, F., Saxena, N., Lerman, K. and Galstyan, A. (2021) A survey on bias and fairness in machine learning. *ACM Computing Surveys* 54: 115.
Mertens, S., Herberz, M., Hahnel, J.J. and Brosch, T. (2022) The effectiveness of nudging: a meta-analysis of choice architecture interventions across behavioral domains. *Proceedings of the National Academy of Sciences USA* 119: e2107346118.
Nematzadeh, A., Ciampaglia, L.G., Menczer, F. and Flammini, A. (2017) How algorithmic popularity bias hinders or promotes quality. *Scientific Reports* 8: 15951.
O'Neil, C. (2016) *Weapons of Math Destruction: How Big Data Increases Inequality and Threatens Democracy*. Broadway Books, New York.
Papa, V. and Kouros, T. (2023) Do Facebook and Google care about journalism? Mapping the relationship between affordances of GNI and FJP tools and journalistic norms. *Digital Journalism* 11, 1475–1498.
Perez, C.C., (2019) *Invisible Women: Data Bias in a World Designed for Men*. Abrams, New York.
Preston, C.C. and Colman, A.M. (2000) Optimal number of response categories in rating scales: reliability, validity, discriminating power, and respondent preferences. *Acta Psychologica* 104, 1–15.
Reuters (2016) New Zealand Passport Robot Tells Applicant of Asian Descent to Open Eyes. *Reuters*. Available at: www.reuters.com/article/us-newzealand-passport-error-idUSKBN13W0RL (accessed 3 October 2024).
Samuels, R., Stich, S. and Bishop, M. (2002) Ending the rationality wars: how to make disputes about human rationality disappear. In: Elio, R. (ed.) *Common Sense, Reasoning and Rationality*. Oxford University Press, New York, pp. 236–268.
Simon, H.A. (1955) A behavioral model of rational choice. *Quarterly Journal of Economics* 69, 99–118.
Simon, H.A. (1956) Rational choice and the structure of the environment. *Psychological Review* 63, 129–138.
Sturm, T. (2012) The "rationality wars" in psychology: where they are and where they could go. *Inquiry* 55, 66–81.
Suresh, H. and Guttag, J. (2021) A framework for understanding sources of harm throughout the machine learning life cycle. In: *Equity and Access in Algorithms, Mechanisms, and Optimization (EAAMO '21), 5–9 October 2021, New York*. Association for Computing Machinery, New York.
Thaler, R. and Sunstein, C. (2008) *Nudge Improving Decisions About Wealth, and Happiness*. Penguin, London.
Themistocleous, C., Smith, A. and Wagner, C. (2014) The ethical dilemma of implicit vs explicit data collection: examining the factors that influence the voluntary disclosure of information by consumers to commercial

organizations. In: *2014 IEEE International Symposium on Ethics in Science, Technology and Engineering*, Chicago, Illinois. IEEE, Piscataway, New Jersey, pp. 1–6,

Themistocleous, C., Pagiaslis, A., Smith, A. and Wagner, C. (2019) A comparison of scale attributes between interval-valued and semantic differential scales. *International Journal of Market Research* 61, 394–407.

Tjoa, E. and Guan, C. (2021) A survey on explainable artificial intelligence (XAI): toward medical XAI. *IEEE Transactions on Neural Networks and Learning Systems* 32, 4793–4813.

Tversky, A. and Kahneman, D. (1974) Judgment under uncertainty: heuristics and biases. *Science* 185, 1124–1131.

Zou, V.S. and Kalai, A.T. (2016) Man is to computer programmer as woman is to homemaker? Debiasing word embeddings. In: Jordan, M.I., LeCun, Y. and Solla, S.A. (eds) *Advances in Neural Information Processing Systems*. MIT Press, Cambridge, Massachusetts, pp. 4349–4357.

Zuboff, S. (2015) Big other: surveillance capitalism and the prospects of an information civilization. *Journal of Information Technology* 30, 75–89.

12 Rigour in Qualitative and Quantitative Studies that Make Use of Tools: Reliability, Validity, Credibility, Transferability, Dependability and Confirmability Issues

Prokopis A. Christou*
Cyprus University of Technology, Limassol, Cyprus

Abstract
This chapter emphasizes the importance of maintaining strict standards and particularly 'rigour' in research that makes use of AI at any stage of the research process. The chapter provides insights of AI in social research from a 'rigour' theoretical perspective. It progresses by dealing specifically with notions linked to the establishment of rigour in both qualitative and quantitative studies that make use of AI technological means. Issues linked to credibility, transferability, dependability, confirmability, reliability and validity are discussed, while specific suggestions and guidelines are provided for each of these issues, to ensure that any research or study that makes use of AI means adheres to rigorous standards.

Keywords: AI, credibility, confirmability, dependability, reliability, rigour, transferability, validity

12.1 Introduction: The Importance of Rigour in Social Research

The foundation of methodological integrity and precision in social research lies in rigour. Köhler *et al.* (2017, p. 173) defined rigour as 'consistency in conceptual development, epistemological stance, application of analytical tools and transparent reporting of their use, and subsequent interpretation and reporting of findings'. The process involves the methodical, thorough and careful use of different research techniques to guarantee the precision and dependability of the results of any qualitative and/or quantitative study (Johnson *et al.*, 2020; Maula and Stam, 2020; Pesämaa *et al.*, 2021).

The intricate nature of human behaviour and social interactions necessitates the challenging yet crucial application of rigour (Reio, 2021). Essentially, it serves as a protector of quality and reliability, allowing researchers and analysts to navigate the complexities of social phenomena and extract insights that accurately represent the true essence of these phenomena. In addition, rigour is a crucial factor in promoting the progress of theoretical development in any field, including the social sciences field. This is very important as it guarantees that the theories and models formulated are founded on methodically collected and analysed evidence. This facilitates the advancement of social science disciplines, allowing a more profound comprehension of societal structures, relationships and complicated

*E-mail: Prokopis.christou@cut.ac.cy

DOI: 10.1079/9781800626607.0012

processes. None the less, rigour is crucial in the replication of research (Cohen, 2017). The capacity to 'reproduce' studies and achieve consistent outcomes is fundamental to the entirety of the scientific process in social research. Adhering to rigorous research methodologies guarantees that studies can be replicated and verified, thereby confirming the reliability of the findings and enabling the gradual advancement of a consistent and strong body of knowledge.

Moreover, the endeavour to achieve rigour in social research is essential for upholding ethical research standards (Onwuegbuzie and Corrigan, 2014). This is because it entails a dedication to openness, responsibility and moral deliberation, especially when addressing delicate subjects within the social domain.

Conceivably, the significance of rigour in social research extends well beyond the boundaries of academic realms (Gregory and Martin, 1994). Essentially, rigorous research acts as a reliable source of truth, providing guidance to decision makers, policy makers and practitioners as they work towards dealing with or resolving various social issues. When social research is conducted with stringent criteria, the results offer a solid basis for the development of effective policies and interventions (Bryman *et al.*, 2008). Research findings have a direct impact on the lives of individuals and communities in critical areas such as public health, education, social justice, business, tourism and economic development. Furthermore, maintaining a high level of rigour in social research assists in cultivating public trust and confidence in the process of scientific inquiry. Through maintaining rigorous standards, researchers guarantee the durability and validity of their work, thus making valuable contributions to a reliable body of knowledge.

12.2 AI in Social Research: A 'Rigorous' Viewpoint

The introduction of AI tools and means in research methodologies requires a stronger focus on rigour (Christou, 2023a), especially in the field of social research. As AI provides enhanced or novel methods for gathering, analysing and interpreting various forms and/or extensive quantities of data (Vlačić *et al.*, 2021; Chubb *et al.*, 2022), it becomes crucial to prioritize rigour in order to uphold the integrity and relevance of research discoveries. Indeed, the integration of AI tools introduces novel aspects and intricacies, necessitating the meticulous implementation of stringent standards within differing fields of the social sciences (Cheng *et al.*, 2021; Heilinger, 2022). For instance, Lévesque *et al.* (2022) concluded that incorporating the power of AI in entrepreneurship research and managing the associated risks offer new challenges for the field.

The incorporation of readily available AI tools and means in social research emphasizes the necessity for increased precision, particularly considering the dynamic and intricate characteristics of AI technologies. AI systems, with their advanced data-handling capabilities, present unique challenges in maintaining the integrity and validity of research findings when applied in research. It is therefore crucial to maintain strict standards when utilizing these AI tools in order to uphold research quality. In more detail, an overarching issue regarding the utilization of AI tools in research is the possibility of inherent biases being present (Mehrabi *et al.*, 2021; Gichoya *et al.*, 2023). Such biases could stem from the datasets used to train the AI tools or from their design and functionality. In this context, rigorous research involves a meticulous assessment of the results produced by these AI tools, guaranteeing that the derived conclusions are ultimately not affected by concealed biases. In addition, the utilization of AI tools can occasionally obscure the research process, giving rise to concerns regarding transparency and the ability to reproduce the results of a given study. As explained in the following sections in more detail, to ensure rigour in research that utilizes any form of AI technology, it is imperative to meticulously document the utilization of these tools, encompassing their precise use by the researcher, as well as other important information, such as, for example, their algorithms and the characteristics of the data they analyse (Christou, 2023b). Precise documentation is crucial to enhance the comprehensiveness of the conclusions reached, enable replication of the study by other researchers, and make the findings accessible to a wide range of individuals and bodies, including non-experts in the field of AI. None the less, the swift advancement of AI technology necessitates that researchers consistently remain updated and knowledgeable about the most recent advancements and ethical considerations (Nassar and Kamal, 2021; Kamila and Jasrotia, 2025). Maintaining rigour in this context entails both adhering to established research standards and remaining adaptable and vigilant regarding the potential impact of various AI tools and capabilities on research outcomes. Overall, the implementation of AI tools in social research introduces additional layers of intricacy, necessitating a strengthened dedication to meticulousness. This involves a meticulous and discerning utilization of these instruments, guaranteeing openness and flexibility to technological progress, thus preserving the dependability, ethical soundness and societal significance of research within the social sciences.

12.3 Ensuring Rigour in Qualitative Research that Uses AI Tools and Means

Rigour has been thoroughly and extensively covered as well as debated within the qualitative research domain (Krefting, 1991; Sandelowski, 1993; Grodal *et al.*, 2021). It is that crucial element in qualitative social research that guarantees the credibility, transferability, dependability and confirmability of any study of qualitative nature, with researchers (e.g. Johnson *et al.*, 2020) insisting on and calling for enhancing rigour in qualitative research.

12.3.1 Credibility

Credibility refers to the level of confidence one can have in the accuracy and truthfulness of the research findings, as perceived by the research participants. In qualitative research, credibility can be established by employing certain techniques (Patton, 1999; Barbour, 2003; Liao and Hitchcock, 2018; Shufutinsky, 2020) such as prolonged engagement, which involves dedicating ample time to fully comprehend the context, as well as triangulation, which entails using multiple methods or sources to corroborate the findings, and member checking, whereby participants review and validate the researchers' interpretations. This procedure guarantees that the research findings precisely mirror the participants' experiences and viewpoints, thereby augmenting the credibility of the qualitative study. The essence of credibility in qualitative research lies in guaranteeing that the findings reflect the participants' opinions, experiences and perspectives.

To uphold credibility standards, it is necessary to follow certain strategies when incorporating AI tools into the research process, such as comprehending the abilities but also the constraints of AI tools, being transparent in reporting (e.g. providing clear and open information regarding the utilization of any AI tools), and engaging in self-reflection to understand the true impact of an AI system/tool on the research process. None the less, there is the crucial and key consideration of verification. Although AI can significantly improve the efficiency of data analysis, depending exclusively on AI may entail the possibility of disregarding nuances that would be detected through manual analysis. In addition, it is recommended to utilize AI tools in conjunction with conventional qualitative analysis methods. For instance, for a thematic analysis, AI can identify codes and themes in interview transcripts, which can then be cross-verified by the researcher or a research team through manual coding (for further implications and details regarding this issue of thematic analysis and AI, you may refer to the study by Christou, 2024). Despite this, verification can be ensured via study participants. In more detail, member checking, also referred to as participant confirmation, entails presenting the research findings to the participants for validation. Ensuring that this step is undertaken is of utmost importance, particularly when employing AI tools for the purpose of data analysis. Researchers, for instance, should communicate the interpretations obtained from AI-processed data to the participants in order to validate the accuracy of these interpretations in reflecting their opinions, perspectives or experiences on a given topic. Direct and exact quotes derived from participants (e.g. in the case of an ethnographic study) can add further value and possibly support visual results such as graphs presented through an AI tool.

12.3.2 Transferability

Transferability pertains to the extent to which the conclusions drawn from qualitative studies can be extrapolated to different contexts or environments (Nassaji, 2020; Stahl and King, 2020). In contrast to generalizability in quantitative research, this does not suggest universal applicability of findings but rather their relevance in similar contexts. Researchers establish transferability by offering detailed and comprehensive descriptions of the research context, enabling others to assess the degree to which the findings can be applied to different settings. When incorporating AI tools into the research process, especially in cases where the researcher has limited influence over the algorithms, it is advisable to implement certain strategies, such as a detailed disclosure of AI tool utilization, an evaluation of bias and verification of AI-produced results. Despite these, there are additionally the key considerations of elaboration, comprehensive presentation of information and examination of varied viewpoints. In more detail, the methodological section of a qualitative study should encompass details regarding the individuals (i.e. study participants) involved, the environment in which the study took place and the specific conditions in which the data was collected. For example, when employing AI for data acquisition, such as extracting information from online sources or examining social media posts, besides ethical clearance, it is imperative to record the precise origins, the duration of data collection and the characteristics of the collected content. Providing such a high level of detail enables other researchers to comprehend the precise conditions under which the study was conducted and evaluate the extent to which the findings can be applied to different situations. Furthermore, when presenting findings, it is important to ensure that the data is comprehensive and thorough. This may entail incorporating verbatim statements from participants (i.e. if interviews or focus groups were employed in the research methodology) and providing comprehensive illustrations of the data scrutinized by the AI tools. The objective is to present a thorough perspective of the data, allowing others to grasp the extent and scope of the information gathered. For example, a visual graph presented by an AI tool should be accompanied by relevant quotes that were derived from the study informants.

Researchers must furthermore guarantee that the data gathered and evaluated by AI encompasses a diverse range of viewpoints within the specific context of the study. Presentation of varied viewpoints is extremely important in any qualitative study, such as for example the study by Christou *et al.* (2019), which provided a detailed account of informants' perspectives regarding the expression of emotions within a service encounter context. In another study, Christou and Simillidou (2020) provided direct quotes from various informants while describing their differing experiences and the comforting role of travel on melancholy. It is crucial to consider this aspect, especially when employing AI for data extraction, as algorithms might unintentionally prioritize data sources that are more widespread or readily available. Such varied viewpoints may be presented in a qualitative study (in the form of detailed quotes derived from informants) in order to support or complement the outcomes presented via AI means.

12.3.3 Dependability

Dependability is also a key consideration in qualitative research (Amin *et al.*, 2020; Johnson *et al.*, 2020; Janis, 2022). It pertains to the reliability and consistency of the research process over a period of time. Although it shares similarities with reliability in quantitative methods, it acknowledges the dynamic nature of the social world and the researcher's interpretation. In order to ensure reliability, researchers may employ a comprehensive documentation of the data-collection process, derivation of categories and decision-making procedures employed throughout the research process.

There are certain aspects to take into consideration when employing AI technology. For instance, verifying AI-produced data or conclusions with alternative sources of data or methodologies, acknowledging AI system constraints, and practising self-reflection and adjusting accordingly, such as contemplating the potential impact of utilizing AI tools on the research process and study outcomes. None the less, there is a key consideration that involves the thorough research process documentation. Researchers may maintain a comprehensive and open documentation of every phase of the research procedure. This encompasses the process of recording the research study plan, the techniques employed for gathering data, any modifications made throughout the study and obviously the utilization of any AI tool. For instance, when utilizing an AI tool for data analysis, it is important to document the precise tool employed, including its version, the chosen settings or parameters, and the reasoning behind these decisions. When presenting the research results, it is important to ensure transparency regarding the function and influence of AI tools in the research procedure (e.g. the analysis process). This entails examining the impact of AI tools on the gathering, examination and understanding of the data, as well as any measures implemented to guarantee the reliability of these procedures. Furthermore, researchers may choose to establish an 'audit trail', which involves the comprehensive and systematic documentation of the decisions and actions undertaken throughout the research process. This entails recording the process of integrating the AI tools into the research, the manner in which the data was processed using specific AI tools and the approach taken to interpret the resulting outputs. Researchers may choose to include this in a diagrammatical form in their study methods section.

12.3.4 Confirmability

Confirmability refers to the extent to which the findings of a study are derived from the experiences, viewpoints and ideas of the participants, rather than being influenced by the researcher's personal preferences, opinions and/or beliefs (Shenton, 2004; Clissett, 2008; Johnson *et al.*, 2020). Confirmability in qualitative research is attained through the practice of reflexivity, wherein researchers consistently analyse and record their own biases and the potential impact these biases may have on the research (more evident in ethnographic studies). The researcher must substantiate the conclusions and interpretations with data, particularly when utilizing AI tools where the researcher may lack control over the algorithms. To ensure confirmability in such circumstances, a researcher can follow certain guidelines. This may involve a clear record of the precise AI tools used, how these facilitated the research process, how constraints and prejudices of AI were mitigated, and a report supported by details and supportive evidence from the data derived (e.g. representative reviews from those shared online, or from participants involved in a qualitative study).

Within the research findings, the researcher may present a comprehensive explanation of the process by which conclusions were derived, explicitly establishing a connection between them and the collected data. Concrete instances of unprocessed data, such as selected portions from recorded conversations that corroborate the conclusions may be provided, along with an analysis and presentation of the role of AI tools in facilitating these interpretations and the conclusions made. Researchers are furthermore encouraged to ensure the maintenance of a comprehensive audit trail encompassing the research process, decision making, utilization of AI tools and any modifications made throughout the research. Although academics have argued about the usefulness of audit trails as a means to achieve confirmability (Cutcliffe and McKenna, 2004), researchers may none the less document clearly how AI was used in the research process (e.g. processing, and output stages managed by AI). Within this context, reflexivity may also be somehow demonstrated, in which the researcher may explain the process of active engagement (and evaluation) with the AI tools, and how these impacted on research outcomes and conclusions.

12.4 Ensuring Rigour in Quantitative Research that Uses AI Tools and Means

Rigour is regarded as a crucial element in quantitative social research, given that it secures the reliability and validity of any study that uses quantitative methodological means (Winter, 2000; Heale and Twycross, 2015; Scrutton and Beames, 2015; Maula and Stam, 2020; Sürücü and Maslakçi, 2020). Its importance is even more emphasized in studies that combine both qualitative and quantitative methodological approaches.

12.4.1 Reliability

Reliability plays a key role in social science research and applied testing situations (Meyer, 2010; Drost, 2011; Revelle and Condon, 2019).

In quantitative research, reliability refers to the degree to which an instrument consistently measures what it is supposed to measure. Depending on how they are applied, AI tools have a substantial impact on a quantitative study's reliability in both positive and negative ways. On the positive side, AI systems are capable of processing huge datasets with great accuracy, which lowers the possibility of human error. This can improve the dependability of the processing and collection of data. Furthermore, the reliability of the analysis may be enhanced when AI tools are able to apply the same analysis criteria consistently across various datasets. In addition, AI can make complex measurement instruments possible, such as ML algorithms for image analysis or data pattern recognition, which can raise measurement accuracy. On the negative side, there may be the case of algorithmic bias (Osoba and Welser, 2017; Panch *et al.*, 2019). For instance, in the case where an AI tool is trained on biased data, it is possible to generate biased results, which would compromise the accuracy of the findings. In addition, because of their complexity, some AI models may lack transparency, which can make it difficult to understand how decisions or analyses were generated.

Therefore, it is imperative that researchers and analysts implement various essential tactics when incorporating AI tools, or any sort of AI technology, in their research process. It is essential for researchers to acquire a comprehensive comprehension of the AI tools being utilized, including their functionality, constraints and any acknowledged prejudices. When dealing with AI tools that incorporate ML components (which are powerful and sophisticated means for analysing large datasets, making predictions, identifying patterns and extracting insights), it is important to comprehend the characteristics of the training and validation data employed for the AI model. The representativeness and quality of this data can greatly influence the dependability of the tool. Researchers should furthermore exercise caution when it comes to automatic updates for AI tools, as they have the potential to alter the tool's functionality and consequently impact research outcomes. If feasible, researchers are advised to employ a consistent iteration of the AI tool throughout the research process, or to meticulously record any modifications and their potential ramifications. Information regarding the specifics of an AI tool can be recorded along with specific information about the utilization of the tools (e.g. configurations, versions and methods of data input). Ensuring this degree of transparency is essential in order to demonstrate the dependability of the tools and the subsequent analysis of data. Researchers are also encouraged to ensure the uniform implementation of AI tools throughout the research process, which entails employing the identical instrument, with identical configurations or criteria, for all pertinent aspects of the investigation. In addition, researchers may utilize cross-validation to compare the outcomes derived from AI tools with conventional approaches to data collection and analysis (e.g. alternative statistical software), whenever feasible. In addition, in order to ensure test–retest reliability, it is advisable to utilize the AI tool on the identical dataset on multiple occasions, if possible. The AI tool's reliability is enhanced by consistent results, which in turn impacts confidence in the study results. To evaluate the consistency of ratings or observations, analysts can ensure that all raters or observers use exactly the same tools or algorithms for their analysis, hence minimizing the variability that may be caused by different interpretation methods. To address parallel-forms reliability (involving the use of two different but equivalent versions of a measure), researchers may run two different AI models that are nevertheless designed to measure the same construct. Researchers may run these models on the same data, and eventually compare their output, to check for consistency.

12.4.2 Validity

In quantitative research, validity pertains to the extent to which a research instrument accurately assesses the intended construct, such as how well a study measures or reflects the real-world phenomena it is designed to investigate (Rourke and Anderson, 2004; Taylor, 2013). Within the context of quantitative research, validity is often broadly categorized into internal and external validity (Cahit, 2015; Johnson *et al.*, 2019; Duckett, 2021).

Both internal and external validity are deemed important for consideration during various phases of a study, for example during an experimental design phase (McDermott, 2011). In more detail, internal validity pertains to the degree to which a study justifiably supports a causal conclusion, as determined by the extent to which systematic error or bias is minimized in the study. The credibility of the relationship between the independent and dependent variables is dependent on the rigour of the research design and methodology. For example, a study is conducted to assess the effectiveness of a new job-training program on employment rates. The researchers in this hypothetical scenario aim to establish a causal link between participation in the program and subsequent employment success. To ensure internal validity, the researchers may use a randomized controlled trial design in which participants are randomly assigned to either the job-training program or a control group that does not receive the training. This randomization helps control for certain confounding variables (e.g. prior work experience or education level). This ensures that any differences in employment rates between the groups can be attributed more confidently to the job-training program itself. In another example within a differing context, assume that researchers are exploring whether high usage of social media negatively affects mental health, specifically looking at symptoms of anxiety and depression in adults. The study design includes longitudinal tracking of a cohort of adults, monitoring their social media usage and mental health status over several years. To enhance internal validity, the researchers control for certain potential confounding variables (e.g. family background, existing mental health conditions and offline social interactions). This control is achieved through careful data collection and statistical analysis techniques that isolate the effect of social media usage from these other factors.

External validity refers to the degree to which the results of a study can be applied to different populations, environments, time periods and measurement methods. The concept pertains to the degree to which the findings of a research study accurately reflect the actual conditions of the world. As Findley *et al.* (2021) noted, external validity captures the extent to which inferences drawn from a given sample apply to a broader population. Strategies to improve external validity involve employing random sampling methods and ensuring that the study sample, settings and procedures accurately reflect the characteristics of the overall population. For example, a public health study investigates the effectiveness of a new health campaign in promoting healthy eating habits among adolescents. The study is conducted in a specific area (i.e. urban) with a diverse population. In order to enhance external validity, the researchers employ random sampling methods to select participants from various demographics within the urban area (i.e. ethnic backgrounds, and socio-economic status). This diverse sample helps ensure that the study's findings are not limited to a specific subgroup and can be generalized to a broader population. Additionally, the researchers may consider replicating the study in other settings (e.g. rural areas) to compare results and assess the applicability of the campaign in varied environments.

AI tools can provide a useful means to address both internal and external validity issues. For instance, they can identify and control for confounding variables (e.g. ML algorithms can assist in detecting hidden confounders in the data), assist in analysing the representativeness of the sample, analyse how well the findings of a study can be generalized, and perform sensitivity analyses to determine how changes in data or model parameters may affect the results. None the less, there are some key aspects that researchers and analysts should take into consideration if AI technology is used for whatever purpose in any quantitative study. Researchers are encouraged to select AI models and algorithms that are suitable for the specific type of data and research question, while becoming aware of the limitations of these models. Conceivably, the comprehensive knowledge of a specific AI tool is crucial for interpreting the results correctly. Researchers may conduct thorough testing and validation of the AI model by using a portion of their data, hence ensuring that the specific model is stable and reliable. A justification of the model selection rationale should furthermore be provided for transparency and reproducibility purposes. Researchers must be mindful that AI algorithms might oversimplify or even misunderstand complex relationships between variables. Additionally, researchers could assess the AI tool's performance and dependability in diverse scenarios by subjecting it to rigorous testing with a range of datasets. It is also important to consistently observe, monitor and record the performance of the AI tool throughout the study. It may be beneficial to incorporate manual evaluations or expert assessments to complement the AI's analysis. Analysts should furthermore be cautious in interpreting any AI-identified patterns, ensuring that these are meaningful and relevant to the research question.

12.5 Conclusion

It has been advocated that in the current era, in which people and society have grown increasingly reliant on AI technologies, there is a need for socially responsible AI algorithms (Cheng *et al.*, 2021). There is a growing need to establish rigour in cases in which the researcher or analyst makes use of AI technology for research purposes. Rigour is an essential component in qualitative social research that ensures the credibility, transferability, dependability and confirmability of any qualitative study. It is also an essential component in quantitative social research, ensuring the reliability and validity of studies that employ quantitative methods. The incorporation of AI tools and means into research methodologies and studies necessitates a heightened emphasis on rigour, particularly in the realm of social research. Undoubtedly, the incorporation of AI tools brings about idiosyncrasies and new complexities, requiring the careful application of rigorous standards. Given that AI offers improved (or at least differing) and/or innovative techniques for extracting, collecting, analysing and interpreting diverse forms of data, it is essential to emphasize rigour in order to maintain the integrity, reliability and validity of research findings and outcomes. Furthermore, the rapid progress of AI technology requires researchers to consistently stay informed and well versed in the latest advancements and ethical considerations considering the employment of AI in any research study. Ensuring rigour in this context involves following established procedures and certain guidelines, while simultaneously staying flexible, as well as being mindful of the potential influence of AI technologies and capabilities on study methods and research results. This chapter has presented some recommendations and principles for addressing these crucial issues in order to secure a rigorous study procedure. Although the chapter has addressed several issues linked to rigour, it has not provided a detailed account of this matter, and I acknowledge this as the author of this chapter. As AI systems, tools and means advance rapidly, academics specifically studying qualitative and quantitative research methods will continually be required to provide more detailed and further direct guidelines on how researchers should address important issues. I trust that this chapter will serve as a foundation for future further and more in-depth inquiries into this significant matter linked to the nexus of AI and social research.

References

Amin, M.E.K., Nørgaard, L.S., Cavaco, A.M., Witry, M.J., Hillman, L. *et al.* (2020) Establishing trustworthiness and authenticity in qualitative pharmacy research. *Research in Social and Administrative Pharmacy* 16, 1472–1482.

Barbour, R.S. (2003) The newfound credibility of qualitative research? Tales of technical essentialism and co-option. *Qualitative Health Research* 13, 1019–1027.

Bryman, A., Becker, S. and Sempik, J. (2008) Quality criteria for quantitative, qualitative and mixed methods research: a view from social policy. *International Journal of Social Research Methodology* 11, 261–276.

Cahit, K. (2015) Internal validity: a must in research designs. *Educational Research and Reviews* 10, 111–118.

Cheng, L., Varshney, K.R. and Liu, H. (2021) Socially responsible AI algorithms: issues, purposes, and challenges. *Journal of Artificial Intelligence Research* 71, 1137–1181.

Christou, P. and Simillidou, A. (2020) Tourist experience: the catalyst role of tourism in comforting melancholy, or not. *Journal of Hospitality and Tourism Management* 42, 210–221.

Christou, P., Avloniti, A. and Farmaki, A. (2019) Guests' perceptions of emotionally expressive and non-expressive service providers within the hospitality context. *International Journal of Hospitality Management* 76, 152–162.

Christou, P.A. (2023a) How to use artificial intelligence (AI) as a resource, methodological and analysis tool in qualitative research? *The Qualitative Report* 28, 1968–1980.

Christou, P.A. (2023b) A critical perspective over whether and how to acknowledge the use of artificial intelligence (AI) in qualitative studies. *The Qualitative Report* 28, 1981–1991.

Christou, P.A. (2024) Thematic analysis through artificial intelligence (AI). *The Qualitative Report* 29, 560–576.

Chubb, J., Cowling, P. and Reed, D. (2022) Speeding up to keep up: exploring the use of AI in the research process. *AI & Society* 37, 1439–1457.

Clissett, P. (2008) Evaluating qualitative research. *Journal of Orthopaedic Nursing* 12, 99–105.

Cohen, M.X. (2017) Rigor and replication in time-frequency analyses of cognitive electrophysiology data. *International Journal of Psychophysiology* 111, 80–87.

Cutcliffe, J.R. and McKenna, H.P. (2004) Expert qualitative researchers and the use of audit trails. *Journal of Advanced Nursing* 45, 126–133.

Drost, E.A. (2011) Validity and reliability in social science research. *Education Research and Perspectives* 38, 105–123.

Duckett, L.J. (2021) Quantitative research excellence: study design and reliable and valid measurement of variables. *Journal of Human Lactation* 37, 456–463.

Findley, M.G., Kikuta, K. and Denly, M. (2021) External validity. *Annual Review of Political Science* 24, 365–393.

Gichoya, J.W., Thomas, K., Celi, L.A., Safdar, N., Banerjee, I. *et al.* (2023) AI pitfalls and what not to do: mitigating bias in AI. *British Journal of Radiology* 96: 20230023.

Gregory, D. and Martin, S. (1994) Crafting evaluation research in the public sector: reconciling rigour and relevance. *British Journal of Management* 5, S43–S52.

Grodal, S., Anteby, M. and Holm, A.L. (2021) Achieving rigor in qualitative analysis: the role of active categorization in theory building. *Academy of Management Review* 46, 591–612.

Heale, R. and Twycross, A. (2015) Validity and reliability in quantitative studies. *Evidence-based Nursing* 18, 66–67.

Heilinger, J.C. (2022) The ethics of AI ethics. A constructive critique. *Philosophy & Technology* 35: 61.

Janis, I. (2022) Strategies for establishing dependability between two qualitative intrinsic case studies: a reflexive thematic analysis. *Field Methods* 34, 240–255.

Johnson, F.R., Yang, J.C. and Reed, S.D. (2019) The internal validity of discrete choice experiment data: a testing tool for quantitative assessments. *Value in Health* 22, 157–160.

Johnson, J.L., Adkins, D. and Chauvin, S. (2020) A review of the quality indicators of rigor in qualitative research. *American Journal of Pharmaceutical Education* 84: 7120.

Kamila, M.K. and Jasrotia, S.S. (2025) Ethical issues in the development of artificial intelligence: recognizing the risks. *International Journal of Ethics and Systems* 41, 45–63.

Köhler, T., Landis, R.S. and Cortina, J.M. (2017) From the editors: Establishing methodological rigor in quantitative management learning and education research: the role of design, statistical methods, and reporting standards. *Academy of Management Learning & Education* 16, 173–192.

Krefting, L. (1991) Rigor in qualitative research: the assessment of trustworthiness. *American Journal of Occupational Therapy* 45, 214–222.

Lévesque, M., Obschonka, M. and Nambisan, S. (2022) Pursuing impactful entrepreneurship research using artificial intelligence. *Entrepreneurship Theory and Practice* 46, 803–832.

Liao, H. and Hitchcock, J. (2018) Reported credibility techniques in higher education evaluation studies that use qualitative methods: a research synthesis. *Evaluation and Program Planning* 68, 157–165.

Maula, M. and Stam, W. (2020) Enhancing rigor in quantitative entrepreneurship research. *Entrepreneurship Theory and Practice* 44, 1059–1090.

McDermott, R. (2011) Internal and external validity. In: Druckman, J.N., Green, D.P., Kuklinski, J.H. and Lupia, A. (eds) *Cambridge Handbook of Experimental Political Science*. Cambridge University Press, New York.

Mehrabi, N., Morstatter, F., Saxena, N., Lerman, K. and Galstyan, A. (2021) A survey on bias and fairness in machine learning. *ACM Computing Surveys* 54: 115.

Meyer, P. (2010) *Understanding Measurement: Reliability*. Oxford University Press, New York.

Nassaji, H. (2020) Good qualitative research. *Language Teaching Research* 24, 427–431.

Nassar, A. and Kamal, M. (2021) Ethical dilemmas in AI-powered decision-making: a deep dive into big data-driven ethical considerations. *International Journal of Responsible Artificial Intelligence* 11, 1–11.

Onwuegbuzie, A.J. and Corrigan, J.A. (2014) Improving the quality of mixed research reports in the field of human resource development and beyond: a call for rigor as an ethical practice. *Human Resource Development Quarterly* 25, 273–299.

Osoba, O.A. and Welser, W., IV (2017) *An Intelligence in Our Image: The Risks of Bias and Errors in Artificial Intelligence*. Rand Corporation, Santa Monica, California.

Panch, T., Mattie, H. and Atun, R. (2019) Artificial intelligence and algorithmic bias: implications for health systems. *Journal of Global Health* 9: 010318.

Patton, M.Q. (1999) Enhancing the quality and credibility of qualitative analysis. *Health Services Research* 34, 1189–1208.

Pesämaa, O., Zwikael, O., Hair, J.F., Jr and Huemann, M. (2021) Publishing quantitative papers with rigor and transparency. *International Journal of Project Management* 39, 217–222.

Reio, T.G., Jr (2021) The ten research questions: an analytic tool for critiquing empirical studies and teaching research rigor. *Human Resource Development Review* 20, 374–390.

Revelle, W. and Condon, D.M. (2019) Reliability from α to ω: a tutorial. *Psychological Assessment* 31, 1395–1411.

Rourke, L. and Anderson, T. (2004) Validity in quantitative content analysis. *Educational Technology Research and Development* 52, 5–18.

Sandelowski, M. (1993) Rigor or rigor mortis: the problem of rigor in qualitative research revisited. *Advances in Nursing Science* 16, 1–8.

Scrutton, R. and Beames, S. (2015) Measuring the unmeasurable: upholding rigor in quantitative studies of personal and social development in outdoor adventure education. *Journal of Experiential Education* 38, 8–25.

Shenton, A.K. (2004) Strategies for ensuring trustworthiness in qualitative research projects. *Education for Information* 22, 63–75.

Shufutinsky, A. (2020) Employing use of self for transparency, rigor, trustworthiness, and credibility in qualitative organizational research methods. *Organization Development Review* 52, 50–58.

Stahl, N.A. and King, J.R. (2020) Expanding approaches for research: understanding and using trustworthiness in qualitative research. *Journal of Developmental Education* 44, 26–28.

Sürücü, L. and Maslakçi, A. (2020) Validity and reliability in quantitative research. *Business & Management Studies* 8, 2694–2726.

Taylor, C.S. (2013) *Validity and Validation: Understanding Statistics*. Oxford University Press, New York.

Vlačić, B., Corbo, L., Costa e Silva, S.C. and Dabić, M. (2021) The evolving role of artificial intelligence in marketing: a review and research agenda. *Journal of Business Research* 128, 187–203.

Winter, G. (2000) A comparative discussion of the notion of validity in qualitative and quantitative research. *The Qualitative Report* 4: 4.

13 The Ethical Implications of Using AI in Qualitative Research

Danielle Hitch[1]*, Kieva Richards[2], Adyya Gupta[3], Urvi Thanekar[4], Jacqueline Edwards[1] and Sophie Goldingay[1]

[1]*Deakin University, Geelong, Victoria, Australia;* [2]*LaTrobe University, Bundoora, Victoria, Australia;* [3]*Global Centre for Preventive Health and Nutrition (GLOBE) within the Institute for Health Transformation at Deakin University, Bundoora, Victoria, Australia;* [4]*Deakin University, Bundoora, Victoria, Australia*

Abstract

This chapter explores the ethical implications of using artificial intelligence (AI) to augment human intelligence in qualitative social science research. A lack of clear guidelines, standards and AI specific research training presents a high risk of ethical breaches in this new and rapidly developing area. The chapter explores the intersection of AI, ethics and qualitative research, highlighting the critical role of human oversight and accountability. It systematically addresses key ethical principles – respect for individuals, confidentiality, integrity, beneficence and justice – illustrated with real-world and hypothetical examples. The chapter concludes with best-practice guidelines for ethical AI augmented social science qualitative research, and emphasizes the importance of iterative critical engagement and interdisciplinary collaboration. These guidelines aim to help researchers navigate the ethical complexities of AI and ensure that their work upholds the rights of participants.

Keywords: dilemmas, ethics, frameworks, guidelines, qualitative research

13.1 Introduction

Artificial intelligence (AI) is rapidly transforming qualitative research in social sciences, reshaping the ethical principles and frameworks upon which all studies are founded. Ethical research transcends theoretical principles; it can only be realized in the practice of researchers within their unique contexts (Pieper, 1998). While institutional and structural changes are necessary to support ethical AI in qualitative research (Walsh, 2022), this chapter focuses on equipping individual researchers with the knowledge and tools they need for responsible practice.

The chapter begins with an introduction to the applications of AI in various stages of qualitative research, highlighting its potential to enhance and disrupt traditional research practices. The intersection of ethics, AI and research is then explored, emphasizing the crucial role of human oversight and accountability. A critical analysis of AI specific ethical issues follows, aligned to five key research ethics principles, and complemented by hypothetical and real-world examples. Following a summary of relevant ethical frameworks and guidelines, the chapter concludes with a best-practice guideline for social researchers engaging in ethical AI augmented

*E-mail: dani.hitch@deakin.edu.au

DOI: 10.1079/9781800626607.0013

qualitative research. Hypothetical and real-life vignettes and examples are provided in boxed text to highlight key issues and describe responses to ethical issues associated with AI in qualitative research.

13.2 The Intersection of Ethics, AI and Research

Research ethics guide researcher behaviour, decision making and conflict resolution based on principles of right and wrong influenced by cultural, religious or philosophical beliefs (Govia, 2020). Their purpose is to collectively foster safety, trust, integrity and professionalism. Ethical reasoning shapes moral obligations, drives human interactions, and influences notions of fairness, transparency, privacy and social justice. These principles are embedded in the codes of conduct and research guidelines that inform resource allocation, organizational standards, legal regulations and policies, and engagement with marginalized groups at both local and national levels (Buolamwini and Gebru, 2018; Govia, 2020).

Technological advancements challenge ethical frameworks, especially concerning privacy, data accessibility, unlawful data use or ethnocentrism. Ethical reflection requires consciousness, a quality that AI lacks despite its goal of emulating human cognitive functions (Asaro, 2023; Roberts *et al.*, 2024). Ethical reasoning is also founded on reflection, critique and introspection, which current AI systems cannot achieve. However, AI may play a role in enabling deeper and more complex ethical conversations between multiple interdisciplinary stakeholders, including researchers, developers, governments, industry, ethicists, advocacy groups, legal experts and the public.

AI can present significant security risks in an increasingly digital world when used to disseminate manipulated information or promote clandestine agendas (Hasselberger, 2019). It has an exponentially growing presence in academia, research and development (Jeyaraman *et al.*, 2023), but its presence and influences are not always obvious. Determining what has been produced by real human intelligence versus artificial creation is becoming more difficult, increasing the risk of non-existent facts and misinformation being perceived as credible (Hasselberger, 2019).

Guidelines for ethical AI augmented research aspire to establish boundaries around a technology that has until now operated with little, if any, inherent or formalized limits (Zhuo *et al.*, 2023a,b). Existing ethical frameworks were developed long before AI became commonly available and have not caught up with the rapid changes in this field. It is entirely possible for a social research study to meet these long-standing ethical standards, while still being ethically problematic due to the specific issues related to AI use. While frameworks exist for the use of AI in other sectors (Arcilla *et al.*, 2023), they are not addressed in detail in national research codes or guidelines, and are therefore not evaluated by ethics committees (Thompson and Morgan, 2020; Bouhouita-Guermech *et al.*, 2023).

While ethics guidelines with AI specific clauses are in development, they alone cannot improve ethical AI practice in social research. AI augmented social research published to date has been criticized for its poor methodological design, delivery and reporting (Ibrahim *et al.*, 2021), and the mitigation of ethical risks is heavily dependent on the unique context of individual studies (Govia, 2020). Some also argue that these guidelines can create or reinforce power imbalances or serve as a form of 'ethics washing' if superficially promoted without meaningful realization in practice (Hagendorff, 2020; Asaro, 2023).

Social researchers play an important role in investigating the impact of AI on moral, political, economic and other aspects of human life (Davis and Scherz, 2019). Both research ethics and social science values are deeply embedded in societal relationships and contexts (Asaro, 2023). AI in social research can disrupt or promote conformity, which necessitates ethical practices and research methodologies that respect participant rights, avoid harm, amplify marginalized voices and capture contextual meaning. AI may complement the work of social researchers but cannot replace their data-interpretation skills (Hitch, 2023). These interpretive skills are crucial for critically evaluating AI outputs and reflecting on human–AI interactions, both of which inform the growing need for a sustainable balance between the capacities of both human and AI intelligences.

13.3 Dilemmas and Considerations for Ethical AI Augmented Qualitative Research

Modern research ethics frameworks have evolved since the mid-20th century (Lock, 1995), and now place greater emphasis on social justice, participant autonomy and transparency (Thakur and Lahiry, 2019). However, their core principles – respect for the individual, confidentiality and privacy, integrity, beneficence and justice – remain unchanged. The challenge of practising ethical AI augmented research therefore demands reinterpretation and modification of existing frameworks, rather than completely new approaches.

13.3.1 Respect for the individual

Recognizing individual agency in making personal decisions is a cornerstone of research ethics and is crucial to protecting human rights and welfare, especially for vulnerable communities (King and Churchill, 2000; Artal and Rubenfeld, 2017). This ethical principle supports personal autonomy, allowing individuals to make their own informed and voluntary decisions about research participation. Transparency in qualitative studies is crucial to establishing methodological trustworthiness and rigour (Liamputtong, 2019), and is the foundation for respecting individual participants.

A key challenge to autonomy for social science qualitative research is a general lack of AI literacy. While the public is increasingly aware of AI, most lack understanding of its characteristics and capacities (Merenkov *et al.*, 2021), and many hold negative or mistrustful perceptions and attitudes towards it (McCradden *et al.*, 2020). Social scientists must critically reflect on the gap between their and the general public's understanding of AI.

Participants cannot exercise autonomy without truly informed consent. Secondary data use by AI systems means researchers must obtain unspecified extended consent (Shaw *et al.*, 2024). This entails two distinct consent processes: (i) consent for data to contribute to AI system training; and (ii) consent to participate in the research study. Participants will receive limited (or probably no) information about future studies using AI system outputs, which are at least partially built from their own data. They may be giving complete control over their data to the AI system, which can use it for any future purpose. While some participants will be comfortable with these conditions, much depends on individual familiarity with that specific AI system and with AI more generally.

Given the extent of consent required for ethical AI research, its terms and conditions must be explicitly and accessibly explained and documented. Respecting the autonomy of individual participants involves enabling real choice, without which they may experience harm.

A 'co-pilot' mental health support program developed a human-supervised AI support platform (Kokobot) (Grohol, 2023). Researchers reported that participants rated AI generated messages as better than human-generated messages and experienced significantly better response times. However, not all participants were fully aware that their data contributed to AI system training and that some responses were AI generated. This led to feelings of anger and distress, and many stopped using Kokobot as they perceived AI generated responses as simulated empathy that lacked authenticity and credibility.

Another unique AI challenge to autonomy is its rapid evolution. Participants must be informed about significant changes to AI systems during the study, and informed consent may need to be renegotiated. As a result, informed consent may become an ongoing process for AI augmented research, particularly for longitudinal studies.

Chris is studying the long-term effects of remote working on employee well-being and productivity. She utilizes a web-based qualitative analysis platform and wants to use a new AI feature that makes coding suggestions. The feature requires contributing data to train the system and will be altering her analytical approach. Chris updates the participants; most re-consent, some opt for manual coding off the platform, and two withdraw entirely.

Ensuring robust informed consent for ethical AI research goes beyond legal compliance; it respects and protects participant dignity and rights. It may also affect retention if participants are uncomfortable with AI use during the study.

Therefore, critical and iterative reflection on the pros and cons of this technology against the long-established core principals of ethical research is critical while developing social science study protocols to ensure appropriate and high-quality governance.

13.3.2 Confidentiality and privacy

Safeguarding personal, sensitive and health data while using AI in social research is essential for ethical practice, and closely aligns with the principle of respect for the individual. However, the interface between confidentiality, privacy and technology is challenging. AI algorithms may compromise privacy by reproducing and disclosing personally identifiable data input by users when formulating outputs for others (Aldoseri *et al.*, 2023).

A not-for-profit organization develops a mobile app named Friend Online to monitor loneliness and support users in improving social connectedness. Users input sensitive, health and personal information, which an AI algorithm analyses to provide personalized recommendations. The algorithm also generates anonymized reports to inform research and policy about social inclusion. A user inputted detailed information about their unique social and medical circumstances, which the system is supposed to securely anonymize and aggregate with other users' data. However, the reader of a research report identified details from this user (their cousin), which disclosed previously unknown information about their health.

Social researchers must carefully anonymize and encrypt any data entered into AI systems to protect participant identity and preserve data integrity. In the example above, the researchers could train the AI algorithm to automatically redact, recode or replace identifying information such as names, locations and specific diagnoses before analysis (Su *et al.*, 2022). Alternatively, researchers can anonymize data before it is inputted if it is not being collected on AI enabled platforms.

Data breaches and unauthorized access to sensitive information on AI systems can cause significant harm to participants (Morgan, 2023). Open-source AI models may be particularly vulnerable to breaches due to their source code availability, potentially exposing user chat histories (Poremba, 2023). Therefore, data being anonymized by the AI model itself may remain vulnerable to disclosure if the original input remains available on the system. Conversely, data anonymized 'offline' prior to its input into the system is at lower risk. Researchers must ensure robust security measures for AI systems and conduct regular audits for platforms they develop. Predicting how AI systems may reuse data is difficult as the models improve and change in complex ways with further training (Morgan, 2023). As algorithms become increasingly sophisticated, new data breach risks may emerge.

Another mitigation strategy is withdrawing data from AI systems at the conclusion of research studies. However, this is rarely feasible due to system complexity and data-retention policies. Social researchers must therefore pay particular attention to privacy-preserving techniques, robust data security and management measures, and secure data transfer and storage guidelines to uphold participant confidentiality and privacy while practising ethical AI augmented social research (Bouhouita-Guermech *et al.*, 2023).

Balancing individual privacy with public benefits was highlighted during the COVID-19 pandemic. Researchers and public health officials monitored social media to understand public behaviour regarding the virus, and COVID social media surveillance was effective in early detection of pandemic trends (Wang *et al.*, 2020). However, these studies have the potential to contravene local online privacy laws (Flores and Young, 2022) and may provoke concerns for individual privacy. Clear distinctions must be drawn between data use for public health surveillance and social research (Zeng *et al.*, 2021). Without rigorous and transparent measures to protect confidentiality, unethical use of AI in research could cause mistrust and ultimately reduce cooperation with public health measures (Eichengreen *et al.*, 2021).

Social researchers must consider cultural norms and expectations related to privacy and confidentiality. Previous research indicates that participants from collectivist cultures are more sensitive to the risks of unintentional disclosure (Fleming *et al.*, 2021), but are also more willing to prioritize community benefits over their personal privacy (Alashoor *et al.*, 2015). Culturally sensitive ethical practices are essential, especially when working with marginalized communities that have experienced historical exploitation (Liamputtong, 2019).

A qualitative study of First Nations and other Australians explored why participants agree to take part in research (Guillemin *et al.*, 2016). First Nations participants considered privacy issues carefully and iteratively to protect community well-being and safety. Privacy was important to their entire participation experience, resulting in active decision making during data collection about what and how much to disclose. First Nations participants appreciated researchers taking their confidentiality seriously and having robust measures in place to protect it.

13.3.3 Integrity

Integrity is the foundation of the researcher–participant relationship, promoting accuracy, honesty and transparency throughout the research process (National Health and Medical Research Council, 2023). Researchers must be transparent about the role of AI in their methodologies and data sources, potential conflicts of interest, limitations, and biases within AI systems and in their reporting of results. However, social researchers may be reluctant to report AI use due to concerns about external criticism of the data standards and analytical practices, potentially leading to rejection from peer-reviewed journals (Christou, 2023). AI is also often seen as an all-knowing entity in the public imagination (Kidd and Birhane, 2023), and doubts about the integrity of AI may be shared by researchers, participants and the broader community alike.

Some unease about AI in qualitative research stems from concerns about output quality and potential plagiarism in academic writing (Christou, 2023). These concerns are not unfounded and may have serious ramifications for researchers. The efficiency of AI systems may also tempt scientists to prioritize speed over quality due to workload pressures or the struggles related to the 'publish or perish' mantra (Dolunay and Temel, 2024).

In the case of Roberto Mata versus Avianca Inc. (Weiser, 2023), a lawyer utilized ChatGPT to conduct legal research. The outputs included both non-existent judicial decisions and fabricated quotations. This information was subsequently submitted to the court and had significant legal and professional repercussions for both the individual lawyer and the legal profession more broadly.

Initially envisioned as 'stochastic parrots' (Bender *et al.*, 2021), AI systems can now hallucinate plausible yet false information and sycophantically echo what they think users want to hear (Roberts *et al.*, 2024). They also mimic other deceptive human traits, increasing the risk of misinformation and challenging our view of computers as passive productivity tools. AI systems process data based on their syntax or tangible properties, and do not understand their semantics or meaning (Roberts *et al.*, 2024). They can, however, selectively filter and emphasize information that reinforces perspectives adopted during training, which may reflect and even amplify existing biases (Ohagi, 2024). It is important to remember that AI systems have no ethical values or reasoning of their own, and they lack reflective self-awareness about the limits of their knowledge. As remarked by Harari (2023) in his YouTube address, AI gives the impression of knowing things when it does not and can create a feeling that it cares when it cannot.

AI systems have the potential to both spread and combat misinformation, although most ethical debate has focused on integrity problems to date. Researchers must verify AI outputs and critically analyse their rigour and quality; nothing can be taken for granted. Implicit biases and poor transparency across many AI systems create opportunities for manipulation (or even weaponization) of information during the training process (Sharma, 2023). Many AI systems function as 'black boxes' with opaque internal workings (Sharma, 2023; Limongi, 2024), all of which can undermine research integrity. Open-source AI models practice transparency by making their source code and decision-making processes freely available to the public (Limongi, 2024). However, addressing implicit biases within AI systems is a far more complex undertaking.

A perceived lack of integrity erodes trust in AI systems, and this is particularly problematic for social science research. In this field, the complexities of human behaviour and social structures are the key concern, and high-quality analysis demands a deep and nuanced understanding of diverse human perspectives and moral judgement. As this is currently far beyond the capacity of AI systems (Hasselberger, 2019), many question the integrity of both what AI systems do and how they do it.

13.3.4 Beneficence

Beneficence poses a dilemma of opposing moral duties to both 'do no harm' (non-maleficence) and 'maximize benefits' in the public sphere (Grant, 2018). AI systems may make very different decisions about how to strike this balance compared with humans, with several published examples suggesting that AI tends to take a utilitarian stance (Rachels and Rachels, 2006).

Researchers at the Center for Artificial Intelligence in Society at the University of Southern California worked on a drug abuse prevention program for homeless youth in shelters. The team included social work researchers using an AI agent designed to minimize peer encouragement of illicit drug use. After training intended to design the intervention, the AI agent recommended grouping all 'high-risk' youth together to minimize population-level risk (Grant, 2018). Placing homeless youth at high risk of illicit drug use together for research purposes is highly likely to exacerbate their already significant vulnerability and risk of harm.

The beneficence dilemma is particularly salient in research with children, balancing potential present harm against future benefits to other children. Grant (2018) highlighted that questions remain about the ability of AI systems to produce nuanced outputs regarding social vulnerabilities for some people who may have criminalized or marginalized identities. In this case, this limitation in the AI system may have resulted in predictive tools that did not align with culturally important and meaningful values and expectations about beneficence.

Grant (2018) went on to question whether proceeding with possibly harmful AI mediated interventions can ever be morally or ethically justified, and proposed a framework founded on the moral duties of necessity, proportionality and trade-off optimization. In his view, 'human judgement will always be required' (p. 245) when considering beneficence dilemmas posed by AI augmentation in social research.

However, AI augmented research also holds the potential to promote beneficence. Grant (2018) found that the AI agent also identified risks to individuals that the human researchers did not consider, which may increase the accuracy of risk predictions. The potential for AI to offer novel and alternative perspectives on social research issues was also experienced by Hitch (2023), who found that ChatGPT identified a theme in data from people with long COVID that had not emerged in her analysis. The 'other' intelligence provided by AI systems therefore has the potential to challenge and stimulate human intelligence in ways that may serve as a catalyst for deeper critical analysis and reflection.

13.3.5 Justice

Justice demands fair distribution of burdens and benefits, equal treatment of participants, inclusivity across diverse groups, and cultural sensitivity to the contexts and traditions of participant groups from study conception to dissemination (National Health and Medical Research Council, 2023). Freely accessible generative AI (genAI) platforms hold the promise of information democratization, but disparities in digital access (also known as the 'digital divide') persist. The key drivers of this divide, including demographic, socio-economic, cultural and geographic factors, are also important topics in social research (Law, 2015; Cruz-Jesus *et al.*, 2018). Not everyone has access to digital devices and internet connections, let alone cutting-edge AI platforms.

The increasing use of AI in qualitative social research might worsen digital exclusion, further marginalizing vulnerable populations and deepening socio-economic divides (Bentley *et al.*, 2024). While some AI platforms are available for little or no cost, these versions often have significant constraints and limitations that negatively impact information access, research quality and overall productivity.

Femi is researching the impact of mobile banking on economic development in rural communities. He has free access to ChatGPT, which he uses for tasks such as summarizing online documents prior to reading the full text. However, this version has usage limits, and frequent internet outages in his area further reduce platform availability. He has considered upgrading to the paid versions, which have higher usage limits, but they are beyond his budget.

The language models that form the basis of many AI systems are also mostly trained on English language sources, limiting their effectiveness and accessibility for speakers of other languages (Zhuo *et al.*, 2023a,b). This amplifies wealthier Euro-Western perspectives; in the words of Roberts *et al.* (2024, p. 8), 'many voices are routinely suppressed, ignored, or choose to remain silent and hence never achieve a presence in the manufactured homogeneity of training data'. While developers include restrictions to protect users from harmful content, inherent biases in training data shape AI outputs and potentially produce unfair or prejudiced responses and material (Sharma, 2023; Limongi, 2024).

A popular image-generation model called Stable Diffusion often portrays a world skewed by racial and gender stereotypes (Nicoletti and Bass, 2023). White male figures predominate as CEOs, women are rarely represented in high-status positions, and black men are disproportionately depicted committing crimes. As the authors state, 'Humans are biased. Generative AI is even worse.'

All these issues challenge the ability of qualitative social researchers to support justice and equity. Access to advanced AI systems remains inequitable, disadvantaging researchers and participants in lower-income or rural areas, and in marginalized communities. While AI may be seen as 'the way of the future', its adoption risks worsening the social inequities often addressed by research. A critical examination of its capacity to uphold justice is essential to ensure equitable experiences for participants and researchers alike.

13.4 Frameworks for Ethical AI Augmented Qualitative Research

Research ethics are guided by multiple frameworks, including professional codes of conduct, institutional guidelines, and national and international frameworks for the responsible conduct of research. These frameworks are generally consistent in their content and recommendations, frequently reflecting the core ethics principles discussed in this chapter. However, notable variation is reported in their application by research ethics committees (Nicholls *et al.*, 2015). Ethical AI in qualitative social science research demands a re-evaluation and enhancement of traditional practices. As AI technologies advance, ethical frameworks must evolve to protect participants and ensure the technology adheres to the core ethical principles described in the relevant codes and guidelines.

The role of AI in research is yet to be specifically addressed in research ethics frameworks, but relevant guidelines are emerging to manage the potential risks of this technology. International organizations, governments, major private companies and academic institutions have all developed general principles and guidelines around the implementation of AI (Boza and Evgeniou, 2021). There is growing (but not complete) consensus around the importance of privacy, accountability and professional responsibility, safety and security, transparency, fairness and non-discrimination, human control of technology and promotion of human values (Fjeld *et al.*, 2020). The United Nations Educational, Scientific and Cultural Organization recommends that AI must enable inclusivity, prevent discrimination, ensure diverse representation, respect cultural contexts and be based on fairness (UNESCO, 2024). While these guidelines suggest that the ethical implications of AI are recognized internationally, frameworks for their application to research are less common.

The Nuffield Foundation produced a roadmap for the ethical and societal implications of AI, including recommendations for research (Whittlestone *et al.*, 2019). These include transparency and accountability mechanisms, accessible explanation of AI systems, bias detection and management strategies, robust data governance practices, promotion of AI literacy and thorough impact assessments. They also recommend interdisciplinary collaboration to reflect and incorporate diverse perspectives and experiences from the humanities, social sciences, technical disciplines and AI practitioners. Dolunay and Temel (2024) also asserted that ethicists play an important role in developing frameworks for ethical AI augmented qualitative research.

The only area with detailed frameworks for ethical AI use is academic writing. There is a consensus that AI systems cannot be listed as authors of academic papers, and that researchers are responsible for all manuscript contents, including AI generated content (Council of Publication Ethics, 2023). The World Association of Medical Editors (2023) has detailed recommendations on using chatbots and genAI, recently updated to address their use in manuscript review. Many journals and publishers, such Elsevier (2024) and Springer (2023), have their own policies on using genAI. GenAI (GPT-4o) was utilized as a writing support tool during the preparation of this chapter, for assistance with rephrasing, topics generation and overall structure. However, all content was conceived and written by the human authors.

13.5 A Good Practice Guideline for Ethical AI Augmented Qualitative Research

We propose the following best-practice guidelines to assist researchers in designing, developing and delivering responsible AI augmented research (Table 13.1). These recommendations were developed from the analysis presented in this chapter, and also from the author's own professional experience of AI implementation. The guideline is arranged around five key topics: governance, methodology, participant understanding and consent, reporting and dissemination, and researcher capacity and training. This guideline helps to identify important ethical issues within the context of individual studies and suggests mitigation and management strategies. Not all elements will be relevant to every study, but they illustrate what ethical AI augmented qualitative research looks like.

13.6 Conclusion

This chapter presents a comprehensive discussion of the ethical implications of using AI in qualitative social science research. AI offers many opportunities and possibilities for qualitative researchers, and its growing presence in society cannot be ignored. Ethical practice in AI augmented social science research is a dynamic and ongoing process, rather than a one-off meeting of formalized requirements. Critical engagement and re-engagement with its potential possibilities and problems should happen at every stage of the study, to keep up with the speed of developments in this field.

Researchers need to reflect deeply on their own assumptions and knowledge about AI prior to adopting it into practice. Researchers may also need to provide education and additional information to their participants as part of the informed consent process. Many will need to upskill themselves about AI capabilities in general and the specific system they are implementing to ensure that their practices are ethical and responsible, and to regularly update their skill set over time. AI implementation therefore requires additional resources and time in the short term, but this may reduce in the future as practices become standardized and more resources are developed to support both researchers and participants.

There is an urgent need for the development and refinement of ethical standards for AI in qualitative research, particularly related to the topics of bias mitigation, data security and participant engagement. Interdisciplinary collaboration will support the development of comprehensive guidelines that are translatable across the full diversity of social science research. However, participants and the public are the key stakeholders in this process, because AI implementation may entail asking participants to give up individual rights for the greater good derived from research. It is incumbent on researchers to fulfil their side of the social contract by protecting rights and freedoms and upholding the ethics principals discussed in this chapter.

The use of AI in qualitative social sciences research undoubtedly poses new ethical challenges and dilemmas, but they can be critically considered and resolved through reflection on long-established ethical principles. Authentic commitment to ethical practice will ensure that researchers utilize AI to augment human intelligence in ways that promote respect, beneficence, justice and integrity. The deep contextual engagement of science researchers leaves them well placed to leverage the benefits of AI while also safeguarding rights and dignity for their participants. The AI genie is well and truly out of the bottle, and proactive engagement with its complexities and opportunities is the only way forward.

Table 13.1. Best-practice guidelines for designing, developing and delivering responsible AI augmented research.

Guideline	Comments
Governance	Clear identification of the person responsible for errors or ethical breaches resulting from AI use in the study. Disclosure and documentation of potential perceived or actual conflicts of interest related to AI. Formal data management plan identifying the measures in place to secure data used by AI system from breaches, unauthorized access, or other unlawful use. Standing items for team meetings regarding: • audit of ethical implications and success of existing mitigation strategies, including ethical breaches or concerns; • reflection on the risk of reinforcing societal marginalization or discrimination due to AI system biases; • emerging longer-term implications or unintended consequences for participants and their communities, including the need to modify the study; • presentation of latest research or guidance regarding AI ethics practice to keep abreast of interdisciplinary developments; and • relevant regulatory changes and updates.
Methodology	Anonymization and encryption of sensitive participant data before AI system input. Clear reporting in protocol of compliance with relevant local, national, and international regulations and guidelines for the ethical use of AI in research. Collaboration with ethicists, technologists and other interdisciplinary stakeholders to inform and improve ethical AI implementation during protocol development. Consideration of the digital divide on the accessibility and fairness of the study, including: • access by researchers and participants to internet services and devices; • cultural and linguistic appropriateness of AI systems; and • clear reporting of who the AI system (or associated technology) excludes from the study. Development of an AI risk-management plan identifying all foreseeable risks and their mitigation strategies. Engagement with participants and communities during the study design process to: • understand their perceptions and expectations of proposed AI use; and • incorporate feedback into protocol development. Researcher-developed AI systems undergo regular security audits. Include mechanisms for participants to provide feedback about their experiences with AI during the study, to inform continuous improvement. Withdrawal of data from AI system at conclusion of study (if possible).

Continued

Table 13.1. Continued.

Guideline	Comments
Participant understanding and consent	Develop an iterative consent strategy, including clear and continuous communication strategies with participants about changes to AI systems (and/or resulting changes to methodology) during the study. Evaluate participants' understanding of AI and its use within the study by preparing additional materials for participants who want more information or need additional education for informed consent. Obtain separate and explicit consent for the use of data: • in the study for research purposes; and • by the AI system for training purposes. Ensure there are processes for obtaining renewed consent in response to changes in the AI system or methodology. Provide accessible participant information about: • the overall role of AI in the study; • how their data will be used by the AI system for both the study and ongoing training; and • potential risks and benefits associated with contributing their data to the AI system.
Reporting and dissemination	Document all ethical breaches or concerns and report them promptly to appropriate authorities. Review and comply with all institutional or publisher guidelines. Ensure transparent reporting of limitations and potential biases of the AI system.
Researcher capacity and training	Researcher capacity building for all team members specific to the implemented AI systems, including: • design, functionality, and decision-making processes of algorithms; • training procedure and datasets; • potential sources of bias; • impact of data-retention policies on participant privacy; and • policies around withdrawal of data. Team reflection on and planning for sustainable and adaptable use of AI in the study. Transparency of AI system developers around ethical standards, algorithms and other practices.

References

Alashoor, T., Keil, M., Liu, L.A. and Smith, H.J. (2015) How values shape concerns about privacy for self and others. In: *Proceedings of International Conference on Interaction Sciences, 9–13 November 2015, Seattle, Washington*. Association for Computing Machinery, New York.

Aldoseri, A., Khalifa, K.N.A. and Hamouda, A.M. (2023) Re-thinking data strategy and integration for artificial intelligence: concepts, opportunities, and challenges. *Applied Sciences* 13: 7082.

Arcilla, A., Espallardo, A., Gomez, C., Viado, E., Ladion, V. *et al*. (2023) Ethics in AI governance: comparative analysis, implication, and policy recommendations for the Philippines. In: *2023 27th International Computer Science and Engineering Conference (ICSEC), 9–13 November 2023, Seattle, Washington.* Association for Computing Machinery, New York, pp. 319–326.

Artal, R. and Rubenfeld, S. (2017) Ethical issues in research. *Best Practice & Research. Clinical Obstetrics & Gynaecology* 43, 107–114.

Asaro, P.M. (2023) Politicizing data: AI ethics as a social critique of algorithms. *Social Research* 90, 675–703.

Bender, E., Gebru, T., McMillan-Major, A. and Shmitchell, S. (2021) On the dangers of stochastic parrots: can language models be too big? In: *Proceedings of the 2021 ACM Conference on Fairness, Accountability, and Transparency*, 3–10 March, Virtual Event. Association for Computing Machinery, New York, pp. 610–623.

Bentley, S.V., Naughtin, C.K., McGrath, M.J., Irons, J.L. and Cooper, P.S. (2024) The digital divide in action: how experiences of digital technology shape future relationships with artificial intelligence. *AI and Ethics* 4, 901–915.

Bouhouita-Guermech, S., Gogognon, P. and Bélisle-Pipon, J. (2023) Specific challenges posed by artificial intelligence in research ethics. *Frontiers in Artifical Intelligence* 6: 1149082.

Boza, P., and Evgeniou, T. (2021) Implementing AI principles: frameworks, processes and tools. INSEAD Working Paper No. 2021/04/DSC/TOM. Social Science Research Network. Available at: https://papers.ssrn.com/sol3/papers.cfm?abstract_id=3783124 (accessed 3 October 2024).

Buolamwini, J. and Gebru, T. (2018) Gender shades: intersectional accuracy disparities in commercial gender classification. *Proceedings of Machine Learning Research* 81, 77–91.

Christou, P. (2023) A critical perspective over whether and how to acknowledge the use of artificial intelligence (AI) in qualitative studies. *The Qualitative Report* 28, 1981–1991.

Council of Publication Ethics (2023) Authorship and AI tools. Council of Publication Ethics, Eastleigh, UK. Available at: https://publicationethics.org/cope-position-statements/ai-author (accessed 3 October 2024).

Cruz-Jesus, F., Oliveira, T. and Bacao, F. (2018) The global digital divide. *Journal of Global Information Management* 26, 1–26.

Davis, J.E. and Scherz, P. (eds) (2019) Persons without qualities: algorithms, AI, and the reshaping of ourselves. *Social Research* 86, xxxiii–xxxix.

Dolunay, A. and Temel, A.C. (2024) The relationship between personal and professional goals and emotional state in academia: a study on unethical use of artificial intelligence. *Frontiers in Psychology* 15: 1363174.

Eichengreen, B., Aksoy, C.G. and Saka, O. (2021) Revenge of the experts: will COVID-19 renew or diminish public trust in science? *Journal of Public Economics* 193:104343.

Elsevier (2024) Publishing Ethics. Available at: www.elsevier.com/en-au/about/policies-and-standards/publishing-ethics (accessed 3 October 2024).

Fjeld, J., Achten, N., Hilligoss, H., Nagy, Á. and Srikumar, M. (2020) *Principled Artificial Intelligence: Mapping Consensus in Ethical and Rights-Based Approaches to Principles for AI*. Berkman Klein Centre for Internet and Society, Harvard, Cambridge, Massachusetts.

Fleming, P., Bayliss, A.P., Edwards, S.G. and Seger, C.R. (2021) The role of personal data value, culture and self-construal in online privacy behaviour. *PLOS ONE* 16: e0253568.

Flores, L. and Young, S.D. (2022) Ethical considerations in the application of artificial intelligence to monitor social media for COVID-19 data. *Minds and Machines* 32, 759–768.

Govia, L. (2020) Coproduction, ethics and artificial intelligence. *Journal of Digital Social Research* 2, 42–64.

Grant, D.G. (2018) Ethics and artificial intelligence in public health social work. In: Tambe, M. and Rice, E. (eds) *Artificial Intelligence for Social Good*. Cambridge University Press, Cambridge, UK, pp. 1–23.

Grohol, J. (2023) Koko Used GPT-3 AI without Informed Consent from Users. *New England Psychologist.* Available at: www.nepsy.com/articles/leading-stories/koko-used-gpt-3-ai-without-informed-consent-from-users/ (accessed 3 October 2024).

Guillemin, M., Gillam, L., Barnard, E., Stewart, P., Walker, H. *et al.* (2016) "We're checking them out": indigenous and non-indigenous research participants' accounts of deciding to be involved in research. *International Journal for Equity in Health* 15: 8.

Hagendorff, T. (2020) The ethics of AI ethics: an evaluation of guidelines. *Minds and Machines* 30, 99–120.

Harari, Y.N. (2023) AI and the Future of Humanity. YouTube. Available at: www.youtube.com/watch?v=L-WiM-LuRe6w (accessed 3 October 2024).

Hasselberger, W. (2019) Ethics beyond computation: why we can't (and shouldn't) replace human moral judgment with algorithms. *Social Research* 86, 977–999.

Hitch, D. (2023) Artificial intelligence augmented qualitative analysis: the way of the future? *Qualitative Health Research* 34, 595–606.

Ibrahim, H., Liu, X. and Denniston, A.K. (2021) Reporting guidelines for artificial intelligence in healthcare research. *Clinical & Experimental Ophthalmology* 49, 470–476.

Jeyaraman, M., Ramasubramanian, S., Balaji, S., Jeyaraman, N., Nallakumarasamy, A. *et al.* (2023) ChatGPT in action: harnessing artificial intelligence potential and addressing ethical challenges in medicine, education, and scientific research. *World Journal of Methodology* 13, 170–178.

Kidd, C. and Birhane, A. (2023) How AI can distort human beliefs: models can convey biases and false information to users. *Science* 380, 1222–1223.

King, N.M.P. and Churchill, L.R. (2000) Ethical principles guiding research on child and adolescent subjects. *Journal of Interpersonal Violence* 15, 710–724.

Law, R. (2015) The global digital divides: explaining change. *Information Technology & Tourism* 15, 185–187.

Liamputtong, P. (2019) *Qualitative Research Methods*. Oxford University Press, London.

Limongi, R. (2024) The use of artificial intelligence in scientific research with integrity and ethics. *Review of Artificial Intelligence in Education* 16: e845.

Lock, S. (1995) Research ethics – a brief historical review to 1965. *Journal of Internal Medicine* 238, 513–520.

McCradden, M.D., Sarker, T. and Paprica, P.A. (2020) Conditionally positive: a qualitative study of public perceptions about using health data for artificial intelligence research. *BMJ Open* 10: e039798.

Merenkov, A.V., Campa, R. and Dronishinets, N.P. (2021) Public opinion on artificial intelligence culture development. In: *XXIV International Conference on Culture, Personality, Society in the Conditions of Digitalization: Methodology and Experience of Empirical Research, 19–21 March 2021,* Yekaterinburg, Russia. KnE Open, Dubai, United Arab Emirates, pp. 565–574.

Morgan, D.L. (2023) Exploring the use of artificial intelligence for qualitative data analysis: the case of ChatGPT. *International Journal of Qualitative Methods* 22: 16094069231211248.

National Health and Medical Research Council (2023) *National Statement on Ethical Conduct in Human Research*. National Health and Medical Research Council, Canberra.

Nicholls, S.G., Hayes, T.P., Brehaut, J.C., McDonald, M., Weijer, C. *et al.* (2015) A scoping review of empirical research relating to quality and effectiveness of research ethics review. *PLOS ONE* 10: e0133639.

Nicoletti, L. and Bass, D. (2023) Humans are biased. Generative AI is even worse. *Bloomberg*. Available at: www.bloomberg.com/graphics/2023-generative-ai-bias/ (accessed 3 October 2024).

Ohagi, M. (2024) Polarization of autonomous generative AI agents under echo chambers. arXiv preprint. Available at: https://arxiv.org/abs/2402.12212 (accessed 3 October 2024).

Pieper, J. (1998) *Happiness and Contemplation*. Translated by Clara Winston and Richard Winston. St Augustine's Press, South Bend, Indiana.

Poremba, S. (2023) ChatGPT Confirms Data Breach, Raising Security Concerns. IBM Security Intelligence. Available at: https://securityintelligence.com/articles/chatgpt-confirms-data-breach/ (accessed 3 October 2024).

Rachels, J. and Rachels, S. (2006) *The Elements of Moral Philosophy*. McGraw Hill, New York.

Roberts, J., Baker, M. and Andrew, J. (2024) Artificial intelligence and qualitative research: the promise and perils of large language model (LLM) assistance. *Critical Perspectives on Accounting* 99: 102722.

Sharma, K. (2023) Compromised integrity in the era of AI? A critical examination of transparency and ethical dilemmas of academic research. *Gyankosh* 6, 78–93.

Shaw, J., Ali, J., Atuire, C.A., Cheah, P.Y., Español, A.G. *et al.* (2024) Research ethics and artificial intelligence for global health: perspectives from the global forum on bioethics in research. *BMC Medical Ethics* 25: 46.

Springer (2023) Artificial Intelligence (AI). Available at: www.springer.com/gp/editorial-policies/artificial-intelligence--ai-/25428500#:~:text=While%20legal%20issues%20relating%20to,in%20a%20legally%20acceptable%20manner (accessed 3 October 2024).

Su, Z., Cheshmehzangi, A., McDonnell, D., Chen, H., Ahmad, J. *et al.* (2022) Technology-based mental health interventions for domestic violence victims amid COVID-19. *International Journal of Environmental Research and Public Health* 19: 4286.

Thakur, S. and Lahiry, S. (2019) Research ethics in the modern era. *Indian Journal of Dermatology, Venereology and Leprology* 85, 351–354.

Thompson, C.L. and Morgan, H.M. (2020) Ethical barriers to artificial intelligence in the National Health Service, United Kingdom of Great Britain and Northern Ireland. *Bulletin of the World Health Organization* 98, 293–295.

UNESCO (2024) Ethics of Artificial Intelligence. UNESCO, Paris. Available at: www.unesco.org/en/artificial-intelligence/recommendation-ethics (accessed 3 October 2024).

Walsh, D. (2022) Timnit Gebru: Ethical AI Requires Institutional and Structural Change. *Stanford University Human-centered Artificial Intelligence.* Available at: https://hai.stanford.edu/news/timnit-gebru-ethical-ai-requires-institutional-and-structural-change (accessed 3 October 2024).

Wang, W., Wang, Y., Zhang, X., Jia, X., Li, Y. *et al.* (2020) Using WeChat, a Chinese social media app, for early detection of the COVID-19 outbreak in December 2019: retrospective study. *JMIR mHealth and uHealth* 8: e19589.

Weiser, B. (2023) Here's What Happens When Your Lawyer Uses ChatGPT. *New York Times.* Available at: https://www.nytimes.com/2023/05/27/nyregion/avianca-airline-lawsuit-chatgpt.html (accessed 31 May 2024).

Whittlestone, J., Nyrup, R., Alexandrova, A., Dihal, K. and Cave, S. (2019) *Ethical and Societal Implications of Algorithms, Data, and Artificial Intelligence: A Roadmap for Research*. Nuffield Foundation, London.

World Association of Medical Editors (2023) Chatbots, Generative AI, and Scholarly Manuscripts*:* WAME Recommendations on Chatbots and Generative Artificial Intelligence in Relation to Scholarly Publications. World Association of Medical Editors. Available at: https://wame.org/page3.php?id=106 (accessed 3 October 2024).

Zeng, D., Cao, Z. and Neill, D.B. (2021) Artificial intelligence-enabled public health surveillance – from local detection to global epidemic monitoring and control. In: Xing, L., Giger, M.L. and Min, J.K. (eds) *Artificial Intelligence in Medicine: Technical Basis and Clinical Applications*. Academic Press, London, pp. 437–453.

Zhuo, T., Huang, Y., Chen, C. and Xing, Z. (2023a) Red teaming ChatGPT via jailbreaking: bias, robustness, reliability and toxicity. arXiv preprint. Available at: https://arxiv.org/abs/2301.12867 (accessed 3 October 2024).

Zhuo, T., Huang, Y., Chen, C. and Xing, Z. (2023b) Exploring AI ethics of ChatGPT: a diagnostic analysis. arXiv preprint. Available at: https://arxiv.org/abs/2301.12867v3 (accessed 3 October 2024).

14 Precision Nudging: The Future of Behaviour Change?

Christos Themistocleous* and Evangelos Karapanos
Department of Communication & Marketing, Cyprus University of Technology, Limassol, Cyprus

Abstract

Behavioural science literature has seen the recent emergence of nudge theory, a proposition that behaviour change can be achieved by altering the 'choice architecture' of our physical and digital environments while considering the boundaries of human rationality. This chapter advocates the term 'precision nudging', the use of artificial intelligence to advance the efficacy of nudges while mitigating their adverse effects. It discusses two methods of precision nudging, tailoring and timing, and their potential in addressing adverse effects, in particular, behavioural spillovers and misfires. In doing so, the authors categorize nudges as reactive ones that aim at improving adverse effects and proactive ones that aim to shield individuals from future spillovers and misfires.

Keywords: behavioural spillover, just-in-time adaptive intervention, mobile health (mHealth), nudge theory, reinforcement learning

14.1 Introduction

Artificial intelligence (AI) has recently gained much attention for its prospect of advancing the efficacy of behaviour change technology. A prominent tool in behavioural sciences with the aim of steering individuals' decisions towards more beneficial, healthy alternatives is 'nudge', proposed in 2008 by Thaler and Sunstein. Since its conception, nudges have attracted much attention in terms of their types, contextual applications and effectiveness. Remaining under academic scrutiny, nudges have the potential of reshaping behavioural and social sciences. We attempt to make the case for how AI-mediated nudges can help address some of their downsides while enhancing their effectiveness.

The chapter is structured as follows. First, we provide an overview of what nudge theory entails and what qualifies as a nudge, and review its latest developments in social, behavioural and computer science literature. Second, we identify new ways in which AI can enhance the use of nudges by improving their effectiveness through two elements, namely, tailoring and timing, thus leading to 'precision nudging'. We present occasions where AI can identify nudge failures in the form of misfires and spillovers. Finally, we make recommendations on how AI can provide corrective courses for nudge failures while covering implications for behavioural, social and computer science research. Throughout the chapter, we employ behavioural pathways, visual representations of trajectories

*E-mail: c.themistocleous@cut.ac.cy

 Artificial Intelligence (AI) in Social Research (P.A. Christou ed.)
DOI: 10.1079/9781800626607.0014

that demonstrate intended and unintended behavioural changes. In these pathways we highlight AI-mediated corrective courses for when nudges create unintended adverse effects.

In terms of contextual application for our ideas, we use the example of smartwatches as fitness and well-being devices that provide visual, sound and haptic information that nudge users towards more beneficial behaviours through reminders, social comparison statistics and more. We note that beneficial behaviours are defined as behaviours that enhance individual and societal welfare. Concrete examples of the latter include exercising, more movement after large intervals of being idle for improved blood circulation, and sugar intake reduction in cases where the average intake significantly exceeds levels recommended by physicians.

14.2 Nudging for Behavioural Change

Nudge theory serves as the behavioural birth child of the heuristics and biases programme named after Tversky and Kahneman's *Science* paper (Tversky and Kahneman, 1974). They posited that heuristics (i.e. availability, representation and anchoring), frugal as they might be, can give rise to biases that hinder individuals from optimal decisions. This perspective on human rationality generated research streams that descended from their work and isolated occasions in which heuristics can lead to systematic errors. Although it is difficult to unsee such biases, Kahneman (2011) proposed that slow and analytical thinking processes can lead to better decisions compared with ones made by heuristics. Nudges are based on the assumption that human decisions aim to maximize expected utility in the most efficient, heuristic-based way. As such, the effort required to analytically evaluate the presented alternatives in a decision-making context is significant and can have ego-depleting effects (Baumeister *et al.*, 1998). In this context, nudging can help individuals make better, more efficient decisions in a chosen environment.

Thaler and Sunstein (2008, p. 6) defined nudges as: 'Any aspect of the choice architecture that alters people's behaviour in a predictable way without forbidding any options or significantly changing their economic incentives. To count as a mere nudge, the intervention must be easy and cheap to avoid. Nudges are not mandates.'

Choice architecture refers to the design of the different ways in which choices are presented to decision makers. A choice architect aiming at bettering the individual's well-being can present choices in ways that steer individuals towards beneficial outcomes, without restricting choices. Some examples of nudges are smart disclosures, default options, alternative suggestions, reminders, sequencing effects and opt-out policies, among others. Since its introduction, the concept of nudging has been eagerly explored in behavioural sciences and beyond, in a variety of contexts including welfare improvement, law compliance and disclosure decisions (Loewenstein *et al.*, 2014; Themistocleous *et al.*, 2014; Steffel *et al.*, 2016; Caraban *et al.*, 2019).

Nudges are set to lead individuals into more beneficial behaviours compared with the trajectory of behaviour where such nudges are absent. For example, an individual that has been idle for a prolonged period of time can be nudged towards a more beneficial behaviour – standing up and moving – compared with the continuation of the existing behaviour, which is remaining sedentary. Figure 14.1 visualizes the hypothesized use of nudges. Embedded in their design and philosophical positioning, nudges are not mandates, and thus one can choose to ignore them. The epitome of a nudge is that the expected utility of the nudged behaviour will exceed that of the projected behaviour.

Several empirical studies have shown nudging to be an effective behaviour change strategy (e.g. Hummel and Maedche, 2019). For instance, research found that a simple change to a default of double-sided printing led to a 15% paper reduction compared with the default counterpart of single-sided printing (Egebark and Ekström, 2016). In another example, the US company Opower found that their social comparison nudges, such as comparing one's energy consumption with that of one's neighbours, lead to a 2% reduction in energy consumption (Loewenstein *et al.*, 2014).

Nudges, nevertheless, may fail and may even produce adverse effects for a number of reasons – for example, due to the provision of complex or confusing information, repeated exposure or compensating behaviours (Sunstein,

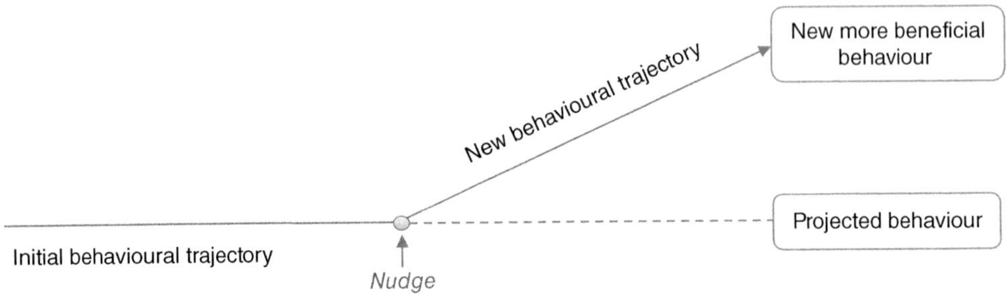

Fig. 14.1. A nudge behavioural pathway. An individual can ignore the nudge and continue with the projected behaviour.

2017). In human–computer interactions, Caraban *et al.* (2019) reviewed the use of nudging and identified seven reasons for nudge failures, such as their lack of educational effects (i.e. nudges working without depleting individuals' cognitive resources but their effects becoming obsolete once nudges are removed) or failing due to individuals' strong preferences and established habits. Choosing a nudge type in a given situation, or for a given individual, is also important. For instance, some individuals may be more prone to follow a social comparison nudge, while others might be more inclined to follow a nudge that explains the reasons or the benefits acquired from following the target behaviour, instead of what others are doing on the subject matter.

AI can help here. The aim of the following section is to show how AI can improve the effectiveness of nudges, focusing on two main dimensions: tailoring (i.e. selecting the right nudge type for a given individual or occasion) and timing (i.e. selecting the right point in time to deliver a nudge).

14.3 AI-mediated Nudges

Machine learning (ML) has enabled social, behavioural and data scientists to migrate from a one-size-fits-all approach in technology design towards a more tailored one, founded on psychographic insights and repeated behavioural patterns of users in a given environment. In the case of nudging, we suggest that AI can increase effectiveness by addressing two main questions: how to nudge (tailoring) and when to nudge (timing). Here, both timing and tailoring can enhance nudging in terms of its precision. Thus, we propose the term 'precision nudging' to describe AI-mediated nudges that are enhanced in terms of the point in time that they are presented and the form they take, dependent on the individual and the environment in which the behaviour occurs.

14.3.1 Tailoring

Tailoring refers to adapting the type of nudge, mode of delivery or any other aspect of the nudge's function, with the goal of increasing its effectiveness in a given situation, or for a given individual. As accurately pointed out by Kaptein *et al.* (2015), the following two statements '70% of users run at least twice a week' and 'fitness experts recommend that you run at least twice a week' are fundamentally different in the way they nudge. Some individuals might be more prone to follow social comparisons (first statement), while others might prefer prompts of exercise that stem from experts' opinions (second statement).

To delineate tailoring, consider an example where we are designing alternative nudges that aim at breaking individuals' sedentary behaviour through their smartwatches (e.g. see Gouveia *et al.*, 2016). Which heuristic do we attempt to tap into, and which type of nudge do we leverage? Individuals may vary in their susceptibility to different persuasion techniques, and as such, some nudges may be suitable for some individuals but not others. Individual differences in terms of need for cognition, scientific reasoning, numeracy, personality traits or general decision-making style will influence the effectiveness of different types of nudge for different individuals (Warberg *et al.*, 2019).

While measuring individuals' susceptibility to different cognitive biases psychometrically may be unrealistic, AI offers a pragmatic approach, that of reinforcement learning (RL). In its simplest form, RL is a technique that identifies the optimal behaviour in order to obtain the maximum reward. In essence, an AI agent is trained through interactions with the environment and the accumulation of observations and responses. Agents, through RL, learn as users interact with the model. A particular implementation of RL that is applicable to nudging is multi-armed bandits. In the example given above, assume that we have designed five different types of nudging to break sedentary behaviour. Each time we decide to nudge the individual to stand up and move, we select one of the five nudges. The individual is completely unknown to us – there are no prior data that describe their behavioural patterns, no information highlighting persuasion tactics that are more likely to be effective and no nudge type that is more favourable over another. Because of this, each nudge has an equal chance of being delivered (20% change). At each trial, we monitor a proximal behavioural variable (e.g. did the individual stand up and move for 50 steps or more during the 5 minutes following the delivery of the nudge?). This informs the model and thus, in each subsequent delivery, we have more knowledge about which of the five types of nudges is more likely to steer this individual to break their sedentary behaviour. The greater the sample of observations, the greater the certainty of nudge type effectiveness.

In the early steps, it may be more fruitful to 'explore' by trying out different types of nudges to acquire knowledge about the individual. Once sufficient knowledge is gathered (e.g. we know that a given type of nudge is significantly more likely than others to steer the individual's behaviour), we can exploit this information (i.e. use a particular nudge type over the others). Multi-armed bandits define the strategy and the mechanisms for this exploration versus exploitation dilemma and have been used effectively in both research and industry. For instance, Kaptein *et al.* (2015) leveraged Cialdini's principles of persuasion (Cialdini, 2009) to suggest the notion of persuasion profiles: while some of us may be more susceptible to the principle of reciprocity (i.e. to return a favour made to us), others may be more susceptible to the principle of scarcity (i.e. to be attracted by an offering whose availability is limited).

14.3.2 Timing

We propose that timing, or the selection of an appropriate point in time to deliver a nudge, is the second method of precision nudging. A time-to-stand-up nudge might be irrelevant when one engages in long drives, and a nudge for taking a walk outdoors might be more effective on a sunny instead of a rainy day. Timing should aim to infer variables from the individual's internal state and environment conditions so that the nudge is delivered at opportune moments. Interventions provided just in time will in essence both maximize their effectiveness and make a change in behaviour more attractive and beneficial. Consider having worked for 3 hours with no break from sedentary activity. This not only implies that a break is much needed but also that a nudge to have a break has a high likelihood of being successful.

Timing is a central tenet in just-in-time adaptive interventions (JITAIs), defined as 'intervention design(s) aiming to provide just-in-time support, by adapting the dynamics of an individual's internal state and context' (Nahum-Shani *et al.*, 2018, p. 448). In their work, they described how inferring with the individuals' internal state and behaviour, such as their mood, medication adherence, sleep, hallucination coping and social functioning, can help in providing schizophrenia patients with a timely and tailored intervention on how to cope when at a psychological peak, a time when help is most needed. Beyond JITAIs, inferring opportune moments for interventions has been a topic of considerable interest across various domains. For instance, Pielot *et al.* (2015) aimed at optimizing users' engagement with mobile phone notifications. They did so by inferring moments of boredom from a wide range of mobile phone sensor data and behavioural logs, and envisioned 'boredom-triggered proactive recommender systems that attune their users' level of attention and need for stimulation' (p. 1). In essence, they aim to influence and persuade an individual at a time when they are more receptive to a recommendation.

In a different line of work, psychologist Mihaly Csikszentmihalyi employed experience sampling, also known as ecological momentary assessment, where individuals were beeped around eight times a day in order to complete a short questionnaire about their feelings, thereby mitigating recall and other biases present in global measures of well-being (Csikszentmihalyi, 2002; Schwarz *et al.*, 2009). The tool aimed to address the challenge of the remembering self and the experiencing self. Prompting you to think how happy you felt the last time you played a guitar can create a misalignment compared with true emotions at the point of playing and the emotions you were just prompted to remember. By identifying opportune moments for triggering a survey during the day, experience sampling is aimed at reducing the chronological difference between the actual experience and the remembering of that experience, increasing recall accuracy.

While tackling these measurement challenges, experience sampling introduces new problems relating to the intrusiveness of the prompt, as participants need to stop their ongoing activity and complete the questionnaire. Recent efforts have attempted to utilize sensor data from smartphones to identify opportune moments to trigger experience sampling surveys, thereby reducing intrusiveness and maximizing the likelihood of a response, yet abiding to the chronological proximity requirements of experience sampling (Mehrotra *et al.*, 2015).

All in all, precision nudging can draw on these past efforts to tailor and time the delivery of nudges. However, these two methods of precision nudging, tailoring and timing, can be further used in mitigating the unintended consequences of nudging. What if someone follows the nudge, but a follow-up, unintended adverse behaviour is triggered? What if there is a misfire and the nudge does not trigger the right behaviour? What if the intervention nudges an individual to a worse-off situation? In the next section, we elaborate on two frequent unintended consequences, spillovers and misfires, and provide recommendations on how precision nudges can address them.

14.4 Mitigating Nudge Failures through AI

14.4.1 Nudge spillovers and AI

Spillovers in psychology relate to a person's behaviours, emotions and attitudes in one domain that can unintendedly flow into another (Zedeck, 1992) and can have either adverse or positive effects (Bell *et al.*, 2012). Detecting spillovers, in the context of nudging, is particularly important, as a seemingly beneficial behaviour triggered from a nudge can lead to an unintended adverse behaviour. Dolan and Galizzi (2015) echoed this argument and made an analogy between behavioural spillovers and ripples in a pond, prompting researchers to 'capture all ripples of behaviour when a pebble of intervention is thrown in the pond' (p. 2). In essence, once following a nudge, the new behavioural trajectory might lead the individual to a subsequent unintended adverse behaviour. We call this a nudge spillover with Fig. 14.2 depicting the respective behavioural pathway. The two behaviours, both intended and unintended, can cancel out the overall expected utility, ultimately leading to a

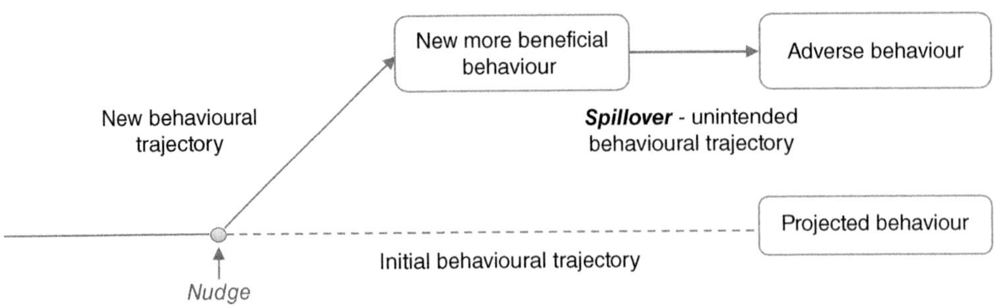

Fig. 14.2. A nudge spillover behavioural pathway.

worse-off situation for the individual. In this case, the nudge might end up doing more harm than good.

As an example, imagine that, following a prolonged period of sitting, an individual is nudged by their smartwatch to stand up. Adopting this behaviour is beneficial for the individual as prolonged periods of sedentarism have detrimental effects on blood circulation (Perdomo *et al.*, 2019), and correlate with all-cause mortality independent of leisure time (Katzmarzyk *et al.*, 2009). Imagine that the user responds to the nudge and stands up for their 1 minute walk; however, she walks into the office's kitchen and consume a few biscuits. A repetition of this behaviour creates a pattern with adverse effects: the individual uses the stand-up nudge as a biscuit reminder, making it a habit in the process. Assuming that the calorie intake from the biscuit is not desirable for the user, the nudge is seemingly effective in its purpose (to prompt movement), but it results in an unexpected negative effect, the unwanted increase in calorie intake.

AI can undertake a mitigating role here. First, assuming the presence of a continuous glucose-monitoring device, ML models can detect an emerging causal relationship between the nudge behaviour (i.e. standing up) and the spillover (i.e. calorie intake as inferred from the glucose monitor), and the contextual factors that play a role in such causal relationships. For example, this spillover might take place only in specific locations, such as the office due to the availability of biscuits in the office's kitchen, or at specific points in time, such as after lunch due to reactive hypoglycaemia. Second, once a spillover is identified, we propose two main courses of action: one that aims at preventing similar adverse effects in the future, a proactive nudge correction, and one that corrects current adverse behaviour, a reactive nudge correction. The two main tools for these adjustments are, as mentioned previously, timing and tailoring.

Figure 14.3 reflects how, following the AI-mediated identification of the spillover, the two types of nudge correction are triggered, proaction and reaction. A proactive nudge is aimed at future spillover prevention. As the present type of nudge was ineffective in preventing the spillover, what is needed is to identify a different type of nudge that is equally effective in achieving the intended behaviour but avoids the negative effect. In this case, a smart disclosure nudge that explains the benefits of standing up while simultaneously highlighting the negatives of sugar intake can reinforce the intended behaviour of standing and avoiding biscuit consumption. Timing, in contrast, aims to trigger this type of nudge at times where the probability of a spillover is low, especially if the utility of standing up is overshadowed by the sugar intake. This timing readjustment for precision nudging can be used tactically to break bad habits while steering the reinforcement of beneficial ones.

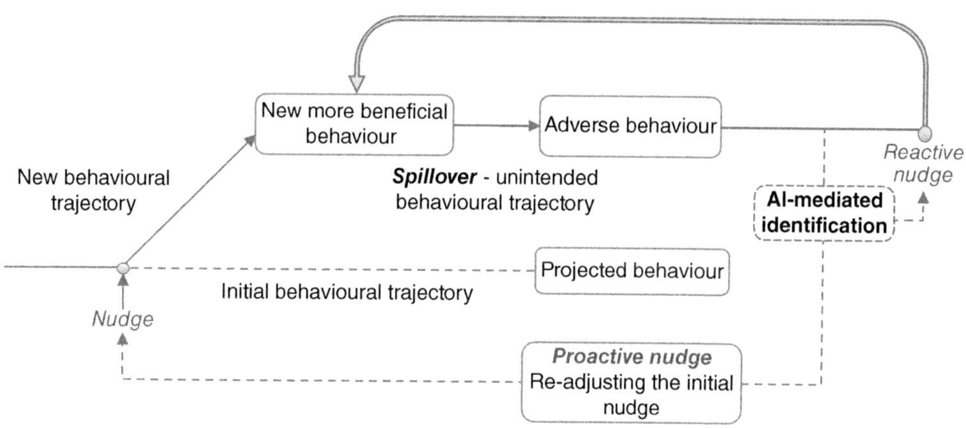

Fig. 14.3. AI-mediated identification and corrective courses for nudge spillovers.

A reactive nudge aims at correcting the current adverse behaviour caused from the spillover. This requires a new nudge and relates to the stage after the biscuit consumption and upon the user's return to her desk. The user can be met with a new nudge prompting her to measure her sugar levels, contrasting those figures with the desirable daily intake tailored to her case. The sugar level nudge timed after biscuit consumption can prompt the user to both readjust the sugar intake for the remainder of the day, reduce further consumption and simultaneously passively call for a behaviour re-evaluation that can affect the next behavioural cycle. Alternatives can also be offered in relation to other nudge types that mitigate this spillover effect or bypass the stand-up nudge during certain hours when biscuit consumption seems imminent.

14.4.2 Nudge misfires and AI

Nudges need to be tested to ensure they do what they are supposed to do (Thaler, 2015), but due to reasons pertaining to emotional states of individuals at the time of the nudge or the frequency of nudges, they can lead to reactance. Certain adverse behaviours might be triggered that deviate from the intended nudged trajectory. We call this a nudge misfire, as the initial nudge can lead directly to an unintended adverse behaviour, putting the individual at a deficit when compared with their initial behavioural trajectory. Figure 14.4 depicts the nudge misfire pathway.

As an example, a smartwatch-wearing user receives a nudge with the aim of prompting them to exercise. Here, the type of nudge was a social comparison nudge (similar to the one used by Opower mentioned earlier) where the targeted individual is nudged with information that facilitates comparisons with others in similar situations. As such, the user is met with information indicating that her calorie-burning performance is in the lowest quartile (bottom 25%) from a similar pool of other smartwatch users – 'Out of 1000 similar users, you are ranked 920th for your calorie-burning performance.' Although some findings report favourable comparative effects (i.e. Loewenstein *et al.*, 2014), others report adverse ones (Samra *et al.*, 2022), as comparisons can lead to low self-esteem and depressing states (White *et al.*, 2006).

The social comparison nudge here could have been effective for individuals in the top quartile putting them in a favourable, motivated position, but individuals being informed of their position in the lowest tiers might not only lead them to disregard the exercise nudge but also to enter a negative mood state. In this moment, the misfire took effect, making the user worse off. Specifically, the individual might balance out the negative emotional effects with consumption of unhealthy sugar-rich foods, an association

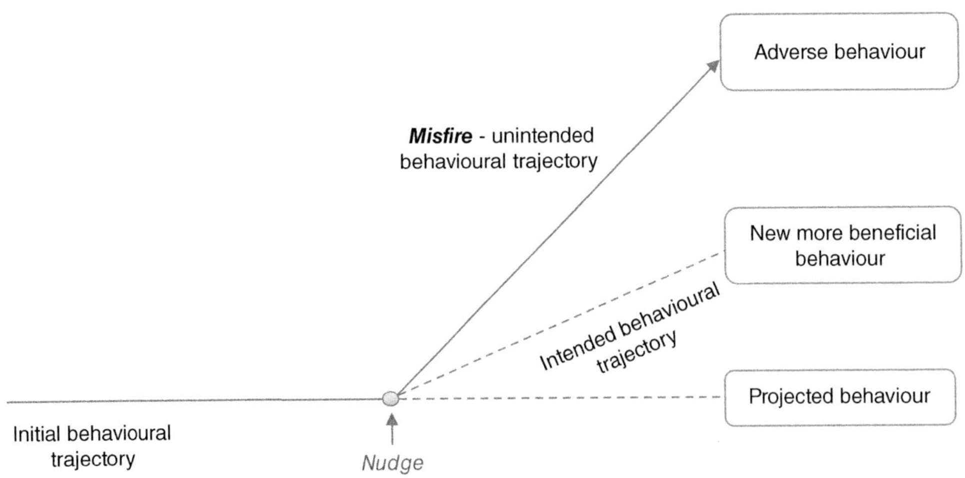

Fig. 14.4. A nudge misfire behavioural pathway.

that is systematically documented in psychological and nutritional research (Heatherton and Baumeister, 1991; Paans *et al.*, 2018). Here, the nudge failed to direct the user into a better behaviour, making things worse off for her in the process.

Similar to spillovers, triangulating the effects from multiple sources including the smartwatch and sugar meter is essential. In detecting phases of low self-esteem, multiple markers can be employed. Two examples include sugar intake and heart rate. Low self-esteem and depressive states are associated with sugary comfort food consumption (Paans *et al.*, 2018). Cardiovascular activity and specifically low heart rate, under certain conditions, is linked with low self-esteem levels (O'Donnell *et al.*, 2008). The inclusion of this and other parameters in the ML process can allow an AI agent to detect occasions where adverse effects have been recorded as a result of the initial nudge, primarily in the immediate phase after it. Following the identification, proactive and reactive nudge corrections are required. Figure 14.5 summarizes the two AI-mediated corrections.

The proactive correction requires a re-evaluation of the nudge type and its timing. In the previous example, the social comparison nudge was responsible for the misfire and thus needs to be substituted with a different nudge type. A nudge in the form of a reminder such as 'Let's exercise' can be more effective in facilitating a beneficial behaviour and mitigating the chance of an adverse unintended one. Timing wise, a social comparison nudge can be resumed when individuals have made their way to the first quartile (top 25%) of similar performers where comparisons with others are likely to work favourably in reinforcing intended behaviours.

The reactive nudge aims to correct the adverse effects caused by the first nudge and complement the proactive one. Once an individual enters the low self-esteem stage as a result of the nudge misfire, although challenging, a new nudge needs to reinstate self-esteem and confidence. In this case, a nudge prompting the user to take a moment to reflect on past successes and practising mindfulness can improve the adverse effects caused. A follow-up prompt to exercise, describing the benefits of exercising, can lead back to the initial beneficial behaviour and correct the adverse course caused (Randal *et al.*, 2015).

14.5 Conclusion

With the ability to analyse behavioural data, identify patterns and provide tailored interventions at the right time, AI offers the promise of more effective and precise behavioural interventions. In this chapter, we discussed how AI, and in particular, RL, can improve the effectiveness of

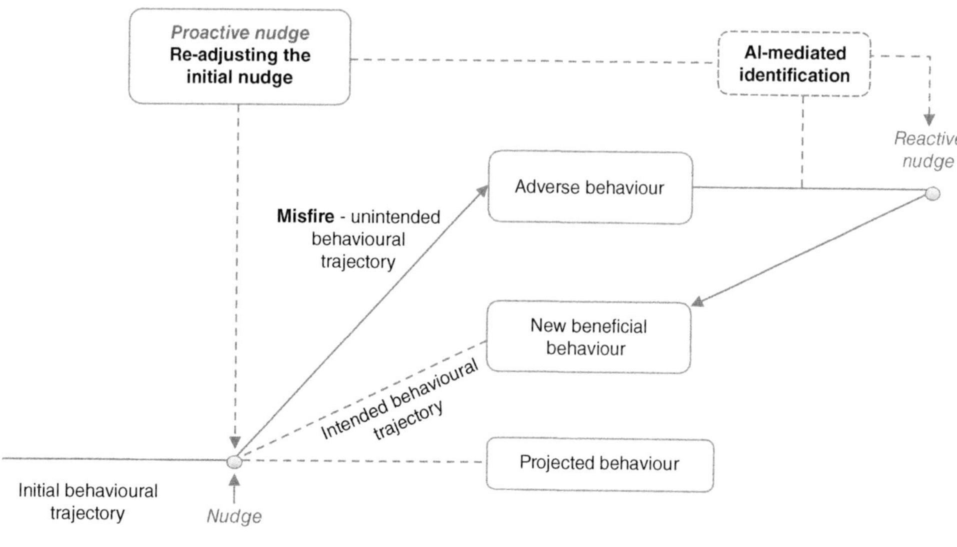

Fig. 14.5. AI-mediated identification and corrective courses for nudge misfires.

nudging while mitigating some of its downfalls, namely spillovers and misfires. We analysed the use of two methods, tailoring and timing, and exemplified their application using the conceptual tool of behavioural pathways.

As with all behavioural tools, nudges can fail. An individual might heed the call of a nudge but end up in a worse-off situation as a consequence. Likewise, a nudge might be ignored, but its type or timing might lead to a miscalculated adverse effect, generating a misfire. Better nudging serves as a seemingly straightforward solution to both problems, but the implementation is not. Identifying the exact moment when a nudge might be needed and heeded is challenging with conventional means. Here, we discussed a pragmatic approach offered by RL, and particularly multi-armed bandits, for the delivery of tailored and just-in-time nudging interventions. The implications of the proposed ideas are linked to persuasive technology designs and can further advance policy making that heightens an individual's benefit based on behavioural insights. Furthermore, precision nudges can also revolutionize sustainable marketing practices for the promotion of environmental, economic and societal well-being (Themistocleous, 2018, 2023) by tailoring nudge types based on consumer data and psychological profiling, nudging individuals to reconsider consumption or recycling patterns.

Our analysis highlights a number of implications and directions for future research. We have conceptualized the terms of reactive and proactive nudges when handling misfires and spillovers. Future empirical research should explore how reactive, corrective nudges can help mitigate adverse effects of a previously delivered nudge. When individuals enter induced nudge spillover and misfire situations, tests can be conducted to examine the effectiveness of reactive nudges for resolving the issues caused. Mapping certain nudge types that equalize the adverse effects of others can provide social and computer researchers with a nudge recovery toolbox for when nudges fail, while multi-armed bandits can generate precision nudges that provide solutions regarding when and in which form nudges can assist with future spillover and misfire prevention.

References

Baumeister, R.F., Bratslavsky, E., Muraven, M. and Tice, D.M. (1998) Ego depletion: is the active self a limited resource? *Journal of Personality and Social Psychology* 74, 1252–1265.

Bell, A.S., Rajendran, D. and Theiler, S. (2012) Job stress, wellbeing, work-life balance and work–life conflict among Australian academics. *E-Journal of Applied Psychology* 8, 25–37.

Caraban, A., Karapanos, E., Gonçalves, D. and Campos, R. (2019) 23 ways to nudge: a review of technology-mediated nudging in human–computer interaction. In: *CHI Conference on Human Factors in Computing Systems Proceedings (CHI 2019), 4–9 May, 2019*, Glasgow, UK, Article 503.

Cialdini, R.B. (2009) *Influence: Science and Practice*. Pearson Education, Boston, Massachusetts.

Csikszentmihalyi, M. (2002) *Flow: The Classic Work on How to Achieve Happiness*. Rider, London.

Dolan, P. and Galizzi, M.M. (2015) Like ripples on a pond: behavioral spillovers and their implications for research and policy. *Journal of Economic Psychology* 47, 1–16.

Egebark, J. and Ekström, M. (2016) Can indifference make the world greener? *Journal of Environmental Economics and Management* 76, 1–13.

Gouveia, R., Pereira, F., Karapanos, E., Munson, S.A. and Hassenzahl, M. (2016) Exploring the design space of glanceable feedback for physical activity trackers. In: *2016 ACM International Joint Conference on Pervasive and Ubiquitous Computing (UbiComp 2016), 12–16 September 2016, Heidelberg, Germany*, pp. 144–155.

Heatherton, T.F. and Baumeister, R.F. (1991) Binge eating as escape from self-awareness. *Psychological Bulletin* 110, 86–108.

Hummel, D. and Maedche, A. (2019) How effective is nudging? A quantitative review on the effect sizes and limits of empirical nudging studies. *Journal of Behavioral and Experimental Economics* 80, 47–58.

Kahneman, D. (2011) *Thinking, Fast and Slow*. Penguin Books, London.

Kaptein, M., Markopoulos, P., de Ruyter, B. and Aarts, E. (2015) Personalizing persuasive technologies: explicit and implicit personalization using persuasion profiles. *International Journal of Human–Computer Studies* 77, 38–51.

Katzmarzyk, P.T., Church, T.S., Craig, C.L. and Bouchard, C. (2009) Sitting time and mortality from all causes, cardiovascular disease, and cancer. *Medicine & Science in Sports & Exercise* 41, 998–1005.

Loewenstein, G., Sunstein, C.R. and Golman, R. (2014) Disclosure: psychology changes everything. *Annual Review of Economics* 6, 391–419.

Mehrotra, A., Vermeulen, J., Pejovic, V. and Musolesi, M. (2015) Ask, but don't interrupt. In: *Adjunct Proceedings of the 2015 ACM International Joint Conference on Pervasive and Ubiquitous Computing and Proceedings of the 2015 ACM International Symposium on Wearable Computers, 7–11 September 2015, Osaka, Japan*, pp. 723–232.

Nahum-Shani, I., Smith, S.N., Spring, B.J., Collins, L.M., Witkiewitz, K. *et al.* (2018) Just-in-time adaptive interventions (JITAIs) in mobile health: key components and design principles for ongoing health behavior support. *Annals of Behavioral Medicine* 52, 446–462.

O'Donnell, K., Brydon, L., Wright, C.E. and Steptoe, A. (2008) Self-esteem levels and cardiovascular and inflammatory responses to acute stress. *Brain, Behavior, and Immunity* 22, 1241–1247.

Paans, N.P.G., Bot, M., Brouwer, I.A., Visser, M., Roca, M. *et al.* (2018) The association between depression and eating styles in four European countries: the MooDFOOD Prevention Study. *Journal of Psychosomatic Research* 108, 85–92.

Perdomo, S.J., Gibbs, B.B., Kowalsky, R.J., Taormina, J.M. and Balzer, J.R. (2019) Effects of alternating standing and sitting compared to prolonged sitting on cerebrovascular hemodynamics. *Sport Sciences for Health* 15, 375–383.

Pielot, M., Dingler, T., Pedro, J.S. and Oliver, N. (2015) When attention is not scarce – detecting boredom from mobile phone usage. In: *Proceedings of the 2015 ACM International Joint Conference on Pervasive and Ubiquitous Computing* (UbiComp 2015), 7–11 September 2015, *Osaka, Japan*, pp. 825–836.

Randal, C., Pratt, D. and Bucci, S. (2015) Mindfulness and self-esteem: a systematic review. *Mindfulness* 6, 1366–1378.

Samra, A., Warburton, W.A. and Collins, A.M. (2022) Social comparisons: a potential mechanism linking problematic social media use with depression. *Journal of Behavioral Addictions* 11, 607–614.

Schwarz, N., Kahneman, D., Xu, J., Belli, R., Stafford, F. *et al.* (2009) Global and episodic reports of hedonic experience. In: *Using Calendar and Diary Methods in Life Events Research*. Sage Publications, Thousand Oaks, California, pp. 157–174.

Steffel, M., Williams, E.F. and Pogacar, R. (2016) Ethically deployed defaults: transparency and consumer protection through disclosure and preference articulation. *Journal of Marketing Research* 53, 865–880.

Sunstein, C.R. (2017) Nudges that fail. *Behavioural Public Policy* 1, 4–25.

Thaler, R. (2015) *Misbehaving: The Making of Behavioural Economics*. W.W. Norton & Company, New York.

Thaler, R. and Sunstein, C. (2008) *Nudge: Improving Decisions About Wealth, and Happiness*. Penguin Books, London.

Themistocleous, C. (2018) Customer data: contemporary issues of privacy and trust. In: Vrontis, D., Weber, Y., Thrassou, A., Shams, S. and Tsoukatos, E. (eds) *Innovation and Capacity Building*. Palgrave Macmillan, Cham, Switzerland, pp. 167–185.

Themistocleous, C. (2023) Sustainable marketing. In: *Concise Encyclopaedia of Corporate Social Responsibility*. Edward Elgar Publishing, London, pp. 215–218.

Themistocleous, C., Smith, A. and Wagner, C. (2014) The ethical dilemma of implicit vs explicit data collection: examining the factors that influence the voluntary disclosure of information by consumers to commercial organizations. In: *2014 IEEE International Symposium on Ethics in Engineering, Science, and Technology (ETHICS), 23 May 2014, Chicago, Illinois*. IEEE Press, Piscataway, New Jersey, Article 37.

Tversky, A. and Kahneman, D. (1974) Judgment under uncertainty: heuristics and biases. *Science* 185, 1124–1131.

Warberg, L., Acquisti, A. and Sicker, D. (2019) Can privacy nudges be tailored to individuals' decision making and personality traits? In: *Proceedings of the 2019 ACM SIGSAC Conference on Computer and Communications Security (CCS 2019), 11–15 November 2019, London*. Association for Computing Machinery, New York, pp. 175–197.

White, J.B., Langer, E.J., Yariv, L. and Welch, J.C. (2006) Frequent social comparisons and destructive emotions and behaviors: the dark side of social comparisons. *Journal of Adult Development* 13, 36–44.

Zedeck, S. (ed.) (1992) *Work, Families, and Organizations*. Jossey-Bass Publishers, San Francisco, California.

15 Competence Frameworks for Exploring Generative AI in Education

Pablo Burneo[1], António P. Costa[2*], Isabel Pinho[2], Aline B.X. Muniz[3] and Eduardo A.D. Moresi[3]

[1]*Universidad San Francisco de Quito, Quito, Ecuador;* [2]*University of Aveiro, Aveiro, Portugal;* [3]*Catholic University of Brasília, Taguatinga, Brazil*

Abstract

This chapter explores the integration of generative artificial intelligence (genAI) tools in higher education, focusing on designing competence frameworks for equitable and inclusive implementation. It discusses the challenges associated with assessing competences and highlights the ResearchComp framework developed by the European Commission as a valuable tool for researchers. The chapter proposes a model for competence frameworks, emphasizing critical thinking, problem solving, collaboration, ethics and continuous learning as key competencies for genAI integration. It underscores the importance of transparency, ethical decision making and collaboration among stakeholders involved in AI education. Ensuring inclusivity and equity is crucial, considering cultural influences and incorporating diverse perspectives in curriculum development. The chapter concludes by addressing challenges and opportunities in integrating genAI tools in educational settings, emphasizing the need for comprehensive training, motivation and ongoing support for educators and students. Overall, the chapter promotes the responsible use of genAI to enhance learning experiences and foster inclusive education.

Keywords: educational research, higher education, responsible AI

15.1 Introduction

Competences are complex ability constructs that are context specific, trainable and closely related to real life, highlighting the challenges in their assessment and the need for more interdisciplinary research (Koeppen *et al.*, 2008). Competences are crucial for researchers, allowing them to conduct high-quality research to succeed in a competitive research environment (Alasadi and Baiz, 2023; van Dis *et al.*, 2023). In this context, the European Commission made available the ResearchComp framework (de Coen and Núñez, 2022), divided into seven areas of competence (cognitive abilities, doing research, managing research, managing research tools, making an impact, working with others and self-management).

The *Mentoring Handbook* by Boden and Teperi (2024) presents, beyond the ResearchComp framework, some proposals for tools to analyse (academic) skills and competencies and the potential to improve them. For example, the University of Edinburgh Research Careers Tool helps researchers select and prioritize their activities to further their research careers. This resource raises concern about the competencies researchers must develop to have successful

*E-mail: apcosta@ua.pt

DOI: 10.1079/9781800626607.0015

careers, enhance research quality, formulate policy, and contribute to the research community and society in general (Alasadi and Baiz, 2023; Bahroun *et al.*, 2023; Lim *et al.*, 2023; Stokel-Walker and van Noorden, 2023; van Dis *et al.*, 2023).

In education research, Khan (2021) stressed the importance of technical and non-technical abilities, such as research conduct, workplace skills and discipline-specific knowledge. Anderson *et al.* (2018) and Ciraso-Calí *et al.* (2022) proposed models for research competencies, with the former focusing on skills in reviewing research, methodology, reflection, communication and content knowledge, and the latter identifying state-of-the-art reviewing and communicative skills as areas for improvement. Some authors have addressed enhancing competencies, such as Vasetskaya *et al.* (2018), who provided a model for training university staff in research and teaching. That research project emphasized the importance of developing appropriate competencies for university staff in research and teaching roles, such as professors, teachers and researchers. It proposed an innovative framework that included personal, social, ethical and professional competencies (Alasadi and Baiz, 2023; Wach *et al.*, 2023). Developing these skills is relevant for researchers, teachers and students, as they influence each other. However, Prosekov *et al.* (2020) concentrated on developing research activities to improve research competency in students. They introduced a comprehensive set of criteria indicators for evaluating students' research competence, with findings indicating heightened motivation and enhanced gnoseological development among students.

Moreover, more advanced operational and personal components correlate with improved research reports and the quality of scientific publications. Koeppen *et al.* (2008) offered a comprehensive view of models for research competencies and skills as intricate ability structures specific to a particular situation that can be developed through training. Finally, the ethical guidelines regarding artificial intelligence (AI) and data usage in education must aim to assist educators in comprehending the benefits and risks associated with utilizing AI and data in teaching and learning, enabling them to engage with AI systems in a positive, critical and ethical manner to maximize their potential (European Commission, Directorate-General for Education, Youth, Sport, and Culture, 2022).

As this chapter does not discuss the different definitions of competence, competency, competent and competencies inside and outside of academia, the difference needs to be clarified, with no universally agreed-upon definition. According to Arifin (2021), a hierarchy between these concepts based on their specificity and application can be established to understand these terms better and distinguish them from each other. While the terms 'competency' and 'competence' are related and often used interchangeably, different authors (Teodorescu, 2006; Birnbaum and Daily, 2009; Guthrie, 2009; Moghabghab *et al.*, 2018; Arifin, 2021) may have varying interpretations or perspectives on their definitions and relationships. In our chapter, we will follow the definition used by ResearchComp, which uses competence or competences as a combination of knowledge, skills and attitudes (de Coen and Núñez, 2022).

With the abrupt growth of generative AI (genAI), several authors have already highlighted the need for a competence framework for researchers (Miracchi, 2019; Faruqe *et al.*, 2022; Muttaqin, 2022; Sattelmaier and Pawlowski, 2023). Miracchi (2019) presented a theoretical and methodological framework for studying 'artificial minded intelligence'. The work also presents a comprehensive methodological called 'generative methodology' and a specific variant of this technique known as the 'Competence Framework for AI research'. These two frameworks aim to guide students in effectively using genAI, preserving the development of essential competences and providing a methodological approach to AI research, respectively. To responsibly employ AI in educational contexts, it is crucial to balance utilizing its advantages, addressing hazards, and incorporating human oversight and morals (Le Borgne *et al.*, 2024).

This chapter delves into the possibilities that genAI offers within the education landscape. It is structured to seek to understand how best to structure the integration of genAI in higher education and, at the same time, enhance competence development in this era. Subsequently, we examine the formulation of competence frameworks tailored for genAI integration in educational settings. This segment exposes what is mentioned as essential proficiencies requisite for adeptly incorporating genAI into educational landscapes through thoroughly examining pertinent literature and analysing existing frameworks. It emphasizes the need to promote inclusivity and justice by implementing these tools and developing competences.

We explore the integration of genAI tools within educational settings from diverse perspectives, underlining initiatives geared towards professional development among educators and strategies aimed at fostering student engagement with AI tools. We envision future avenues of research and praxis, underscoring the imperative of cultivating a beta version of a genAI competence framework. We advocate for sustained endeavours to refine competence frameworks, examine the nexus between genAI and educational equity and inclusion, and confront institutions' unique challenges in embracing genAI-driven paradigms.

15.2 Understanding GenAI in Higher Education

Higher education has a growing recognition of the importance of cultivating competencies and AI literacy to navigate the evolving educational terrain (Al-Zahrani, 2023; UNESCO, 2023; Xia *et al.*, 2024). Integrating AI into educational practices has become increasingly prevalent, prompting educators and researchers to reconsider traditional approaches to curriculum design and pedagogy (Chiu, 2023; Kadaruddin, 2023). This evolution necessitates not only a revaluation of educational content but also a reflection within scientific research, as well as among students, teachers and researchers in higher education, to acquire the competencies needed to engage meaningfully with AI (Baidoo-Anu and Ansah, 2023; Zekaj, 2023; Messeri and Crockett, 2024).

The educational ecosystem has been incorporating AI, with different intensities, at varying levels of education systems. Education must be based on four pillars: learning to know, learning to do, learning to live together and learning to be (International Commission on Education for the Twenty-first Century, 1996). GenAI forces us to rethink how educational content is designed, personalized and delivered. Another essential reflection concerns how to foster the development of students' skills to use genAI responsibly and effectively (Chauncey and McKenna, 2023; Halaweh, 2023). GenAI must ensure it aligns with the pedagogical missions of inspiring curiosity, ensuring equity and fostering deep, meaningful learning. This nuanced exploration ventures into the matrix of algorithmic learning initiatives to answer the question: What are the fundamental principles behind genAI in educational settings?

GenAI in educational settings is a multidimensional and evolving field, focusing on social interaction, personalized learning and ethical considerations (Zhai *et al.*, 2021; Christou, 2023; Kadaruddin, 2023). It impacts instructional strategies, such as personalized learning experiences and interactive content creation (Kadaruddin, 2023). This renewed vision of education advocates the redefinition of pedagogy, incorporating fundamental principles of cooperation, collaboration and solidarity; it also proposes curricula emphasizing ecological, intercultural and interdisciplinary learning (Chiu, 2024), empowering students to access and produce knowledge.

Similarly, the report *Technology in Education: A Tool on Whose Terms?* by UNESCO (2023) addresses the importance of intelligently addressing the inclusion of AI tools. This report presents the challenges faced in incorporating technology into educational processes. Even though the technology is presented as a hope for providing solutions to academic challenges, it highlights the need for more evidence of the results of the improvements that these systems have generated. In this perspective, Chiu (2023) argued that the educational future needs to include relevant studies delineating how education should be conceived. Lim *et al.* (2023) highlighted that the transformation of education is still slow compared with the rapidly emerging trends in technological development. However, Cao and Dede (2023), in a more encouraging perspective, proposed a look at how education should be conceived, suggesting an approach to education focused on the process and not on the product, as they consider that 'the essence of learning is the process' (p. 3). This change implies the inclusion of AI as an interlocutor and requires reforms in educational curricula where, in this new proposal, AI is incorporated within the academic plan (Cao and Dede, 2023).

However, concerns about data privacy, algorithmic bias and the role of educators in AI-driven learning experiences must be addressed (Kadaruddin, 2023). Higher education institutions are joining other companies and organizations in embracing AI in several ways: (i) administrative support; (ii) teaching; (iii) learning: and (iv) research support (Moresi *et al.*, 2024).

The use of genAI in computing education has been explored, focusing on prompt engineering and the perspectives of students and instructors (Hutson and Robertson, 2023; Zastudil *et al.*, 2023). The design of genAI applications should consider principles such as multiple outcomes, exploration, control and potential harm (Weisz *et al.*, 2023).

GenAI can improve traditional educational approaches by enhancing instructional design, personalizing learning experiences and creating interactive content (Kadaruddin, 2023; Ruiz-Rojas *et al.*, 2023). However, its widespread use in higher education also presents challenges, such as the need for digital literacy and ethical use (Walczak and Cellary, 2023). Software development education has suggested tools to assess genAI use or results to help learners understand the subject material (Petrovska *et al.*, 2024). GenAI has also been evaluated for various scenarios in programming education, with GPT-4 showing promising performance (Phung *et al.*, 2023).

This leads us to AI literacy, which appeals to transversal and specific skills (Laupichler *et al.*, 2022, 2023; Carolus *et al.*, 2023). At a research level, a relevant starting point is to read the ResearchComp framework described in de Coen and Núñez (2022). This document was built to provide a shared vision of the knowledge, skills and attitudes researchers need for a successful research career inside and outside academia. This framework provides a helpful tool for monitoring skills and training at the institutional level by clarifying what competences researchers need and how these competencies could evolve from a foundational to an expert level. The ResearchComp framework comprises seven competence areas (cognitive abilities, doing research, managing research, managing research tools, making an impact, working with others and self-management) and 38 competences, with 389 learning outcomes along four proficiency levels (foundational, intermediate, advanced and expert) (Fig. 15.1).

The ResearchComp framework is an umbrella tool for helping researchers identify their competences and training needs. These must be considered when using AI to improve the quality of research.

In short, we must go beyond the debate of whether to use AI and emphasize the responsible use of genAI through acquiring digital competences based on ethical principles and respect for human rights. These are the driving ideas for developing competence frameworks for genAI in education. The following section explains the initial phase of the proposal for this framework.

15.3 Competence Frameworks for GenAI in Education

This section will explore competence frameworks that can be used with genAI in education. While the term 'competence' can apply to a wide range of abilities, knowledge and attitudes, we will concentrate on a 'competence' framework that focuses on the specific talents and traits required for proficiency in integrating genAI into educational settings (Teodorescu, 2006; Guthrie, 2009; Arifin, 2021). Using a competence framework approach, we hope to provide a deep and focused study of the critical competences tailored for each segment: educators, researchers and students required to apply genAI in education effectively. This approach enables us to discover and prioritize essential skills and traits necessary to use genAI successfully for educational purposes.

Various competence frameworks have been proposed using genAI for distinct purposes. Brauner *et al.* (2025) identified five key competence categories for AI professionals, including data science and AI product development. The proposed competence frameworks for genAI, as determined by Brauner *et al.* (2025), intersect with the broader study of competencies, which encompasses principles, methods and dimensions elucidated by Le Boterf (2003), where competence is conceptualized as the integration of knowledge, skills and attitudes yielding competent actions aligned with objectives.

In this conceptual line, competence frameworks in genAI in education should be aligned

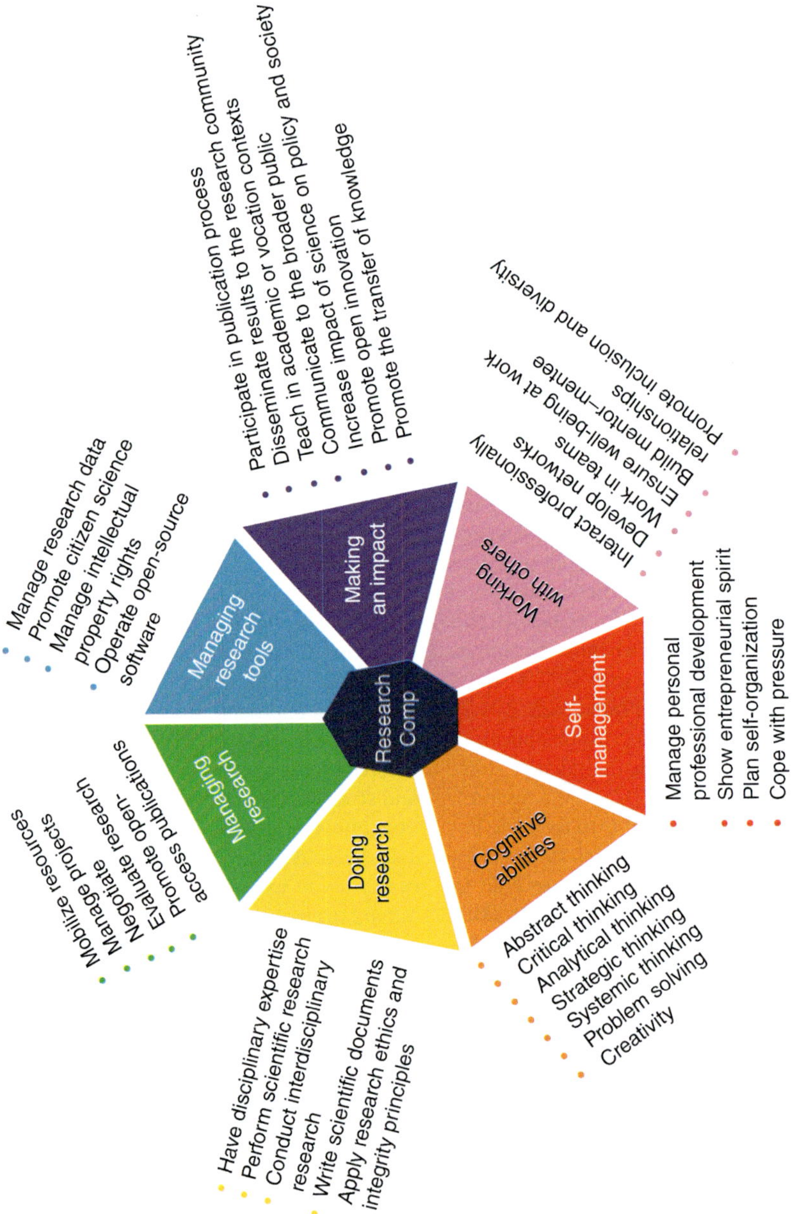

Fig. 15.1. The ResearchComp framework. From de Coen and Núñez (2022, p. 14).

with these structures, distancing themselves from technicist concepts of competences. The theoretical assumptions of Bloom's taxonomy are a viable way of structuring competence frameworks (Bloom *et al.*, 1956). According to Conklin (2005), Bloom's taxonomy and its hierarchical classification of learning objectives are surprisingly aligned between the technical and the reflective, covering high levels of reasoning and abstractions without distancing themselves from the educational purpose. Thanh *et al.* (2023) developed a framework for assessing the capabilities of genAI tools, finding that they perform well at lower levels of Bloom's taxonomy.

Taxonomies can be used to construct competence frameworks to guide educational objectives. Competencies are targeted according to the stages of maturation. The hierarchical structure comprises knowledge, comprehension, application, analysis, synthesis and evaluation. One example of innovation in taxonomy studies is including metacognitive knowledge in the knowledge category (Conklin, 2005).

This emerging need for genAI competences and their integration into the evolving educational landscape is forcing researchers and teachers to reshape their working strategies. Models such as GPT-4 (or older free versions such aş GPT 3.5) have exemplified the transforming evidence and potential to facilitate personalized learning experiences and adaptive assessments (Kadaruddin, 2023; Phung *et al.*, 2023) and offer capabilities for content creation, personalization and adaptive learning (Lim *et al.*, 2023; Sætra, 2023).

While these benefits are clear, the problems and challenges are taking shape, as there are evident drawbacks, such as the need for digital literacy, ethical control of the creation of content and the need for a new digital literacy (Walczak and Cellary, 2023). Identifying the critical capabilities and knowledge needed for genAI involves understanding this technology's technical and ethical aspects and promoting a continuous learning approach (Alasadi and Baiz, 2023).

Quality education (goal 4) is also included in the Sustainable Development Goals (SDGs) plan of the United Nations. Scott (2015) mentioned that 21st-century skills can be organized into pillars of education. He described the respective skills within these pillars. He also stated that, 'Above all, these competencies emphasize active learning' (p. 4). This classification from Scott (2015) is presented in Table 15.1. In addition, according to the ResearchComp framework (de Coen and Núñez, 2022), training should be focused on core research activities, as transferable skills are essential for career development.

This procedure of promoting interactive and adaptive learning and aligning it with a sustainable quality education must be aligned with the needs of the social context, so several proposals seek to define what is conceived as the competences of the 21st century. In 2021, the World Economic Forum published its report in which it reconceptualized the taxonomy of the language of skills and competences needed for the future. Ruiz-Rojas *et al.* (2023) emphasized the potential of genAI in education. They highlighted the importance of an instructional design matrix, which serves as a blueprint for structuring digital content creation experiences that effectively integrate generative AI technologies. Sanusi *et al.* (2022a) delved deeper into the competences needed for AI education, emphasizing cognitive abilities, human–tool collaboration, self-learning, technical competence and ethical considerations. These competencies were also explored among other competences such as personalized learning processes, providing enhanced knowledge acquisition experiences, real-time formative assessment, interactive and adaptive learning, and elimination of language barriers, among other benefits (Alasadi and Baiz, 2023; Baidoo-Anu and Ansah, 2023; Cao and Dede, 2023; Llorens-Largo *et al.*, 2023; Mujiono, 2023; Qadir, 2023; Zhai *et al.*, 2024). From a constructive perspective, it is undeniable that genAI has the potential to transform education by providing personalized learning experiences; in a world where education must be connected to the natural environment, both students and educators must understand not only the use of AI but also its nature and social consequences (Chassignol *et al.*, 2018).

Furthermore, Faruqe *et al.* (2022) built on this by advocating for a competence model approach to AI literacy, which could guide instructional content development. These studies underscore the need for a competence framework tailored to explore genAI in education, which should incorporate the GenAI Content

Table 15.1. Learning competences and skills for 21st century. Based on Scott (2015); European Commission, Directorate-General for Education, Youth, Sport, and Culture (2022) and Holmes and Miao (2023).

Pillar	Description	Competences and skills
Learning to know	Mastery of core subjects and learning related to the thematic areas, aligned with experience	Knowledge of fundamental subjects such as grammar, language, languages, mathematics, economics, culture and humanities, among others
Learning to do	Linking knowledge and skills, learning and competences and turning them into valuable skills	Transferable skills • Critical thinking • Problem solving • Analytical thinking Technological literacy • Managing research tools Doing and managing research • Perform scientific research Writing research documents Knowledge transfer Creativity and innovation Communication and collaboration
Learning to be	Personal qualities that shape identities guide their responses to failure and prepare individuals to face difficulties and problems	Cognitive skills • Social and intercultural competences • Sense-making competences Self-management: initiative, autonomy and personal responsibility • Cope with pressure • Plan self-organization Metacognitive competences Lifelong learning and learning habits throughout life
Learning to live together	Collaborative learning and knowledge creation to reach higher thinking levels	Working with others: teamwork and interconnectedness • Develop networks • Work in teams • Promote inclusion and diversity Global competence • Understanding the context Seeking and valuing diversity Ethics and privacy • Data privacy • Hallucination identification

Generation Framework, an instructional design matrix, and the identified competencies for AI education.

These discussions underscore the need for a higher education competence framework tailored for exploring genAI in education, which should incorporate a content framework or an instructional design matrix and a set of the top identified competencies for AI education. A competence framework is a comprehensive set of knowledge, skills and attitudes that students, educators and researchers must possess to carry out their professional duties effectively. This framework typically includes domains such as pedagogical, personal, social and professional competencies (Kadaruddin, 2023). The specific competences within these domains can vary but often include knowledge, understanding, values and attitudes. The development of such a framework can be influenced by theoretical perspectives, research trends, and existing and developing literature (Miracchi, 2019).

While several authors (Alasadi and Baiz, 2023; Qadir, 2023; Ruiz-Rojas *et al.*, 2023) have discussed the need to develop a competence framework aligned to the changing needs in genAI, not all of them have defined clear structures and proposals on how to approach the creation of this framework in this new context. Table 15.2 summarizes the proposed approaches and the competences identified as key to this transformative process.

In designing and implementing competence frameworks for genAI researchers, as presented in Table 15.2, the approach and steps are not the only ones to be aligned to obtain a robust framework. These tools should be aligned with desired goals, such as the SDGs outlined by the United Nations, and supported by the essential competencies within the analysis field. Within the genAI integration, competences aligned with the 'Learning to do' category described in Table 15.1 are continuously mentioned as essential. In addition, it is necessary to ensure inclusivity and equity in designing and implementing competence frameworks for genAI, so this raises a new question: How can researchers, higher education professors and students ensure inclusivity and equity in designing and implementing competence frameworks for genAI?

15.4 Ensuring Inclusivity and Equity in the Integration of GenAI

Alasadi and Baiz (2023) explored the promising possibilities of incorporating genAI into educational practices and research, highlighting the need to guarantee equity and inclusivity in the context of genAI and education. To ensure transparent use in academic and research processes, it is necessary to understand the technology involved in genAI and the biases associated with the structure of the creation of these systems. This may promote transparent and ethical uses of the tools, guaranteeing equitable access to the developed educational resources. These biases can be linked not only to the generative access but also to the data used in the training process, perpetuating inequalities or reinforcing existing disparities if not carefully addressed (Baidoo-Anu and Ansah, 2023; Cao and Dede, 2023; Llorens-Largo *et al.*, 2023; Qadir, 2023).

In parallel, Shanto *et al.* (2023) and Nixon *et al.* (2024) highlighted the capability of genAI tools in STEM (science, technology, engineering and mathematics)-aligned careers. Nixon *et al.* (2024) promoted achieving an inclusive space in STEM with two approaches using genAI. First is the need to establish joint assessment guidelines, and second, the use of adaptive and personalized AI systems to ensure that all users of genAI tools have a voice in the process; this is because collaborative problem solving is a crucial skill as findings demonstrate the subjective nature of human evaluation on teamwork, and necessitates more equitable components for future collaborative learning assessment' (Nixon *et al.*, 2024, p. 87). Kinnula *et al.* (2021) further explored the challenges and opportunities that must be addressed in creating accessible and inclusive AI. Some of the key challenges identified in the document as 'current trends in AI [that] might not be inclusive or accessible' (p. 2) included algorithmic bias, lack of diversity in data representation, limited user-centric design, responsibility distribution, and ethical concerns such as privacy and simulated data.

Kadaruddin (2023), Lee *et al.* (2021), and Sattelmaier and Pawlowski (2023) made an effort to further the conversation about the necessity for ethical conditions and frameworks in the use of genAI tools. As educators and researchers are the ones who can handle these evolving technologies with the maturity required to develop an awareness of the potential ethical implications, their work sought to underline how important it is to incorporate processes from their side. For Kadaruddin (2023), creating and putting ethical frameworks into place is crucial as it can lessen the effects by ensuring the welfare and rights of users. Furthermore, this study stressed the responsible incorporation of genAI into education, highlighting the need to address issues such as data privacy, algorithmic bias and the educator's role in directing AI-driven learning experiences.

Regarding the crucial role of educators and researchers, it is necessary to equip educators with the knowledge and skills required to leverage genAI in their teaching practices. These insights underscore the importance of a collaborative, inclusive and ethical approach to designing

Table 15.2. Comparative analysis of approaches, framework steps and desired competences.

Study title	Reference	Approach	Framework steps	Competences
'Empowering education with generative artificial intelligence tools: approach with an instructional design matrix'	Ruiz-Rojas *et al.* (2023)	4PADAFE instructional design matrix • Training and professional development • Personalization and customization • Curriculum design and planning • Evaluation and feedback (assessment) • Ethical and privacy considerations	4PADAFE [4] stands for Academic Project, Strategic Plan, Instructional Planning, Instructional Material Production (4P), Teaching Action (AD), Formative Adjustments (AF), and Evaluation (E)	• Understanding of AI and educational technology (technical proficiency) • Instructional design skills (goal setting, assessment) • Critical thinking and problem solving • Ethical awareness • Collaboration and communication • Adaptability and continuous learning
'Investigating learners' competencies for artificial intelligence education in an African K-12 setting'	Sanusi *et al.* (2022a)	The proposed framework of competences for AI education: knowledge, skills, disposition (attitudes), personal characteristics, interactions with others, work performance, context-situatedness, cognitive abilities and ethics		• Cultural context and humanistic thinking • Teamwork competence • Human–tool collaboration • Self-learning competence (independent analysis, exploration, practice, questioning and creation)
'Competence model approach to AI literacy: research-based path from initial framework to model'	Faruqe *et al.* (2022)			• Recognizing AI • Understanding AI • Ethics • Programmability
'Empowering education through generative AI: innovative instructional strategies for tomorrow's learners'	Kadaruddin (2023)	Essential components • Knowledge base (technical and pedagogical) • Skills (technical and pedagogical) • Behaviours and attitudes (ethics) • Collaboration (teamwork) • Continuous learning and development		• Technical proficiency (AI literacy, data literacy, programming skills) • Pedagogical competencies (curriculum integration, differentiated instruction, assessment design) • Ethical competencies (data privacy awareness, algorithmic bias awareness, transparency and accountability) • Thinking (creativity, critical, problem solving)
'Necessary to increase teacher competence in facing the artificial intelligence era'	Muttaqin (2022)	Does not explicitly mention or propose a specific framework		• Pedagogical competence • Digital competence • Continuous learning • Adaptability and innovation • Collaboration and communication • Thinking (creativity, critical thinking, problem solving)

and implementing competence frameworks for genAI in education.

Furthermore, continuous, transparent collaboration among educators, researchers, policy makers and AI developers, as emphasized by Walczak and Cellary (2023), is integral to ensuring the ethical and equitable implementation of genAI in education. This collaborative effort involves sharing best practices, piloting new strategies, and establishing guidelines and standards for using genAI in educational settings. A collaborative effort between users emerged as a pivotal strategy in fostering inclusivity and equity in the design and implementation of AI, embodying a shared vision by several authors (Kinnula *et al.*, 2021; Faruqe *et al.*, 2022; Gibellini *et al.*, 2023; Brauner *et al.*, 2025) and also 'between AI and human expertise [that] would ensure that the integrity and creativity of scientific publications are preserved while harnessing the potential of AI to enhance the efficiency and accessibility of scientific communication' (Alasadi and Baiz, 2023, p. 2968).

Additionally, insights from Sanusi *et al.* (2022b) underscored the importance of considering cultural influences in curriculum development for inclusive AI learning. They emphasized involving students in the design process to ensure that their perspectives and needs are considered. They also provided teacher training and support to address diversity, equity and inclusion in AI education. Moreover, Sanusi *et al.* (2022b) highlighted the crucial steps of ensuring equitable resource allocation and integrating discussions on ethics, bias and fairness in AI technologies to foster a culture of inclusivity and equity in AI education. Sanusi *et al.* (2022b) also emphasized the importance of developing assessment strategies that are fair, unbiased and inclusive of diverse student populations.

Walczak and Cellary (2023) further discussed the challenges and opportunities of genAI in higher education, emphasizing the need for digital literacy and ethical use. The idea of 'truth-relevant and truth-irrelevant content' presented emphasized the close relationship necessary in the genAI era between AI literacy and ethics as 'A person without knowledge cannot distinguish between the right and wrong parts of the generated text' (p. 11).

15.5 Integration of GenAI Tools in Educational Settings

The integration of genAI tools in educational settings has been explored in various studies from diverse perspectives. Kadaruddin (2023) pointed out that genAI integration into educational settings can be executed in different approaches, namely professional development as its primary requirement or approach, as educators should receive adequate training and support to integrate genAI into instructional strategies effectively. Kadaruddin (2023, p. 622) reinforced the benefits of genAI: 'Professional development programs should equip educators with AI knowledge, pedagogical best practices, and ethical considerations.' For this, it is mentioned that educators could utilize the genAI tool to develop personalized learning and interactive and immersive experiences. For Kadaruddin (2023), this is reachable if, during this process, a collaborative strategy between educators and other educational stakeholders is in place, promoting transparent AI decision-making processes and periodic audits. Muttaqin (2022) agreed with the conclusions of Kadaruddin (2023) and emphasized that educators can enhance their teaching process by participating in appropriate training programs focused on AI technologies in education. He suggested creating pilot training and learning programs where those involved can continuously experiment with different tools and strategies, always considering ethical considerations, such as data privacy, bias mitigation and inclusiveness.

For Lin (2023), it is not only a matter of training teachers to strengthen and develop their competencies; the integration of genAI also forces educators to motivate students to actively use these tools, to motivate exploration and the need to create learning materials that enhance the learning process, and to encourage interaction between peers with the tools 'providing assistance and resources to extend students' learning beyond what they could achieve alone in using' (p. 9). Gomathi *et al.* (2022) and Soelistiono (2023) highlighted AI's potential in teaching, with Gomathi *et al.* (2022) proposing a model that uses AI to test and enhance each understanding. The proposed model by Gomathi *et al.* (2022) integrates AI in two phases: a first phase of information gathering and a second phase of creation. AI allows teachers and researchers to collect data on everyone for later evaluation and analysis. This is followed by a personalized content creation process based on the individual analysis of each student. In contrast, Soelistiono (2023) discussed the benefits of AI-based learning systems in promoting self-directed learning, as it allows, through computerized systems, the creation of individualized content, personalized follow-up and the generation of individual feedback. This integration requires a flexible system where learning occurs within a classroom and in personal spaces such as each home.

French *et al.* (2023) provided a practical example of integrating OpenAI tools in game development education, demonstrating their value in refining students' skills. Zastudil *et al.* (2023) underscored the need to address concerns and align the preferences of students and instructors in integrating genAI tools in computing education. Perceptions of the use and benefit of genAI tools demonstrate that integrating these systems requires stakeholders to consider their counterparts actively. These studies collectively underscore the potential of genAI tools in education, highlighting the need for careful integration and consideration of ethical implications.

In contrast, Williamson *et al.* (2023) did not limit their analysis to how implementation is or should be done but centred their attention on what the future will be and foresaw that, shortly, the amount of debate around using these tools in educational environments will increase, mainly focused on practical evaluation, academic cheating and ethical responsibility. This is primarily because of the number of tools the education sector is being ravaged by and the trend of datafication in education. This may promote a new research direction involving AI and education. Other authors have also emphasized the need to promote collaboration between users and integrate it into the educational curriculum. Table 15.3 summarizes the main approaches.

Table 15.3. GenAI integration approach.

Integration approach/ need	Explanation	Reference(s)
The quest for professional development	To emphasize the need for educators to receive comprehensive training and support in effectively integrating genAI tools into educational settings	Chassignol *et al.* (2018); Muttaqin (2022); Sanusi *et al.* (2022a); Chiu (2023); Kadaruddin (2023); Walczak and Cellary (2023)
The harmonious alignment	To highlight the importance of actively motivating students to use AI tools and ensuring alignment with their preferences during integration processes	Lin (2023); Williamson *et al.* (2023); Zastudil *et al.* (2023)
Personalized learning with AI assistance	To propose innovative models and systems that facilitate personalized learning experiences with AI assistance, thereby enhancing individual student engagement and outcomes	Gomathi *et al.* (2022); French *et al.* (2023); Ruiz-Rojas *et al.* (2023); Soelistiono (2023)
The practical wisdom of examples	To provide tangible examples demonstrating how genAI tools can be effectively integrated into specific educational contexts	French *et al.* (2023)
The collaborative journey	To foster collaboration between students and teachers by leveraging genAI tools, promoting interactive and inclusive learning environments	Sanusi *et al.* (2022a,b)
The curriculum inclusion	Exploring ways to embed genAI tools into existing educational curriculum structures	Chiu (2023, 2024); Walczak and Cellary (2023)

15.6 Conclusion

This chapter has highlighted the challenges in assessing competencies and developing competency frameworks to promote equitable and ethical usage of genAI tools in educational contexts. The European Commission's ResearchComp framework acts as a model, guiding academics towards an understanding of the capabilities required for genAI integration. This paradigm promotes critical thinking, problem solving, teamwork, ethics and continuous learning, and guides educators, researchers and educational leaders as they embark on the journey to genAI integration.

In order to achieve effective integration of genAI in education, it is essential to consider the ethical implications it encompasses to ensure inclusion and equity. Ethical and transparent decision making to encourage and promote the use of genAI requires ongoing collaboration among key stakeholders in higher education such as instructors, researchers, policy makers and AI developers. Moreover, it is crucial to acknowledge the impact of cultural influences on curriculum development, particularly in ensuring content that embraces diversity and inclusiveness.

While challenges abound, comprehensive training, ongoing support and motivation of educators and students are imperative. From fostering algorithmic thinking to promoting adaptability and innovation, educators must be equipped with the skills necessary to navigate genAI integration effectively. Likewise, students need guidance and encouragement to harness the power of genAI in their educational journey.

Looking ahead, the vision for education with genAI embraces a commitment to holistic development, where responsible integration is combined with ethical considerations. By prioritizing inclusion, equity and continuous competency development, educators can leverage genAI to create dynamic, personalized learning environments that meet the diverse needs of all learners.

In conclusion, genAI presents a wide array of opportunities for educational enrichment. Through responsible integration, researchers and educators can unlock the transformative potential of genAI, paving the way for a future in which learning is not only enhanced but also truly inclusive and equitable. As educators and researchers continue to navigate the changing landscape of genAI integration, it is imperative to remain vigilant, adaptive and collaborative. By embracing these principles, educators can ensure that genAI integration continues to be a catalyst for positive change, empowering students and shaping a brighter future for education.

15.7 Acknowledgement

We thank the Catholic University of Brasília and the University of Aveiro for their partnership in preparing this article. The PPI Softex program supported this project, Agreement No. TPA/194/SOFTEX/UCB – Residência em TIC 04B – TIC em Trilhas, financed by the Ministry of Science, Technology, and Innovation with funds from Law No. 8,248 of 23 October 1991. National funds funded the work of the second author through FCT – Fundação para a Ciência e a Tecnologia, I.P., under the Scientific Employment Stimulus – Institutional Call – [CDL-CTTRI-248-SGRH/2022] and the CIDTFF (projects UIDB/00194/2020 and UIDP/00194/2020).

15.8 References

Alasadi, E.A. and Baiz, C.R. (2023) Generative AI in education and research: opportunities, concerns, and solutions. *Journal of Chemical Education* 100, 2965–2971.

Al-Zahrani, A.M. (2023) The impact of generative AI tools on researchers and research: implications for academia in higher education. *Innovations in Education and Teaching International* 61, 1029–1043.

Anderson, M., Mitchell, B., Northcote, M., Williams, A., Petrie, K. *et al.* (2018) The construction of a postgraduate student and supervisor support framework: using stakeholder voices to promote effective postgraduate teaching and learning practice. *Journal of University Teaching and Learning Practice* 75, 91–110.

Arifin, M.A. (2021) Competence, competency, and competencies: a misunderstanding in theory and practice for future reference. *International Journal of Academic Research in Business and Social Sciences* 11, 755–764.

Bahroun, Z., Anane, C., Ahmed, V. and Zacca, A. (2023) Transforming education: a comprehensive review of generative artificial intelligence in educational settings through bibliometric and content analysis. *Sustainability* 15: 12983.

Baïdoo-Anu, D. and Ansah, L.O. (2023) Education in the era of generative artificial intelligence (AI): understanding the potential benefits of ChatGPT in promoting teaching and learning. *Journal of AI* 7, 52–62.

Birnbaum, M.L. and Daily, E.K. (2009) Competency and competence. *Prehospital and Disaster Medicine* 24, 1–2.

Bloom, B.S., Krathwohl, D.R. and Masia, B.B. (1956) *Taxonomy of Educational Objectives, Handbook I: The Cognitive Domain*. David McKay Co., New York.

Boden, R. and Teperi, J. (2024) *Tampere Institute for Advanced Study: Mentoring Handbook, Version 2.0*. Tampere University, Tampere, Finland. Available at: https://trepo.tuni.fi/bitstream/handle/10024/154473/978-952-03-3280-8.pdf?sequence=2 (accessed 7 October 2024).

Brauner, S., Murawski, M. and Bick, M. (2025) The development of a competence framework for artificial intelligence professionals using probabilistic topic modelling. *Journal of Enterprise Information Management* 38, 197–218.

Cao, L. and Dede, C. (2023) *Navigating a World of Generative AI: Suggestions for Educators*. Next Level Lab, Harvard Graduate School of Education, Cambridge, Massachusetts.

Carolus, A., Koch, M.J., Straka, S., Latoschik, M.E. and Wienrich, C. (2023) MAILS – meta AI literacy scale: development and testing of an AI literacy questionnaire based on well-founded competency models and psychological change- and meta-competencies. *Computers in Human Behavior* 1: 100014.

Chassignol, M., Khoroshavin, A., Klimova, A. and Bilyatdinova, A. (2018) Artificial intelligence trends in education: a narrative overview. *Procedia Computer Science* 136, 16–24.

Chauncey, S.A. and McKenna, H.P. (2023) A framework and exemplars for ethical and responsible use of AI chatbot technology to support teaching and learning. *Computers and Education* 5: 100182.

Chiu, T.K.F. (2023) The impact of generative AI (GenAI) on practices, policies and research direction in education: a case of ChatGPT and Midjourney. *Interactive Learning Environments* 32, 6187–6203.

Chiu, T.K.F. (2024) Future research recommendations for transforming higher education with generative AI. *Computers and Education* 6: 100197.

Christou, P.A. (2023) A critical perspective over whether and how to acknowledge the use of artificial intelligence (AI) in qualitative studies. *The Qualitative Report* 28, 1981–1991.

Ciraso-Calí, A., Martínez-Fernández, J.R., París-Mañas, G., Sánchez-Martí, A. and García-Ravidá, L.B. (2022) The research competence: acquisition and development among undergraduates in education sciences. *Frontiers in Education* 7: 836165.

Conklin, J. (2005) *A Taxonomy for Learning, Teaching and Assessing: A Revision of Blooms' Taxonomy of Educational Objectives. In: Educational Horizons, Vol. 83, The Quest for Strengths: The Dawn of a Talent-Based Approach to K-12 Education*. Phi Delta Kappa International, Arlington, Virginia, pp. 154–159.

de Coen, A. and Núñez, L. (eds) (2022) Knowledge ecosystems in the new era: using a competence-based approach for career development in academia and beyond. European Commission, Directorate-General for Research and Innovation, Publications Office of the European Union. Available at: https://data.europa.eu/doi/10.2777/150763 (accessed 7 October 2024).

European Commission, Directorate-General for Education, Youth, Sport, and Culture (2022) Ethical guidelines on using artificial intelligence (AI) and data in teaching and learning for educators. Publications Office of the European Union. Available at: https://data.europa.eu/doi/10.2766/153756 (accessed 7 October 2024).

Faruqe, F., Watkins, R. and Medsker, L. (2022) Competency model approach to AI literacy: research-based path from initial framework to model. *Advances in Artificial Intelligence and Machine Learning* 2, 580–587.

French, F., Levi, D., Maczo, C., Simonaityte, A., Triantafyllidis, S. *et al.* (2023) Creative use of OpenAI in education: case studies from game development. *Multimodal Technologies and Interaction* 7: 81.

Gibellini, G., Fabretti, V. and Schiavo, G. (2023) AI education from the educator's perspective: best practices for an inclusive AI curriculum for middle school. In: *Extended Abstracts of the 2023 CHI Conference on Human Factors in Computing Systems (CHI EA 202), 23–28 April 2023, Hamburg, Germany*. Association for Computing Machinery, New York, Article 27.

Gomathi, R.D., Maheswaran, S., Sathesh, S., Murugesan, G., Duraisamy, P. and Nandita, S. (2022) The roll [sic] of artificial intelligence in teaching pedagogy: challenges and prospects for sustainable growth in education. In: *2022 13th International Conference on Computing Communication and Networking Technologies (ICCCNT), 3–5 October 2022, Kharagpur, India*. IEEE, Piscataway, New Jersey, pp. 1–7.

Guthrie, H. (2009) *Competence and Competency-Based Training: What the Literature Says*. National Centre for Vocational Education Research, Adelaide, Australia.

Halaweh, M. (2023) ChatGPT in education: strategies for responsible implementation. *Contemporary Educational Technology* 15: ep421.

Holmes, W. and Miao, F. (2023) *Guidance for Generative AI in Education and Research*. UNESCO Publishing, Paris.

Hutson, J. and Robertson, B. (2023) Exploring the educational potential of AI generative art in 3D design fundamentals: a case study on prompt engineering and creative workflows. *Global Journal of Human–Social Science* 23. Available at: https://digitalcommons.lindenwood.edu/faculty-research-papers/485/ (accessed 7 October 2024).

International Commission on Education for the Twenty-first Century (1996) Learning: The Treasure Within: Report to UNESCO of the International Commission on Education for the Twenty-first Century. UNESCO Publishing, Paris. Available at: https://unesdoc.unesco.org/ark:/48223/pf0000109590 (accessed 7 October 2024).

Kadaruddin, K. (2023) Empowering education through generative AI: innovative instructional strategies for tomorrow's learners. *International Journal of Business, Law, and Education* 4, 618–625.

Khan, R.A. (2021) Achieving the competencies of an educational researcher. *Health Professions Educator Journal* 4: 6.

Kinnula, M., Iivari, N., Sharma, S., Eden, G., Turunen, M. *et al.* (2021) Researchers' toolbox for the future: understanding and designing accessible and inclusive artificial intelligence (AIAI). In: *Academic Mindtrek 2021: Proceedings of the 24th International Academic Mindtrek Conference, 1–3 June 2021, Tampere/Virtual Finland*. Association for Computing Machinery, New York, pp. 41–48.

Koeppen, K., Hartig, J., Klieme, E. and Leutner, D. (2008) Current issues in competence modeling and assessment. *Journal of Psychology* 216, 61–73.

Laupichler, M.C., Aster, A., Schirch, J. and Raupach, T. (2022) Artificial intelligence literacy in higher and adult education: a scoping literature review. *Computers and Education* 3: 100101.

Laupichler, M.C., Aster, A., Perschewski, J.-O. and Schleiss, J. (2023) Evaluating AI courses: a valid and reliable instrument for assessing artificial-intelligence learning through comparative self-assessment. *Education Sciences* 13: 978.

Le Borgne, Y.-A., Bellas, F., Dara, C., Riina, V. *et al.* (2024) *AI report*. Royal College of Surgeons in Ireland, Dublin. Available at: https://repository.rcsi.com/articles/report/AI_report/25021193?file=44112797 (accessed 7 October 2024).

Le Boterf, G. (2003) *Desenvolvendo a Competência dos Profissionais [Developing the Competence of Professionals]*, 3rd edn. Artmed Editora, Porto Alegre, Sao Paulo.

Lee, I., Ali, S., Zhang, H., DiPaola, D. and Breazeal, C. (2021) Developing middle school students' AI literacy. In: *SIGCSE 2021: Proceedings of the 52nd ACM Technical Symposium on Computer Science Education, 13–20 March 2021, Virtual Event USA*. Association for Computing Machinery, New York, pp. 191–197.

Lim, W.M., Gunasekara, A., Pallant, J.L., Pallant, J.I. and Pechenkina, E. (2023) Generative AI and the future of education: ragnarök or reformation? A paradoxical perspective from management educators. *International Journal of Management Education* 21: 100790.

Lin, Z. (2023) Why and how to embrace AI such as ChatGPT in your academic life. Royal Society Publishing, London. Available at: https://royalsocietypublishing.org/doi/10.1098/rsos.230658 (accessed 7 October 2024).

Llorens-Largo, F., Vidal, J. and García-Peñalvo, F.J. (2023) Ya llegó, ya está aquí, y nadie puede esconderse: la inteligencia artificial generativa en educación. *Aula Magna*. Available at: https://cuedespyd.hypotheses.org/14389 (accessed 7 October 2024).

Messeri, L. and Crockett, M.J. (2024) Artificial intelligence and illusions of understanding in scientific research. *Nature* 627, 49–58.

Miracchi, L. (2019) A competence framework for artificial intelligence research. *Philosophical Psychology* 32, 588–633.

Moghabghab, R., Tong, A., Hallaran, A. and Anderson, J. (2018) The difference between competency and competence: a regulatory perspective. *Journal of Nursing Regulation* 9, 54–59.

Moresi, E., Burneo, P., Pinho, I., Costa, A., Machado, L. *et al.* (2024) Bibliometric and comparative analysis of generative artificial intelligence in education research. In: *19th Iberian Conference on Information Systems and Technologies (CISTI 2024), 25–28 June 2024, Salamanca, Spain*. IEEE, Piscataway, New Jersey.

Mujiono, M. (2023) Educational collaboration: teachers and artificial intelligence. *Jurnal Kependidikan* 9: 618.

Muttaqin, I. (2022) Necessary to increase teacher competency in facing the artificial intelligence era. *Al-Hayat* 6: 549.

Nixon, N., Lin, Y. and Snow, L. (2024) Catalyzing equity in STEM teams: harnessing generative AI for inclusion and diversity. *Policy Insights from the Behavioral and Brain Sciences* 11, 85–92.

Petrovska, O., Clift, L., Moller, F. and Pearsall, R. (2024) Incorporating generative AI into software development education. In: *Proceedings of the 8th Conference on Computing Education Practice (CEP 2024), 5 January 2024, Durham, UK*. Association for Computing Machinery, New York, pp. 37–40.

Phung, T., Pădurean, V.-A., Cambronero, J., Gulwani, S., Kohn, T. *et al.* (2023) Generative AI for programming education: benchmarking ChatGPT, GPT-4, and human tutors. In *ICER 2023: Proceedings of the 2023 ACM Conference on International Computing Education Research, 7–11 August, Chicago, Illinois, Vol.* 2 Association for Computing Machinery, USA, pp. 41–42.

Prosekov, A., Morozova, I. and Filatova, E. (2020) A case study of developing research competency in university students. *European Journal of Contemporary Education* 9, 592–602.

Qadir, J. (2023) Engineering education in the era of ChatGPT: promise and pitfalls of generative AI for education. In: *2023 IEEE Global Engineering Education Conference (EDUCON), 1–4 May 2023, Kuwait*. IEEE, Piscataway, New Jersey, pp. 1–9.

Ruiz-Rojas, L.I., Acosta-Vargas, P., De-Moreta-Llovet, J. and Gonzalez-Rodriguez, M. (2023) Empowering education with generative artificial intelligence tools: approach with an instructional design matrix. *Sustainability* 15: 11524.

Sætra, H.S. (2023) Generative AI: here to stay, but for good? *Technology in Society* 75: 102372.

Sanusi, I.T., Olaleye, S.A., Agbo, F.J. and Chiu, T.K.F. (2022a) The role of learners' competencies in artificial intelligence education. *Computers and Education: Artificial Intelligence* 3: 100098.

Sanusi, I.T., Olaleye, S.A., Oyelere, S.S. and Dixon, R.A. (2022b) Investigating learners' competencies for artificial intelligence education in an African K-12 setting. *Computers and Education Open* 3: 100083.

Sattelmaier, L. and Pawlowski, J.M. (2023) Towards a generative artificial intelligence competence framework for schools. In: *Proceedings of the International Conference on Enterprise and Industrial Systems (ICOEINS 2023), 4–5 October 2023, Badung, Bali*. Atlantis Press, Amsterdam, Netherlands, pp. 291–307.

Scott, C.L. (2015) El Futuro del aprendizaje ¿Qué tipo de aprendizaje se necesita en el siglo XXI? [The future of learning. What kind of learning is needed in the 21st century?]. UNESCO Publishing, Paris. Available at: https://unesdoc.unesco.org/ark:/48223/pf0000242996_spa (accessed 7 October 2024).

Shanto, S.S., Ahmed, Z. and Jony, A.I. (2023) PAIGE: a generative AI-based framework for promoting assignment integrity in higher education. *STEM Education* 3, 288–305.

Soelistiono, S. (2023) Educational technology innovation: AI-integrated learning system design in AILS-based education. *Influence: International Journal of Science Review* 5, 470–480.

Stokel-Walker, C. and van Noorden, R. (2023) What ChatGPT and generative AI mean for science. *Nature* 614, 214–216.

Teodorescu, T. (2006) Competence versus competency: what is the difference? *Performance Improvement* 45, 27–30.

Thanh, B.N., Vo, D.T.H., Nhat, M.N., Pham, T.T.T., Trung, H.T. and Xuan, S.H. (2023) Race with the machines: assessing the capability of generative AI in solving authentic assessments. *Australasian Journal of Educational Technology* 39, 59–81.

UNESCO (United Nations Educational, Scientific, and Cultural Organization) (2023) *Global Education Monitoring Report, 2023: Technology in Education: A Tool on Whose Terms?* Global Education Monitoring Report Team. UNESCO, Paris. Available at: https://doi.org/10.54676/UZQV8501 (accessed 15 October 2024).

van Dis, E.A.M., Bollen, J., Zuidema, W., van Rooij, R. and Bockting, C.L. (2023) ChatGPT: five priorities for research. *Nature* 614, 224–226.

Vasetskaya, N.O., Glukhov, V.V. and Burdakov, S.F. (2018) The elaboration of the model of competences of the research and teaching university staff. In: *2018 XVII Russian Scientific and Practical Conference on Planning and Teaching Engineering Staff for the Industrial and Economic Complex of the Region (PTES), 14–15 November 2018, St Petersburg, Russia*. IEEE, Piscataway, New Jersey, pp. 98–101.

Wach, K., Duong, C.D., Ejdys, J., Kazlauskaite, R., Korynski, P. *et al*. (2023) The dark side of generative artificial intelligence: a critical analysis of controversies and risks of ChatGPT. *Entrepreneurial Business and Economics Review* 11, 7–30.

Walczak, K. and Cellary, W. (2023) Challenges for higher education in the era of widespread access to generative AI. *Economics and Business Review* 9, 71–100.

Weisz, J.D., Muller, M., He, J. and Houde, S. (2023) Toward general design principles for generative AI applications. In: *Joint Proceedings of the ACM IUI Workshops 2023, March 2023, Sydney, Australia*. Available at: https://ceur-ws.org/Vol-3359/paper14.pdf (accessed 7 October 2024).

Williamson, B., MacGilchrist, F. and Potter, J. (2023) Re-examining AI, automation and datafication in education. *Learning, Media and Technology* 48, 1–5.

Xia, Q., Weng, X., Ouyang, F., Lin, T.J. and Chiu, T.K.F. (2024) A scoping review on how generative artificial intelligence transforms assessment in higher education. *International Journal of Educational Technology in Higher Education* 21: 40.

Zastudil, C., Rogalska, M., Kapp, C., Vaughn, J. and MacNeil, S. (2023) Generative AI in computing education: perspectives of students and instructors. In: *2023 IEEE Frontiers in Education Conference (FIE), 18–21 October 2023, Cellege Station, Texas*. IEEE, Piscataway, New Jersey, pp. 1–9.

Zekaj, R. (2023) AI language models as educational allies: enhancing instructional support in higher education. *International Journal of Learning, Teaching and Educational Research* 22, 120–134.

Zhai, X., Chu, X., Chai, C.S., Jong, M.S.Y. and Istenic, A. (2021) A review of artificial intelligence (AI) in education from 2010 to 2020. *Complexity* 2021: 8812542.

Zhai, X., Nyaaba, M. and Ma, W. (2024) Can generative AI and ChatGPT outperform humans on cognitive-demanding problem-solving tasks in science? *Science & Education* 2024. https://doi.org/10.1007/s11191-024-00496-1

16 Data Collection Methods in the Age of Artificial Intelligence: Insights from a Survey-based Study on College Students' Perceptions and Use of AI

Terrell L. Strayhorn[1]* and J'Quen Johnson[2]
[1]*Virginia Union University, Richmond, Virginia, USA;* [2]*University of the Cumberlands, Williamsburg, Kentucky, USA*

Abstract
Artificial intelligence (AI) is everywhere. As more and more people frequently interact with AI, social researchers must expand knowledge about the importance and challenges associated with generative AI technologies based on studies using rigorous data collection methods. This chapter discusses data collection methodologies, including quantitative, qualitative and mixed methods to study AI in social science research. Employing a cross-sectional case study comprising over 400 college students' knowledge, perception and use of AI technologies, the results showed that most respondents used ChatGPT. Although participants utilized other AI tools, concerns ranged from accuracy and reliability of information to issues of academic integrity.

Keywords: artificial intelligence, data collection, case study, college students, research design

16.1 Introduction

Artificial intelligence (AI) is ubiquitous and rapidly advancing in its pervasive use across all aspects of everyday life, from autonomous (i.e. self-driving) vehicles such as Google's Waymo or Tesla's autopiloted Model 3 to Roomba's smart vacuum (iRobot), sophisticated chatbots within Fintech's CashApp and Google's smart home manager, Nest, that allows users to enjoy the benefits of multi-device automation (e.g. thermostats, cameras, speakers) via natural language programming (NLPs) and simple voice-activated commands. Indeed, AI is seemingly everywhere, in all things.

For the purposes of this chapter, AI refers to a set of computer systems or programs that imitate human behaviours, learn from experience and perform tasks independently that are normally attributed to humans such as problem-solving, thinking and learning (Alzahrani, 2023). AI technologies can be used to solve problems, execute complex tasks, and improve complicated or convoluted processes. AI use is growing exponentially, and it is projected to be a dominant part of the global economy in the future. Estimates indicate that the global AI market will grow to over US$2 trillion by 2028 (Catsaros, 2023).

The growth of AI's presence and use significantly impacts society. Interestingly, approximately one-third of Americans report not using AI in their daily life, although data show that 77% of

*E-mail: tlstrayhorn@vuu.edu

DOI: 10.1079/9781800626607.0016

them actually do, revealing how omnipresent and pervasive AI has become. It has become embedded in aspects of everyday life in obvious and hidden ways. For instance, everyone who has a smartphone (iPhone or Android) has AI, literally in the palms of their hands. AI technologies run the gamut including highly visible and popular voice assistants such as Alexa and Siri, but also include wearable fitness trackers (and watches), and NLP such as Google Translate and Elicit, as well as more basic programs and tools such as spellcheck, algorithmic playlist recommendations like Pandora and spam filters.

AI's rising prevalence and widespread use in society has significantly disrupted the status quo – extending across industries too. The AI revolution is not only transforming business operations but also changing the job market. As a result, there is a rising demand for AI experts and AI-related jobs. According to reports, 2.6 million new jobs in information technology (IT) fields alone are expected to be AI related, and the number of AI and machine learning specialists is projected to increase 40% by 2027 (TestGorilla, 2024). Several of the emerging 'hot jobs' are directly related to AI, including data engineer, machine learning engineer, cybersecurity specialist and big data analyst. Integration of AI technologies in core business operations has reshaped the nature of work for many jobs and roles, such as customer service (56%), inventory management (40%) and even healthcare. Several leading global companies use AI-powered chatbots acting as virtual customer service assistants, handling routine queries, managing complex datasets and providing personalized recommendations (National University, 2024). In the healthcare sector, AI algorithms assist in diagnosing diseases, analysing patient data and establishing treatment plans, to name but a few uses (Ayyappan and Coffin, 2024).

AI's prevalence, rapid adoption and use in daily life provoke varying public opinions about its novelty and safety. As generative AI tools become increasingly sophisticated and capable of performing tasks that were once exclusively within the human domain, they have ignited concerns among some groups about potential threats, including economic disruption, job displacement and lack of authenticity/reliability of created content (Delello *et al.*, 2023). Other concerns include ethical issues and potential security risks related to AI use. In terms of ethics, some critics are apprehensive about AI's (cap-)ability to make reasonable and reliable decisions that might significantly impact human lives, especially in fields such as criminal justice, finance and healthcare. Other questions swirl around accountability and transparency of AI-generated information and security vulnerabilities that expose complex systems to potential exploitation by malicious actors. Consider, for instance, a security breach in early 2024 that affected 37 million T-Mobile customers where an expert hacker used an application programming interface (API) with AI capabilities to gain unauthorized access to sensitive information including clients' full names, phone numbers and personal identification numbers (PINs), among others.

Despite concerns surrounding AI, there is also significant support for AI's potential to improve and streamline various processes, ultimately easing the workload shouldered by humans. A recent report revealed the top ways consumers use AI, including 45% responding to email, 43% answering financial questions and 38% planning travel itineraries with AI tools, to mention a few (National University, 2024). AI has been proven to enhance efficiency by automating repetitive and mundane tasks, freeing up human resources to focus on more complex and creative initiatives. Two-thirds of business owners believe that AI can improve customer relationships and 97% believe ChatGPT can improve their business (Haan, 2023).

AI is also shaping educational settings. According to a study by Anthology (2023), US college students report that AI has the potential to play a significant role in higher education. They believe AI can help in generating new or revising existing ideas. They also think that AI can improve student engagement and transform teaching and learning approaches. As AI capabilities continue to evolve, its integration into deep-learning contexts holds promise for improving the nature and accessibility of primary, secondary and post-secondary education.

So, the evidence is clear that AI is becoming a common part of social life, with remarkable prevalence in business and education. Much of what we know about AI's growing presence, changing perceptions, and expanding use in daily life and specific sectors (e.g. legal consulting) comes from evidence-based studies in social science research. Social science scholars who study AI often emphasize its transformative impact on the job market, robot interactions with humans, and methods that can be used effectively to explore AI use and its impact on key outcomes in domains of life (e.g. Alharthi, 2020). Education researchers, in contrast, who study AI concentrate mostly on the impact AI has on educational outcomes, students' attitudes towards AI tools and the increasing use of AI technologies in educational settings such as classrooms and laboratories (e.g. Al Shamsi *et al.*, 2022; Alzahrani, 2023). Rarely do writers address the 'murky middle' that lies at the intersection of these literatures (Fig. 16.1).

Indeed, much more information is needed to understand the full potential, power and problems associated with AI's growing presence, adoption and use in education, social science research and broader society. That insight should be drawn from rigorous, high-quality research studies that collect data from appropriate samples, informants and subjects. It follows, then, that we need to explore methods for data collection in AI-related research. This is the focus of the current chapter.

The purpose of this chapter is to provide an overview of the importance and challenges associated with studying the prevalence, perceptions and use of AI among diverse social populations, most notably college students. The chapter aims to address methods for collecting data in social science research generally and AI-focused college student studies specifically. Key questions that guide our approach to this chapter's topic include:

1. What are appropriate data-collection methods that can be used to study AI tools and applications in social settings, including education contexts?
2. How might social researchers use such data-collection methods to explore college students' prevalence, perceptions and use of AI in academic settings?

16.2 What Is Known About AI

To deeply engage with the central focus of this book chapter, we found it necessary to read,

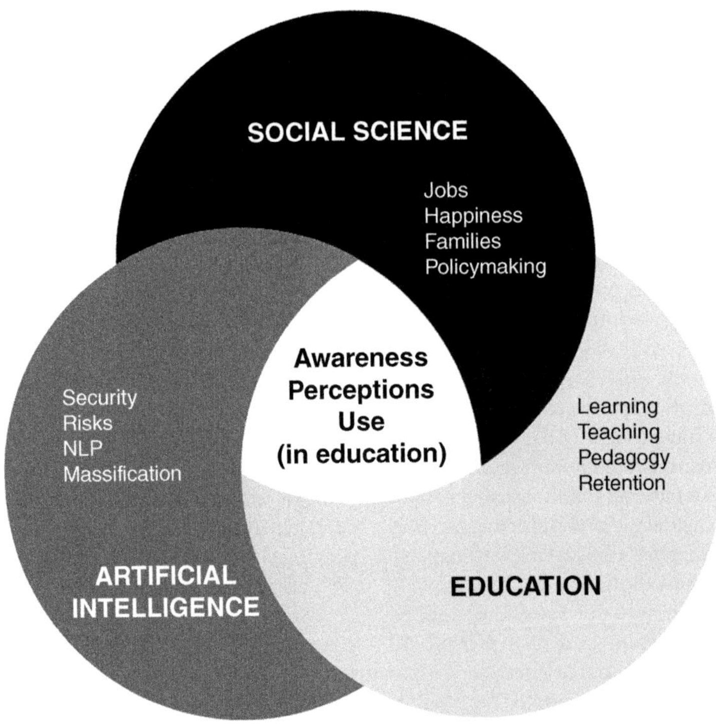

Fig. 16.1. Venn diagram of the 'murky middle' in extant literature. NLP, natural language programming.

review and familiarize ourselves with the existing literature on AI in social research generally and education specifically. To this end, we conducted substantive searches of existing research databases including ProQuest, ScienceDirect and Google Scholar, to name a few. Initial queries yielded over 4 million results or 'hits' that included published books, chapters, scientific abstracts and peer-reviewed journal articles. We filtered the list to include retrievable studies only, notably peer-reviewed journal articles, online abstracts and book chapters (as pdfs). The finalized list of published studies could be organized into three major categories: studies addressing AI awareness, attitudes and perceptions, and use. Consequently, our literature review follows this flow of information.

16.2.1 Awareness of AI

Previous studies and systematic reviews have focused on assessing college students' awareness of and knowledge about AI. For example, Delello *et al.* (2023) conducted a mixed-methods study of 165 undergraduate and graduate students at a 4-year university using an online survey. The sample comprised a majority of women who were white and aged 18–29 years. They found that awareness and knowledge of AI was greater than ChatGPT knowledge; and awareness and knowledge increased with years in school. Significant differences related to AI were noted between business and education/psychology majors.

16.2.2 Attitudes towards AI

Several studies have explored college students' attitudes towards AI, shedding light on potential factors that influence their thoughts about integrating AI into academic settings. For instance, Mousavi Baigi *et al.* (2023) conducted a systematic review of published studies from a variety of databases (e.g. PubMed, SCOPUS) using PRISMA (Preferred Reporting Items for Systematic Reviews and Meta-Analyses) to examine healthcare students' attitudes, knowledge and skills in AI from full-text, cross-sectional studies examining these aspects, among others. Most studies included in the review found evidence of positive and promising attitudes towards AI among healthcare science students, although the results indicated generally low knowledge, skills and use of AI. Low knowledge and skills were attributed to lack of training and relevant coursework.

16.2.3 Perceptions of AI

A growing body of research has examined college students' perceptions and understanding of AI, providing insights into how this emerging technology is viewed and interpreted by those pursuing postsecondary education. Keleş and Aydın (2021) conducted an independent word association test to determine the perception of the concept of AI among 130 university students using a snowball sampling method. Participants were given 40 seconds to write the first eight words that came to mind regarding AI. Findings revealed that students studying education were more aware of AI, producing 273 words. Notably, the category with the lowest frequency across all sample groups was positive aspects of AI, whereas the highest frequency referred to where AI was used. More recently, Ngo (2023) collected data from 200 college student survey respondents and 30 interview participants to investigate their perceptions of ChatGPT usage for learning. The findings suggested generally positive attitudes towards ChatGPT. Participants reported that ChatGPT saves time, offers personalized feedback and sparks new ideas for writing, to mention a few.

16.2.4 Use of AI

Researchers have investigated the extent to which college students use AI tools and technologies, including factors that influence their adoption of AI in academic contexts. For example, Alzahrani (2023) collected data from 350 undergraduate students attending a business administration college at a public university using a 33-item web-based survey. The survey was designed to elicit information related to six factors closely aligned with variables identified in the widely acclaimed technology adoption model (TAM; see Chapter 10, this volume): perceived risk (PR), performance expectancy (PE), effort expectancy (EE), facilitating conditions (FC), awareness and attitude. Analysing data using structural equation modelling, they found that several factors influence college students' attitudes and expected or intended use of AI including PR and FC. Attitudes towards AI are influenced by EE and PE, meaning that college students evaluate the trade-off between the effort required to learn and use AI tools versus the expected performance benefits they may gain. It was concluded that 'system resources, the accessibility of infrastructure, and expertise work together to facilitate use of AI in higher education' (Alzahrani, 2023, p. 71). Other studies support these conclusions (e.g. Kuleto *et al.*, 2021; Al Shamsi *et al.*, 2022).

While useful previous studies have focused on AI and differences in prevalence, perceptions and use among college students (e.g. Kuleto *et al.*, 2021; Alzahrani, 2023), there is a need for more scholarship examining data-collection methods in social research on AI in education. This is the gap addressed in this chapter.

16.2.5 Revisiting the purpose of the chapter

Recall that the purpose of this chapter is to provide a brief overview of the importance and challenges associated with studying the prevalence, perceptions and use of AI among diverse social populations, such as college students, paying close attention to effective data-collection methods in social research generally and education studies specifically. The next section describes prominent data-collection methods in social research before introducing the exploratory study that sits at the centre of this discussion.

16.3 Data Collection Methods in Social Research

16.3.1 On research design

A variety of data-collection methods exist in social science research. Data-collection methods can be organized into three major categories: quantitative, qualitative and mixed-methods approaches. Quantitative designs refer to statistical approaches that aim to explain phenomena through the collection of numerical data, which is then analysed using mathematically based methods (Creswell, 2014).

There are four main quantitative research types: correlation, descriptive, experimental and causal–comparative/quasi-experimental. Correlation research includes determining relationships, trends and patterns between two or more variables. Descriptive statistics can be used to summarize, describe and interpret an identified variable. Experimental studies are characterized by their ability to establish cause–effect relationships between variables by the researcher manipulating one or more independent variables to observe the effect on an outcome while controlling for potential confounding variables. Causal–comparative and quasi-experimental designs involve comparing groups to examine relationships between variables. However, causal–comparative designs rely on naturally occurring differences between groups without manipulation, whereas quasi-experimental research manipulates independent variables. Both designs aim to establish cause–effect relationships without the researcher manipulating independent variables to determine the effect on the dependent variable (Vogt, 1999).

Qualitative or naturalistic designs refer to a family of methodologies that aim to understand social phenomena in depth using appropriate methods for data collection and analytic techniques that yield insights '*in vivo*' (i.e. in life or 'living colour') that could not be easily matched using other designs. Qualitative approaches focus on the quality, context, nature and richness of data rather than emphasizing numerical measurements, sample sizes or statistical associations (Denzin and Lincoln, 2002).

Leading designs include case study, grounded theory, phenomenology, narrative inquiry and portraiture. For example, case study has been defined in many ways, one of which is that it is 'a problem to be studied, which will reveal in-depth understandings of a "case" or bounded system, which involves understanding an event, activity, process, or one or more individuals' (Creswell, 2002, p. 61). Known for their richness and detail (Flyvbjerg, 2011), there are different types of case study, such as exploratory, multisite, critical and ethnographic, to name but a few (VanWynsberghe and Khan, 2007). Grounded theory, however, goes beyond mere description to understand and explain a concept using 'precise coding [that] allows for generation of categories that represent relations among and across categories within a [emerging] model' (Arminio and Hultgren, 2002, p. 453). Multiple methods exist for collecting qualitative data, including interviews, observations and document analysis.

Mixed-methods approaches include the combination of quantitative and qualitative methodologies in a single study, providing a more comprehensive understanding of the research questions or phenomena than either method alone can offer. Investigators can choose between conducting mixed-methods studies sequentially, where one phase of data collection and analysis precedes the other, or in a concurrent manner, where both types of data are collected simultaneously. Triangulation approaches are used when comparing findings from both quantitative and qualitative analyses to validate results, enhance reliability and provide a more robust interpretation of the data (Clark and Creswell, 2008).

16.3.2 On methods

Observational studies allow researchers to capture real-time interactions in their natural settings, providing contextually rich data and insights. Collection of rich data and insights from observational methods can derive from both quantitative and qualitative studies, depending on the research questions and methods used. Such studies can be longitudinal (i.e. conducted over time) or cross-sectional (i.e. at a single point in time). Observational studies vary in type, including, but not limited to, behavioural, clinical, ecological and ethnographic. There are two main types of observation: participant and non-participant. Participant observation involves researchers immersing themselves in the context being studied by directly interacting with informants. In contrast, non-participant observation requires researchers to remain separate with no direct interaction with the study participants (Dallos, 2006).

In-depth interviews are one way to collect data in qualitative studies. Interviews provide rich naturalistic insights into the personal experiences and attitudes of people, notably educators and students in academic and school settings. Kvale (1996, p. 19) simply said: 'The research interview is a specific form of conversation.' In this way, individual or focus group interviews involve an interchange of views between people conversing about a topic of mutual interest. To facilitate the dialogue, researchers craft and present a series of questions, along with probing follow-ups, that unearth and draw out the respondent's thoughts, feelings, dreams and worries in ways that connect to the primary research objective.

In many quantitative and qualitative designs, social scientists use surveys to elicit data about a concept from information-rich participants in a target sample. Survey researchers use the sample and well-designed questions (i.e. items) to make inferences about the broader population or concept(s) under study. Among their many advantages, surveys offer a scalable and efficient method for gathering extensive data on people's awareness, perceptions and 'the distribution and correlates of attitudes in a population by collecting reports from a representative sample' (Schwarz *et al.*, 1998, p. 158). Like all methods, surveys have limits and challenges as well, including social desirability bias, self-presentation concerns and lack of face validity, especially when questions are poorly worded, unclear or open to the reader's interpretation.

With these critical perspectives in mind about a suite of data-collection methods, let us turn attention to an illustrative case demonstrating how survey methods can be used to study AI-related matters. But first, a few words to justify the methods we used in this study.

16.3.3 Justification of our methods

Our methods can be justified in three ways. First, considering time and resources, case study was an appropriate choice. In terms of time, generative tools change rapidly, requiring researchers to adjust their study procedures within a limited time frame. Updates to AI tools occur frequently, with new versions being released weekly, if not daily. In contrast, due to lack of financial and human resources, a quantitative case study enabled us to gather and analyse data from a relatively large sample on a small budget with just two researchers.

Second, the study's research questions supported our faith in using a quantitative case study to accomplish our objectives. Quantitative case study research design is perfectly suited for answering 'how' and 'why' questions. In this chapter, we wanted to illustrate how researchers could collect data using an online survey to examine how college students use AI, and why they use it.

Third, focusing on a specific subject group, namely college students, justifies our decision to employ a quantitative case-study research design. A quantitative case-study approach is appropriate to gain in-depth insights into a single population. It allows us to evaluate, describe and understand various aspects of complex phenomena in social settings.

Taken together, a quantitative case-study approach benefited us and yielded several positive results, which we discuss in the next section.

16.4 A Case Study: College Student Project

Building on the existing body of research, our exploration of AI in education reveals significant gaps in our understanding of how college students perceive, learn about and engage with AI technologies. While the literature highlights various dimensions of AI and technology integration, a paucity of empirical data regarding college students' awareness, perceptions and utilization of AI remains, particularly in the context of voice assistants and generative AI.

To address this topic, the lead author designed an online survey aimed at collecting comprehensive data from college students. The survey consisted of 12 multi-part items, eliciting students' levels of awareness, their perceptions of AI and their patterns of use, with a specific focus on voice assistants and generative AI. For example, one survey item asked: 'Have you ever used these AI tools?' Response options varied including ChatGPT (OpenAi), Grammarly, Otter.ai and Alexa, among others. Some other items employed a 5-point Likert-type response scale, ranging from 1 (not at all) to 5 (very much). By delving into these areas, our exploratory study aims to contribute nuanced insights to the ongoing discourse on AI in social research and educational settings.

At the time of this writing, 456 college students have responded to the study's survey. Almost half are women (49%) and 64% identify as white, 10% as black and 12% as Latinx (pronounced Lat-TEEN-ex; this is a gender-neutral reference to people of Latin American heritage first appearing in 2004 and most frequently adopted by young Latin American descendants living in the USA (Brammer, 2019), as described elsewhere (Strayhorn, 2023)). Half of the responding sample currently attend or attended a 4-year public university, whereas 17% attend or attended a 2-year institution or community college. Figure 16.2 presents a summary.

As an illustrative case study, we have limited the reporting of results to a few examples that reflect how relevant data can be collected using social science survey methods. For example, 72% of respondents indicated that they had used ChatGPT, whereas only 27% had used Microsoft Co-pilot and 22% Otter.ai, in keeping with previous studies (Ngo, 2023).

Opinions about AI use varied across the sample. Generally, 35% of responding students strongly agreed that AI tools/technology 'can improve [their] productivity'. Overwhelmingly, 80% of the analytical sample reported using voice assistants, while 37% felt that AI tools could 'help [them] finish tasks/assignments quickly'.

One-third (33%) believed that AI tools could be trusted. However, survey insights also revealed that some students were worried about AI: top concerns ranged from the accuracy and reliability of AI-generated information to data security, ethics and issues of academic integrity (i.e. plagiarism).

While more information is needed to fully understand what aspects of AI created the greatest concerns for students, survey methods were effective in our study for eliciting different kinds of information (i.e. perceptions, attitudes, use) from a large number of students across various institutions and campus types. Administering the survey online also facilitated easy distribution through institutional email lists, listservs, learning management systems and social media.

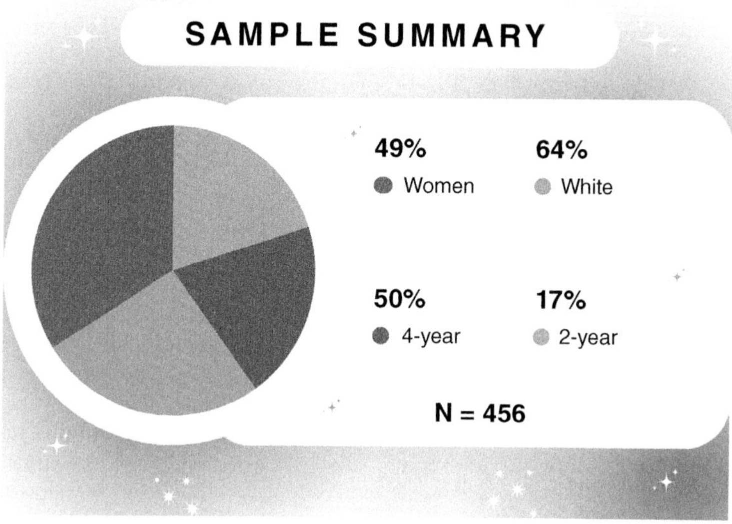

Fig. 16.2. Sample summary.

16.5 Discussion

Recall that the purpose of this chapter was to provide an overview of the importance and challenges associated with studying the prevalence, perceptions and use of AI among diverse social populations, most notably college students. We sought to address methods for collecting data in social research generally and AI-focused college student studies specifically.

Two questions guided our approach to the chapter's topic. First, we addressed the need for using scientific data-collection methods to study AI tools, application, and subjects such as people's awareness, perceptions and use of such technologies. Approaches can be organized into three major categories: quantitative, qualitative and mixed methods. Typically, social scientists use existing datasets, test scores, questionnaires or surveys (administered in person, by phone or online) to elicit information from relevant samples – such as college students – about their general awareness, perceptions and use of AI. Several such studies are cited in our literature review (e.g. Ngo, 2023) and we highlight a case study in the previous section.

Results from our case study yielded important conclusions. For instance, some study respondents reported concerns around trust, but one-third strongly believed that AI could be trusted. Here is what we know: AI can generate a lot of content in little time. But let us not mistake quantity for quality. Dozens of reports show that AI is still learning from us and thus produces material that varies in terms of originality, accuracy and relevance. End-users such as college students would do well to develop a healthy habit of fact checking, verifying and assessing the validity of AI-generated content. There have been far too many embarrassing moments where college graduates turned, say, attorneys in New York use AI tools to write legal briefs that include six fake cases (Milmo, 2023). In our opinion, the error is not in being resourceful and using available tools and devices to stimulate new thoughts, get something 'on screen' or identify key sources that you would later explore more fully; rather, the error is taking information straight from AI – hook, line and sinker – and copying into a document without ever vetting its legitimacy or looking at its logic.

Information provided in this chapter is relevant in terms of future research, policy and practice. We explained that qualitative data can be collected in several ways. For example, methodologists recommend the value that one-on-one interviews, focus groups, observations and document analysis add to naturalistic investigations of people's AI beliefs, knowledge and adoption. Building on our case study, future researchers might develop an interview protocol to unearth the reasoning and rationale between college students' concerns about AI safety, security and accuracy. For example, they might ask students to recall a time when they worried about AI and/or its accuracy. How did they address these concerns? What is the underlying root cause? And how have those worries influenced their current or future perceptions and use of AI?

There are other directions for future research on AI among social scientists, education researchers and scholars. One promising avenue involves exploring the ethical implications and societal impacts of AI deployment in and across various industries, such as business, healthcare, finance and criminal justice. With the rapid expansion and advance of AI technologies, researchers would do well to explore growing awareness of new, emergent, and existing AI apps and tools. For example, researchers might survey, interview or analyse documents (e.g. journal reflections) about people's knowledge and use of ChatGPT, Otter.ai, voice-enabled assistants (e.g. Alexa, Siri), chatbots or algorithmic playlists. Open-ended questions can be used to invite information about new or relatively unknown AI technologies.

Researchers can also delve into the gaps that exist in AI awareness and adoption across different demographic groups. Building on some of the differences that characterize our study's sample, future social researchers might pay close attention to how factors such as age, gender, socio-economic status and geographical location influence awareness, perceptions and usage patterns. Moreover, longitudinal studies could provide valuable insights into how attitudes and interactions with AI evolve over time, particularly in education.

Another critical area of investigation is the role of media and communication in shaping public understanding and sentiment towards AI. By employing a mix of qualitative and quantitative methods, social researchers can uncover nuanced perspectives and contribute to developing frameworks for responsible AI governance and public policy. Additionally, interdisciplinary collaborations with technologists and ethicists can enrich the research enterprise, fostering a more holistic understanding of AI's place in society.

16.6 Conclusion

In conclusion, the study of AI awareness, perceptions and use through social research data-collection methods is vital for understanding the broader societal implications of this transformative technology. AI is certainly helpful, and over 30% of our case study sample agreed that it can improve productivity. But it is not perfect, and it can be used with malicious, unethical and illegal intent. In the wrong hands, AI can be used to generate false documents, hack secured systems and wire fraudulent funds into off-shore accounts, all with disastrous repercussions. Clearly, studying how often people use AI is not enough. Studies must also inform responsible use of AI, in ways that ensure our collective safety and security. Employing a diverse array of methodologies, from surveys and interviews to ethnographic studies and content analysis, enables researchers to capture a comprehensive picture of how different populations interact with and perceive AI. Diverse data-collection methods not only illuminate current trends and disparities but also help track future shifts in public sentiment and behaviour. By integrating qualitative, quantitative and mixed-methods insights, social scientists can provide robust evidence to inform pedagogical practices, program development and policy making to ensure ethical AI use. As AI technologies continue to evolve and permeate various aspects of daily life, ongoing research in this field will be crucial for navigating the complex interplay between technological innovation and societal impact. It is hoped that insights from this chapter and book will help guide the way.

References

Al Shamsi, J.H., Al-Emran, M. and Shaalan, K. (2022) Understanding key drivers affecting students' use of artificial intelligence-based voice assistants. *Education & Information Technologies* 27, 8071–8091.

Alharthi, H. (2020) Predicting the level of generalized anxiety disorder of the coronavirus pandemic among college age students using artificial intelligence technology. In: *2020 19th International Symposium on Distributed Computing and Applications for Business Engineering and Science (DCABES), 16–19 October 2020, Xuzhou, China.* IEEE, Piscataway, New Jersey, pp. 218–221.

Alzahrani, L. (2023) Analyzing students' attitudes and behavior toward artificial intelligence technologies in higher education. *International Journal of Recent Technology & Engineering* 11, 65–73.

Anthology (2023) Anthology Survey Reveals University Students and Leaders Slow to Adopt, but Cautiously Optimistic about AI. Anthology.com. Available at: www.anthology.com/news/anthology-survey-reveals-university-students-and-leaders-slow-to-adopt-but-cautiously (accessed 8 October 2024).

Arminio, J.L. and Hultgren, F.H. (2002) Breaking out from the shadow: the question of criteria in qualitative research. *Journal of College Student Development* 43, 446–460.

Ayyappan, V. and Coffin, J. (2024) Artificial intelligence in diagnosing medical conditions and impact on healthcare. Medical Group Management Association, Englewood, Colorado. Available at: www.mgma.com/articles/artificial-intelligence-in-diagnosing-medical-conditions-and-impact-on-healthcare (accessed 8 October 2024).

Brammer, J.P. (2019) Digging Into the Messy History of "Latinx" Helped Me Embrace My Complex Identity. *Mother Jones*. Available at: www.motherjones.com/media/2019/06/digging-into-the-messy-history-of-latinx-helped-me-embrace-my-complex-identity/ (accessed 8 October 2024).

Catsaros, O. (2023) Generative AI to Become a $1.3 Trillion Market by 2032, Research Finds. *Bloomberg News*. Available at: www.bloomberg.com/company/press/generative-ai-to-become-a-1-3-trillion-market-by-2032-research-finds/ (accessed 7 October 2024).

Clark, V.L.P. and Creswell, J.W. (2008) *The Mixed Methods Reader*. Sage Publications, Thousand Oaks, California.

Creswell, J. (2002) *Educational Research: Planning, Conducting, and Evaluating Quantitative and Qualitative Research*. Merrill Prentice Hall, Upper Saddle River, New Jersey.

Cresswell, J.W. (2014) *Research Design: Qualitative, Quantitative and Mixed Methods Approaches*, 4th edn. Sage Publications, Thousand Oaks, California.

Dallos, R. (2006) Observational methods. *Research Methods in Psychology* 3, 124–145.

Delello, J.A., Woonhee, S., Mokhtari, K. and Giuseppe, T.D. (2023). Exploring college students' awareness of AI and ChatGPT: unveiling perceived benefits and risks. *Journal of Inclusive Methodology and Technology in Learning and Teaching* 3, 1–25.

Denzin, N.K. and Lincoln, Y.S. (eds) (2002) *The Qualitative Enquiry Reader*. Sage Publications, Thousand Oaks, California.

Flyvbjerg, B. (2011) Case study. In: Denzin, N.K. and Lincoln, Y.S. (eds) *The Sage Handbook of Qualitative Research*, 4th edn. Sage Publications, Thousand Oaks, pp. 301–316.

Haan, K. (2023) How Businesses Are Using Artificial Intelligence in 2024. Forbes Advisor. Available at; www.forbes.com/advisor/business/software/ai-in-business/ (accessed 7 October 2024).

Keleş, P.U. and Aydın, S. (2021) University students' perceptions about artificial intelligence. *Shanlax International Journal of Education* 9, 212–220.

Kuleto, V., Illic, M., Dedic, V. and Raketic, K. (2021) Application of artificial intelligence and machine learning in higher education. *EdTech* 1, 24–28.

Kvale, S. (1996) *Interview Views: An Introduction to Qualitative Research Interviewing*. Sage Publications, Thousand Oaks, California.

Milmo, D. (2023) Two US Lawyers Fined for Submitting Fake Court Citations from ChatGPT. *The Guardian*. Available at: www.theguardian.com/technology/2023/jun/23/two-us-lawyers-fined-submitting-fake-court-citations-chatgpt (accessed 15 October 2023).

Mousavi Baigi, S.F., Sarbaz, M., Ghaddaripouri, K., Ghaddaripouri, M. and Mousavi, A.S. (2023) Attitudes, knowledge, and skills towards artificial intelligence among healthcare students: a systematic review. *Health Science Reports* 6: e1138.

National University (2024) 131 AI Statistics and Trends for 2024. National University blog. Available at: www.nu.edu/blog/ai-statistics-trends/ (accessed 8 October 2024).

Ngo, T.T.A. (2023) The perception by university students of the use of ChatGPT in education. *International Journal of Emerging Technologies in Learning* 18, 4–19.

Schwarz, N., Groves, R.M. and Schuman, H. (1998) Survey methods. In: *The Handbook of Social Psychology*, 4th edn. McGraw-Hill, New York, pp. 143–179.

Strayhorn, T.L. (2023) "Tellin' the truth in their own words": a critical race qualitative analysis of ethnic minority law school students' experiences. *American Journal of Qualitative Research* 7, 25–45.

TestGorilla (2024) 7 roles that are on the rise because of AI. TestGorilla blog. Available at: www.testgorilla.com/blog/roles-on-rise-because-ai/ (accessed 8 October 2024).

VanWynsberghe, R. and Khan, S. (2007) Redefining case study. *International Journal of Qualitative Methods* 6, 80–94.

Vogt, W.P. (1999) *Dictionary of Statistics and Methodology: A Non-technical Guide for the Social Sciences*. Sage Publications, Thousand Oaks, California.

17 AI and International Business

Anthi Avloniti*
University of Central Lancashire, Pyla, Cyprus

Abstract
This chapter explores artificial intelligence (AI) and international business, and considers five perspectives in their interplay: intelligence, interconnectedness, complexity, mindset and foresight. It begins with an exploration of human and machine intelligence, as foundations in learning and adapting to complex business environments. The discussion then centres around the interconnectedness of the networked world, reflecting on the interplay between globalization, AI advancement and multinational companies creating a dynamic cycle of growth. By distinguishing between complicated and complex through different analogies, the intricacy of the networked company is highlighted. It then analyses the mindset for complicated and complex problems – inductive reasoning for the former and abductive logic for the latter – and the machine learning and deep-learning tools relevant to each. Finally, the 'race condition' is discussed, presenting foresight into the prospects of AI and international business, and concludes by highlighting the key insights of the chapter along with some directions for future research.

Keywords: abductive logic, artificial intelligence, complicated, complex, deep learning, inductive reasoning, interconnectedness, international business, machine learning, multinational enterprises

17.1 Intelligence: Human, Machine and Business

> The measure of intelligence is the ability to change.
> Albert Einstein

There is a consensus among researchers and philosophers that intelligence is defined by the capacity to learn and adapt to dynamic and complex environments, with various intellectual abilities often interlinked in fascinating ways (Sternberg, 2012). The modern study of intelligence includes several prominent theories: the Cattell–Horn–Carroll theory of broad and narrow capabilities, which forms the basis for IQ tests (Kamphaus *et al.*, 1997); Gardner's (2006) theory of multiple intelligences; and Sternberg's (2003) triarchic theory, which categorizes intelligence into analytical, creative and practical components. Intelligence lies at the core of humanity's existential journey as it empowers problem solving, adaptation, innovation and creativity, and drives societal progress. While crucial, intelligence is not the sole determinant of survival, but its influence on our ability to thrive and shape the future of the world is undeniable, anchoring progress and advancements across all domains.

*E-mail: aavloniti@uclan.ac.uk

DOI: 10.1079/9781800626607.0017

Human intelligence can partially be explained by the brain's biology, particularly the functioning of the prefrontal cortex, and while brain size has a modest correlation with intelligence, neural efficiency, reflected in the speed and complexity of brain activity, is a more significant factor (Neubauer *et al.*, 2002). Similarly to human intelligence, artificial intelligence (AI), coined in 1956 by John McCarthy and others (Shao *et al.*, 2022), can mimic human cognitive functions by relying on the efficiency of its algorithms and processing power to learn and adapt to new information. Following Cattell–Horn–Carroll's theory of intelligence, AI can be divided into narrow AI, which focuses on specialized tasks, and general AI, which aims to emulate overall cognitive functions. The Turing test, originally termed the imitation game, by Alan Turing in 1950, determines the ability of a machine to exhibit intelligent behaviour equivalent to or indistinguishable from that of a human (French, 2000).

AI began with breakthroughs in symbolic logic and early programs such as ELIZA in the 1960s (Weizenbaum, 1966), and advancements in heuristic search and computer vision in the 1970s (Marr, 1976). The 1980s marked progress in machine learning (ML), while the 1990s introduced the semantic web (Berners-Lee *et al.*, 1998) and statistical ML techniques, such as support vector machines, which enabled the analysis of datasets to identify patterns and make predictions (Cortes and Vapnik, 1995). In the 2000s, AI research focused on knowledge-based systems, with IBM's Deep Blue simulating human intelligence and performing complicated tasks such as playing chess (Campbell *et al.*, 2002). The third wave of AI was characterized by deep learning (DL), which involves multiple layers of neural networks involving multiple layers (hence 'deep') that can detect and extract intricate patterns in big data (Emmert-Streib *et al.*, 2020). The explosion of AI is partly due to its optimization techniques (Shao *et al.*, 2022), and the democratization of AI. The controversial and multi-debated 'democratization' of AI, through its widespread accessibility on the Internet, allows access of individuals and organizations to ML and DL tools, spanning from complex high-tech equipment to personalized exclusive tools to end users (Vuppalapati, 2021).

As DL continues to progress rapidly, it is expected to transform industries and human–machine interactions, potentially becoming vastly more intelligent than humans within the next decade, as described by Pearson in 2018 speaking on a panel hosted by CNBC at the World Government Summit in Dubai. At its current state, both ML and DL, as subsets of AI, learn from data, make predictions or decisions without being explicitly programmed for every task or step in the process, and adapt to changes and the environment they are operating in to improve their performance. Therefore, it can support organizations in multiple tasks across various fields. In the field of international business (IB), this capability has the potential to remodel or transform how international companies manage the intricacies of global markets, enhancing their ability to respond swiftly to dynamic changes and competitive pressures.

IB is a multi-faceted field comprising all activities and transactions across national borders involving the movement of goods, services, capital, technology and people with the aim of maximizing economic value by leveraging global resources and markets to achieve competitive advantages and sustainable growth. Diverse regulatory environments, cultural differences, fluctuating economic conditions, labour market variation, technological disparities, supply chain disruptions and geopolitical factors are among the many challenges that multinational companies must navigate to survive or succeed globally. Therefore, the inherent complexity of the IB field can be described in the multitude of entities, and the diversity of interactions between them in a dynamic and constantly evolving global system (Eden and Nielsen, 2020).

Intelligence, both human and artificial, plays a crucial role in managing complexity in multinational companies. Human intelligence drives strategic vision, creative problem solving and innovative thinking, while AI's capacity to process and analyse enormous amounts of data can enable more informed decision making and strategic planning (Jaiswal *et al.*, 2022). The synergetic interplay between human creativity and AI's computational power presents a new form of intelligence that has the potential to enhance the capacity to learn rapidly and adapt efficiently in an increasingly interconnected and interdependent world.

17.2 Interconnectedness: a 'Networked World'

It is both essential and challenging to approach the interconnectedness of things. In the IB field, the interplay between technological advancements and globalization has been researched as a catalyst driving the integration of economies, financial systems, value chains, capital flows, trade networks, markets, cultures and societies on a global scale (Ghauri *et al.*, 2021). Some researchers argue that the world has become so interconnected and interdependent that no single country can efficiently manufacture a product entirely on its own, necessitating the exchange of components, services and goods with other nations (Buckley and Ghauri, 2004). While some governments adopt a protectionism approach in the form of tariffs, trade barriers, restricting immigration and emphasizing national sovereignty over international collaboration (a phenomenon referred to as deglobalization), the forces of globalization, particularly 'digital globalization' (i.e. globalization of firms enabled by digital assets) (Verbeke and Hutzschenreuter, 2021, p. 606), persist, rapidly evolve and further deepen interconnectedness.

Multinational enterprises (MNEs), driven by technology and increasing digitalization (Autio *et al.*, 2021), engage in cross-national activities, transfers, and sharing and exchanges of information and technology more than ever before. This contributes to a 'networked world', where knowledge, information, ideas and goods flow across borders with limited or no interruptions. An interconnected networked world means that people and organizations, irrespective of their location on the map, are fractions in a complex web of relationships and interactions, and as AI technology continues to evolve rapidly, this interconnectedness will grow wider, deeper and more intricate. Business success increasingly lies in the coordination and management of relationships because 'in a networked world, more money can be made from managing interactions than in performing tasks' (Sawhney and Parikh, 2001, p. 82).

As AI's capabilities have evolved from basic data processing to advanced ML, predictive analytics, natural language processing (NLP) and generative technologies, they enable real-time collaboration and information exchange across various digital platforms (Shao *et al.*, 2022). Now more than ever, a single individual action in a remote location of the world can have wide-ranging and far-reaching implications. For example, a scientist in a remote research station discovers a new species of local plant with medicinal properties. Global interconnectedness facilitates the spread of this discovery through global trade networks, scientific collaborations and market demand, enabling its distribution and adoption in diverse healthcare systems worldwide. AI expedites the dissemination of the new plant's medicinal properties through its ability to facilitate rapid research analysis, global collaboration, optimized cultivation techniques and accelerated drug discovery. Its capacity to process vast datasets and predict outcomes amplifies the pace and scale of scientific advancements, driving the plant's impact on global healthcare.

While the evolution of AI involves a diverse array of stakeholders, including academic researchers, start-ups and government-funded initiatives, MNEs are at the forefront of leading AI development, significantly contributing to the range, depth and speed in which AI is developed, while integrating these technologies to enhance user experience and the functionality of their products. Powerful MNEs are a formidable force in AI advancement by utilizing their extensive resources, expertise, innovation capacity and global reach, while making substantial investments in logic and knowledge-based AI tools (Jaiswal *et al.*, 2022) and acquisitions of AI start-ups, thus generating digital monopolies. As Ghauri *et al.* (2021) explained in their paper critically reviewing new realities in IB, the more AI is developed and efficiently employed by MNEs, the more value it generates for the brand, and the bigger the company gets.

Google is considered among the leaders of AI research and development of AI-powered tools and projects, such as Google Brain and DeepMind. Microsoft has invested heavily in AI with a variety of initiatives and the acquisition of AI start-ups. The company has delivered various AI solutions, such as Cortana, Azure AI and Microsoft Cognitive Services. IBM has a long history of AI development with solutions across multiple industries such as cybersecurity and healthcare. Amazon is another key player in AI with products such as Alexa and Amazon Rekognition. Facebook (Meta Platforms Inc.)

utilizes AI for content, personalized recommendation and facial recognition technologies. Apple integrates AI in products such as Siri and develops on-device ML algorithms for personalized experiences and privacy preservation. NVIDIA is a leading tech company involved in AI hardware and software in areas such as DL and autonomous vehicles. Intel channels major investments in AI through various partnerships and develops AI hardware and software solutions. Alibaba Group utilizes AI for cloud computing, smart cities, e-commerce platforms and logistics. Tencent develops AI NLP, computer vision and gaming.

Alongside these giants, AI start-ups are emerging at record rates (Weber *et al.*, 2022), because for new businesses, access to capital is no longer a problem anymore; rather, it is the access to data that provides competitive advantage (Mayer-Schonberger and Cukier, 2013). AI start-ups are each eager to innovate and transform industries, with many embracing a global mindset and targeting international markets from their inception, namely, born-global companies. These start-ups play a significant role in advancing AI by introducing a diversity of innovative AI uses as well as new technologies, algorithms and applications, thus breaking new ground and redefining possibilities. One such example is OpenAI, which, although now functions as a research institute, started as a born-global AI start-up with a mission that transcended national boundaries, dedicated to advancing AI through products such as ChatGPT.

Many other start-ups or smaller organizations are acquired by larger MNEs as a strategic move to access innovative technologies, talent or market share. In 2019, Tesla acquired DeepScale, a computer vision start-up for developing AI perception systems for autonomous vehicles. In 2022, Microsoft acquired Nuance Communications, a leading provider of conversational AI and speech recognition for US$19.7 billion, bringing together 'Nuance's best-in-class conversational AI and ambient intelligence with Microsoft's secure and trusted industry cloud offerings' (Microsoft News Center, 2022).

As these giants, along with many other MNEs across industries, continue to expand through acquisitions, investments, partnerships and strategic alliances, their networks become increasingly powerful and complex (Ghauri *et al.*, 2021). Discoveries, knowledge, skills, expertise, synergies and advancements shared within the networks of these multinational companies, with operations spanning across countries in the form of branches, affiliates, subsidiaries, outlets and strategic partnerships, speed up AI advancements internationally and spread global interconnectedness. Therefore, within the IB context, global interconnectedness and AI mutually reinforce and amplify one another's effects, leading to transformative shifts in industries, modern business, innovation and global business dynamics. And at the core of this interplay are MNEs, whose operations, networks and external environments are becoming increasingly complex.

17.3 Complexity: the 'Networked Multinational Enterprise'

To comprehend the complexity inherent in the network of a multinational company, we must first clearly define the term 'complex' and distinguish it from related concepts. Tony Robbins, an American author with around 2 million YouTube subscribers, explained that complexity is the enemy of execution, while simplicity prompts action. As explored next, while simplicity can indeed drive action, it is not the right approach for complexity.

Consider this question: Which is more complex? A pile of sand, a mechanical music box or a baby? The obvious answer is the baby. But it is not as simple as that. The pile of sand appears simple and unchanging; however, each grain has its unique structure and composition, involving complex interactions and granular physics. The dynamics within the sand pile can exhibit self-organization, altered by forces such as moisture, gravity and friction. Its complexity arises from these interactions, leading to emergent behaviours that cannot be fully understood by examining a grain in isolation.

The mechanical music box illustrates intricate engineering, consisting of a winding mechanism, gear, rotating cylinder or disc, and combs. Its intricacy lies in the design and synchronization required to produce music through precise mechanical interactions. However, although mechanically complicated, it operates through a fixed set of interactions in a predetermined manner, lacking the adaptive interactions of complex systems, and is thus considered complicated rather than complex.

A baby is a living organism with cells, tissues and systems synchronized collectively with immense complexity in its biological structure, genetic information and environmental interactions. The biological networks within a baby's body, such as the nervous, circulatory and immune systems, are intricately interconnected to sustain life and development. The neural networks in a baby's brain, comprising billions of interconnected neurons, facilitate learning, behaviour and cognitive growth.

While multiple insights can be derived from the above analogies, the focus next will be on two elements that are relevant to the topic of this chapter. The first is the distinction between complex and complicated (Nason, 2011), illustrated in the pile of sand and the music box. While the music box may be *complicated* due to its intricate mechanical design, the sand grains demonstrate *complex* behaviour in emergent properties, dynamic interactions, self-organization and non-linearity. While the words 'complex' and 'complicated' are often used as synonyms (Kinni, 2017), this distinction is critical because it influences how they can be approached in an interconnected world. In his book *It's Not Complicated: The Art and Science of Complexity for Business*, Rick Nason (2017) emphasized the critical distinction between simple, complicated and complex systems, arguing that approaching a complex phenomenon as complicated is the source of many business failures. This distinction is important because complex problems involve numerous interrelated factors and unknowns that cannot be resolved with straightforward rules and processes, unlike complicated problems, which, while challenging, can be addressed with predefined algorithms and structures.

Simple systems can range from straightforward tasks, such as brewing a cup of coffee, to more difficult ones, such as making a free throw in basketball, or time-consuming ones, such as making a challenging math calculation. With the use of basic AI algorithms, some simple tasks can be automated or completed much faster and easier, such as using a smartphone calculator, which can quickly process mathematical operations and provide accurate results in a fraction of the time. *Complicated* systems, such as the music box, consist of many interconnected parts that can be analysed and understood through logical processes. These systems follow rules and predictable patterns and can often be managed with checklists, procedures and standard operating protocols, such as accounting and manufacturing. While complicated problems can be highly challenging to solve, they can be tackled by rules and formulas, such as the ML algorithms used for the ads shown when scrolling through an Instagram feed.

Complexity, in contrast, cannot be fully understood or solved but, to a certain degree, it can be managed. *Complex* systems are characterized by the dynamic interactions among their components, such as in the pile of sand, as well as unpredictability due to numerous unknowns and interdependencies that lead to emergent behaviour. Complexity considers the interconnected nature of elements and how this interconnectedness gives rise to intriguing features such as adaptive behaviour and self-organization without central control. Being adaptive means that the actions of each element in a complex system influence the others, prompting changes that are perpetual and evolving.

Nason (2017) emphasized that complex problems require a holistic approach and adaptive management strategies, as they cannot be fully understood through reductionist methods or controlled through algorithms. Kinni (2017) talked about avoiding the arrogance of complicated thinking, as it leads managers into thinking that they are acting purposefully when in fact they are not, potentially causing more harm than good. The same applies for the use of AI in complex problems. While ML can be valuable in complicated problems, it inherently lacks the capacity to fully account for the dynamic interactions in complex systems or phenomena. The integration of DL in managing complex problems is an ongoing endeavour; however, along with its advancement, it is increasingly being used in harnessing the power of data, advanced computational techniques and pattern recognition. However, its role in managing different forms of complexity is yet to be determined.

This leads to the second insight from the analogies of the complexity in a pile of sand and a baby, illustrating the critical impact of the mindset towards complexity. Complexity presents itself in a diverse multitude of forms, encompassing structural intricacies, functional diversity, dynamic interactions and emergent phenomena, as well as adaptive and developmental capabilities within systems. While both analogies exhibit complexity in emergence and interconnectedness, the baby involves cognitive processes, emotional expressions and social interactions, while its growth is dynamically influenced by genetic predispositions, environmental stimuli and the intricate development of neural networks. The networks of MNEs are highly complex, consisting of an intricate web of foreign subsidiaries, supply chains spanning multiple countries, diversified portfolios across markets, extensive interactions with numerous stakeholders across social, cultural, regulatory and economic environments, and the need to steer across evolving global dynamics and geopolitical changes in sustaining advantage and growth.

Therefore, much of the complexity for MNEs arises from the simultaneous pressures for local responsiveness and pressures for global integration (Meyer *et al.*, 2023). Global integration enables the leveraging of economies of scale and standardization, reducing costs and maintaining central control. Local responsiveness enables meeting the unique needs of each market and stronger relationships with local stakeholders. Furthermore, while MNEs face local, international and global complexities, the lack of clearly defined boundaries of their networks introduces additional layers of complexity. As Edwards *et al.* (2022, p. 207) noted, the 'fluid and contested nature of the internationally integrated multinational, involving frequent instances of restructuring and reinvention, means that boundaries between different sections or parts of MNCs are often blurred or unclear'. For this reason, researchers should avoid presuming that structures or processes of one MNE mirror those of another, while exploring the sources of complexity could be useful.

Andrews *et al.* (2023) in their study published in the *Journal of International Business Studies* explained the three sources of complexity in MNE networks of subsidiaries: multiplicity, multiplexity and dynamism. Multiplicity refers to the diverse range of entities/actors involved in shaping subsidiary research, ranging from employees and managers to industries and regions, at national, international and global levels. Multiplexity describes the intricate interactions among the multitude of actors within MNEs. Multiplexity arises when there are 'networks of networks', leading to systemic issues such as cross-level effects, feedback loops and diffusion. Subsidiaries, especially those geographically dispersed and functionally distributed, exhibit complex structures and systems of routines and workflows that are influenced by interactions between home and host markets. Dynamism refers to the ever-evolving nature of global and MNE systems over time. Trends, business cycles and external events such as the COVID-19 pandemic or geopolitical tensions continuously shape structures and interactions.

While the sources, boundaries and forms of complexity are significant, the frame in which complexity is perceived is crucial. Kurtz and Snowden (2003) argued that separating individuals into two groups – a complex thinking space and a knowledgeable space – and asking them to frame the same subject, namely 'the influence of the Internet on globalization', would lead to diverse perspectives emerging from both groups, each potentially enriching our understanding of the topic. While we can comprehend the usefulness of these different approaches, the difference is that the act of complex thinking involves creativity and neural efficiency, whereas knowing entails retrieving information. Both are components of intelligence but serve different functions. Einstein was a genius and a complex thinker, while Walther Mayer, who performed many of the calculations needed for Einstein's theoretical explorations, is considered a proficient mathematician and complicated thinker.

However, as Kinni (2017) explained, what differentiates a complexity mindset from the rest is acknowledgement of the existence of complexity, recognition of the unique approach required, acceptance of the limitations, and embracing the inherent challenges and opportunities. In essence, complexity in the IB field can potentially be managed, but it cannot be solved, which creates a very interesting space for the contribution of AI, and particularly DL neural networks, as will be discussed next.

17.4 Mindset: Inductive Reasoning and Abductive Logic

In the IB field, complexity has often been researched through the lens of complicated approaches, without adequately distinguishing between complex and complicated. Although complicated approaches can provide useful insights for complex problems, they limit our ability to fully capture the dynamic and interdependent complexity of global business networks and may constrain the effective application of AI tools and techniques. While high complexity is a fundamental aspect in IB, it is crucial to recognize that both complex and complicated problems exist, each requiring a different mindset: abductive logic or inductive reasoning. Both will be discussed next, along with the role of AI in supporting these mindsets for MNEs. The intention here is not to compile an exhaustive list of complicated and complex problems, as context plays a central role in IB and is unique to each MNE (Knight *et al.*, 2022); rather, we will focus on the two insights from complexity: the distinction between complex and complicated, and complexity mindset.

To limit generalized discussions, an industry example is used. Construction MNEs embarking on international projects are selected for multiple reasons: (i) their significant global presence; (ii) the high-stake capital-intensive nature of operations making the selection of the appropriate project management approach and mindset vital (Viswanathan and Jha, 2020); (iii) the involvement of multiple stakeholders and sensitivity to technological and institutional changes, e.g. regulatory and cultural (Han and Diekmann, 2001); and (iv) their sensitivity to supply chain disruptions and resource availability (Habibi and Kermanshachi, 2018). The international risks and problems were identified in Viswanathan and Jha's (2020) review of existing research on construction MNEs. The list of variables capturing these risks and problems is extracted from their comprehensive study and separated into complicated and complex to facilitate the discussion.

17.4.1 Complicated, inductive reasoning and ML

Examples of complicated problems for construction MNEs according to Viswanathan and Jha (2020) include the following: regulatory compliance in different countries, detailed financial analysis, language barriers, low labour productivity, untimely payment from the client, tight project schedules, inaccuracies in competitor analysis, improper cost estimation, poor subcontractor management and the non-availability of quality materials in host countries. These problems are considered complicated because they involve multiple interdependent components that require detailed planning, precise execution and systematic management. Each issue, while intricate, operates in predictable ways and can be broken down into manageable parts to be addressed through meticulous analysis and control.

The mindset that could be applied to solve such complicated issues is inductive reasoning. Hayes *et al.* (2010) analysed inductive reasoning in their advanced review paper and explained it as the process of involving existing knowledge or observations to make predictions about novel cases and incorporating 'a range of cognitive activities such as categorization, probability judgment, analogical reasoning, scientific inference, and decision making' (p. 278). Inductive reasoning would be well suited for the complicated problems listed above, as it relies on analysing data to derive insights. Such data could include regulatory compliance data, financial performance metrics, subcontractor performance reviews, client payment histories, cost estimation records, local labour productivity data and past project data to predict costs, timelines and resource needs.

The AI technique that can be implemented to support inductive reasoning is ML. Bosma and van Witteloostuijn (2024) recently explored the use of ML in IB, and argued that ML provides a very efficient and effective toolbox for the inductive exploration of complicated issues; therefore, it is ideal for identifying complicated patterns in high-dimensional data. Using ML algorithms, the MNE can, for example, predict project risks and fluctuations in the price of construction materials and ensure adherence to safety regulations by analysing historical and current data. Some specific AI tools that can be incorporated are support vector machines, which are useful for classifications problems (Awad and Khanna, 2015), such as identifying patterns in regulatory compliance data, and K-means clustering, which is one of the popular algorithms for segmenting data into meaningful groups (Mucherino *et al.*, 2009), such as analysing subcontractor performance and categorizing different types of client payment histories.

Overall, the inductive reasoning's focus on data and consistent patterns makes it appropriate for addressing complicated problems. ML complements and enhances inductive reasoning by efficiently processing big data and increasing the reliability and accuracy of the identified patterns, clusters and predictions. However, managerial oversight is required in this process to avoid overfitting (models excessively tailored to specific training data failing to generalize to new or unobserved data) and oversimplifications (models overly simplify complications overlooking other contextual factors), as well as critically assessing the quality and availability of the data (inaccurate or incomplete data) (Whang *et al.*, 2023).

17.4.2 Complex, abductive logic and DL

The complex problems identified from Viswanathan and Jha's (2020) study involved unpredictable, interconnected and interdependent elements. These include: cross-cultural organizational behaviour, cultural differences, host country government instability, international economic instability, supply chain disruptions, dispute(s) with local construction labour, increased geopolitical risks in the country or region, frequent currency fluctuations, dynamic pressures for sustainability, and community opposition. These can be considered complex due to their intrinsic uncertainty, the need for adaptive strategies and the intricate interplay of multiple influencing factors. Within each of these complex problems, the actions of one element affect the others, resulting in continuous and reciprocal adjustments.

The mindset that could be used for these complicated issues is abductive logic. Drawing from Charles Peirce's philosophic views, Timmermans and Tavory (2012) defined abductive logic as a creative inferential process designed to generate new hypotheses and theories in response to unexpected research findings, which is therefore linked to Sternberg's (2003) triarchic theory of analytical, creative and practical intelligence. In the IB field, this approach has been suggested by Edwards *et al.* (2022, p. 207), who stated that to 'capture the complexity of the reality on the ground', the abductive logic must be embraced. The abductive logic starts with an incomplete set of observations and seeks the most likely explanation for them. It is therefore suited for complex problems because it allows the generation of plausible explanations in situations where data is incomplete, ambiguous or rapidly changing. The process followed for abductive logic is observing surprising facts, generating multiple hypotheses, and following a method of constant experimentation and refinement.

Experimentation, however, is not a one-off process. In the words of Jeff Bezos, 'Our success here at Amazon is a function of how many experiments we do per year, per month, per day', reflecting the growing popularity of this mindset in organizations. Experimentation can also be found in processes such as growth hacking, which involves rapid, iterative, systematic, data-driven experimentation for growth (Bargoni *et al.*, 2024), adopted in companies such as Google, Amazon, Netflix, Spotify and Uber (Bohnsack and Liesner, 2019). Experimentation and refinement facilitate rapid learning from both successes and failures, as understanding potential pitfalls is as crucial as recognizing what works; however, the speed of this learning process is what sets the winners apart. Experimentation should be iterative, with each cycle involving changes and adjustments that progressively enhance the process, ultimately enabling companies to become more agile and innovative (Feiz *et al.*, 2021).

DL could be useful across different phases of the abductive logic process: observing, hypothesizing, experimenting and refining. In observing and hypothesizing, different types of neural networks can be utilized (e.g. convolutional neural networks), which can uncover hidden structures and relationships that might not be apparent through traditional analysis (Li *et al.*, 2022). Furthermore, diverse DL techniques can be utilized for observing and hypothesizing for complex problems in the industry. For cross-cultural communication issues, NLP techniques can be used to understand sentiment in different languages. For understanding cultural norms, preferences and community views generative adversarial networks can process and analyse vast amounts of social media data, local news and cultural content (Malik, 2020). For political and economic instability observations, DL tools such as sentiment analysis models and reinforcement learning algorithms can monitor political news, social media and economic indicators in real time. Furthermore, time-series forecasting models can be used to predict currency fluctuations and economic trends (Yang *et al.*, 2022).

While there is no standard process in experimenting and refining in the abductive mindset, companies could develop and sustain a searchable central repository of previous iterations of experiments, including successes, setbacks and final decisions, to enable the systematic improvement of the process. DL can enhance this central repository by automating the categorization of experimental data, making it easier to search and retrieve relevant information. DL algorithms can identify patterns and trends across different experiments, offer predictive insights, and detect anomalies, unusual results or significant deviations. Therefore, DL could enhance the mindset and application of abductive logic in dealing with complexity by providing increasingly sophisticated tools for big-data analysis. However, as discussed next, there are many critical considerations for IB by taking into account the current stage of DL capabilities.

First, AI is 'data hungry' (Dessimoz and Thomas, 2024), and DL models perform best with vast datasets, which may not always be available. Considering the multiplicity of entities, multiplexity of interactions and dynamic nature from which the complex IB environment is composed, the amounts of data required are immense, and are needed from diverse sources and formats to capture the full range of interdependent elements and their continuous interactions. Second, DL requires substantial computational power and resources, which can be a limiting factor for many organizations (Shrestha *et al.*, 2021). While for large MNEs the cost and infrastructure needed for DL may not be prohibitive, for smaller international organizations it can be overly burdensome. Third, the newness of AI technology and its scalability across different national and cultural contexts is a challenging issue for MNEs to consider. For example, when scaling AI solutions in developing countries, the novelty of the technology and the need to adapt it to the cultural and institutional environment may be a complex process (Tatarinov *et al.*, 2023), due to the lack of formal institutions and the corruption often present in disadvantaged communities (Sartor and Beamish, 2014).

Fourth, critical considerations of AI in IB are related to data biases, managerial oversight and creativity. Biases in the training data may be amplified in DL models, raising ethical concerns, particularly in relation to culturally sensitive data across countries. While AI's speed is one of its main advantages, its effectiveness is constrained by the quality of its training data. However, this limitation can potentially be mitigated by incorporating the out-of-sample expertise of human specialists (Autio *et al.*, 2021). Nevertheless, the synergy between human abductive judgement and DL is not straightforward. DL models, particularly deep neural networks, often function as 'black boxes' (Shrestha *et al.*, 2021), which complicates understanding on how they reach conclusions and critical decision-making processes. While this may be less challenging during the observation and hypotheses phases, it may hinder creative experimentation and organizational learning through trial and error.

Iterative experimentation, as part of the observation, hypothesize and refinement abductive mindset, is becoming even more critical in the digital age. Due to the perpetual exponential growth of AI and its role in rapid innovations across products, services and markets, the key for competitive edge lies in the agility, resilience and creativity that can be exerted from a culture and a mentality of constant experimentation. Overall, the complex dynamic nature of IB necessitates adaptability and flexibility in combining inductive reasoning in complicated problems with abductive logic in complex issues, as the nature of the problems is constantly changing and evolving. While the increasingly networked and digital world provides MNEs with greater opportunities for global integration, the pressures for local adaptation across borders will continue to persist as a crucial institutional contextual factor (Meyer *et al.*, 2023). The slower adjustment of some countries to AI development in relation to the rapid adoption and utilization in others may create additional barriers for AI scalability by MNEs in cross-border operations, as well as reinforcing inequalities in economic disparities, bias, discrimination and the digital divide.

17.5 Foresight: The 'Race Condition'

At the rate AI is developing, it is impossible to talk about AI in the IB field without considering its future advancement in the next 5, 10 or 20 years, along with the role of MNEs in such developments. However, the future of AI is largely perplexing. Computer and data scientists, technologists, AI experts, engineers, business leaders, entrepreneurs, researchers, educators and philosophers all discuss the short-term and long-term implications of AI advancements. While their predictions and speculations are highly diverse, most of them agree on a specific premise: AI transcends the boundaries of any industrial revolution the world has ever experienced and, more importantly, can recalibrate the framework and core principles of our life and our society.

While the role of MNEs in driving AI development and integration across countries is undeniable, little is known about the ethical standards in which this development is framed. What is known is that companies, particularly MNEs and tech giants, are in a 'race condition' fuelled by their competitiveness to capitalize on the immense potential of AI. This logic of 'if I don't do it, someone else will' brings about concerns about the concentration of AI power in the hands of a few dominant players and giving rise to digital monopolies. On this subject, Ghauri *et al.* (2021, p. 6) stated that 'it seems we do not mind or are unable to stop/control these monopolies', despite the urgent need for ethical AI development and equitable AI deployment.

The current rise of AI has been characterized as 'an Oppenheimer moment' due to its magnitude and pivotal role in the history of humanity, emphasizing the immense impact of the choices faced in how AI technology is developed and deployed now and in the future. AI advocates and evangelists endorse the substantial benefits of AI related to unprecedented global advancements in healthcare, actionable solutions in environmental sustainability and poverty mitigation, enhanced productivity, personalized experiences, innovation and creativity. Sceptics and critics discuss pitfalls of AI ranging from job displacement, loss of control, privacy invasion and security risk to existential risk.

Even the key companies and individuals closest to the development of AI struggle to explain and elaborate on how AI will evolve and unfold in the future. In this context, many of these individuals share their expert views on AI advancement in interviews and podcasts watched by millions of viewers. Mustafa Suleyman, a primary architect of many of the AI models used today and developed for the future, argues that 'there is no upper limit to AI's potential intelligence', constantly stressing the importance of the 'pessimism aversion trap (optimism bias)' and 'precautionary discipline' in the sense that containment of AI is necessary to avoid pitfalls and capitalize its potential 'before it gets out of control'. Sam Harris, American philosopher and neuroscientist, says 'we can't put the genie back in the bottle'.

While this is true and the potential of AI is truly unimaginable, it is no longer a matter of 'pausing' its rapid advancement or restricting the powerful MNEs steering its development; it could be a matter of containing, controlling and managing. For example, one of the many concerns of AI relates to the scale and speed through which fake news can spread through AI algorithms, which can generate and disseminate misleading information. As a countermeasure, we observe the development of online platforms with AI algorithms, which can compare news from multiple sources globally and evaluate their reliability, bias, accuracy, political sentiment and propaganda (Iqbal *et al.*, 2023). AI necessitates adaptive approaches, such as in the abductive logic, to effectively steer through the multiplicity, multiplexity and dynamic features in complex IB systems and phenomena.

17.6 Conclusion

The main conclusions and insights derived from this chapter are summarized here, along with future research directions for researchers and students to consider.

- *Combine data science with in-depth IB knowledge.* Human intelligence and AI are both critical for researching complex phenomena in IB, but integration of both should be the foundation of any progress in researching complex IB phenomena. AI, particularly through ML and DL, excels in processing vast datasets, identifying patterns and making data-driven predictions. Human intelligence drives creative problem solving, innovative thinking and unconventional experimentation. Therefore, a balance between the two will assist in making substantial progress in dealing with IB complexity. For researchers and students, the practical application involves developing interdisciplinary approaches and skills that combine data science with deep IB knowledge. Without in-depth IB knowledge, the insights gained from AI data science may lack the necessary context and understanding. IB knowledge ensures that insights from data-driven strategies are relevant and aligned with the IB complexities that are crucial for formulating hypotheses and looking beyond the metrics and numbers.

- *Understand the uniqueness of interconnectedness in each MNE.* While it is impossible to research IB complexity and AI integration without considering its interconnected and interdependent nature, it is also crucial to consider the uniqueness within and across MNE networks. Each MNE operates within a distinct context and network of relationships, which means that AI applications must be tailored to fit these specific dynamics. While this personalized approach allows more accurate and effective implementation of AI tools, such tools require extensive customization, which can be resource intensive and time consuming. To gain deeper insights into the uniqueness of each MNE and improve AI implementation, future research should focus on detailed and comprehensive case studies. Most of the research in IB consists of extensive samples and large-scale examinations. By examining specific instances of AI integration in diverse MNEs through case studies, researchers and students can uncover significant insights. Examples of such research could include: the scalability of AI tools across an MNE's networks, institutional contexts and countries; and addressing issues in the immense cross-country data needed to research the multiplicity, multiplexity and dynamic nature of an MNE for ML and DL algorithms to produce useful insights.
- *Distinguish between complex and complicated problems in IB for enhanced AI tool integration.* The IB environment is undeniably highly complex, yet it contains both complicated and complex problems. While IB researchers have been discussing complexity for years, recently with even more attention, there is limited discussion about distinguishing between complex and complicated. Future research should focus on developing frameworks to differentiate and address complicated and complex issues appropriately. Practically, this means adopting specific AI tools and methodologies tailored to the nature of the problem. ML can be highly effective for the inductive reasoning process in solving complicated IB problems due to the effectiveness and efficiency of ML algorithms that can analyse an MNE's historical data to predict future trends. DL can be complimentary to the human-led process of abductive logic for managing complex IB problems due to its capacity to uncover hidden patterns and relationships in large, convoluted datasets. Further research could adopt this approach to validate and deliver new insights.
- *Examine the role of MNEs in the rapid development of AI.* The role of MNEs and tech giants in accelerating the development and deployment of AI leading to digital monopolies is crucial. For researchers and students, it is important to study how MNEs influence AI trends, contribute to technological advancements and shape global business practices. This involves analysing case studies to understand the leading AI strategies of MNEs and assessing the broader implications of their AI initiatives on global business dynamics. The ethical implications of AI deployment by these corporations, including concerns about privacy, surveillance and job displacement, should be considered.

The far-reaching implications of AI for every human underscore the need for research into these emerging issues involving MNEs. Mohammad Gawdat, an AI expert who served as a

CBO of Google X for years, talked about humanity in the age of the machines and stated: 'AI machines are pure potential; the threat is how we will use them.' Research on facilitating the synergetic interactions between human and machine intelligence, understanding the interconnectedness of things in IB and critically adopting complexity mindsets could be a way to manage AI's potential in addressing some of the most pressing challenges in our networked world.

References

Andrews, D.S., Nell, P.C., Schotter, A.P.J. and Laamanen, T. (2023) And the subsidiary lives on: harnessing complex realities in the contemporary MNE. *Journal of International Business Studies* 54, 538–549.

Autio, E., Mudambi, R. and Yoo, Y. (2021) Digitalization and globalization in a turbulent world: centrifugal and centripetal forces. *Global Strategy Journal* 11, 3–16.

Awad, M. and Khanna, R. (2015) Support vector machines for classification. In: *Efficient Learning Machines*. Apress, Berkeley, California, pp. 39–66.

Bargoni, A., Smrčka, L., Santoro, G. and Ferraris, A. (2024) Highway to hell or paradise city? Exploring the role of growth hacking in learning from innovation failure. *Technovation* 131: 102945.

Berners-Lee, T., *et al.* (1998) Semantic Web Road Map. World Wide Web Consortium (W3C). Available at: www.w3.org/DesignIssues/Semantic.html (accessed 7 October 2024).

Bohnsack, R. and Liesner, M.M. (2019) What the hack? A growth hacking taxonomy and practical applications for firms. *Business Horizons* 62, 799–818.

Bosma, B. and van Witteloostuijn, A. (2024) Machine learning in international business. *Journal of International Business Studies* 55, 676–702.

Buckley, P. and Ghauri, P. (2004) Globalisation, economic geography, and the strategy of multinational enterprises. *Journal of International Business Studies* 35, 81–98.

Campbell, M., Hoane, A.J., Jr and Hsu, F.-H. (2002) Deep blue. *Artificial Intelligence* 134, 57–83.

Cortes, C. and Vapnik, V. (1995) Support-vector networks. *Machine Learning* 20, 273–297.

Dessimoz, C. and Thomas, P.D. (2024) AI and the democratization of knowledge. *Scientific Data* 11: 268.

Eden, L. and Nielsen, B.B. (2020) Research methods in international business: the challenge of complexity. *Journal of International Business Studies* 51, 1609–1620.

Edwards, T., Svystunova, L., Almond, P., Kern, P., Kim, K. *et al.* (2022) Whither national subsidiaries? The need to refocus international management research on structures and processes that matter. *Journal of International Business Studies* 53, 203–210.

Emmert-Streib, F., Yang, Z., Feng, H., Tripathi, S. and Dehmer, M. (2020) An introductory review of deep learning for prediction models with big data. *Frontiers in Artificial Intelligence* 3: 4.

Feiz, D., Zarei, A., Mibashrazgah, M.M. and Shaabani, A. (2021) Typology of growth hacking strategies along the growth hacking funnel. *Iranian Journal of Management Studies* 14, 331–346.

French, R.M. (2000) The Turing test: the first 50 years. *Trends in Cognitive Sciences* 4, 115–122.

Gardner, H. (2006) *Multiple Intelligences: New Horizons*, revised edn. Basic Books, New York.

Ghauri, P., Strange, R. and Cooke, F.L. (2021) Research on international business: the new realities. *International Business Review* 30: 101794.

Habibi, M. and Kermanshachi, S. (2018) Phase-based analysis of key cost and schedule performance causes and preventive strategies: research trends and implications. *Engineering, Construction and Architectural Management* 25, 1009–1033.

Han, S.H. and Diekmann, J.E. (2001) Making a risk-based bid decision for overseas construction projects. *Construction Management and Economics* 19, 765–776.

Hayes, B.K., Heit, E. and Swendsen, H. (2010) Inductive reasoning. *Wiley Interdisciplinary Reviews: Cognitive Science* 1, 278–292.

Iqbal, A., Shahzad, K., Khan, S.A. and Chaudhry, M.S. (2023) The relationship of artificial intelligence (AI) with fake news detection (FND): a systematic literature review. *Global Knowledge, Memory and Communication* (in press). Available at: www.emerald.com/insight/content/doi/10.1108/GKMC-07-2023-0264/full/html (accessed 7 October 2024).

Jaiswal, A., Arun, C.J. and Varma, A. (2022) Rebooting employees: upskilling for artificial intelligence in multinational corporations. *International Journal of Human Resource Management* 33, 1179–1208.

Kamphaus, R.W., Winsor, A.P., Rowe, E.W., Kim, S., Flanagan, D.P. *et al.* (1997) A history of intelligence test interpretation. In: *Contemporary Intellectual Assessment: Theories, Tests, and Issues*. The Guilford Press, New York, pp. 32–47.

Kinni, T. (2017) The Critical Difference Between Complex and Complicated. *MIT Sloan Management Review*. Available at: https://sloanreview.mit.edu/article/the-critical-difference-between-complex-and-complicated/ (accessed 7 October 2024).
Knight, G., Chidlow, A. and Minbaeva, D. (2022) Methodological fit for empirical research in international business: a contingency framework. *Journal of International Business Studies* 53, 39–52.
Kurtz, C.F. and Snowden, D.J. (2003) The new dynamics of strategy: sense-making in a complex and complicated world. *IBM Systems Journal* 42, 462–483.
Li, Z., Liu, F., Yang, W., Peng, S. and Zhou, J. (2022) A survey of convolutional neural networks: analysis, applications, and prospects. *IEEE Transactions on Neural Networks and Learning Systems* 33, 6999–7019.
Malik, A. (2020) Survey paper on applications of generative adversarial networks in the field of social media. *International Journal of Computer Applications* 175: 13.
Marr, D. (1976) Early processing of visual information. *Philosophical Transactions of the Royal Society of London B: Biological Sciences* 275, 483–519.
Mayer-Schonberger, V. and Cukier, K. (2013) *Big Data: A Revolution That Will Transform How We Live, Work and Think*. Houghton Mifflin Harcourt, Boston, Massachusetts.
Meyer, K.E., Li, J., Brouthers, K.D. and Jean, R.-J. "Bryan" (2023) International business in the digital age: global strategies in a world of national institutions. *Journal of International Business Studies* 54, 577–598.
Microsoft News Center (2022) Microsoft Completes Acquisition of Nuance, Ushering in New Era of Outcomes-based AI. Microsoft. Available at: https://news.microsoft.com/2022/03/04/microsoft-completes-acquisition-of-nuance-ushering-in-new-era-of-outcomes-based-ai/ (accessed 7 October 2024).
Mucherino, A., Papajorgji, P.J. and Pardalos, P.M. (2009) Clustering by *k*-means. In: *Data Mining in Agriculture*. Springer, New York, pp. 47–82.
Nason, R. (2011) It's not complicated. *RMA Journal* 93: 66.
Nason, R. (2017) *It's Not Complicated: The Art and Science of Complexity in Business*. University of Toronto Press, Toronto, Ontario, Canada.
Neubauer, A.C., Fink, A. and Schrausser, D.G. (2002) Intelligence and neural efficiency: the influence of task content and sex on the brain–IQ relationship. *Intelligence* 30, 515–536.
Sartor, M.A. and Beamish, P.W. (2014) Offshoring innovation to emerging markets: organizational control and informal institutional distance. *Journal of International Business Studies* 45, 1072–1095.
Sawhney, M. and Parikh, D. (2001) Where value lives in a networked world. *Harvard Business Review* 79, 79–86.
Shao, Z., Zhao, R., Yuan, S., Ding, M., Wang, Y. *et al.* (2022) Tracing the evolution of AI in the past decade and forecasting the emerging trends. *Expert Systems with Applications* 209: 118221.
Shrestha, Y.R., Krishna, V. and Krogh, G. (2021) Augmenting organizational decision-making with deep learning algorithms: principles, promises, and challenges. *Journal of Business Research* 123, 588–603.
Sternberg, R.J. (2003) *Wisdom, Intelligence, and Creativity Synthesized*. Cambridge University Press, Cambridge, UK.
Sternberg, R.J. (2012) Intelligence. *Dialogues in Clinical Neuroscience* 14, 19–27.
Tatarinov, K., Ambos, T.C. and Tschang, F.T. (2023) Scaling digital solutions for wicked problems: ecosystem versatility. *Journal of International Business Studies* 54, 631–656.
Timmermans, S. and Tavory, I. (2012) Theory construction in qualitative research: from grounded theory to abductive analysis. *Sociological Theory* 30, 167–186.
Turing, A.M. (1950) Computing machinery and intelligence. *Mind* 59, 433–460.
Verbeke, A. and Hutzschenreuter, T. (2021) The dark side of digital globalization. *Academy of Management Perspectives* 35, 606–621.
Viswanathan, S.K. and Jha, K.N. (2020) Critical risk factors in international construction projects: an Indian perspective. *Engineering, Construction and Architectural Management* 27, 1169–1190.
Vuppalapati, C. (2021) *Democratization of Artificial Intelligence for the Future of Humanity*, 1st edn. CRC Press, Boca Raton, Florida.
Weber, M., Beutter, M., Weking, J., Böhm, M. and Krcmar, H. (2022) AI startup business models. *Business & Information Systems Engineering* 64, 91–109.
Weizenbaum, J. (1966) ELIZA – a computer program for the study of natural language communication between man and machine. *Communications of the ACM* 9, 36–45.
Whang, S.E., Roh, Y., Song, H. and Lee, J.G. (2023) Data collection and quality challenges in deep learning: a data-centric AI perspective. *VLDB Journal* 32, 791–813.
Yang, M., Jiang, B., Wang, Y., Hao, T. and Liu, Y. (2022) News text mining-based business sentiment analysis and its significance in economy. *Frontiers in Psychology* 13: 918447.

18 AI Systems Employed in Archaeological Research for Ancient Artefacts – A Dilemma

Annita Antoniadou*
Independent Researcher/Cyprus University of Technology, Limassol, Cyprus

Abstract
Traditional investigation methods for sites and ancient artefacts have been time consuming and are no longer adequate. Recent reports highlight the successful collaboration between archaeologists and artificial intelligence (AI) systems, which utilize techniques such as aerial image classification and site pattern recognition to detect new sites and restore specific artefacts. AI is a game-changer for archaeologists seeking to unravel the mysteries of our past, although it requires a strategic approach. This chapter provides a concise overview of the evolution of archaeological science, delves into the use of AI for research support, and investigates the potential for managing and categorizing artefact data using these systems. It also raises concerns about ensuring the alignment of results from these technologies with accepted archaeological interpretations. Furthermore, it discusses the dilemma of creating AI systems that rely on data from online archaeological sources for academic and research purposes, while ensuring the accuracy of the derived information.

Keywords: AI systems, artificial intelligence, archaeology

18.1 Introduction

Archaeology has always been a captivating field, focusing on the study of human beings and past civilizations, offering a glimpse of humanity's past. It employs a wide range of methods and techniques derived from social sciences to gain insights into historical aspects (Boissinot, 2017; Price and Knudson, 2018). Archaeologists use artefacts, structures and remnants from ancient civilizations to uncover the history of societies and cultures. Through excavation and analysis, archaeology sheds light on human evolution and progress (Renfrew and Bahn, 2000). The evolution of archaeology into a multi-disciplinary domain has resulted in the integration of state-of-the-art methods, with geoarchaeology being one of the key additions to the traditional toolkit of excavation practices (Antoniadou, 2012).

Artificial intelligence (AI) has been a topic of discussion since its inception, with many focusing on its potential to revolutionize numerous aspects of society. The discussion often revolves around its ability to lead to significant changes in fields such as art, technology and humanity as a whole (Echterhölter *et al.*, 2022). To date, AI systems have not been specifically designed for use in the field of archaeology. There are various recent studies, however, that document the outcomes of collaborations between archaeologists and AI systems, assist in detecting ancient ruins from aerial photos, site pattern recognition

*E-mail: drannitaantoniadou@gmail.com

 Artificial Intelligence (AI) in Social Research (P.A. Christou ed.)
DOI: 10.1079/9781800626607.0018

and documentation, as well as artefact identification and restoration (Sharafi *et al.*, 2016; Casini *et al.*, 2023; Kerig *et al.*, 2023; Pavlidis, 2023). The capability of AI to identify new findings can be greatly enhanced by employing further research beyond image classification methods. Integrating AI with online databases for specific locations can further amplify its effectiveness.

This chapter discusses the evolution of archaeological science, explores the application of AI in research, and examines the feasibility of organizing and classifying artefact data through these platforms. It also examines the dilemma of designing AI systems that rely on data from online sources, while ensuring the accuracy of the derived information, and raises concerns about ensuring the alignment of results from these technologies with established research from social sciences.

18.2 The Development of Archaeological Science

Archaeology is a multi-disciplinary area that draws inputs from several sciences in order to dive into the past (Murray and Evans, 2008; Antoniadou, 2012); it proposes hypotheses, and tests and validates them, often through laboratory work. It encompasses a significantly broader range than history, which is limited to the period in which written records appeared. In its early stages, archaeology evolved around exploration and the pursuit of valuables, with minimal emphasis on documentation. The cradle of modern archaeology dates to the Renaissance in Europe, when an interest for collection of sculptures and relics and their study appeared in the upper social classes (Renfrew and Bahn, 2000). This resulted in unearthing of structures and priceless artefacts that lacked a scientific approach, without any comprehension regarding chronology or historical context. The curiosity rush for the ancient past and its subsequent study has witnessed a remarkable growth in Europe and North America that paved the way for numerous expeditions.

Archaeology as a discipline did not emerge until early 20th century, and was marked by astonishing discoveries such as the Sphinx, the city of Pompeii and the Palace of Knossos (Renfrew and Bahn, 2000). Objects of historical and artistic interest were often collected and traded, and some were displayed in private collections. Over time, these collections evolved into remarkable institutions, such as the Louvre and the British Museum, now housing an extensive array of captivating pieces that offer invaluable insights into humanity's evolution, and displaying the artistic and intellectual achievements of ancient civilizations. In addition, ancient literature was successfully employed to discover lost cities – from Homer's Troy at Hisarlik, Turkey, in 1871 by Heinrich Schliemann and Frank Calvert (Uslu, 2017; Solly, 2022; Martins, 2023) to the tomb of Tutankhamen in Egypt by Howard Carter in 1922 (Marchant, 2023). In the years that followed, unearthing of significant historical sites continued in the absence of systematic approaches; a prime example is the accidental discovery of the Terracotta Army in Shaanxi Province, China, in 1974 (Cartwright, 2017).

From its initial days of only discovering treasures, without recording their context, archaeological survey has witnessed tremendous transformation as complex features of human processes have revealed themselves. Excavation is the basic tool, and the development of field techniques was an important step towards the understanding of cultural practices, with major contributors such as Pitt Rivers, a pioneer in recording techniques; William Flinders Petrie, known for thorough excavation, recording techniques and sequence dating; and Mortimer Wheeler for the extensive use of grid-square stratigraphy, to name a few (Renfrew and Bahn, 2000; Carver, 2014). Archaeological sites are discovered by systematic ground and air surveys and by accident (Murray and Evans, 2008), often relying on the expertise and even the intuition of the archaeologist. Prior to embarking on a fieldwork expedition, in order to evaluate the potentiality of a chosen geographical zone for the presence of archaeological remains, archaeologists must gather an extensive amount of information including old maps, references from ancient literature and previous works that relate to the specific area. In this regard, old maps are useful as they often identify ground remains from the period in which they were prepared, and even dried-up rivers often are marked. In the present day, macro- and microdata obtained from excavations across the landscape can be investigated with sophisticated equipment and include aspects such as migration, origin studies and palaeoclimate (Renfrew and Bahn, 2000; Antoniadou, 2012; Carver, 2014).

18.3 Cutting-edge Technologies for Locating Sites and Handling Assemblages

Since the 1960s when archaeologists started to use computers for research, machine learning (ML) has rapidly been adopted for analysing large datasets efficiently related to geospatial and material culture and for simulating restoration. ML algorithms can be trained to recognize and classify features on artefact assemblages, which can save time and enhance the accuracy of cataloguing findings (Anichini *et al.*, 2021; Bickler, 2021). The advancement of archaeology has incorporated cutting-edge techniques, with geoarchaeology enhancing excavation methods (Antoniadou, 2012). Medium-resolution, multi-spectral satellite imagery open-access software offers great potential for monitoring natural events such as sand dune movements in deserts due to its frequent revisits. Depending on the nature of the landscape and terrain, surveying entire landscapes enables the identification of agricultural activities and hidden infrastructures, and appropriate statistical methodologies can be applied (Renfrew and Bahn, 2000; Banning, 2002; Oxoli and Brovelli, 2022). Furthermore, results obtained using pre-trained semantic segmentation deep-learning models using openly available satellite imagery for the detection of archaeological sites, for example within the Mesopotamian floodplains, have shown that the best model reaches a detection accuracy of 80% (Casini *et al.*, 2023), reasoning that an inaccurate prediction by human–machine collaboration can be useful when put into context and interpreted by a trained archaeologist (Casini *et al.*, 2023). Nevertheless, locating sites and artefacts remains a challenge. Innovative strategies, such as remote sensing technologies (Oxoli and Brovelli, 2022), geophysical instruments, semi-automated methodologies (Agapiou and Lysandrou, 2022), and automatic recognition of lithics and ceramics from photographs (Anichini *et al.*, 2021; Di Maida *et al.*, 2023) are being used to address these problems.

AI has a direct impact on shaping how information is presented and analysed in historical research, improving efficiency and accuracy in archaeological studies (Pavlidis, 2023). Could the utilization of AI be the revolutionary means archaeologists and researchers employ in order to understand our past?

18.3.1 Spatial survey

An archaeological site is an area where there are physical remains of past human activities; this includes villages, stone quarries, rock shelters, campsites and megalithic monuments. A site can be as small as a pile of chipped stone tools left by a prehistoric hunter, or as large and complex as a city (Renfrew and Bahn, 2000). AI is now playing a crucial role in automating and improving the process of site discovery (Oxoli and Brovelli, 2022) by analysing satellite imagery, and light detection and ranging (LiDAR), which uses laser pulses to create detailed three-dimensional (3D) maps of terrain and vegetation, and reveals hidden structures even beneath dense forests, and other geospatial information. AI algorithms can identify features and patterns that may indicate the presence of archaeological sites, assisting in the planning, logistics and time management of excavations. Drones and AI-powered image analysis can assist in the identification and documentation of archaeological sites, enabling researchers to cover larger areas efficiently. These can process large datasets quickly, aiding in the analysis of archaeological data and identifying patterns that might be challenging for humans to discern (Radak and Akhgar, 2023). Free and open access to satellite imagery is a result of the open-data policies embraced by some of the leading national and international Earth Observation programmes (Wulder *et al.*, 2012; Oxoli and Brovelli, 2022).

AI algorithms study vast amounts of data, sifting through historical and geographical information to identify potential archaeological sites, and provide insights into the most efficient and effective excavation strategies. This reduces speculation and increases the possibility of uncovering hidden treasures (Bickler, 2021), optimizing the allocation of resources and time, increasing the chances of discovering, and enhancing the overall excavation process. Archaeologists streamline the process of sifting through millions of documents by utilizing neural networks, which efficiently organize spatial information using specific algorithms, analysing images and providing pattern recognition (Sharafi *et al.*, 2016; Echterhölter *et al.*, 2022). Ground surveys are essential to validate the findings of remote sensing analysis (Quintus *et al.*, 2017; Argyrou and Agapiou, 2022), without which our understanding remains limited to a theoretical standpoint. While there may be situations where automated surveys are not suitable, it is important to acknowledge that ground surveys, manual evaluations and automated detection algorithms are valuable tools for archaeologists, each with their own advantages and disadvantages.

18.3.2 Artefact documentation

Excavating, handling and classifying artefacts is a fundamental aspect of archaeological research (Renfrew and Bahn, 2000). When artefacts are removed from their original context, their scientific value diminishes, as context is crucial for comprehending the relationships among objects and archaeological sites, shedding light on past behaviours. Algorithms can detect subtle patterns, classify artefacts based on shape and material, and determine their cultural purpose, and have the capability to simulate and reconstruct artefacts, offering new perspectives on the past (Pavlidis, 2023). In the absence of organic material to allow carbon dating, pottery classification provides an indispensable tool for dating excavated content. Much of the work on automated identification of sherds is based on 3D scanning or multi-view reconstruction technologies (Arnaoutoglou *et al.*, 2003; Pavlidis, 2023). Recent developments in 3D digitization and visualization technologies, combined with network technologies, offer new possibilities for the integrated and complete description of typological characteristics for cultural objects; however, their adoption has been very limited due to the challenges of 3D acquisition in the field (Arnaoutoglou *et al.*, 2003). Cutmarks on ancient bones from published images representing ancient hominin presence in Africa, America and Europe tested by AI models provided high accuracy in classification, with the research suggesting that collective learning is typically more concise and well-rounded compared with individual models (Domínguez-Rodrigo *et al.*, 2020).

Automatic analysis of profiles of potsherds has been studied using classical computer vision methods (Itkin *et al.*, 2019). This research concluded that none of these systems is robust enough to be applied automatically on a varied set of excavated sherds, and much of it was only applied to complete profiles. Some years later, there was a study of automatic recognition of ceramics using only a photo, called the ArchAIDE app for tablets and smartphones, which was employed during both fieldwork and post-excavation analysis (Anichini *et al.*, 2021). This was a collaborative work of archaeological and technical experts creating a pipeline where potsherds were photographed, their characteristics were compared against a trained neural network, and the results suggested matches from a comparative collection of typical pottery types and characteristics. Once the correct type was identified, information was linked to the artefact and saved within a database that could be shared online (Anichini *et al.*, 2021).

This author argues that it is essential to generate high-quality data that closely mirrors real-world data in order to effectively train an automated model. Archaeological classification should not rely solely on fracture shape, emphasizing the necessity of domain expertise to consider factors such as location, other artefacts present and other relevant considerations. Despite this, research so far indicates that the gap in distinguishing potsherds based on shape between automated methods and human archaeologists is likely to be minimal. In addition, AI employed in archaeological research can assist in the restoration and reconstruction of damaged or fragmented pieces. By analysing digital scans and employing ML algorithms, AI systems can suggest potential connections and reconstruct missing parts, allowing researchers to gain a better understanding of the artefact's original form and purpose. For example, the Big Exchange project recently investigated large-scale exchange systems in Eurasia and Africa (8000–1 BC) based on raw materials sources. The network analysis enabled the formulation of statements regarding the correlation between the concurrent distribution of various goods and the varying levels of access that individuals have to raw materials, and it appeared that the integration of datasets containing different raw materials enabled the reconstruction of more complex relationships, including economic decisions, in which specific raw materials are exchanged for automation and to meet domain-specific and research data management requirements (Knappet, 2021; Kerig *et al.*, 2023). Furthermore Resler *et al.* (2024) focused on the exploration and comparison of pre-trained convolutional neural networks (CNNs), loss functions and evaluation metrics for automated age estimation of archaeological artefacts. CNN models are designed to automatically learn features from images by utilizing numerous layers of convolutional filters, and can automatically identify patterns and styles, while also extracting features from input images that are subsequently utilized by additional computational layers to categorize valuable information from input data related to the periodic differentiation of lithic assemblages (Itkin *et al.*, 2019; Resler *et al.*, 2024). This allows them to uncover complex patterns and details from visual data related to age estimation of archaeological artefacts. In the view of the author, the most effective approach involves feeding AI systems with data and parameters, which enables researchers to analyse patterns and trends. Consequently, they can develop virtual models that shed light on the socio-political, economic and cultural factors that have influenced historical developments.

With regard to artefacts bearing inscriptions, AI is automating and accelerating the process of reading ancient languages and scripts, as researchers have developed algorithms that can recognize patterns, identify symbols and decode ancient texts more efficiently, providing insights into social and religious beliefs. Ithaca, a unique deep neural network working with Greek inscriptions, was trained to simultaneously perform the tasks of textual restoration, geographical attribution and chronological attribution (Assael *et al.*, 2022). However, this first epigraphic restoration and attribution model of its kind requires enhancement in terms of precision and efficiency, as acknowledged by its creators.

18.3.3 Data interpretation

The analysis of methods for the classification of fragments, artefacts and mobile assemblages generates vast amounts of data, including excavation records, scientific analyses and historical documents. Managing and interpreting these data can be a daunting task. It is suggested that archaeological data is better described as 'slow data' (Heitman *et al.*, 2017); whereas 'big data' approaches focus on managing data flowing in on a continuous or near-continuous basis, archaeological data can be very slow to create – taking years or decades – and delivered in big groups of complex contextualized information (Bickler, 2021). ML processes large amounts of data, builds models and uses analysis to understand future data, as well as organizing new data, learning from it and incorporating findings into interpretations. This tool is effective with well-organized datasets but can also be used to analyse disorganized and incomplete datasets, although archaeologists focus primarily on numerical and/or categorical data, textual data, images and geospatial data (Bickler, 2021; Di Maida *et al.*, 2023).

Regarding big data, a recent study by Iyer and Franklin (2022) on a curated dataset of 55,000 ancient artefact images from over 343 different cultures was aimed at origin culture classification using two CNN models (InceptionResNetV2 and VGG-19). The dataset consisted of samples from different regions and was built using the British Museum's online collection of over 3 million artefact images, aiming to assess the precision of AI in categorizing and recognizing their cultural origins. Both AI models demonstrated effectiveness in estimating the origin of artefacts recovered from excavation sites, and for the artefacts of unknown origin, the culture suggestion was reasonable. With images of artefacts widely accessible online, including the British Museum's website, the process involved grouping them into classes with minimal effort and creating a dataset of these artefact images. Indeed, recent developments in CNN technology now enable the utilization of more robust models, resulting in significantly higher training and validation accuracy; however, one may argue that, despite undergoing thorough testing, the ML approach is not yet suitable for practical use, as basic CNN models do not have the complexity required to be trained on the dataset.

18.3.4 How AI is revolutionizing studies of ancient artefacts

Archaeologists examine artefacts to gain insights into the individuals who crafted them, and a wealth of significant information can be found even in the tiniest archaeological context. To safeguard context, archaeologists record the exact position of the artefact before extracting it for preservation purposes. Features such as soil discolorations that indicate former presence (i.e. storage pits, buildings or walls) are also studied. Ecofacts, which are natural remnants linked to human actions, such as plant and animal remains, aid in comprehending dietary habits. Once all data is collected, archaeologists assess the importance of the information collected (Renfrew and Bahn, 2000). When evaluating the historical significance of an artefact, various factors are considered. Archaeologists often find fragments during excavations. Identifying and categorizing artefacts used to require extensive training and expertise. The abundance of data from excavations, historical records and scientific research can be overwhelming for researchers. Technology can help in organizing and analysing this data, identifying trends and providing valuable insights. By using image-recognition algorithms, researchers can quickly categorize, draw connections and evaluate artefacts, leading to more accurate analysis.

In the author's opinion, the evidence suggests that, if AI is applied in an effective manner early in the excavation process, it could detect and monitor new discoveries through image classification techniques, and propose potential reconstructions by considering shapes and material properties. Automated object identification could accelerate the cataloguing process, enabling excavators to focus on deeper analysis. For instance, the importance of a gold ring discovered in a Mycenaean megalithic tomb in Pylos, Greece, is determined by its ability to provide insights into the past. The ring has the ability to serve as a time capsule, capturing a glimpse of the technology and culture of the era when it was interred alongside its wearer. Dating archaeological finds is essential for establishing the chronological context of civilizations and understanding their development over time. The author argues for an early integration of AI based on the flexibility of excavation and the efficiency of data, but this adaptability would depend on the applied environment and the specialist's training for data import.

18.4 The Dilemma

AI is revolutionizing the way we approach archaeology and ancient history, by converting physical documents into digital formats, enhancing their searchability and availability, and safeguarding significant information while establishing precise timelines. On the one hand, virtual collections help scholars to remotely study artefacts, reducing the need for physical handling and preserving delicate items for the future, in addition to uncovering new insights by identifying correlations and anomalies that may have been missed by human researchers; on the other hand, in order to ensure accurate and reliable data, archaeologists are required to conduct a thorough primary analysis of the typology, context, profile, shape, etc.

The process of classification involves a transformation from raw facts to finds and features, so by providing detailed information and utilizing a comparable scale factor, features and measures, a well-documented set of data is more likely to yield consistent results when compared with findings from around the world. Currently, there is a lack of dedicated systems that are specifically designed to handle and offer such information. Advances in the application of ML techniques to computational archaeology highlight the importance of careful selection and empirical testing of the systems first. The objective of applied AI is to build computer models that replicate specific physical processes, allowing a deeper understanding of the domain and the ability to forecast future trends and events (Pavlidis, 2023). The introduction of AI tools could have an influence on the methods and therefore on the way the results are produced. The use of open and free AI systems in such archaeological research presents both opportunities and challenges, leading to a dilemma, a situation of options, each with both positive and negative consequences, that researchers must navigate when classifying.

18.4.1 Accuracy and reliability

Data quality is crucial for accurate analysis. Ensuring that collected data is reliable, consistent and representative is challenging. For example, a requirement that relates to correctness is the reliability of input. Meeting this demand is extremely challenging, as it relies solely on the user's preferences and choices. The user's input is crucial in fulfilling this requirement, making it the most arduous to satisfy. This is achieved by providing pre-programmed multiple-choice options for the user to select from. The validity of the input, however, is hardly verifiable. Validation of input is often not possible due to the lack of consistency between the descriptions of two variables, especially when there is a dependency present. The reason lies in the subjectivity of the observations of the wear traces on the object.

Recent reports have detailed the successful partnership between archaeologists and AI systems, enabling archaeologists to exploit a vast amount of data to come to decisions on excavation strategies, preservation and protection, as well as to identify optimal excavation locations. The accuracy of AI analyses for artefacts that draw information from online databases available for each archaeological site relies heavily on the quality and representativeness of the data. A well-documented set is more likely to produce reliable results when compared with another across the world. AI algorithms require a large volume of data for training. Collecting sufficient artefact data can be time consuming and resource intensive. With regard to the need for accuracy, it can be inferred that even with efforts to regulate incoming data, there will inevitably be instances where incorrect interpretations occur. An example of this would be when a description is provided that follows the correct procedures and is therefore permitted by the system but does not align with the observed traces. Despite this mismatch, an interpretation is still made. In such a scenario, the interpretation may be procedurally correct, but it is unrelated to the specific implementation being discussed. This leads to the conclusion that if a user is not capable of providing reliable input, the output will not be reliable either (van den Dries, 1998).

18.4.2 Quality and objectivity

To improve objectivity, a variety of quantitative variables are employed, including the width of a polish or the number of striations. However, the author argues that most variables relate to qualitative observations; for instance, the texture of the polish or the degree of edge rounding on a stone tool, a dagger or an amphora cannot be measured. Thus, in order to enhance objectivity, numerous quantitative variables are utilized, such as the width of a polish or the number of striations. A well-documented collection of stone tools from the middle Stone Age in North Africa is expected to yield more reliable results than a similar collection from South Africa or China of the same typology. Nevertheless, there are currently no dedicated systems for managing and disseminating information about artefacts such as prehistoric microliths, Bronze Age jewellery and ancient pottery used for cooking. Classification is the conversion of raw data into findings and characteristics. AI models are not tailored for use in archaeological qualitative studies and generate quantitative human-like text based on the input provided to them.

ML is heavily influenced by the data the system is trained on, resulting in models that classify objects or assemblages based only on known categories. Diverse artefact samples are essential to develop reliable models and avoid bias, as the latter makes them vulnerable. In addition, categorizing ancient objects into predetermined groups can lead to overlooking rare and unique items. For instance, a researcher may overlook a classical period ceramic vessel, only to later discover its unique surface treatment upon closer examination. ML assessments may also overlook the bigger picture because of insufficient contextual information in the training data, especially in image-based situations, or because of the use of a limited set of predetermined variables that may not cover sufficient data to distinguish between important (e.g. archaeologically important) categories.

18.4.3 Accessibility and distribution

Sharing project data is increasingly vital for research advancement, and the availability of digital databases enhances collaborative efforts in understanding human history across geographical and cultural barriers. Implementing AI with the potential to aid in sample identification requires a strategic approach and an understanding of technological capabilities. Training the tool on biased or incomplete datasets can reinforce existing biases in the interpretation, and hence information must be described accurately with metadata. Overcoming bias in classification and clustering involves using diverse training data and carefully selecting features and variables for training the model. This requires a diverse dataset that represents different contexts, regions and periods to reduce bias and avoid stereotypes. Interdisciplinary collaborations could validate the results.

Despite the challenges encountered, the results provide a promising direction for further exploration and application of deep learning in the field of archaeology (Resler *et al.*, 2024), increased accuracy and advanced cultural heritage conservation, leading to economic gains. However, there is a risk of over-reliance on AI-generated information, leading to potential inaccuracies or misinterpretations, and therefore it is important to carefully consider social and practical factors before using AI. Archaeologists face the significant challenge of acquiring the necessary skills to effectively manage this extensive and varied information (Kansa and Kansa, 2021, 2013). One could argue that archaeologists bring critical contextual knowledge; consequently, AI should complement rather than replace this expertise, requiring validation and comparison of generated results with reliable references. It is crucial to achieve a balance between AI-assisted processes and human expertise, ensuring that human researchers retain the ultimate authority in interpreting archaeological discoveries. Integrating these outcomes into academic and cultural resource management frameworks will be a revolutionary task.

18.4.4 Limits and efficiency

The integration of AI is changing research methodology and shaping the future of archaeology. From deciphering ancient languages to historical simulations and predictions, AI is reshaping the landscape of social sciences.

Consequently, it becomes increasingly important to improve our educational and analytical skills through alternative methods to ensure successful outcomes. In this respect, for an academically accepted case, we have to create literate end-users, but there is a lack of focus on understanding end-users' attitudes and needs for knowledge-based systems in archaeology. Improving the functionality may not ensure success in minimizing the costs and time-consuming efforts of surveying and excavating landscape areas, as field archaeologists rarely use a fully functional application.

Embracing AI has the potential to improve the efficiency of research endeavours and promote increased public involvement. However, implementing AI technologies can be costly, limiting their accessibility for researchers in certain regions or with limited funding, potentially exacerbating global disparities in archaeological research. The integration of AI in archaeological studies raises ethical concerns including data privacy, cultural sensitivity and preservation of cultural heritage, and hence ensuring ethical AI practices is crucial. Digital reproductions of artefacts may raise questions about intellectual property rights and cultural ownership. AI developers and archaeologists must navigate these ethical complexities to ensure the respectful representation and preservation of cultural heritage. Moreover, copyright issues must be resolved before such data are used, and cultural heritage professionals need to learn how to navigate this complex terrain skilfully.

18.5 Conclusion

According to the above, one could argue that AI is transforming the study of archaeology as its lack of emotion, biases and ideological beliefs enhances pre-existing methodologies and can provide more objective judgements compared with humans, focusing on optimizing parameters rather than engaging in ideological disputes, and ensuring a neutral treatment for the data involved. Nevertheless, developing educational and reference materials for collections post-excavation highlights the importance of creating organized excavation reports by archaeologists working on similar sites and managing them systematically within the same framework. This could create a unique dataset, preventing inconsistencies in overlapping site information, and eliminating the risk of losing valuable data.

The advancement of AI offers archaeologists the chance to unravel the mysteries of our past. To fully understand the archaeological landscape, automated analysis, manual evaluation and field testing are necessary. This chapter suggests that sharing datasets and training information could improve the ability of AI models to detect archaeological features, empowering archaeologists globally to utilize diverse methods and data for overcoming obstacles in archaeology. AI systems can assist in processing and analysing vast amounts of textual data more efficiently. They can aid in tasks such as literature reviews, data summarization and information extraction. By providing alternative perspectives or insights, AI systems may even inspire archaeologists to explore new research questions or adopt advanced approaches. The use of AI has the potential to be highly effective in detecting and monitoring new discoveries in the archaeological world through image classification techniques, especially when there are online databases for each site. Furthermore, OpenAI technologies have the potential to play a significant role in the development of captivating and interactive tools that can be utilized for public outreach and educational purposes. By leveraging virtual assistants, chatbots and interactive applications, it becomes possible to effectively communicate information regarding ancient artefacts to a wider audience, thereby enhancing engagement and facilitating learning opportunities for individuals of all backgrounds and ages. The potential for a promising future lies in the collaboration between AI and archaeology.

It is acknowledged by the author that the continued development of AI has the potential to revolutionize the way we study and interpret our historical heritage. Incorporating AI tools in archaeological research can enhance precision and productivity in excavation, exploration, identification and data management, eventually enhancing our understanding of past civilizations. The future shows promise. By providing education to future archaeologists on how to effectively utilize AI technologies, we can ensure that they are equipped with the necessary skills to succeed and address ethical concerns in their work implications. Ultimately, this collaboration between technology and social sciences has the potential to preserve and share the fascinating stories of ancient civilizations for future generations.

References

Agapiou, A. and Lysandrou, V. (2022) Remote sensing studies on monitoring natural hazards over cultural heritage sites in Cyprus. In: Saud, M.M. (ed.) *Applications of Space Techniques on the Natural Hazards in the MENA Region*. Springer, Cham, Switzerland, pp. 167–194.

Anichini, F., Dershowitz, N., Dubbini, N., Gattiglia, G., Itkin, B. *et al.* (2021) The automatic recognition of ceramics from only one photo: the ArchAIDE app. *Journal of Archaeological Science* 36: 102788.

Antoniadou, A. (2012) The geoarchaeology of Cyrenaica, Libya. PhD thesis, Queen's University Belfast, Belfast, UK.

Arnaoutoglou, F., Evagelidis, V., Pavlidis, G., Tsirliganis, N. and Chamzas, C. (2003) 3D-GIS: new ways in digitization and visualization of cultural objects. In: *Workshop on the Digitization of Cultural Content, 27–28 June 2003, Corfu, Greece*, p. 27.

Argyrou, A. and Agapiou, A. (2022) A review of artificial intelligence and remote sensing for archaeological research. *Remote Sensing* 14: 6000.

Assael, Y., Sommerschield, T., Shillingford, B., Bordbar, M., Pavlopoulos, J. *et al.* (2022) Restoring and attributing ancient texts using deep neural networks. *Nature* 603, 280–283.

Banning, E. (2002) *Archaeological Survey. Manuals in Archaeological Method, Theory and Technique*, *Vol. 1*. Springer, New York.

Bickler, S.H. (2021) Machine learning arrives in archaeology. *Advances in Archaeological Practice* 9, 186–191.

Boissinot, P. (2017) Why archaeology, in all of its components, is a social science? *Archéologie et Sciences Sociales* 9, 1–24.

Cartwright, M. (2017) Terracotta Army. World History Encyclopedia. Available at: www.worldhistory.org/Terracotta_Army/ (accessed 14 October 2024).

Carver, M. (2014) Field method in archaeology: overview. In: Smith, C. (ed.) *Encyclopedia of Global Archaeology*. Springer, New York.

Casini, L., Orrù, V., Montanucci, A, Marchetti, N. and Roccetti, M. (2023) *Archaeological Sites Detection with a Human–AI Collaboration Workflow*. arXiv preprint. Available at: https://arxiv.org/abs/2302.05286 (accessed 14 October 2024).

Di Maida, G.D., Hattermann, M. and Delpiano, D. (2023) 3D models of lithic artefacts: a test on their efficacy. *Digital Applications in Archaeology and Cultural Heritage* 30: e00279.

Domínguez-Rodrigo, M., Cifuentes-Alcobendas, G., Jiménez-García, B., Abellán, N., Pizarro-Monzo, M. *et al.* (2020) Artificial intelligence provides greater accuracy in the classification of modern and ancient bone surface modifications. *Scientific Reports* 10: 18862.

Echterhölter, A., Schröter, J. and Sudmann, A. (2022) How is artificial intelligence changing science? Research in the era of learning algorithms. MediArXiv Preprint. Available at: https://osf.io/preprints/mediarxiv/28pnx (accessed 14 October 2024).

Heitman, C., Worthy, M. and Plog, S. (2017) Innovation through large-scale integration of legacy records: assessing the "value added" in cultural heritage resources. *Journal on Computing and Cultural Heritage* 10: 17.

Itkin, B., Wolf, L. and Dershowitz, N. (2019) Computational ceramicology. arXiv preprint. Available at: https://arxiv.org/abs/1911.09960 (accessed 14 October 2024).

Iyer, A. and Franklin, M. (2022) Determining the origin culture of various ancient artifacts using machine learning. *Journal of Student Research* 11: 2465.

Kansa, E.C. and Kansa, S.W. (2013) We all know that a 14 is a sheep: data publication and professionalism in archaeological communication. *Journal of Eastern Mediterranean Archaeology and Heritage Studies* 1, 88–97.

Kansa, E.C. and Kansa, S.W. (2021) Digital data and data literacy in archaeology now and in the new decade. *Advances in Archaeological Practice* 9, 81–85.

Kerig, T., Hilpert, J., Strohm, S., Berger, D. and Denis, S. (2023) Interlinking research: the *Big Exchange* project. *Antiquity* 97: e22.

Knappet, C. (2021) Networks in archaeology. In: Light, R. (ed.) *The Oxford Handbook of Social Networks*. Oxford University Press, Oxford, pp. 443–466.

Marchant, J. (2023) How Howard Carter Discovered King Tut's Golden Tomb. *Smithsonian Magazine*. Available at: www.smithsonianmag.com/history/how-howard-carter-discovered-king-tuts-golden-tomb-180981052/ (accessed 14 October 2024).

Martins, K. (2023) Discovery of Troy. *World History Encyclopedia*. Available at: www.worldhistory.org/article/2196/discovery-of-troy/ (accessed 14 October 2024).

Murray, T. and Evans, C. (2008) *Histories of Archaeology: A Reader in the History of Archaeology*. Oxford University Press, Oxford, UK.

Oxoli, D. and Brovelli, M.A. (2022) Open data and tools for multispectral satellite analysis of desert sand dunes migration: case studies in the MENA region. In: Saud, M.M. (ed.) *Applications of Space Techniques on the Natural Hazards in the MENA Region*. Springer, Cham, Switzerland.

Pavlidis, G. (2023) From digital recording to advanced AI applications in archaeology and cultural heritage. In: Ben-Yosef, E. and Jones, I. (eds) *"And in Length of Days Understanding": (Job 12:12): Essays on Archaeology in the Eastern Mediterranean and Beyond in Honor of Thomas E. Levy.* Interdisciplinary Contributions to Archaeology. Springer, New York.

Price, T.D. and Knudson, K. (2018) *Principles of Archaeology: An Introduction to Archaeology that Helps Students Think Like Archaeologists*, 2nd edn. Thames & Hudson, London.

Quintus, S., Day, S.S. and Smith, N.J. (2017) The efficacy and analytical importance of manual feature extraction using lidar datasets. *Advances in Archaeological Practice* 5, 351–364.

Radak, M. and Akhgar, A. (2023) Image processing on images of ancient artifacts with the help of methods based on artificial intelligence. *Journal of Anthropological Archaeology* 5, 27–39.

Renfrew, C. and Bahn, P. (2000) *Archaeology: Theories, Methods and Practice*, 3rd edn. Thames & Hudson, London.

Resler, A., Yeshurun, R., Natalio, F. and Giryes, R. (2024) A deep-learning model for predictive archaeology and archaeological community detection. *Humanities and Social Sciences Communications* 7, 185–194.

Sharafi, S., Fouladvand, S., Simpson, I. and Alvarez, J.A.B. (2016) Application of pattern recognition in detection of buried archaeological sites based on analysing environmental variables, Khorramabad Plain, West Iran. *Journal of Archaeological Science* 8, 206–215.

Solly, M. (2022) The Many Myths of the Man Who 'Discovered' – and Nearly Destroyed – Troy. *Smithsonian Magazine.* Available at: www.smithsonianmag.com/smart-news/the-many-myths-of-the-man-who-discoveredand-nearly-destroyedtroy-180980102/ (accessed 14 October 2024).

Uslu, G. (2017) The discovery of Troy: Schliemann and the Ottomans in the 1870s. In: *In Homer, Troy and the Turks*. Amsterdam University Press, Amsterdam, Netherlands, pp. 35–82.

van den Dries, H.M. (1998) Archaeology and the application of artificial intelligence: case-studies on use-wear analysis of prehistoric flint tools. PhD thesis, Faculty of Archaeology, Leiden University, Leiden, Netherlands.

Wulder, M.A., Masek, J.G., Cohen, W.B., Loveland, T.R. and Woodcock, C.E. (2012) Opening the archive: how free data has enabled the science and monitoring promise of Landsat. *Remote Sensing of Environment* 122, 2–10.

19 Conclusion

Prokopis A. Christou*
Cyprus University of Technology, Limassol, Cyprus

Artificial intelligence (AI) has emerged as a transformative force in numerous fields, and its impact on social research is profound and multifaceted. This book, *Artificial Intelligence (AI) in Social Research*, has explored various ways in which AI technologies can enhance, challenge and reshape the landscape of social research. As we conclude, it is important to reflect on the opportunities and perils associated with AI in this context and to underscore once more the importance of this book in navigating the complex interplay between AI and social research.

As noted in the introductory part of this book, the field of social research is characterized by its broad scope and interdisciplinary nature, encompassing the examination of human behavior, societies and facets of social existence and social exchange. It embraces a diverse array of disciplines and domains of inquiry, such as sociology, psychology, anthropology, economics, political sciences, education, communication studies, public health, geography, social policy, management, and cultural, family and gender studies. The advent of AI has swiftly emerged as a catalyst for significant change in these domains. The applications of this technological advancement in social inquiry have experienced substantial growth and increased attention from the research community, providing novel tools for the collection, analysis and interpretation of data. The utilization of AI in the field of social research encompasses a broad spectrum of applications, augmenting the abilities of researchers while delivering different or even new perspectives on social phenomena. One of the most significant advantages is the ability to handle vast amounts of data with increased speed and efficiency. Generative AI facilitates creativity and automates time-consuming tasks. AI's potential to augment quantitative and qualitative analysis is another area of immense promise. Despite this and other opportunities, it is important to acknowledge the accompanying dilemmas involved in AI, as well as the constraints, risks and limitations of its utilization in social research. One notable limitation pertains to the inherent opacity of specific AI models, impeding researchers' comprehension of the underlying processes by which AI systems reach specific outcomes and conclusions. This 'black box' nature of AI systems can make it difficult to ensure transparency and accountability in research findings. Rigor in AI-assisted research are paramount. Ensuring reliability, validity, credibility, transferability, dependability and confirmability in studies employing AI tools is essential for maintaining the integrity of research findings. This is something that has been stressed in this book. Ethical implications are another critical area of concern. Researchers must

*E-mail: Prokopis.christou@cut.ac.cy

DOI: 10.1079/9781800626607.0019

navigate various ethical challenges to ensure that the use of AI respects the rights and dignity of research subjects and upholds the highest standards of ethical conduct. Addressing such issues effectively requires a commitment to specific principles and frameworks, ongoing dialogue and reflexivity within the research community.

The extent to which the cognitive input and evaluative skills of the researcher are demonstrated in AI-assisted research, such as during the interpretation process and in reaching conclusions following analysis performed by an AI system, is also a matter of concern. It is emphasized that the reliance on AI should not overshadow the critical thinking and interpretative skills that human researchers bring to the table. It is the synergy between AI's computational power and human insight that holds the most promise for advancing social research.

This book serves as a guide for researchers, scholars and practitioners navigating the integration of AI in social research. By compiling diverse perspectives and expertise, it provides a balanced view of the opportunities and challenges presented by AI technologies. The initial chapters of the book laid the foundation by exploring the interconnections between AI and social research. They set the stage for understanding how AI can enhance research capabilities. The chapters on generative AI, qualitative and quantitative analysis, and ethnographic research offered both theoretical and practical insights that demonstrate the practical applications of AI in various research tasks and processes. The chapters addressing rigor, bias and ethics ensured that researchers are equipped with the knowledge and tools to conduct AI-assisted research responsibly and ethically. By highlighting potential pitfalls and offering solutions, this part of the book serves as a crucial resource for maintaining the integrity and credibility of social research. The case studies showcased in the latter part of the book illustrate the application of AI in diverse social contexts. These chapters, ranging from behaviour change and education to international business and archaeology, demonstrate the versatility and breadth of AI applications. They not only provide practical insights but also inspire researchers to explore new frontiers linked to AI and research, in their work and their own domains.

As the editor of this book, I extend my gratitude to the contributors whose expertise and dedication have made this book possible. Their insights and research have significantly enriched our understanding of AI's role in social research. Each chapter reflects the hard work and commitment of scholars who are at the forefront of integrating AI into their respective fields. Their contributions advance academic discourse and provide both theoretical and practical guidance for researchers and analysts worldwide.

In conclusion, *Artificial Intelligence (AI) in Social Research* stands as a testament to the transformative potential of AI technologies, while highlighting both the opportunities and challenges that come with integrating AI into research. This book serves as an invaluable resource for researchers aiming to harness the power of AI while maintaining the rigour and ethical standards of social research. As we move forward, it is our (editor and contributors) hope that this book will inspire further exploration, innovation and thoughtful application of AI in social research, paving the way for new advancements in the field. Further research is crucial to fully appreciate the implications and impacts of AI on research processes, methodologies, ethics and outcomes. As AI continues to evolve, so too must our approaches towards studying and leveraging this powerful technology. The journey of integrating AI into social research is ongoing, and it is through continued inquiry and collaboration that we will unlock its full potential but without marginalizing the 'human element' in this process, whether that refers to the ethical and responsible use of AI in research, or the cognitive and evaluative input of researchers using AI technologies in their research.

Index

abductive logic 193–194
Alibaba Group 189
Amazon 188
annotation bias 120
ANOVA 44, 57
Anthropic and Gemini 1.5 21
anthropology 101–102, 114
  applications in 5
archaeological research, for ancient artifacts 199–200
  accessibility and distribution in 205–206
  accuracy and reliability in 204–205
  archaeological science development and 200–201
  artificial intelligence and 203–204
  cutting-edge technologies to locate sites and handling assemblages and 201–204
  data interpretation and 203
  dilemma in 204
  limits and efficiency in 206
  quality and objectivity in 205
archaeology, applications in 6
ArchAIDE app 202
artefact documentation 202–203
Artificial Intelligence Learning Intention Scale (AILIS) 106
artificial minded intelligence 161
ATLAS.ti 63
AutoGen Studio (Microsoft) 51, 53, 54
automated object identification 204
automated reporting 52
automated visualization 52

behavioural intention 106–107
beneficence and ethical implications 142
beneficence dilemma 142
BERT 64
bias 117
  genealogy of 114–117
  human rationality and 117–119
  machine learning and 119–121
  mitigation of 119, 120–121, 122–123
  types of 118–123
big data 203
Big Exchange project 202
black box problem 94, 120, 141, 210
blame attribution, by narrative 32, 33
Bloom's taxonomy 165
bounded rationality 117–118

case study, significance of 180, 182
Cattell–Horn–Carroll's theory, of intelligence 187
causal–comparative designs 180
chain-of-thought technique 28
challenges, ethical considerations and risks, AI-linked 16–17
ChatGPT 7, 8, 17, 22, 29, 34, 40–43, 62, 63, 65, 74, 77, 81, 84–85, 105, 106, 110, 141, 142, 179, 189
  as brainstorming tool 91–94
  continuous improvement in AI and 87
  cross-referencing data and 87
  general population, target population, sampling frame and sample and 90–91
  hallucination in AI and 86
  need for transparency and 87, 94, 95
  plot of survey responses generated using 24
  prompt engineering and 85–86
  purpose statement using AI and 88–89
  for qualitative data analysis 94

ChatGPT (*Continued*)
research questions using AI and 89–90
researcher cognitive input and 86–87
research-worthy problems and gaps identification and 87–88
terminology understanding and 90
tool bias acknowledgement and researcher bias 87
choice architecture 151
classical phenomenology 66
classification process, of artefacts 204
Claude 3 21
cluster analysis 44
coding and emergent technologies 74–75
integration into AI technology and anomalies 77–79
need for new perspective 79–80
normal science period and 75–77
resistance and crisis within quality research community 79
transformation of 80–81
cognitive bias 45, 117
cognitive psychology 121
comma-separated values (CSV) file 54
Competence Framework for AI research 161
competence frameworks, to explore gen AI 160–162
comparative analysis of 168
in educational settings 169–170
in higher education, understanding 162–163
inclusivity and equity in 167, 169
significance of 163, 165–167
complex and complicated systems, distinction between 190
complexity 190–191
sources, in MNE networks 191
computational ethnography 5
computer-assisted qualitative data analysis (CAQDAS) software 75, 76–77, 79, 80
confidentiality and privacy and ethical implications 140–141
confirmability and rigour 131
confirmation and framing biases 118–119
constructivist grounded theory (CGT) 65, 67
content analysis 61–62, 67
conversational AI 38–39
data analysis with, concerns and limitations regarding 45–46
conversational approach, to qualitative data analysis 79–80
convolutional neural networks (CNNs) 203
correlation research 180
credibility and rigour 129
CrewAI 53
critical thinking 63, 99
cross-sectional survey 108, 109, 110
cultural studies, applications in 5
data/information collection and analysis, AI impact on 15–16
data analysis and visualization 42–45
data bias 194
data cleaning and formatting 52
data collection methods
AI awareness and 179
AI knowledge and 178–179
AI perception and 179
AI use and 179–180
attitude towards AI and 179
college student project as case study and 182
discussion of 183–184
focus on 181
importance of 176–178
justification of 181–182
on research design 180–181
data interpretation 42
data labelling 40
data manipulation 40–41
data mining and web scraping 52
data quality assurance 52
DataRefiner tool 15–16
decision making 60, 61, 62, 64
deep learning (DL) 4, 187, 190
complex and abductive logic and 193–194
DeepScale 189
deglobalization 188
democratization process 13, 14, 25, 187
dependability and rigour 130–131
dependent variables, identification of 42
descriptive qualitative analysis 62, 67
descriptive statistics 52, 180
diffusion model 107
digital globalization 188
dilemmas, in ethical AI-augmented qualitative research 139–143
discourse analysis 63, 67
discourse and AI 116–117
dynamism 191

ecological momentary assessment 154
economics, applications in 6
education, applications in 6, 14
education research 161
ELIZA 4
Enterprisers Project, The 105
environmental studies and sustainability, applications in 6
epoché 66
ethical implications, in qualitative research 137–138
beneficence and 142
confidentiality and privacy and 140–141
frameworks for 143–144
good practice guideline for 144, 145–146

integrity and 141–142
intersection of AI and research and 138
justice and 142–143
respect for individual and 139–140
ethnography 5, 63–64, 67
AI limitations and perils in anthropology and 101–102
collaboration with AI 102–103
context setting 97–98
project life and AI and 98–101
European Commission 160
evolutionary overview 3–5
2020s and future 4–5
early application in social research 4
machine and deep learning 4
experimental designs 108–109
experimental studies 180
experimentation 193
external validity 133

Facebook 188–189
factor analysis 44–45
FactorAnalyzer library 44
Foucauldian perspective, of power/knowledge 114–117
funnel approach 87
future behaviour predicting and comprehending, AI opportunities on 15

GenAI Content Generation Framework 165–166
generative AI (gen AI) 21–22, 71–72, 98
coding and 74–81
image analysis 30, 32–34
importance of 100
paradigm shift applications and 74
prompting techniques 25–29
reproducibility 34–35
scientific revolutions through Kuhn's perspective and 72–73
text information analysing 29–30
tools, brainstorming with 22–25
generative methodology 161
geospatial analysis 52
Google 188
GPT-4 39, 40, 44, 78, 165
GPT-4o 21, 22
Grammarly 105
grounded theory 180–181

hallucination, in AI 86, 141
heritage conservation, applications in 5–6
heuristics 117–118, 151
historical context technique 29
human–AI interaction and human behaviour comprehension 13–14
human intelligence 186–187
human rationality
human biases and errors and 118–119
perspectives of 117–118
hypothesis building 42

IBM 188
incommensurability paradigm 73
in-context prompting 28
in-depth interviews 181
inductive reasoning 192–193
inductive thematic analysis 94
InfraNodus tool 16
integrity and ethical implications 141–142
Intel 189
interferential statistics 52
internal validity 133
international business 186–187
inductive reasoning and abductive logic and 191–194
interconnectedness and 188–189
networked multinational enterprises and 189–191
race condition and 195
interpretative phenomenological analysis (IPA) 66
interview guide questions, ChatGPT for 91–92
interviews 181
Ipsos Facto 97, 98
iterative experimentation 194
Ithaca 203

justice and ethical implications 142–143
just-in-time adaptive interventions (JITAIs) 153

label prediction, based on data 41
Langraph Studio 53
large language models (LLMs) 21–22, 25, 26, 27, 28, 30, 34, 38, 42, 43, 45–46, 54, 62, 78, 79
applications, autonomy level in 49
for better prompts creation 29
for data analysis 39–40
guide for qualitative researchers with 84–94
interaction with 50
LinearRegression (Python) 43
linear regression analysis 43
Llama 3 21
logical and sequential processing techniques 27–28
longitudinal studies 184

machine learning (ML) 4, 63, 108, 152, 190, 205
  complicated and inductive reasoning and 192–193
machine learning bias 113–114
  discourse and 116–117
  human rationality and 117–119
  mitigation of 120–121, 122–123
  power–knowledge nexus and 114–116
  significance of 119–120
management and business, applications in 6–7
marketing, applications in 7
matplotlib.pyplot 43
Meta 21
Microsoft 188
missing values, addressing 40–41
mixed-methods approach 181
multi-agent architectures 49
multi-collinearity test 43
multinational enterprises (MNEs) 188
multi-personas technique 28
multiple regression analysis 43–44
multiplexity 191
multiplicity 191
MYCIN 4

natural language, significance of 25
natural language processing (NLP) 4, 5, 12, 13–14, 16, 86, 99, 101, 178
  -GPT model 78
  software use for 61
netnography, significance of 64
networked world, interconnected 188
no-code platforms 38
non-participant observation 181
Nuance Communications 189
nudging 150–151
  AI-mediated 152–154
  for behavioural change 151–152
  failures, mitigating 154–156
  misfires 156–157
Nuffield Foundation 143
NumPy (Python) 37, 43
NVIDIA 189
NVivo 63

observation guide, ChatGPT for 92
observation studies 181
OpenAI 21, 39, 189, 207
outliers, elimination of 41

Pandas 37
participant observation 181
participation observation 92–93
participatory action research (PAR) 64–65, 67
PEGASUS 64
perceived ease of use (PEOU) 106, 107
perceived use (PU) 106, 107
phenomenology 65–66, 67
precision nudging *see* nudging
predictive modelling 52
principal component analysis (PCA) 44–45
PRISMA 179
proactive nudge 155, 157
project life and AI
  analysis of 101
  efficiency and collaboration and 98–99
  research materials 100–101
  sample of 99–100
prompting engineering 25, 27, 32
prompting principles 25–27
prompting techniques 25–29
prompt logging 34–35
psychology, applications in 7
public health, applications in 7
Python 22, 25, 37, 39, 40, 43, 45, 54–56

qualitative analysis, AI-augmented 59–60
  critical questions for 66–67
  design and 61, 64, 66, 67
  methodological compatibility and 60–61
  research across traditions of 61–65
  see also ethical implications, in qualitative research; generative AI
qualitative and naturalistic designs 180
qualitative researchers, LLMs for *see* ChatGPT
quantitative case study approach 182
quantitative data analysis 37–38
  concerns and limitations regarding 45–46
  data analysis and visualization 42–45
  data interpretation and hypothesis building and 42
  data manipulation and 40–41
  LLMs for 39–40
  traditional tools for 38
quantitative designs 180
quantitative social research, AI agents in 48–49
  advanced end-to-end quantitative analysis with 56–57
  benefits of 50
  chain of tasks by 51, 52
  challenges and considerations with 57
  cleaning and preprocessing data with 56
  data collection and analysis with 53–56
  features of 49
  high-level components of 48
  interaction with 50–51
  workflow examples using 51, 53
quasi-experimental designs 108, 109, 180
query-based analysis 80
Quillbot 105

randomization 108, 133
reactive nudge 156, 157
regression analysis 52
reinforcement learning (RL) 153
reliability and rigour 131–132
replacement theory 104–105
replication and valuation studies 52
representativeness bias 118
ResearchComp framework 160, 163, 164, 165, 171
research designs, in social context 104–106
    discussions and implications 109–110
    features, cross comparison of 109
    in social research 108–109
    studies on attitudes towards AI adoption and 106
    studies on behavioural intention and 106–107
    studies on college students and AI and 107
    studies on perceived ease of use and 106
    studies on perceived use and 106
    technology acceptance model and 107–108
research interview 181
responsible AI 88, 134, 144, 145, 184
rigour 127–128
    AI in social research and 128–129
    confirmability and 131
    credibility and 129
    dependability 130–131
    in qualitative research 129–131
    in quantitative research 131–134
    reliability and 131–132
    transferability and 129–130
    validity and 132–134

scientific revolutions, through Kuhn's perspective
    anomalies, occurrence of 72
    crisis state 72–73
    new paradigm birth 73
    normal science, phase of 72
SciPy 44
selection bias 119, 120
self-assessment technique 28–29
simple systems 190
single-agent architectures 48
skeleton-of-thought technique 28, 30
sklearn.cluster function 44
slow data 203
social work, applications in 8
society, AI influence on 12, 13
sociology, applications in 8
spatial survey 201–202
spillovers, nudging 154–156
Stable Diffusion (image-generation model) 143
start-ups 189
structural equation modelling 106
surveys 181
    ChatGPT for 93–94
    design and assistance 52
survivorship bias 119

tailoring and precision nudging 152–153
taxonomies, significance of 165
technology acceptance model (TAM) 107–108, 109, 110
Technology in Education (UNESCO report) 162
technosocial system 114
Tencent 189
Tesla 189
text information analysing and gen AI 29–30
thematic analysis 62, 94, 129
time series analysis 52
timing and precision nudging 153–154
tourism, applications in 8
transcription, AI 66
transferability and rigour 129–130
triangulation approaches 181
T-test 44
Turing test 187

University of Edinburgh Research Careers Tool 160

validity and rigour 132–134
variance inflation factor (VIF) 43
visual ethnography 98
vocabulary technique 29

World Association of Medical Editors 144
World Economic Forum 165

Printed and bound by CPI Group (UK) Ltd, Croydon, CR0 4YY

13/09/2026

14961113-0002